ISLANDERS

Islanders

THE PACIFIC IN THE AGE OF EMPIRE

❖

NICHOLAS THOMAS

YALE UNIVERSITY PRESS
NEW HAVEN AND LONDON

DEC 2010

Published with assistance from the Annie Burr Lewis Fund

For information about this and other Yale University Press publications, please contact:
U.S. Office: sales.press@yale.edu   www.yalebooks.com
Europe Office: sales @yaleup.co.uk   www.yaleup.co.uk

Set in Minion Pro by IDSUK (DataConnection) Ltd
Printed in by Great Britain by TJ International Ltd, Padstow, Cornwall

Library of Congress Cataloging-in-Publication Data

Thomas, Nicholas, 1960–
    Islanders: the age of empire in the Pacific / Nicholas Thomas.
      p. cm.
    Includes bibliographical references and index.
    ISBN 978-0-300-12438-5 (cl:alk. paper)
    1. Islands of the Pacific—History—19th century. 2. Islands of the Pacific—
Colonization. 3. Pacific Islanders—History—19th century. 4. Europe—Colonies—Islands
of the Pacific—History—19th century. 5. Europeans—Islands of the Pacific—History—
19th century. I. Title.
    DU29.T47 2010
    996—dc22

                                                                              2010020777

A catalogue record for this book is available from the British Library.

10 9 8 7 6 5 4 3 2 1

for Keith Thomas
and
in memory of Julia Thomas (1939–2009)

Contents

Illustrations

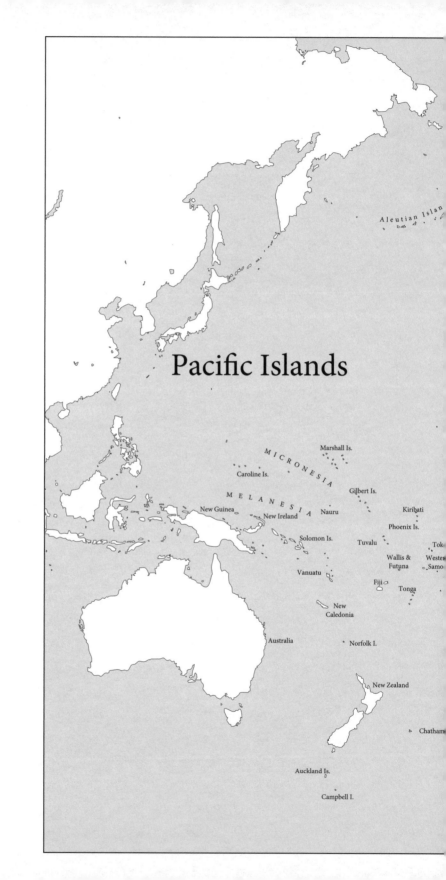

Pacific Islands

Aleutian Islan

MICRONESIA

Marshall Is.

Caroline Is.

MELANESIA

Gilbert Is.

New Guinea

New Ireland

Nauru

Kiribati

Phoenix Is.

Solomon Is.

Tuvalu

Tok

Wallis &
Futuna

Weste

Samo

Vanuatu

Fiji

Tonga

New
Caledonia

Australia

Norfolk I.

New Zealand

Chatham

Auckland Is.

Campbell I.

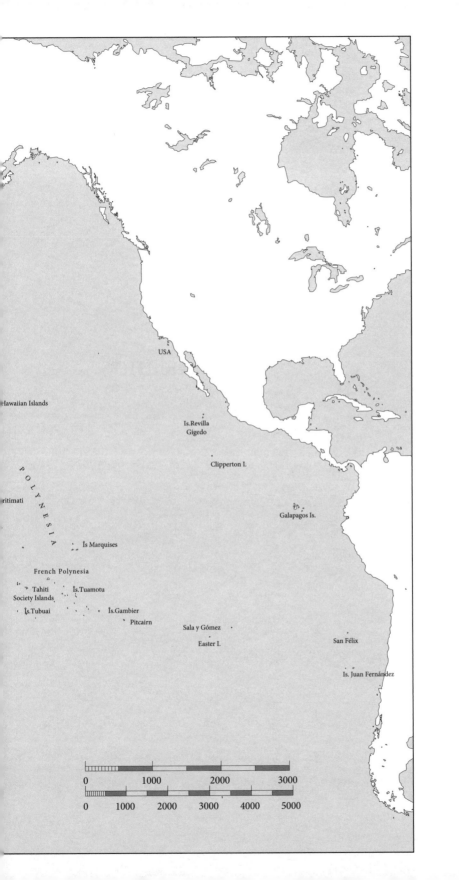

USA

Hawaiian Islands

Is.Revilla
Gigedo

Clipperton I.

P
O
L
Y
N
E
S
I
A

ritimati

Galapagos Is.

Ís Marquises

French Polynesia

Tahiti   Ís.Tuamotu
Society Islands

Ís.Tubuai   Ís.Gambier

Pitcairn   Sala y Gómez

Easter I.   San Félix

Is. Juan Fernández

0   1000   2000   3000

0   1000   2000   3000   4000   5000

Introduction

This book is about the diverse experiences of Pacific Islanders during a century – a long century, embracing the last decades of the eighteenth as well as the beginning of the twentieth. Over this period, European incursions into the lives of the vast ocean's inhabitants became more consequential and injurious. At its beginning, contacts between Europeans and Islanders amounted to little more than sporadic visits. When it ended, virtually every island was under some kind of colonial regime, and on many, there were substantial populations of European settlers, hence sundry sorts of dispossession.

Such a history might begin, most appropriately, in the Pacific itself. But I start with a moment in London and a young man named Kualelo, as a way of drawing attention to the diverse, and maybe unexpected, voyages that make up this story.

* * *

It was the coldest time of the year. Ashen dirty clouds trailed over the city. Snow and sludge along the river's edge melted into the brown tide that surged up past Deptford, Southwark and the City. From warships to watermen's boats, just about every sort of vessel was at anchor or active here. Among them a rowing boat plied back and forth, two tars pulling the oars, two other men at times conversing, at times simply taking in the spectacle and squalor. The younger of these two gestured toward St Paul's Cathedral and observed, 'Hare nui etua' ('The great house of god').

Kualelo was a young Hawaiian, aged around fifteen. On Wednesday, 26 January 1791, he was said to be not himself, a little dejected. He had wanted to return home, and was about to embark on a ship headed for the Pacific Ocean, to that end. But he had been in England for the better part of two years, and the prospect of departure made him melancholy, his companion thought. Archibald Menzies, botanist and surgeon, had encountered Kualelo in China.

The Hawaiian had arrived there on an English trading sloop, the *Princess Royal*, which he'd joined in January 1788 when it stopped for food and water at Molokai, in the Hawaiian archipelago, en route to the north-west coast of America. Having obtained there a cargo of fur for the Asian markets, the *Princess Royal* called at the island again, but Kualelo – out of what Menzies took to be 'instinctive curiosity' – had begged the captain, Charles Duncan, to be taken to Britain rather than deposited at home. In China, therefore, he was transferred to another trader, the *Prince of Wales*, in which one James Johnstone was commander and Menzies both surgeon and naturalist. Menzies had been collecting privately for Sir Joseph Banks, the greatest scientific entrepreneur of the epoch, and he shared Banks's eager curiosity about exotic peoples as well as unfamiliar plants.

On the *Prince of Wales*, Kualelo travelled back to England, and resided largely in Plymouth with Johnstone, where he was inoculated against smallpox and sent to school. He had sailed with Duncan again in the summer of 1790, who on this occasion had been commissioned by the Hudson's Bay Company to make an exploratory voyage, one that seems to have accomplished little, across the Atlantic into far northern waters. Kualelo had returned to London in the autumn; he was now joining, with Johnstone and Menzies, what would in due course be considered one of the great expeditions of the epoch. George Vancouver, one of Captain James Cook's erstwhile lieutenants, was the commander; his ship was the *Discovery*, and discovery was its business, from the European point of view. Yet it would take Kualelo, not into the unknown, but back to his place of birth, to the port where his own voyage had begun.[1]

Vancouver lacked both genuine curiosity and a sense of humour. In his judgement Kualelo 'did not seem in the least to have benefitted by his residence in this country'.[2] Menzies acknowledged that efforts to teach the Hawaiian to read had failed, but he was good at drawing, and might have acquired genuine skill, had his inclinations been less vulgar – his favourite amusement involved dashing off caricatures of friends and acquaintances. Kualelo, it seems, liked pictures. He had equipped himself with a number of prints of great London buildings – Westminster Abbey, Greenwich Hospital and St Paul's – that he wanted to show to his people. The last was the building he had called 'the great house of god', and it was one 'on whose structure & elevation he had often gazed with admiration & astonishment'.[3]

In general, it is assumed that dealings between Europeans and indigenous peoples – whether in the Pacific, the Americas or Africa – have amounted, essentially, to a series of depredations perpetrated by the former upon the latter: the incursions of explorers are followed by those of traders, missionaries and colonial powers, and latterly multinational companies. These are histories, in other words, of 'impact' on peoples who were not themselves mobile. Pacific Islanders were those impacted on, or more benignly visited; they are presumed not to have been visitors, not mobile themselves.[4]

Over the epoch of decolonization, historians came to emphasize that Islanders, among other native peoples, were not merely victims but actors, who resisted colonizers' impositions or creatively accommodated them. This rethinking, stimulated by the political climate of the period, was associated with a broader effort to understand colonial histories as two-sided, and to reconstruct them in a two-sided way, complementing the old emphasis on European policy and practice with an account of the perspectives of the colonized.[5]

The importance, even the necessity of this step, was obvious, though it raised a host of questions, practical and philosophical. What sorts of new methods were needed to reconstruct indigenous perspectives, where direct documentary records were sparse, or non-existent? Was it valid to cobble a counterpart to a European history out of whatever evidence might be assembled, to realize the 'both sides' aspiration? Or did Islander understandings of the past presuppose such different beginnings, epochs and ideas of events, acts and causes, as to be distorted through inclusion? The effort to represent native perspectives was ostensibly a democratizing one – but would there always be something inappropriate, asymmetrical, even residually colonial, in the incorporation of native stories in what, perhaps inevitably, would remain a Western genre of historical narrative?[6]

My concern, just here, is not to struggle further with these much-debated issues. It is rather with the point that the 'both sides' talk tends to preserve the idea that on one of these 'sides' we find indigenous communities, communities that are bounded, firmly situated in place and culturally coherent. The propensity of recent scholarship, which affirms cultural continuities and native resilience, certainly makes Islanders active rather than passive, but reinforces the old notion that Islanders are in situ, they inhabit particular places, they are the 'local' opponents, translators, or recipients of 'global' forces, meanings and commodities, emanating largely from the West.

Kualelo's story seems not to fit this vision, indeed it suggests a Pacific history written around new assumptions. We might start by noting a particular cultural condition, one rarely attributed to native people at all, and never at this early stage of their interactions with the colonial world – that of cosmopolitanism.[7] As Menzies wrote, barely a decade after contacts between Hawaiians and Europeans had been inaugurated by Cook's visits, Kualelo was prompted to visit not only England but 'several other parts of the globe'.[8] He encountered a range of Pacific Islanders, the indigenous peoples of north-west America and the Arctic, the ports of China and Europe, the multicultural decks of naval and merchant ships, and London, a place of starkly unequal social classes, and already in the late eighteenth century, one of diverse immigrants and refugees.

Kualelo's experience would count for little were it his alone. But it was not. As early as 1528, three men, probably from the island of Manus or another in the vicinity, to the north of New Guinea, were abducted by the Spanish voyager Alvaro de Saavedra. They spent time in parts of Micronesia and the Philippines before his ship passed Manus again a year later, when they escaped by leaping overboard and swimming ashore.[9] Most contacts during the sixteenth, seventeenth and early eighteenth centuries were brief and marked by mutual hostility, and though others were abducted – the Spanish explorer Alvaro de Mendaña took six Melanesians to Peru in 1568 – none was repatriated, and Islanders began to travel with Europeans willingly and in greater numbers only with the voyages of the French soldier and explorer Louis-Antoine de Bougainville and Captain Cook from the late 1760s, when contacts became more frequent and familiarity began to grow.[10]

By the end of the eighteenth century, dozens certainly and maybe hundreds of Islanders had joined traders, whalers and other ships.[11] Nearly, but not quite all, were male; most worked as crew, but some were what the navy called supernumeries, the guests of explorers or missionaries. In many cases they visited British outposts like Sydney, and Asian ports such as Canton, Macau and Manila. Some returned to their ships' home bases in New England or Europe. En route, they called variously at Batavia, Bengal, the Cape or Rio, among other places. It is striking that many also became temporary or permanent residents of Pacific Islands other than their own. Around 1800, there were Hawaiians in the Marquesas and Tahiti, Marquesans in Tahiti, and Tahitians in Tonga and New Zealand.[12] On all these islands both travellers and hosts became aware not only of the Europeans entering their world, but of Islanders and Island societies not known to them before. Polynesian chiefs tended to be avidly curious about other Polynesian places. They were excited by the potential of political practices that were akin but distinct, by new rites that might be imported, by unfamiliar and prestigious objects, by the scope for new sorts of trade.

The early visits of Islanders to Europe have not been completely forgotten. Kualelo had two famous predecessors. 'Aotourou', properly Ahutoru, and 'Omai', properly Mai, were both Society Islanders, the first Polynesians to visit France and England respectively. The Tahitian Ahutoru joined Bougainville during his visit of April 1768 and travelled with him back to France, arriving in March 1769. He left to be repatriated in February 1770, and was conveyed

1 Mai famous as 'Omai', the first Pacific Islander to visit England, as depicted by William Hodges, artist on Cook's second voyage.

at first to Mauritius. The navigator Marc-Joseph Marion du Fresne volunteered to take him back to Tahiti from there, but Ahutoru died of smallpox less than a month from port, in November 1771. In Paris he had been drawn into the highest circles of fashionable society, had gone to the opera, wept on encountering Pacific species in the Jardin des Plantes, and met the king, Louis XV. Ahutoru figured in a host of literary works, including Denis Diderot's famous *Supplément au Voyage de Bougainville*. Though that famous dialogue, among others, ostensibly presented Ahutoru's own voice, none in fact did so, rather using the Islander rhetorically to illustrate the virtue of simple society and the corruptions of civilization.[13]

Thanks to Joseph Banks, who had himself been to Tahiti on Cook's first voyage (1768–71), Mai, brought back to England on the *Adventure*, Cook's companion ship on his second voyage (1772–5), was likewise shown to aristocratic society. He became the talk of the town, his tattoos were inspected, his portrait was painted by no less an artist than Joshua Reynolds, as well as by William Hodges, William Parry and Nathaniel Dance. Like Ahutoru, Mai was the subject of a host of satirical works; and in more or less all these contexts he was presented as a noble savage. While Ahutoru has lapsed into obscurity as a historical figure, there has been a revival of interest in Mai, exemplified or maybe driven by the iconic status that his portrait by Reynolds has recently acquired.[14] If the noble-savage notion is always cited as a great myth of the Enlightenment, Mai's new fame paradoxically revives the associations between the Pacific and the romanticized primitivism of Diderot, Jean-Jacques Rousseau and others. Ancient Polynesians are still seen as dignified and noble yet sensual and natural, and their societies as once ideal communities, savagely disrupted by the West.

The interest at the time, and the appeal in hindsight, of the stories of both Ahutoru and 'Omai' turned on the arresting notion, indeed the stark anomaly, of a noble savage in the heart of metropolitan glitz – the presence in a civilized society of its antithesis. These Pacific voyagers were indeed remarkable, but not in this way, as was apparent even in the 1770s to more astute observers such as Cook. He understood perfectly well that Islanders did not live in a state of nature: their societies engaged in trade, people sailed in great seagoing canoes from island to island, there were inter-island patterns of allegiance and subordination that were disputed, and that erupted from time to time in rebellion and warfare. Cook's remarks on these social and political circumstances usually rested on faulty analogies with European feudal kingdoms, but he did understand that Pacific peoples had histories, that their lives were no more 'natural' than those of Parisians or Londoners.[15]

Ahutoru's motivations for joining Bougainville and visiting Europe are obscure, but Mai's are well documented. His family and wider kin group had been dispossessed as a result of ongoing conflict, and he was a refugee seeking to strengthen his hand. For Society Islanders, foreign ideas and goods – cloth, iron, weapons, ornaments – were potent and prestigious. Mai hoped to acquire actual weapons, to ally himself with King George III, and recruit emissaries of the king such as Cook, so he could fight, recover his lands, and humiliate his enemies. During Cook's third voyage (1776–80) he was repatriated, with a host of prestigious things that – Cook and others judged – he did not distribute very strategically. The foreign gambit was one that many Polynesians would follow up, but Mai himself seems to have lacked the status, or maybe just the maturity, to carry it through.

If the real story of Mai tells us something different to the myth of Omai, then Kualelo's biography suggests something different again. Part traveller, motivated by curiosity, part ordinary maritime worker, his imagination and actions appear to have been unconstrained by anything like Mai's project. He was not trying to use foreign experience or alliances to gain some sort of victory at home. On the voyage back to the Pacific the young Hawaiian made connections in Tahiti and sought to stay there. Vancouver, wedded to his instructions, which stipulated that the young man was to be repatriated, forced Kualelo to remain with the expedition until he could return him to Hawaii, under circumstances that turned out to be unpropitious.[16]

This book is concerned with Islanders' voyages, social and conceptual as well as strictly geographic. It is also concerned with the voyages and projects of Europeans in the Pacific, some idiosyncratic and inconsequential, others far-reaching in their ramifications. It deals with the movements across seas, societies and cultures that Kualelo's journeys prefigured. But I need to set the scene, by sketching what led up to his own voyaging in the longer history of the peoples of the Pacific, and in the eighteenth-century encounters that immediately preceded his travels.

* * *

It is ironic that the peoples of Oceania were so often thought to inhabit a state of nature, or one approximating the earliest stages of society, since human beings have been, for all but the most recent chapters in the species' history, confined to the continents, and to islands very close to them. The human colonization of the remote archipelagoes scattered across the world's largest ocean occurred only recently, in the time scale of world prehistory, and there was nothing natural about it. Rather, the business of undertaking voyages to new lands with the makings of a new life, then surviving on them and adapting to them, was a sophisticated effort, and one that demanded both specialist accomplishment and versatility.[17]

This is to jump ahead, however. It is vital to acknowledge that, in archaeo-logical terms, there is an important distinction between the genuinely old and the relatively new, in Pacific prehistory. The island of New Guinea was joined to Australia during the last ice age, which ended about 10,000 years before the present. New Guinea and Australia were settled 40–50,000 years ago by popu-lations that no doubt initially confined themselves to the coastlines of the era and the river systems, but who gradually spread to occupy virtually the entire land mass, settling the harsher regions more sparsely. While their modes of subsistence involved diverse sorts of foraging, these populations became more specialized over time, and the populations of New Guinea and Australia, once separated by rising sea levels, gradually diverged – physically, linguistically and culturally. In the New Guinea highlands, people began practising horticulture at much the same time as peoples did in south-western Asia and the Middle East. In many different ways over succeeding millennia, the people of the Pacific Islands, unlike those of Australia, would be hunter-gatherers no longer but would garden and fish instead.

Remarkably, these peoples also left the security of the continental mainland and settled what in modern times are incongruously known as the Bismarck Islands, to the immediate east and north-east of New Guinea. Their voyages of settlement were undertaken at a time when there is no evidence from anywhere in the world for seagoing boats, though boats of some sort they must have had. These migrations in due course resulted in the early human settlement, further east still, of the whole of the Solomon Islands archipelago.

The watershed in the prehistory of Oceania was, however, the movement of a different population, which originated on the island of Formosa (Taiwan) and began to spread southward and eastward into south-east Asia and Melanesia (there is no 'real' cultural or ethnic boundary) four thousand years or so before the present, mixing with, indeed colonizing, the prior inhabitants of the region. The intruders were speakers of one of the great language families of the world, the Malayo-Polynesian branch of the Austronesian language family. Their broader dispersal, as far as Madagascar to the west, is less relevant to this book than the formation, in the islands to the north-east of New Guinea – in the Bismarck archipelago – of a particular branch of this great family, known as Oceanic. Its early speakers, referred to as Lapita people by archaeologists after a highly distinctive style of pottery excavated from sites across the region, assumed a specific identity, no doubt in the course of mixing with the older occupants of these islands, and began to expand further.

Their subsequent migrations are unlike anything else in world history, for their range and rapidity. Archaeologically, Lapita can be recognized as a culture, through its typical artefacts and decorated pots, as early as 1350 BC, in the Bismarcks. Just two or three hundred years later, around 1150–1050 BC, people move as far as the south-eastern Solomon Islands, Vanuatu and New Caledonia, and then embark to the east, across much greater expanses of open water, to Fiji, Samoa and Tonga. The earliest dates for beach middens and similar sites on these easternmost islands are around 950 BC, indicating that an extraordinary succession of voyages, spanning thousands of kilometres,

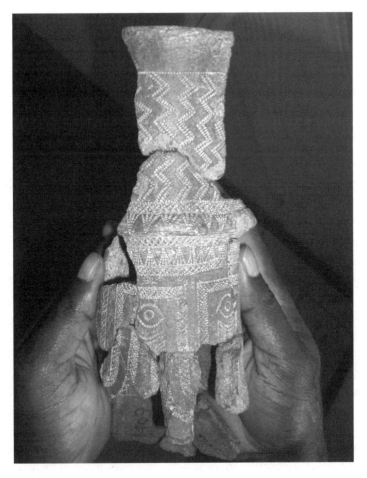

2 Top half of a Lapita dentate-stamped cylinder stand, held by Vanuatu Cultural Centre curator Takaronga Kuautonga, excavated from the Teouma cemetery, Efate, Vanuatu.

and resulting in the settlement of dozens of islands, took place over the course of a century or two. Some nineteenth- and twentieth-century theorists, unable to entertain the thought that ancient Pacific Islanders were capable of long-range navigation, proposed that islands had been settled by accident. Those out fishing, we were invited to believe, might have been blown away in storms, and in due course drifted to new lands. Drift voyages and accidental voyages certainly did take place, not infrequently, in the history of the Pacific. But people out fishing do not typically take with them seedlings, cultivated plants, breeding pairs of pigs and chickens, in other words the makings of a new life.

The pattern of the evidence is unambiguous: these were voyages of settlement, which aimed to establish permanent new homes.

Having reached the extensive and closely connected archipelagoes of Fiji, Tonga and Samoa, this rapid succession of expeditions came to a halt. For fifteen hundred years or so, there was no further expansion, or at any rate none that has yet been documented. Then another series of voyages took place that resulted initially in the settlement of the Cook Islands, the Society Islands and the Marquesas. Rapa Nui (Easter Island) and the Hawaiian Islands were perhaps reached as early as AD 800, and almost certainly by AD 1000. The people who became the Maori settled New Zealand, in all likelihood from somewhere around the Society Islands, between about AD 1200 and 1300.

For most parts of the world, efforts to link ancient peoples and languages quickly become mired by the sheer complexity of movements and interactions that are now remote in time – their reconstruction is perforce more in the realm of antiquarian speculation than real history. But the comparatively recent nature of human movements into and through Oceania makes it possible for us to add social meanings, a sense of the story, to the relics and statistics that constitute the archaeological record. Without going into the technicalities of historical linguistics, methods that trace terms which are common among some or all of the diverse languages spoken historically by the descendants of the Lapita people, who now live more or less everywhere between the fringes of New Guinea and Easter Island, have enabled scholars to partially reconstruct the languages of these peoples' ancestors. They have assembled lists of words, including terms for relationships, institutions and objects that were important in these ancestors' lives. Among them are many words for food plants such as taro and coconuts, and *waqa*, meaning an outrigger canoe, from which words in common use today, like *vaka* in Tahitian and *waka* in Maori, are derived.[18]

Perhaps most suggestively, there is clear evidence that early Oceanic languages made a distinction between senior and junior, in kinship terms. There were no words for 'brother' and 'sister', only words for elder brother and elder sister, and younger brother and younger sister. The likelihood is that these expressed a ranking, not only of siblings, but of siblings' families and their descendants.[19] In small communities there cannot have been sharp divisions between aristocrats and commoners, but there was some sort of hierarchy, a difference of status, at least a sort of precedence accorded to the first-born. This may have been mainly a ritual issue – senior lines performed rites on behalf of the whole community – but spiritual power and political power tended anyway to be closely associated.[20]

If little that is specific can be said about the early forms of rank in Oceanic societies, there is abundant and specific evidence, from oral history as well as archaeology, for the unequal and complex nature of Pacific societies, in the later stages of their pre-European history. The range of this evidence makes it all but certain that in earlier times, status difference was more than just a linguistic convention. If this were not so, it would be a struggle to understand what energized the Lapita voyagers. It is in any case hard to grasp why a particular population, who lived through subsistence fishing and gardening, should over such a relatively short period expand to a host of distant and new lands with all the relentless ambition and energy we would associate with profit-seeking nineteenth-century imperialists. Given the rapidity of movement from one newly settled territory to another, these expeditions and migrations cannot have been driven by a lack of land, or a scarcity of food. The stimuli can only have been social. They very likely stemmed from some political competition, some social instability, and perhaps specifically from a will among those who were junior, among those who possessed ambition but lacked rank, to establish new societies in which they were the founders of temples and lineages.[21]

* * *

The extraordinary story of the first settlement of the islands of the Pacific amounts only to the first chapter of the region's human history. In succeeding centuries, communities grew, the populations of islands became denser, and environments changed, as forests were cleared for gardens, and soils lost or displaced. Needless to say, societies developed in different ways in different regions. Some peoples found themselves on high volcanic islands rich in resources, and big enough to support populations of tens of thousands, that would become divided into distinct language groups. Tribes with common ancestors would come to see each other as ethnically different peoples. Other Islanders became atoll dwellers, with access to reefs but little in the way of land. These diverse situations led to an impressive variety of locally specialized economies, some of which involved elaborate taro irrigation systems, others ways of preserving and storing processed breadfruit, and others still intensive, seasonal fishing practices. Modes of producing food, structuring society and managing rites and spirits developed in locally particular ways, creating wonderfully diverse Pacific identities, yet identities that for all their variety, retained affinities, reflecting a shared history.

A detailed discussion of what can be said of cultural change over the period leading up to European contact is beyond the scope of this book, but it is worth drawing attention to two points. The first is that the process of early settlement did not involve merely one-way voyages of settlement. Rather, those who departed from islands to settle new ones often sustained contact, in some cases over centuries. The presence of relics such as pots and volcanic glass flakes – which in both cases can be traced back to their specific sources – demonstrates that ongoing exchange took place. Intriguingly, this traffic appears to have extended to molluscs: it has been established that one distinctive, delicately white, oddly beautiful tree snail, endemic only to Tahiti, was found historically also in parts of the Cook and Austral Islands – to which it was introduced, probably during the prehistoric period, for use in ornaments such as necklaces.[22]

In a number of cases, during the first centuries of human settlement, ongoing contact and trade embraced archipelagoes that were widely separated. In the early stages of human occupation in the Cook Islands, for example, people seem to have retained contact with the communities in Fiji and elsewhere in western Polynesia, from which the Cooks were settled. Subsequently, no doubt as the population in the Cooks grew, this long-range trade lapsed. An epoch of continuing voyaging that linked widely dispersed, but small populations was followed by one marked by less long-range sea travel, but probably more frequent and intensive interaction, within and among the new communities of particular islands and island groups.

Secondly, for many island groups, ranging from the western Solomons to the Society Islands, the combination of oral history, genealogy and the recent archaeological record tells us that the recent period – the century or so leading up to European contacts – was replete with political drama. Without entering into the specifics of local histories – some of which are touched on later in this book – there are many instances where there is evidence, for example, for the formation of new chiefdoms, sometimes claiming sovereignty over diverse groups of people, spread across numerous islands. There is also much evidence for the late realignment of trading systems, which often involved seasonal voyages, the specialized production of pots, cloth, or food for export, and the traffic of prestigious shell valuables, or other sorts of local 'money'.[23] Similarly, there is evidence for pre-European religious exchanges. Rites, cults, secret knowledge and sacred artefacts were sold, stolen, or imported. Those who controlled particular objects or temples sometimes gained new 'converts', and, since spiritual authority was often at least loosely linked with political authority, they thereby created new chiefdoms, or at least made new alliances.[24]

There are two broader points that emerge. The lives of the peoples of Oceania were already complex, unstable and political, before the arrival of Europeans. The second is that, while the cosmopolitanism that the Hawaiian Kualelo experienced was a product of the early colonial period, it had deep precedents. For as long as there had been Islanders in the Pacific, they had travelled and traded extensively. They had regularly taken great risks to seek out new lands. They had long had dealings with people who were more or less unlike themselves.

* * *

Europeans began to voyage through the Pacific in the sixteenth century, but the earliest circumnavigators, such as the Portuguese Ferdinand Magellan, missed all the larger islands and archipelagoes. Such contacts as did take place were fleeting and hostile. In the course of voyages during the late sixteenth and early seventeenth centuries, Mendaña and Pedro Fernandez de Quiros were responsible for a massacre in the southern Marquesas Islands, and they also killed many during efforts to establish colonies in northern Vanuatu and the Solomons.[25] The most extended of these visits was the 1595 settlement of Santa Cruz, abandoned after forty-seven days. There are no recorded local traditions relating to these events, and none of the localities were visited again by Europeans for more than 150 years, so it is difficult to assess their ramifications.

Over the period up to the 1760s there were further Spanish, Dutch and British voyages, some in search of the rumoured great South Land, thought to exist somewhere in the Southern hemisphere. But they were relatively infrequent, did not involve Spanish-style efforts to establish colonies, and typically involved only brief contacts between Europeans and Islanders. Some of the encounters that took place we count as historically significant because they marked first contacts – the Dutch explorer Jacob Roggeveen, for example, came upon Rapa Nui in April 1722, landed with his men, was involved in a fracas that killed some twelve locals, and made the first European observations of the famous statues.[26] We can be pretty sure that the Islanders did not understand this meeting as marking the beginning of their history – first contact is too easily reified as a founding moment in this sense – but what they did make of it cannot now be reconstructed.

Until the last third of the eighteenth century, the islands and Islanders of the Pacific remained effectively unknown to Europeans. Indeed the lack of precise navigational techniques meant that even those places that had been known, through Quiros or others, were imprecisely situated: a good many islands were found and lost several times in succession. The lack of a commitment to natural historical enquiry meant that both the places and the people were at best haphazardly observed and described. The 1760s marked the beginning of another kind of contact altogether. There was renewed interest in the possibility of a southern continent; natural history and science enjoyed new prestige; a period of peace among the European nations reinvigorated commerce, trade and empire, and incidentally made major expeditions possible. By the time conflicts resumed in the late 1770s, Pacific surveys and projects had gained some momentum of their own, and once the Australian convict settlement was established, it was inevitable that British ships, at least, would regularly enter and cross Pacific waters.

The earlier navigations of the period were British, French and Spanish. Those patronized by George III begin with the voyages of John Byron and Samuel Wallis in the mid 1760s. Neither was notable, but both pointed toward new possibilities in the search for the great South Land, and Wallis happened upon Tahiti, an island considered aesthetically delightful by Europeans, which supported easily the largest Polynesian population that had yet been encountered. Wallis's arrival met local resistance, to which he responded with a violent cannonade of Tahitian canoes and villages. This assault, he considered, had happy results in ceremonies of submission, even friendship. However the events are interpreted, the Tahitians evidently considered it prudent or even desirable to accommodate the intruders. If they must have been at least ambivalent about Wallis, they were indeed generally welcoming to those Europeans who followed – Bougainville, the Spaniard Domingo de Boenechea, Cook, and many successors. An epoch of engagement with Polynesian people had begun.[27]

Pacific intellectuals such as the late anthropologist and writer, Epeli Hau'ofa, have been understandably irritated by the preoccupation with Captain James Cook among the western public and among western historians.[28] Certainly, Cook has been treated as a superstar to an absurd extent, and as a result has arguably been misunderstood by both worshippers and detractors. Yet, if a history that brings Islanders to centre stage has little interest in the cult of Cook's personality, it must reckon with the genuinely remarkable character of his three voyages, and try to come to grips with their varied and sometimes profound consequences.[29]

The voyages were different to any that came before, not because they were exploratory rather than commercial or military – there had been more or less purely investigative expeditions before. Cook's were different because the investigative role was embraced with unprecedented energy, and was not limited to narrowly navigational or geographic enquiries but embedded in a wide-ranging, genuinely curious natural history. Coasts actually were traced systematically, lands and islands were visited and studied, resources were observed, and plants and animals collected. Most importantly, this inquisitiveness extended to people, to their manners and customs, to their institutions, and to their knowledge.

Some degree of interaction was unavoidable in a practical sense, because ships' crews needed food, firewood and fresh water, and it was easier to obtain whatever could be had through negotiation and trade rather than violence and seizure. But both official instructions and the mariners' inclinations prompted not only commerce but social engagement, to whatever extent Islanders would welcome or suffer it. Both the voyagers themselves, and British propaganda of the time, made these meetings out to be benevolent. Though some Islanders trenchantly resisted landings, in the Society Islands and Hawaii, among other places, they had in contrast an interest that converged fortuitously with that of the Europeans. They made the most of their visitors, gifts were exchanged, meals and physical intimacies were shared, ceremonies were performed, people were sketched, wordlists were compiled, artworks, handicrafts and manufactures were collected.

During Cook's first voyage, some four months were spent at Tahiti in order to prepare for and perform the astronomical observations that were ostensibly the voyage's aim. Although the needs were scientific rather than social, the upshot was a far longer period of interaction and observation than any European since Mendaña had had anywhere in the Pacific beforehand – Bougainville, for instance, had spent only nine days at the island. The visit was followed by a complete circuit of both the North and South islands of New Zealand, involving a good deal of contact with Maori at a number of points around the coasts. Though the Spanish who visited, and settled missionaries, on Tahiti's eastern peninsula, would be there for longer, Cook's voyages acquired almost immediate fame, and the publications arising from them were enormously influential for European understandings of Oceania over many decades afterwards. It was his second voyage, especially, that featured a genuinely unprecedented series of meetings with Islanders. Again, encounter was not an aim in itself. Cook was dedicating the southern summers to the search for a continent, but his cruises in the frigid Antarctic waters could not be sustained through the colder months, during which his ships returned to the tropics for refreshment, and as it were incidentally, further exploration. He revisited places he knew such as Tahiti, the Society Islands and New Zealand. He revisited many islands and island groups, which had had some earlier contact with Europeans, among them Rapa Nui, the Marquesas and the Tongan archipelago. Yet in many cases the previous visits had been much earlier – there was, for example, a gap of 180 years between Quiros's visit to the Marquesas in 1595 and Cook's in 1774. And he identified many islands previously unknown to Europeans, and inaugurated contacts with major populations such as the peoples of New Caledonia, the New Hebrides (now Vanuatu) and, during his third voyage, the Hawaiian group. There were both extended and repeat visits to certain places – Tahiti and various other islands in the Society group were visited several times and at length, while Cook called at a favourite harbour, Ship Core, at the northern end of the South Island of New Zealand five times over the decade of the three voyages.

An obvious consequence of these many visits and contacts was a new level of Western knowledge concerning the Pacific. A few of the mariners acquired something approaching fluency in Tahitian, many others acquired some competence in Tongan and Maori among other Polynesian languages. None of the Europeans were equipped, either linguistically or methodologically, to study matters such as religious belief in anything like the systematic fashion of the twentieth-century ethnographer. But with respect to what could be observed or asked about straightforwardly, their accounts were pretty good as far as they went. Subsistence activities, crafts, forms of body decoration and the conduct of rites were all carefully described; political relationships were among the matters that tended to be more roughly translated. But the question of whether the emerging European knowledge of the Pacific was accurate or otherwise is less important than the fact that it did emerge. It created a published literature. Voyagers who followed thought they knew what sorts of people were to be found, in Tahiti or Tonga; they thought they knew what kinds of resources they might traffic in, and what trade would be wanted in return. They thought they knew which islands they would run a risk in visiting, and at which they might count on hospitality.

Equally obviously, Islanders began to know Europeans. Certain Islanders, such as the Tahitian high chief, Tu, or Pomare I, became intimate with particular Europeans such as Cook – and myths of benevolence aside, Tu among a number of others appears to have counted Cook as a true ally, maybe even a friend. More generally, Islanders came to know the effect of European weapons, and their own desires for certain European goods, particularly iron, and manufactured cloth. This they treated, not as a novelty, but as a form of their own barkcloth, which had always expressed not only quotidian but refined forms, associated with prestige, sanctity and sovereignty. Introduced fabrics, for as long as they remained rare, were assimilated to that special class.

A good deal more could be said about various aspects of this emerging mutual knowledge. But, interesting as this two-sided process is, it was not all that was going on. Cook's voyages also enabled Islanders to get to know each other. Pacific peoples such as Tahitians and Maori, who were ancestrally linked, but who had had, in all likelihood, negligible contact for centuries, were reintroduced. Their meetings created another kind of cross-cultural

3 Tu, also known as Pomare I, as sketched by William Hodges, probably in August 1773.

knowledge – a knowledge on the part of Tahitians of such diverse places as Rapa Nui, the Marquesas, New Caledonia and New Zealand, and reciprocally a knowledge of Tahiti, among other places, among the peoples of Rapa Nui, the Marquesas and elsewhere.

Before Cook, Islanders had travelled with Europeans – Ahutoru, as we have seen, had joined Bougainville's voyage, but the Frenchman's contacts with people, hence Ahutoru's observations of them, were cursory on the passage between Tahiti and the Dutch East Indies. On his first voyage, Cook agreed that Tupaia, a Raiatean priest and navigator resident at the time on Tahiti, might, together with a young man described as his 'servant', join the *Endeavour* and visit England. Tupaia was clearly highly knowledgeable, intelligent and stimulated by the British visitors. Indeed he had spent a good deal of time with Joseph Banks and with Banks's artists, and has become famous over the last decade, since an obscure letter found among Banks's very voluminous papers revealed that the Islander was the artist who made a group of European-style drawings, mainly of Tahitians and Tahitian scenes, that had previously been attributed to Banks himself.

Tupaia was already well known, among scholars interested in indigenous Pacific navigation, as the author of a map indicating the islands known to Polynesians, which was presumably stimulated by the geographic enquiries of Cook and others, and which he likewise prepared, emulating the form of Cook's own charts. While Cook had reservations about the propriety of taking Tupaia (agreeing only when Banks promised that he would be responsible), it is not hard to imagine that he might have welcomed the Islander's participation, given

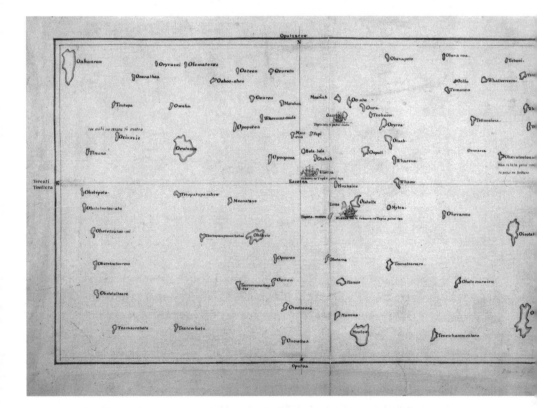

4 Detail of Tupaia's map of the Pacific Islands. No original in Tupaia's own hand is extant; this copy was made by Captain James Cook.

his potential usefulness both as a navigator and a go-between. And Tupaia was not only helpful, but so prominent in New Zealand that he appears to have been taken by Maori to be the leader of the expedition. Sadly, both he and his servant were among the many who perished of fevers in Batavia. Though he neither reached England nor ever returned home, he did become something of a mythic figure among Maori, who enquired after him during Cook's subsequent visits.

On Cook's second voyage Mahine from Raiatea joined the *Resolution* in 1773, intending to travel with the ship back to Britain. In New Zealand he was notably horrified by Maori cannibalism, or rather by a staging of cannibalism, a 'proof' of the practice, orchestrated by some of Cook's officers on the deck of the ship. At Rapa Nui he liked the people, but was shocked by the impoverished state of the land. In the Marquesas he 'was excessively fond' of the Islanders 'on account of the vast similarity between their manners, language and persons, and those of his nation, was continually engaged in conversation with them, and purchased a great number of their ornaments'.[30] When Cook returned to the Society Islands, Mahine decided to remain, but he saw Cook again during his third voyage, dined with Captain Bligh during his 1788–9 visit, prior to Fletcher Christian's *Bounty* mutiny of April 1789, and travelled with Edward Edwards, who had been despatched in the *Pandora* to capture the mutineers.

A year or so before Mahine joined the *Resolution*, the Spanish navigator Boenechea, who had called not at Matavai, the Tahitian harbour customarily visited by the British, but at the eastern peninsula, the base of rival aristocrats and lineages, took four Tahitians to Lima in Peru, of whom two, Pautu and Tetuanui, survived to return, ostensibly baptised, with Catholic missionaries in 1774. While the mission was a failure, and the Islanders soon discarded both their European clothes and the new faith that they signified, Pautu played a key role as a go-between, and must have told his kin much about colonial Spanish life. Maximo Rodriguez, an assistant to the padres in Tahiti, wrote of a convivial time spent with Pautu and others, who enquired just how many countries the Spanish king possessed. 'We all chatted over our countries, and their products, and mode of living, at which they were astonished, and some of them said we must be madmen.'[31] It would be nice to know just which aspects of Spanish life these Tahitians considered crazy; if we cannot, it does seem that at this time they had little admiration for, and little wish to emulate, a European model.

On his third voyage, in addition to repatriating Mai, Cook took two young men, Te Weherua and Koa, from New Zealand to Tahiti where they settled. It is in the nature of these movements that they are frustratingly undocumented – the engagement one would be eager to understand was that which occurred among Polynesians. It did not involve, or only peripherally involved, the mariners whose writings are our sources for these cross-cultural encounters. And rich sources they are, but only for the meetings between Islanders and Europeans: they allude to, but do not describe, cross-cultural encounters among different Islanders, who rediscovered their own affinities centuries after voyages of migration had separated them. While, in the minds of Cook's naturalists, a sort of comparative anthropology was emerging, which regarded the customs of Maori, Tahitians and Tongans as variations upon each other, to be understood, perhaps, as consequences of differing climates, these Islanders were engaged in comparisons of their own. In effect, they rediscovered lost kin, regained a sense of an Oceanic community, and a bigger theatre for their ventures and ambitions. Their discovery of Europeans or of Europe itself was in no sense unimportant. But it went hand in hand with a rediscovery of archipelagoes beyond those they knew and already travelled – a rediscovery of 'a sea of islands' (Epeli Hau'ofa's term) that would suffer colonial tsunami yet remain an Islanders' world.[32]

* * *

The consequences of Cook's voyages were many, they were far-reaching, and they were profound. Among the direct effects was a new awareness among mariners and merchants of commercial opportunities. On the third expedition some men had acquired a few sea-otter furs from the American northwest coast, which they were able to sell at an incredible profit, when fortuitously they called at Macao in southern China on their passage home. The news spread quickly, and by the mid 1780s several British expeditions had departed from Asian ports or Britain itself. The traders' many misadventures are another story: what is germane here is that many followed Cook in using the Hawaiian Islands as a staging post and port of refreshment. Indeed it had been Charles Duncan, one of the early fur traders, who recruited Kualelo from the island of Molokai to the *Princess Royal* and took him to China. By the early 1790s Kealakekua Bay among other Hawaiian harbours was well established as a place of barter. Ominously, it was the first place where firearms and ammunition were regularly traded to Islanders.[33]

By this time, too, the advice of Joseph Banks had been taken up by the British Parliament. The loss of the American colonies and the overcrowding of gaols and prison hulks would be addressed by the establishment of the penal colony of New South Wales. That, again, is another story, but one with many repercussions for the Pacific islands and Pacific peoples. When, for instance, in the early years, the colonists were desperately short of food, voyages were made to obtain and salt pork.[34] A transition from occasional barter to regular provisioning was well under way. It raised issues that would reoccur time and again over the subsequent century on many other islands. If people were trading food they would otherwise have eaten, could they make up their own supplies in another way, or did they suffer from shortages? What impacts did trade have, socially and economically? Was it monopolized and did it exacerbate traditional inequalities?

Joseph Banks had a hand, too, in another venture that had a profound impact on Polynesia. During their Tahitian sojourns, he, Cook and others had considered breadfruit a truly wonderful food plant, an exemplar of Tahiti's bountiful environment. Banks was maybe the most energetic and influential advocate of the transportation of plants and animals to new regions in which they might be economically useful.[35] He promoted the voyage that sought to transplant breadfruit from Tahiti to the plantations of the West Indies – a voyage which, however, was disrupted by the most famous mutiny in world history. Again, the story of the *Bounty* is largely peripheral to the concerns of this book, but it involved the longest visit to Tahiti by any ship up until that time, and for decades afterwards – it took five months to gather and load the botanical cargo.[36] The April 1789 mutiny took place less than a month after departure, not far from the Tongan island of Tofua. Fletcher Christian then tried to colonize the island of Tubuai – sufficiently obscure, he hoped, to avoid the attention of any British naval vessel that might come in search of the mutineers – but local resistance made the plan unsustainable. He called at Tahiti and then, so far as anyone knew for nearly twenty years, vanished into the Pacific, with the ship and thirty-four companions – eight of the mutineers and the rest of the Islanders who for whatever reason wished to go with him. The other mutineers remained on Tahiti for a year and a half before their arrest by the crew of the *Pandora* under Edwards in March 1791. These sixteen men were not in fact the first Pacific beachcombers – individuals and small groups had deserted or survived wrecks from the time of Magellan – but they were the first whose experiences were well documented.

The temporarily resident mutineers moreover shaped events in Tahiti, in ways disproportionate to their numbers, because of what we might call Cook's after-effects. Europeans were not the only people who turned the explorer into a hero, who presented themselves as his posthumous allies or successors (as Bligh certainly did). Cook had been considered a great chief and ally by the Tahitian high chief Tu and others. They had solicited his assistance in local warfare, both because they understood the technological magic of his firearms but also because things European, and things British specifically, had become signs of potency. When asked, Cook generally refused to offer military assistance, and anyway he was never around the islands for long enough to make more than a one-off intervention. But beachcombers such as the mutineers were in an entirely different situation. They were valued by Islanders because they represented British prestige, they held modest supplies of valued items, and they had guns, but without the support and protection of one chief or another they would quickly have been stripped of possessions. They were thus typically incorporated into chiefly households, more or less as privileged servants, meaning, needless to say, that when their chiefs sought services in conflict, beachcombers had to help.[37]

In some cases Europeans fought in these conflicts themselves, in others they prepared and serviced firearms that local warriors used. It was with such borrowed weapons that, in April 1790, Tu's allies on the island of Mo'orea, off Tahiti's north-western coast, decisively resolved a struggle for pre-eminence that had persisted for nearly twenty years.[38] The details are less important than the fact of a sea-change. Conflict and warfare had been features of indigenous history, but rival parties could only draw on the same sorts of resources and do the same kinds of things. If one or the other might have the upper hand at a particular time, things tended not to change too radically. Alliances with prestigious foreigners and their guns might not be easily controlled or monopolized, but when they could be, there was a new potential in indigenous politics. Tribal autonomy, reciprocity, rivalry and competition could be supplanted by centralization, dominance, even exploitation.

If early visitors such as Cook brought new trade goods, resources and ideas to Polynesia, they certainly also subtracted a good deal from indigenous life. Most obviously, lives were lost as a result of introduced disease. The small and relatively isolated populations of the Pacific were vulnerable to a host of infections, including sexually transmitted ones, to which they had never previously been exposed. Individuals died, the health (and hence the labouring capacity) of people generally deteriorated, and populations declined. Just how far they declined is highly debatable, indeed this is one of the most controversial topics in public as well as academic argument about the Pacific past.[39]

While the effects of certain epidemics later in the contact process can be conventionally measured, the assessment of early impact depends on estimates of pre-European populations. Various of Cook's naturalists and officers and other voyagers came up with figures that in some cases were merely impressionistic, in others were arrived at somewhat more methodically, through extrapolation, for example, from the numbers of warriors that districts were believed to be capable of sending into the field. Modern historical demographers tended to be sceptical, and placed greatest weight on the firm evidence of censuses and the like, but these typically only began to be compiled decades after initial contact – after populations had already suffered severe or even catastrophic decline. In a number of contexts, archaeologists recognized that intensive agricultural systems suggested high populations, indeed populations up against the limits of what environments might sustain. But the interpretation of their data is, needless to say, complex and contentious. Hence, whereas the historical demographer claimed that the population of Upolu and Savai'i (which today form the nation of Samoa) was no more than 38,000, today's archaeologist insists that it cannot have been less than 100,000 and may well have been 300,000. On the eve of European contact, there were maybe only 120,000 people, or perhaps as many as one million, in the whole Hawaiian archipelago, depending on whether you favour the low or high estimate.

The issues are political rather than merely demographic. In the Hawaiian case, the higher figures tend to be embraced by native Hawaiians and their supporters, who seek to underscore the tragedy suffered by the people and the need for redress today.[40] But this does not mean that the weight of evidence may not point toward higher numbers. Most importantly, even if the figures are lower, it can only be assumed that incalculable harm was done. Going even on relatively conservative estimates, the population of the Marquesas Islands was reduced by almost half – declining from at least 35,000 to around 20,000 – between about 1800 and 1840. This would imply not merely the loss of family members but the extinction of whole families. Not the death of priests and elders but the loss of priests' knowledge and lore, and of other knowledge – agricultural, maritime, medical and artistic. Not the passing of individual chiefs but more or less the end of the ritual and social life, of everything they had created and struggled over. One can only be astonished both by the protracted awfulness of this damage, and by what remained vital in indigenous life in the Marquesas – during and beyond this horrific process.

Not all populations suffered so badly. But all were disrupted. If change and disruption were features of indigenous life prior to European contact, the disruptions that followed contact were of a new magnitude. Nothing would be the same again.

* * *

To sum up, the last decades, and most especially the last decade, of the eighteenth century marked a great turn in the history of the Pacific. For millennia, Islanders had voyaged and established new communities. Those communities had diversified, voyaged again and evolved. For centuries, there had been sporadic contacts with Europeans. Those contacts had been marked by occasional violence, even by massacres, but for the most part they were fleeting – Europeans had scarcely arrived before they were gone, and once they were gone they generally failed to reappear for decades or longer. The exception that proved the rule was Guam in the Marianas of Micronesia. In the decades following Magellan's visit of 1521, the Spanish sought to conquer and trade from the Philippines, had more or less succeeded in doing so by the 1570s, and began making annual trans-Pacific voyages that linked the archipelago with Acapulco on Mexico's southwestern coast, though the galleons typically aimed to avoid island landfalls and almost always did. From the 1660s onwards Catholic missionaries arrived in the Marianas and over the last thirty years of the seventeenth century the Spanish established themselves, brutally repressing the Chamorro, the people of Guam. A colony was established there but it was one that had surprisingly limited consequences, for the wider Islander world.[41] Neglected, often bypassed, even by the Spanish galleons, it was in no sense the base for commerce and wider engagement that Tahiti and Hawaii both became in the late eighteenth and early nineteenth century. Catastrophic as its impact was, in the Marianas itself, this Spanish intrusion was a sort of insular blockhouse – it was not a catalyst for a more wide-ranging wave of new contact.

In the late 1760s and 1770s, however, in Tahiti, the Society Islands as a whole, in New Zealand and in the Hawaiian and Tongan archipelagoes, Europeans entered the lives of Polynesians. And by the 1790s there was a new momentum to this contact. The visits were no longer being made by great and occasional voyages of discovery, but more frequently, more than once a year, by trading and whaling vessels.[42] Beachcombers had also become a feature of local life, at least on Tahiti, where six to eight and sometimes more were resident, more or less continuously, from the early 1790s on, and on Hawaii, where numbers grew from about ten in 1790 to nearly one hundred in 1806 (by which time they were located not on the island of Hawaii but around the growing port of Honolulu on Oahu).

It is important to stress, however, that the increasing pace of cross-cultural engagement in these places was not reproduced across the Pacific as a whole. In the western islands, particularly, New Guinea and the archipelagoes of the Solomons and Vanuatu saw no frequent visitors for many decades. Though many of the main islands had been sighted by eighteenth-century explorers, their populations were typically cautious and avoided or resisted the visitors. No explorer had had the opportunity to make any extended survey. Of those who passed through the Solomon Islands, for example, few made landings. Of those few, none seem to have ventured any distance inland.[43] The Tahitian enthusiasm for things European and things British, and the mutual familiarity that engendered, had no parallel. There were many peoples – of coastlines less visited for navigational reasons, of river systems, and in the interiors of larger islands – on whose lives Europeans scarcely impinged until the late nineteenth century, in some cases until well into the twentieth.

* * *

This book is about the history of the Pacific from the late eighteenth to the beginning of the twentieth century. It is about the ways Islanders and Europeans came to deal with each other, and put up with each other, in the kind of world we call imperial. It is interested in what empire really was, not so much at the level of colour on the map, or the policy and diplomacy of the metropolitan powers, but in bibles and blood on the beaches of the islands, and in the imaginations that these novel artefacts and intrusions engendered. *Islanders* is about this history, it is not 'the history' or even 'a history' in the sense of a conventional survey that tries to present a general account of an epoch. The book does aim to tell a larger story through individuals' experiences and lives, through events and happenings, some of which were small in the scheme of things, but remain resonant of the kinds of dealings that shaped the colonial relationships and cultures which emerged in the Pacific during the nineteenth century. Some of my characters, such as the Tahitian king Pomare, the missionary John Williams and the navigator Dumont d'Urville, are major figures, considered great men and women in their time. Others such as the Tahitian traveller Tapioi, the Rapa Nui elder Va'e Iko and the Fijian rebel Na Bisiki, were scarcely known beyond the milieux they inhabited, though their acts and interests can be reconstructed from obscure records, and are poignantly, disproportionately resonant of the circumstances and predicaments of their contemporaries.

Over the last twenty-five years it has been my privilege to get to know parts of the Pacific, however unevenly. This book inevitably gives greatest weight to peoples and moments I am most familiar with – the Marquesas and Fiji loom large, I am embarrassed that north-western Oceania does not – but the scenes and stories that I foreground are intended to be broadly representative. New Zealand's history, particularly from 1840 onwards, has been addressed in a strong and substantial literature; points of connection and parallels with Pacific islands' stories enter into this book, but I make no attempt to 'cover' colonial New Zealand in any more extensive sense. The long histories of trade and cosmopolitan contact in north-west New Guinea are very much part of the larger story I seek to tell, but for the bulk of the great island's peoples, colonial encounters and their consequences begin to unfold only from the last years of the nineteenth century onward. They therefore belong to a succeeding book, rather than this one.

There is a kind of watershed in nineteenth-century Oceania, a broad transition from contact and exchange between Islanders who remained essentially autonomous, to confrontation with colonial states and enterprises that would, insofar as they could, claim territory, command labour and presume a responsibility to govern. European acts of annexation were not necessarily the turning points, though needless to say in hindsight they often appear to have been. In any event, those acts fall before 1850 in a few cases and after that date in many others. Hence it has made sense to divide this book into two parts, covering roughly the first and second halves of the century respectively, while bearing in mind that people's lives and many processes, such as the emergence of a migrant labour trade, straddled that date, and therefore the two parts of the book. The chapter order is broadly chronological but essentially thematic, meaning that successive chapters dedicated to particular stories overlap, reflecting the uneven progression of, for example, contact and commerce across the ocean.

* * *

Captain Cook's voyages had an impact on Europeans as well as Islanders. They provided an extraordinary wealth of information about a great world – about peoples, places and societies that had barely before been known. Of course, detailed information concerning parts of the non-European world – the Americas and Asia for instance – had long been available. But a fresh body of knowledge, which was by the standards of the time rich and empirically precise, captured the imagination of a new and broad reading public. While the fascination of the exotic and the romanticization of the noble savage are most commonly mentioned among the responses Cook's *Voyages* stimulated, the Evangelicals who were growing in numbers at the time were more typically appalled to come, as it were, face to face with the reality of heathen societies. Cook had vividly described a human sacrifice that he witnessed on Tahiti during his third voyage; the ceremony was depicted, too, in a fine and graphic engraving after John Webber, published with the narrative of Cook's third voyage but widely reproduced in cheaper forms. Small in numbers peoples such as the Tahitians might have been, but the barbarism of their ceremony excited and horrified the evangelical constituency, and heightened their sense of the evil in the world, which true Christians were bound to actively combat.

These at any rate were the thoughts of William Carey, a Northamptonshire shoemaker and passionate autodidact, born in 1761, who joined evangelical circles and read widely in theology but also in geography and exploration.[44] He drew population estimates from Cook and many others, and compiled an extended statistical table. This calculation of the vast numbers of souls who had never heard God's word was central to his 1792 pamphlet, *An Enquiry into the Obligations of Christians to use means for the Conversion of the Heathens*, more or less the charter document for the formation of the Baptist Missionary Society. Carey felt that the growth of navigation and trade enabled the evangelization of distant populations, which had previously not been feasible, but his imagination was also energized by the novel sense of the world as a great market, and his metaphor was that of a hazardous yet potentially super-profitable trading voyage. Merchants, his readers knew, would venture to the 'utmost limits' of their charter, enter among 'the most barbarous nations', undergo the greatest peril and suffer tremendous anxieties, all because their souls had entered into the spirit of their project; Christians likewise needed to commit themselves to the expansion of Christ's kingdom. 'Their charter is very extensive, their encouragements exceeding great, and the returns promised infinitely superior to all the gains of the most lucrative fellowship.'[45]

While missionary activity was not new, it gained new and dramatic momentum in Britain in the 1790s. If, for modern secular imaginations, missionaries are self-righteous, narrow-minded, pious, indeed ludicrous characters, the stereotype in no sense captures the restless and fervent young men

5 A Human Sacrifice, in a Morai in Otaheite, engraving after John Webber, from James Cook and James King, *A Voyage to the Pacific Ocean*.

and women who were drawn into the enterprise in its early decades. Typically members of the emerging artisanal classes, they were full of aspirations and ambitions, which were not politically revolutionary but were radical in diverse spiritual, cultural and social respects. Carey had thought of establishing a Tahitian mission but turned to India; another body, formed soon afterward, and at first called simply the Missionary Society, would conceive of the South Seas as its field of activity.[46] The wave of evangelical energy paralleled the increasing momentum of contact and commerce in Polynesia. If initially these developments were but loosely linked – inasmuch as the example of the Pacific had stoked evangelical fires – they would very soon become powerfully intertwined.

PART ONE

✦

THE BIBLE AND THE GUN
Contact, Commerce, Conversion

CHAPTER ONE

✦

A plan of great extent and importance

A *Missionary Voyage to the Southern Pacific Ocean, performed in the Years 1796, 1797, and 1798 . . . including details never before published, of the Natural and Civil State of Otaheite*, the first book produced by the London Missionary Society, would also be its most opulent – the handsome and well-illustrated quarto, dedicated to King George III, set a standard that the innumerable subsequent tracts, transactions, reports, catechisms and primers never quite matched.[1] That was perhaps a measure of the extent to which the Society's great expectations came to be, if not exactly diminished, certainly complicated.

The London Missionary Society had been established in 1795. Quickly attracting philanthropists and subscribers, it got off to an enthusiastic start, recruited prospective missionaries, purchased a ship and found a captain. The *Duff*, under James Wilson, a trader friendly to Evangelicals, departed London in August 1796 for Otaheite (Tahiti), with a crew of twenty-two and a missionary party of thirty-nine, including just four ordained ministers. The prior occupations of the twenty-six other men included buckle and harness maker, carpenter, cooper, hatter, tailor, tinworker and weaver. Six were accompanied by their wives; the three children included a sixteen-week-old baby, named Samuel Otuu Hassell in honour of the great Tahitian chief, properly Tu, or Pomare I, whose friendship this odd set of earnest, eager, not quite middle-class men anticipated. Yet the instructions prepared by the LMS directors stressed that the missionaries were to make it clear to their hosts that they, the Islanders, would be recipients of 'advantages' that they ought to desire. The missionaries were not supposed, therefore, to beg for aid or protection; instead, they were to expect chiefs to offer them inducements to stay. In particular, the 'full title' to sufficient land for the missionary party to settle upon 'should not be purchased, but required, as a condition for remaining with them', it was stipulated.[2] The expectation back in London, it seems, was that Christianity's 'advantages' would be readily appreciated, and that appreciation swiftly acted upon.

On one subject, the directions implied greater practicality. A resolution at a meeting of the Society had stated that 'a mission be undertaken to Otaheite, the Friendly Islands, the Marquesas, the Sandwich, and the Pelew Islands'. The instructions affirmed that the plan was one 'of great extent and importance', but acknowledged that it needed to be balanced against strength in numbers, and the desirability perhaps of the missionaries forming one or two parties that would amount to 'models of civilized society, small indeed, but tolerably complete'.[3]

The 'Missionary House and Environs in the Island of Otaheite', the frontispiece engraving to *A Missionary Voyage*, depicts no doubt the kind of model society that the directors had in mind. It may have been intended as a contrast

6 'Missionary House and Environs in the Island of Otaheite', engraving after William Wilson, frontispiece to Wilson, *A Missionary Voyage to the Southern Pacific Ocean*.

to William Hodges's iconic paintings of the same location, Point Venus, on the eastern end of Tahiti at Matavai Bay, which were well known through printed engravings. Hodges, the artist on Cook's second voyage, had evoked voluptuous bodies, a sensual existence and natural luxury – an imagining of Oceania that would later be attributed, above all, to the artist Paul Gauguin and his literary contemporaries, such as Pierre Loti.[4] The associations of the evangelical image were emphatically different. It revealed, not an exotic people, but two peoples, European and Tahitian, seemingly in a state of friendly proximity, if not exactly intimacy. The missionaries and their wives look as though they are politely enjoying an excursion by boat on, say, the Thames at Richmond. A couple of native ladies are seated easily against the missionary house – in neat Islander style, but with a British flag aloft – while another Tahitian figure holds his arms out wide, amazed by one of the Englishmen, who is working a long saw. A white woman and her baby imply that the situation is safe and secure, while, in the centre, a double canoe brings Tahitian gifts – some pigs and a pile of coconuts – and a missionary waves to indicate where these ought to be put. Whereas Hodges accorded some prominence to the carvings of gods often mounted on larger canoes, the engraving includes these figures without detailing them, as it were understating the ongoing, indeed stubborn heathenism of these people.

While the *Duff* remained at Tahiti, the missionaries were able, remarkably, to negotiate what they understood the directors had pressed them to require: the presentation of not only a tract of land, but the whole of Matavai. Certainly people gathered for an oration by the elderly priest Ha'amanemane, which included the genealogies of the chiefs of Tahiti and Moorea among other islands, and a genealogy-like recitation of the ships captained by Wallis, Bougainville and Cook down to Wilson of the *Duff*. This was followed by what the missionaries understood as 'the formal surrender of the district' – the priest observed 'that we might take what houses, trees, fruit, hogs, &c. we thought proper'.[5] But the missionaries' grasp of what was said depended on a beachcomber known as Peter the Swede, who they did not entirely trust, and it is notable that Ha'amanemane promptly then sought the assistance of the captain. The priest wanted to mount an assault against the island of Raiatea, to regain lands from which he had been displaced, and was unhappy and no doubt perplexed to hear that the missionaries would not fight unless they themselves were attacked. Almost certainly, what Ha'amanemane said had nothing to do with any gift of land, but represented a welcome, a rehearsal of the long history of connections between the Islanders and the Europeans,

7 'The cession of the district of Matavai in the island of Otaheite to Captain James
Wilson for the use of the missionaries', acquatint by Bartolozzi after Robert Smirke.

perhaps specifically the British, and an offer of shelter and food, intended to
provide the context for his own request. All this became evident to the
missionaries on the ground soon enough, though at home the Society would
make much of the 'cession' of the lands, going as far as to commission a large
painting commemorating the moment, and printing engravings based
upon it.

* * *

The sense that the missionaries would form 'one or two' main settlements was
more or less adhered to. Eighteen of the men, including all four of those who
were ordained, and all the women and children, remained at Tahiti, while it
was anticipated that two missionaries would settle at the island of Tahuata in
the Marquesas, and the remaining ten go to Tonga. They were nearly all young
men, apart from Seth Kelso, a cotton weaver from Manchester, who would
turn fifty during his residence in Tonga.

On reaching the island of Tahuata one of the missionaries, William Harris, became increasingly uneasy – compared with Tahiti, the island had seen few Europeans. The men were fully tattooed, and no doubt intimidating; and, if the densely gardened and inhabited coastal lands of Tahiti seemed inviting, indeed Arcadian, the Marquesan valleys, hemmed between precipitous mountains and a rough sea, were lacking in idyllic associations, indeed daunting. Harris vacillated, agreed to spend a night ashore, but was woken by women curious to inspect him physically – his earlier refusal to take one as a partner had made them uncertain of his sex. This intrusion horrified or terrified him; he fled immediately to the beach, was robbed of most of his possessions, and once back on the *Duff* refused absolutely to countenance remaining on the island. It is all the more extraordinary that the second missionary, William Pascoe Crook, remained 'steadfast' in his intention to stay on his own. He was struck, perhaps, less by the rugged topography than the groves of august breadfruit trees – which seem to grow larger in the Marquesas than anywhere else in the Pacific – by the music of barkcloth beaters, by intricately carved ivory ornaments and wooden bowls, and by the fine stonemasonry manifest in great house platforms. There were signs of civility for those prepared to look, and Crook seems to have been capable of looking, also perhaps of looking beyond the 'wrapping in images' that constituted tattooing, at the acuity and the humour of the chief Teinae, who offered him a house.[6] Yet the island was seldom called at, and Crook can only have anticipated a gap of a year or more before he might receive support of any sort from a ship. But he was happy and according to Wilson had 'various kinds of garden-seeds, implements, medicines, &c.; an Encyclopedia, and other useful books'.[7]

* * *

Cook had called the Tongan archipelago the Friendly Islands. Readers of the published accounts of this group of islands in his voyage narratives could have formed only favourable impressions. With those of Hawaii, Tongan societies were the most stratified in the Pacific; their institutions seemed those of European kingdoms; aristocrats were treated with great ritual respect, and at times behaved despotically. Some early visitors indeed considered their treatment of people arbitrary and callous; but Cook among others was impressed by the stability and refinement of the social order, and by well-maintained and fenced plantations, implying clearly established relations of property.

All this augured well, the missionaries might have thought, but the civilized polity encountered by the British in the 1770s was not static: it would transpire that it was only temporarily stable. The political structures of Tongan society had been evolving and were continuing to evolve, engendering new tensions. Cook and his companions had been puzzled by the roles and relations among various men of high rank, most baldly by the fact that three individuals were, they were told at different times, the king.

Traditions that were only collated and analyzed subsequently make it apparent that from the late fifteenth century onward the sacred kingship had been distinguished from practical governance: the king, or Tui Tonga, became a religious figurehead, while a lower-ranking aristocrat such as a younger brother was responsible for managing affairs, and held the title of Tui Ha'atakalaua; a hundred or so years later, a further title, Tui Kanokupolu, was created, and the bearer governed the important district of Hihifo.[8] So, what the missionaries were told was right: there were three 'kings', of different sorts. As far as is known, this system had more or less endured through the seventeenth and eighteenth centuries, though the figure of the Tui Ha'atakalaua declined in status, becoming a nominal political leader, while that of the Tui Kanokupolu emerged as the dominant figure. Moreover, although succession to the Tui Tonga title was meant to be strictly hereditary, a group of high-ranking leaders were supposed to elect the other two individuals from members of appropriate families; hence there was much scope for rivalry, as there was for practical meddling on the part of the Tui Tonga, despite the supposed depoliticization of the kingship.

A 'Christian mission': one thinks of European missionaries arriving among non-Europeans, as the party on board the *Duff* had arrived among the Tahitians. However, that arrival was something other than a straightforward meeting of two cultures: among those the missionaries met first were European beachcombers, expatriates living among Polynesians, who would serve as their interpreters. This was so not only in the literal sense that they helped translate conversation: Peter the Swede, among others, interpreted Tahitian circumstances, as best he could, and no doubt did his best, too, to explain the missionaries to the Tahitians. When the *Duff* reached Tongatapu, in April 1797, there was a new assortment of people on board. Captain Wilson had brought along both Peter and another Swede referred to as John, who was ill, aged around forty, and seeking a passage back to Europe, and three Tahitians – a young woman named Tano Manu, who was Peter's companion, a man known only as Tom, and a boy called Harauia. All were helpful to William Crook, who made the most of the passage to the Marquesas via Tonga to improve his understanding of Polynesian languages.[9]

The Tongans who visited the ship soon after its arrival thus encountered Islanders whose speech they could not immediately understand (Tahitian was close to Marquesan but not to Tongan), yet who resembled them physically and perhaps behaviourally. They also met a mixed set of Europeans, some who sought to settle among them, albeit with intentions that differed from those of the white men resident already – for here, too, beachcombers had beaten the missionaries to the beach, and as it were contaminated the indigenous understanding of what contact with civilized society might mean. Of their arrival, Wilson remarks both of the 'unspeakable pleasure' he and the missionaries felt in hearing English spoken so far from home, and on the evident villainy of the speakers: 'in England a well-disposed person would shun them as he would a swindler or a pick-pocket'.[10] Yet Benjamin Ambler, originally of Shadwell, London, and John Connelly, from Cork, would inevitably be there, whether to assist or to frustrate the missionaries remained to be seen.

* * *

The missionary voyage makes mention, in passing, of the fact that some of the chiefs who visited the *Duff* 'regaled themselves with a bowl of kava, which, though a delicious treat to them, was . . . disgusting to us'.[11] Not only did the Europeans not partake, they felt unable to dine, until the business was over. It was perhaps natural to the missionaries to dissociate themselves from the consumption of an apparently unappetizing drink. But kava was more than a refreshment and mild narcotic for these Islanders. In a double sense it was integral to the social life, admittedly not of the population as a whole, but that of high-ranking men. It was never simply prepared and drunk unceremoniously. It was ritually offered to the person of highest rank present, then it was received, blessed and shared.[12] Among a small group of friends, the rites would be performed perhaps cursorily, but they would still be performed, and on many occasions – when guests were present, or when some arrival, departure, gift, or event was being marked – protocol would be minutely observed, and orations might be extended. Once those were concluded, however, those drinking would relax, and there would be much talk. *Talanoa*, casual conversation, loomed large in Polynesian life, especially among men and women of higher social status, who were, partly if not fully, relieved of the labour of subsistence gardening; the common people who occupied their lands also worked them.

Preserved in museum collections from Tonga – as well as Fiji and Samoa – are many fine, large, low circular bowls, as much as a yard across, carved from single blocks of the hardwood called *vesi* in Fijian, more often than not beautifully toned and richly patinated, bearing the traces of many kava drinking

8 Kava bowl, Tonga or eastern Fiji, likely to have been collected on Cook's second or third voyage.

sessions. These great dishes are not just cultural relics, however; more recent examples of much the same size and form will be encountered all over the place – in ordinary people's houses, chiefs' houses, public buildings and government offices – by anyone who spends any time in any of these island nations today. After the garden work is done, sometimes before working, or instead of working, people will drink, stretch out on pandanus mats, talk, and doze off. They will mainly be men, but women may well join them, in talking and dozing if not in drinking.

The point is banal but also basic to what it meant to live in Tonga. To maintain a distance from the kava circle was like spending time with Europeans, without ever sitting down at a dining table. Bowls, like tables, were touched often, were part of the experience of day-to-day interactions and intimacies. It was not inevitable that foreigners were excluded from the rituals of respect and hierarchy that were expressive of higher Tongan social life, or the more informal flow of talanoa, of talk, through which everyday news as well as more extraordinary matters were aired and indeed negotiated. There had long been outsiders, such as Fijians and Samoans, in Tonga – they travelled back and forth, had certain roles and performed particular services. They seated themselves among the group around the vesi bowl; they were included, and actively included themselves, on terms appropriate to *muli*, foreigners, in

Tongan life. The missionaries on the other hand remained outside the circle, looking anxiously in.

* * *

Over the days following the *Duff*'s arrival, the Tahitians and Europeans began to meet prominent men, and prominent women too. Some of the Europeans were struck by the ceremony that surrounded a visit to the vessel of an 'old lady', whose amazing corpulence rendered her coming on board rather difficult' (body size, in Tonga, tended to speak opulence and status). She was accompanied by a considerable party of female and male attendants; Wilson was prompted to remark that the respect paid to her distinguished Tonga from many 'other savage states or tribes' in which women were notably servile. Here, rather, they possessed 'the highest degrees of rank, and support it with a dignity and firmness equal to the men'.[13]

The people the missionaries met were caught up in the latest machinations, in short-term struggles that spoke a deeper danger, an uneasiness in the compromises that constituted the Tongan aristocratic order. The missionaries, needless to say, had no awareness of the genealogies, protocols and innovations that lay behind these circumstances, but did learn bits and pieces. They gathered that the widow of the great chief Paulaho, who had been Tui Tonga at the time of Cook's visit, had tried to assume control of some lands to which she was entitled, on the death of a lesser chief. But a man they called 'Toogahowe' had pre-emptively seized the estate; the lady had called on her supporters to drive him off, but failed to do so; 'Toogahowe' pursued his advantage, and expelled the woman and her party from the island.[14]

The 'widow' of the story, Tupoumoheofo, was in fact far more than a mere consort to Paulaho. She had been responsible for an elaborate ceremony observed by Cook, which had, so far from being a customary rite, involved an unprecedented transgression of conventional taboos – the high chief had shared a meal with their son. This was a subversion of protocol, but one that boldly declared that the young man was elevated, with immediate effect, to the status of king – which was to pre-empt the conventions of election and succession, and consolidate Tupoumoheofo's own centrality in the highest affairs of state. Her strategizing went further when she herself assumed the role of the executive chief, the Tui Kanokupolu, for a period somewhat later, thereby antagonizing various other prominent players, notably Tuku'aho ('Toogahowe'), who made war and forced her to step down in favour of his father, Mumui, an elderly and indeed declining chief, at the time of the arrival of the missionaries. Little did they know, but the dispute over a tract of land reflected long-standing antagonisms between these great title-holders, over matters including the very distinction between sacred and secular authority – specifically, over the issue of whether the customary separation would be sustained.[15]

* * *

On the departure of the *Duff* the missionaries formed several smaller parties, living with various chiefs, labouring to retain their protection and support, and struggling to prevent their property being appropriated, either by locals or by the white beachcombers, who tended increasingly to harass them. If these external threats were demoralizing, the missionary party furthered suffered from defection from within. Even before the ship's departure, George Vason, a twenty-five-year-old bricklayer from Nottingham, was suspected of sexual relations with a local woman, which he at first denied and then acknowledged. Though he initially expressed remorse, the others' hopes that his conduct promised 'recovery' were quickly extinguished – to the contrary, Vason enjoyed 'mingling with the heathen', displaying a strong inclination to learn not only their language but their ways, in which he soon arrived at what his brethren called 'a woeful proficiency'.[16]

Vason went and lived with the family of the high chief Mulikiha'amea, who appears to have been as genuinely fond of him as he was of them. He married, adopted local dress, and was given access to land which he cultivated with care, with a good deal of assistance from the commoner people of the vicinity, who were customarily obliged to work for him. He travelled around the islands with his Tongan friends. He contracted further marriages, not it appears primarily because he wanted more sexual partners, but because people sought alliances with him or for him – the women were the relatives of chiefs who sought an affiliation with Vason, or to strengthen an affiliation with Mulikiha'amea through him.[17] He was, in other words, acting approximately in a Tongan manner, and his experience suggests that there is a distinction to be made between beachcombers such as the group in Tahiti and more exceptional figures such as Vason. In Tahiti, the Swedes and the other Europeans there associated largely with each other, and were incorporated in native society in a peripheral way, but Vason was more genuinely and fully integrated. He was not made at home by people of rank because they wanted him to facilitate contacts with the commanders of visiting ships, or help them get guns. He did neither of these things, yet he was accorded the status of a chief, he learned what was expected of him, and he did it.

* * *

More than a decade later, Vason published a memoir of this time. Although he wrote apologetically, lamenting his 'declension', his conquest by temptation, these declarations ring hollow. Despite Vason's awkward, at any rate formulaic writing, his reader is struck by the aesthetic pleasure, the sense of social stimulation, that pervade this account of experience in Tonga. In the evenings, Vason recounted, if people did not dance, as they often did, they would recline on their mats and talk. 'I have been delighted, for hours,' he wrote, 'in listening to these noctural confabulations, and often very much surprised and improved, by the shrewdness of their observations, and the good sense of their reasoning.' Their etiquette, their gift-giving, their amusements and recreations, their dances, their crafts, their food and fish, all delighted him too. As did his estate: 'With what joy did I contemplate its little pendant groves of coca and plantain trees, and its smooth lawns, diversified by little habitations, which contained the peaceful natives, who now became my subjects and labourers to cultivate my fields for their own subsistence and mine!'[18] From Nottinghamshire working man to Tongan noble was indeed an extraordinary transformation, and one that, in fact, resonated deeply with the yearning for self-advancement and improvement at the heart of the evangelical self. The creation of a utopia in the missionary field, a perfect society free of the disorder and venality of the British metropolis, was also a recurrent motif of the missionary imagination. While the image of a garden – in which souls would be tended, in which the Lord would reap a great harvest – loomed large, the lapsed missionary preferred to garden literally.

For two years Vason enjoyed himself, and no doubt learned a great deal more of Tongan life than he in the end succeeded in conveying through his slim publication. The remainder of the missionary party enjoyed relative security, but struggled to subsist. They were fortunate to adopt one of the several other beachcombers who arrived during their stay, one William Beak, a sober character and a trained blacksmith.[19] He made many iron knives and blades to fit Tongan *toki*, or adzes, which the missionaries exchanged with chiefs for supplies of food, while endeavouring at the same time to establish gardens themselves. The missionaries say nothing of preaching, or of otherwise attempting to communicate the Christian message. Given the extent to which they remained with each other, given their lack of intimacy with Tongans, they probably never acquired the level of linguistic confidence to discourse on gods true and false. But they were also no doubt sufficiently self-aware to grasp that they were no more than marginal figures, mere bystanders, in a society possessed by its own momentum.

On 21 April 1799, Tuakaho, the Tui Kanokupolu, was killed. He had been overbearing, and it was a custom of sorts that despots were disposed of. But this – endorsed by a coalition of conspirators, among them his long-standing antagonists – would be no ordinary assassination. It marked the end of a period of relative tranquillity. If that tranquillity had been uneasy, often disturbed by rivalry, it now gave way to unrestrained war, which was to carry on intermittently for many years. Finau, high chief of Vava'u, the northern-most part of the Tongan group of islands, asserted his pre-eminence. It was at first anticipated that Vason's friend and protector, Mulikiha'amea, would replace Tuakaho, but he allied himself with Finau and was killed by Finau's opponents, as were many individual chiefs and hundreds of common people. Invading and counter-invading parties pillaged the lands of their enemies and enemies' supporters; pigs were seized, houses, gardens and canoes were destroyed, and in some instances those who could not flee – women, children and the elderly – were massacred by warriors. Among those killed were three of the missionaries, Daniel Bowell, Samuel Gaulton and Samuel Harper, in the wrong place at the wrong time. The remainder went from place to place, fearing with good reason for their lives. Though the conflict eased in the latter months of 1799, the catastrophe was blamed by a native priest upon the missionaries' presence, and affairs remained unsettled.[20]

In late January 1800 a ship named the *Betsey* appeared. It was a whaler carrying 'letters of marque', hence authorized to act as a privateer. It had been engaged in actions against Spanish ports on the South American coast, and brought a prize under the command of one Captain Glasse, variously known as *El Plumier* or the *Plumo*; the *Betsey* had called at Tahiti, where the missionary John Harris had joined it, in order to investigate the state of the Tongan mission; he found the missionaries, needless to say, more than ready to depart.[21] There was no ambiguity as to the balance sheet: their part of the Missionary Society's 'great and important' plan had failed, even to create an awareness of Christianity among the Tongans. The enterprise's collapse reflected not so much the intransigence or deep-seatedness of local religion, but the intractable energy of local society. In no sense, at this time, could a few Europeans change what it meant to be Tongan.

* * *

The missionaries made no effort, at the time of their departure, to locate or assist Vason. Associated now with the great chief Finau, he was tattooed and he participated in some military ventures, but he was shocked by the all-out nature of the conflict – by the surprise killings, on some occasions, of hundreds, and by the vigour of the effort to destroy a people's subsistence base. Fighting was renewed after the missionaries' escape, provisions were short everywhere – and Vason, too, seized the opportunity to escape when the *Duff*'s successor, the missionary ship *Royal Admiral*, passed through the islands in August 1801. William Wilson (nephew of James, who had commanded the *Duff*) found that circumstances had again deteriorated, the war:

> continued to rage as violent as ever, and had reduced the people to a starving condition . . . no respectable chiefs remained at Tongataboo, that they were either killed or had fled to other Islands for safety, Lukalalla [Finau] who resided at Harby [Ha'apai] has the strongest party, he is the only chief of consequence that has weathered the storm, all the Northern Islands have submitted to him, but the inhabitants of Tongataboo neither acknowledge him, nor suffer his adherents to land there, therefore the war continues. Cultivation is neglected, there were neither Yams nor Plantains (their staff of life) at Vavow, nor a single Hog on the Island.[22]

The missionaries proceeded to China, where Vason was too ashamed (he at any rate claimed afterwards) to return to his own country, and joined an American vessel instead, which sailed via the Caribbean (calling at Guadeloupe, at the time in the hands of rebel slaves) to New York. By now a professional sailor, Vason joined another voyage to the Caribbean, but then felt he could return to England, and to Nottingham. Despite his full tattoo, he became a member of respectable society, at first responsible for a workhouse, then governor of Nottingham gaol. He married, attended a Baptist church, and was considered a liberal man, though one who retained the appearance of a weather-beaten tar, and, through his middle age, was said to be somewhat irritable and melancholy. His *Authentic Narrative of Four Years' Residence at Tongataboo*, published anonymously in 1810, carries a distinct nostalgia, though one tempered by the recollection of violence. It is not hard to imagine that a man who had experienced such joy and such loss before the age of thirty might subsequently have been prone to depression.

* * *

William Crook did not fare well on Tahuata. The people were not unfriendly, but they faced difficulties of their own: even while the *Duff* had been at the island, there were food shortages, and soon after its departure a breadfruit crop failed. The Islanders did not go out of their way to adopt a foreigner, and Crook had no notion of how he might make himself related. He was also disadvantaged by the particular nature of local interests in what he had to trade. Most Polynesians had manifested strong interests in iron, and the missionaries in Tonga had sustained a food supply by bartering tools, but they had a forge, and were adapting what they had, producing iron versions of the local adze blades. Crook could not do anything similar and 'wished in vain to exchange the Iron ware that was left with him for provisions of any kind'.[23] Only later did he realize that he might have had food had he asked for it; as it was he struggled to feed himself, resorting to fishing with a line in his hand, as he swam out into the deep waters of the bay.

Despite his isolation, the missionary appears to have made a real effort to convey his message. But, he found, people refused to see things other than in their own terms. 'They could compare a book to nothing but a head dress, & letters only to punctures', that is, to tattoos.[24] If one can forgive him his frustration, these were nevertheless potent and intriguing analogies; headdresses, as Crook surely knew, were not mere frippery, but sacred priests' and warriors' wear, while *tatau* armoured the body and marked personal identity.

Rich and confusing as this meeting between missionary and Islander, European artefact and Polynesian perception, certainly was, it was not a two-sided encounter but one that involved other parties, people who were neither Marquesan nor English. The *Duff* had landed not only the missionary Crook but also Harauia, who absconded and remained on the island. Though the Tahitian boy had helped Crook with the language during the ship's passage, they had evidently not remained friends, and the lad swiftly gained fluency in Marquesan (which was and is close to Tahitian) and 'spread various false reports'. Some eight months later, a New England vessel left a Hawaiian or Tahuata. Though Crook understood that his name was something like Owheve, he had been called Sam on board, and this was rendered Tama by the Tahuatans. They 'were highly entertained' by his account of Hawaiian 'manners & notions . . . which were sufficiently similar to their own, to interest and inform them', Crook later observed. The information that he had tried himself to convey was in contrast too remote, too peculiar to be of any interest.

Almost a year after his arrival, Crook sighted a ship off Vaitahu, and joined a few people who paddled out in a canoe. Edmund Fanning was captain of the *Betsy*, not the ship that had taken the missionaries from Tonga, but an American trader that was carrying seal skins for the Chinese market. He had given up the struggle against adverse winds, and already decided to bear off toward Nukuhiva, to seek refreshment there instead.[25] Though his books and few possessions were ashore, Crook decided on the spur of the moment to remain on board. Latterly people had been treating him, he reported, with contempt; they had made Tama their *toa*, or chief warrior, but he, they considered, was good for nothing but poring over a book.

On arriving at Taiohae, a vast amphitheatre of a bay, Crook somehow fell on his feet. Almost immediately, the chief Keatonui demanded that the young missionary exchange names with his grandson, and from that point on he had a place in local life, he was well fed and looked after. Keatonui, Crook believed, was 'a greater Chief than any other in the Island', an assertion that would have been vigorously contested by rivals and opponents in other valleys. But the man, who was some forty to fifty years old, came across as astute, and Crook's careful report of the chief's various kin connections underscores the impression of a politically acute character.[26]

A descriptive manuscript that bears the missionary's name was actually composed later in London, by the London Missionary Society intellectual Samuel Greatheed, on the basis of interviews with Crook and – importantly – the Marquesan boy Temoteitei who in due course returned to London with him. Hence it is unclear whether the curiosity and intelligence of this ethnography is to be credited to the erudite gentleman, the evangelical fieldworker, or the native voyager – or rather to the meeting of the three. In any event, despite its obscurity the 'Account of the Marquesas Islands' was as rich and nuanced as any description of a particular non-European culture composed around this time. Marquesan ideas of *tapu*, or taboo, which continued to boggle the minds of observers for decades, were unravelled with some elegance; but the evocation of Keatonui's power base could have been of special importance for the understanding of Polynesian society. Deceptively simple, it detailed the chief's affiliations and relationships: 'One of Keattonue's sisters, named Taheibu, lives with Pahoutahau, an elderly man, of remarkable stature and strength, . . . & they have the property of the next part of the Bay. . . . Their eldest Son, who is a person of considerable property, is espoused to a beautiful Woman, named Teabu, a daughter of the Chief of Tioa . . .'.[27] And so it went on, a mounting accumulation of affiliations, via adoption, marriage, membership of men's houses and the like.

European travellers in the Pacific notoriously misidentified leaders or exaggerated their power. The manuscript's rendering of Keatonui's network enables an understanding of a Polynesian polity, quite different to the usual clumsy characterization of the hereditary chief, a governor of tribe and territory. Yes, rank was inherited, but not in any straightforward way. Keatonui drew his status from his mother rather than his father. More importantly, there was no formalized sovereignty, even at a local level. Instead, life here was shaped by something like the faction-mongering that proceeds within modern political parties. Connections were drawn upon, gifts, favours and services exchanged, and people mobilized for the cause or the occasion.

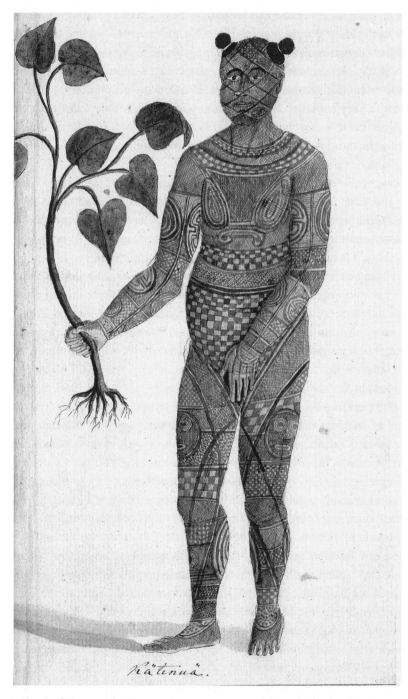

9 Sketch of Keatonui, by Herman Loewenstern, a participant in the first Russian circumnavigation of 1803–6.

Perhaps, this was more starkly so around Taiohae, and in the Marquesas generally, than in the Tongan or Hawaiian Islands, where chiefly office, indeed kingship, was more fully institutionalized.[28] Yet the very practical, negotiable and indeed precarious quality that was so striking in Marquesan political life was also a feature of those overtly more ordered societies – as the awful conflicts in Tonga made all too apparent. And if affairs were negotiable and precarious, prior to any European intrusion or meddling, they could surely only become more dangerous and less predictable afterwards.

* * *

Crook made friends with one of Keatonui's dependants, a man named Hiihui, who helped him negotiate rights to garden and live on a plot of land. He did not marry, at any rate he does not acknowledge any association with a local woman, nor did he become tattooed, but in other respects he began to settle in, as Vason had done. He witnessed feasting and warfare, and kept Keatonui on side, even though the chief got tired of his religious talk, 'objecting that he did not know this or that tree, and how then should he be able to know God?'[29]

Comfortable as the situation had become, Crook however dreamt of the arrival of ships, and found himself agitated by the thought that vessels might pass, and that he would be unable to reach them. In due course, in December 1798, two English whalers did call, anchoring not at Taiohae but close to Taipi, and it was only with difficulty that Crook could persuade people to take him by canoe into this hostile territory; yet they did so without incident. His 'account' presents his decision to leave the island as a considered one. Crook stated that he expected to arrive in England before a second voyage of the *Duff*, and hence to be able to provide the London Missionary Society directors and the new missionary party with valuable information. He may even have persuaded himself, but it is all too clear that the intractable exoticism of Marquesan life had exhausted him. If Crook had found he could live among these people, he had also learned that he was powerless to change them.

Like, it seems, nearly every ship of the epoch, the *Euphrates* and the *Butterworth* carried Islanders, two young men from Tahuata, of whom one chose to remain on Nukuhiva; his place was taken by a Taiohae boy, Hikonaiki. Crook and the other young Marquesan, Temoteitei, reached London in April 1799 on the *Butterworth*; in October 1800, Hikonaiki arrived there on the *Euphrates*; and a month later, Harauia, who had sailed with Crook on the *Duff* and been an irritant to him when first at Tahuata, appeared too, on another whaleship. Temoteitei and Crook meanwhile spent time with the bookish

Greatheed in Buckinghamshire, providing him with the material for the 'Account' and for a Marquesan vocabulary. The last sentence of the 'Account' read 'The Change of Climate much affected the health of these three Islanders.'[30] This seems to have been euphemistic. Temoteitei's death late in 1800 is recorded. What became of the other two Islanders is not.

* * *

If, since Robinson Crusoe, the castaway has been a figure of poignancy and fascination, the beachcomber emerged, during the nineteenth century, as a similarly seductive literary motif. Just as the idea of a man removed from all society was philosophically potent, for theorists of individualism and utilitarianism, the figure of a man between societies, caught up in cross-cultural trade and mistranslation, came to be equally suggestive. Writers such as Robert Louis Stevenson were intrigued by confusions of language and morality at the edge of empire. A century later, postcolonial theorists relished the condition of cultural 'hybridity' for much the same reasons. In the Pacific, historians and anthropologists such as Greg Dening made beachcombers an icon of the toing and froing, the crossings of beaches, that seemed the stuff of these islands' histories.[31]

The ideas were fertile but had their limitations. The beachcomber was canonically a European in the islands. Though the story of Mai, the Polynesian traveller to Europe, had long been considered equally or more fascinating, it was also taken to be exceptional. The true range and diversity of Islanders' own travels are only beginning to be appreciated, as indeed is the extent to which many beachcombers were in fact Islanders rather than Europeans.

The story of one Tahitian was publicized and debated in a limited way about the time Vason's own memoir first appeared anonymously in London. On Friday, 15 July 1808, a curious case came to trial at Hick's Hall, the magistrates' court for the county of Middlesex, which was located in St John Street, Clerkenwell. The trial was brief. It involved nothing as sensational as murder, no substantial sum of money, nor anybody remotely famous, but it did warrant a couple of column inches in the newspaper, the *Morning Chronicle*, a few days later.[32] The accused was Seth Kelso, now aged sixty, one of the missionaries in Tonga. His part in one of the foundational ventures of Protestant evangelism was not highly rated by the paper, however, which described him merely as 'a weaver and *ci-devant* itinerant preacher'. Kelso was before the magistrate because he was accused of having exploited and assaulted a Tahitian, at one time resident with him, a man named Tapioi. The prosecution stated that:

Kelso had seduced this Otaheitian from Captain Wilson's protection, under the profession of teaching him to read, but instead of that, had turned the possession of him to the same purpose as Pidcock does his wild animals, making money by the show of beasts, (royal lions, Bengal tigers, or kangaroos alive,) . . . keeping the poor man in wretched ignorance, and ruling him with a rod of iron. That at last Tapeoe, finding the situation in which he was placed too oppressive to bear, fled for protection to Mr. Gilham, Surgeon, Blackfriars Road . . . [who] interested himself with great humanity and disinterestedness in the poor stranger's case; and as Tapeoe was determined to leave his pretended instructor, Mr. G. went with him to Kelso, to obtain his clothing. Instead of this, Kelso forbad Tapeoe leaving him, refused his clothes, and, on his attempting to take them, seized him and beat him with a chair.

Around 1808–10 the management of the London Missionary Society was under attack. A sometime supporter, the evangelical philanthropist Joseph Fox, had accused the directors of acting dictatorially, like a Vatican clique – a wounding accusation, for a group of dissenters – as well as incompetently on various fronts. Fox rehearsed the story of Tapioi's misadventures and abuse at some length, as an instance of their negligence. Some of the facts are unclear or controversial, but it appears that Tapioi first became known to Europeans shortly after the missionaries' arrival in Tahiti; he was among those who assisted with the construction of their house; and he was the *taio*, or particular friend, of Henry Bicknell, a member of the founding group, as, rather briefly, had been John Gilham, the surgeon who later helped him make his escape from Kelso.[33] Though it was asserted that Tapioi was about twenty at this time, other reports suggest he was somewhat older and already had a wife and child.

Fox's line was that when a whaler called at Tahiti in 1797, the high chief Pomare wanted one of his people to visit England; and Tapioi, supposedly 'having a thirst for knowledge', put himself forward.[34] In fact, he did not leave the island until 1800 – on the first day of the new century, if some muddled records are to be trusted – and there seems to be no evidence that he did so at the chief's behest. Were Pomare to have sent an emissary, he would more likely have despatched a relative of some rank than a commoner, which is what Tapioi seems to have been. On one account, in other words, Tapioi was a young man without responsibilities, enthusiastic to know the world and bring back his knowledge, a potential instructor of his own people; or, on another account, a man indifferent to his family, wanting to be elsewhere.

For whatever reason, Tapioi joined the whaler. The vessel was in fact the *Betsy*, already mentioned, on which the missionary John Harris also sailed.

Their first call was in Tonga, where they took off the missionary survivors, when Tapioi would have made the acquaintance of Kelso. They then travelled to Sydney where Tapioi met the governor, the prominent missionary Samuel Marsden, and a number of others there. He left on the *Betsy* which first spent a few days in New Zealand, then called again at the Tongan archipelago. Here, he happened to encounter another Tahitian, and decided that he would rather return home than go on to England. Tapioi therefore stayed on in Tonga, presumably hoping to find a passage to Tahiti on another passing ship, but from this point his voyage became almost unbelievably protracted and circuitous; it truly reads like the vicissitudes of a Polynesian Odysseus.

Captain Wilson reported that, shortly before he had picked up Vason, he met 'An Otaheitan one of Otoo's servants [who] had been left at these Islands by a whaler, and not being used to such hard living, begd earnestly for me to take him onboard, to which in gratitude to his country I consented'.[35] This was not Tapioi; but it was probably the 'countryman' whom Tapioi had chosen to stay with. Tapioi himself was picked up soon afterwards by the *Plumo*, or *El Plumier*, previously Glasse's South American prize, which had been sold in Sydney and had made an extended trading visit to northern New Zealand. However, it promptly struck a reef in the notoriously dangerous Fijian seas; the ship was saved, it was later claimed, primarily because Tapioi's ability to dive enabled him to stop up the worst leaks. The crew were able partially to repair the vessel and get under way again; they then mutinied, and made sail for Macao. In difficulties, however, they put into the Spanish port of Guam in Micronesia, where all were promptly imprisoned.[36] Tapioi among others was able after a few months to obtain his release and a passage to Manila, where he met some prior associates from whaleships who were now seeking bêche-de-mer for the lucrative China trade. He worked as a diver on voyages to Palau and elsewhere to collect the sea slugs but was again wrecked, this time off Great Banda in the Moluccas. He was rescued by another English trader, with whom he travelled extensively in the East Indies, before eventually being brought to England in September 1806 by Henry Wilson, the captain of an East Indiaman. This Wilson – though unrelated to either James or William, who had commanded the London Missionary Society's ships – had had dealings with the LMS, and thought that it might provide for Tapioi.[37]

The Society declined – and later rejected the story that Tapioi had travelled specifically to seek knowledge and instruction – but since the Tahitian said that he knew James Wilson, by then in rural retirement, his nephew William came forward and accommodated the Islander, until Kelso appeared with promises that he would support and educate Tapioi, as Tapioi apparently earnestly wished, while all along Kelso intended only to raise cash by exhibiting him.

The involvement of the LMS in Tapioi's sorry history was peripheral, since Kelso had long ceased to have any official connection or employment with it. But its involvement had implications that were still clearer from the story of another Islander, which Fox also reported in detail. This young Tahitian, one Toma ('Tomma'), had arrived in London a year later than Tapioi on a ship bringing a cargo of sealskins. He had worked throughout the voyage, but when the crew were discharged was told he was due no pay. He somehow met Tapioi, now being supported by a committee Fox had established, and educated at Lancaster's Free School on the Borough Road in Southwark, a progressive Quaker establishment. Tapioi was, we are told, by now 'sufficiently acquainted with the laws of civilized society to know, that labour performed, gave title to the recompense of wages', and thus pressed his philanthropic friends to take up the cause, which they indeed did, going to the trouble of interviewing other seamen from the seal-hunting voyage.[38] They were convinced of the justice of the case; they sought to interest the LMS, presumably on the grounds that the Society had committed itself to benefacting the people of the Pacific, and was indeed the only British institution that had established any kind of presence in the Pacific Islands at this time. Yet the LMS declined to get involved. Intriguingly, supporters of the Society drew attention to the fact that Islanders were now arriving in London so regularly that the LMS simply could not assist or support them all. Fox noted that Toma's treatment threatened to establish 'in the persons of South Sea Islanders, a slavery like unto that, under which Africa had so long groaned', and went so far as to seek the support of the famous abolitionist, Granville Sharp, in the campaign to get Toma paid his wages, which eventually succeeded.[39]

Kelso was in court, on 15 July, only briefly. He was treated leniently by the magistrate, because he had already spent a week in prison. It was counted in his favour, too, that he made no attempt to preach in the courtroom. But with respect to the London Missionary Society, the jury was still out. Were the missionaries genuinely committed to the improvement of the Polynesians? Were they true benefactors, or were they somehow complicit in, or at any rate shamefully indifferent to, the use of Pacific Islanders as exhibits, as quasi-slaves?

The publicity generated interest in Tapioi himself, and Joseph Banks, among others, contributed handsomely to a fund to enable the Tahitian to be repatriated, along with a range of useful goods, including tools for carpentry – a move that they hoped would strengthen the positive image of Britain in the minds of the Tahitians. He was supplied, too, with drawing paper, pencils and 'a large box of colours'. Like Kualelo, he had taken to drawing, but while the Hawaiian had indulged in caricature, Tapioi impressed his evangelical friends with views around Tahiti, Tonga and Sydney, places he had not seen for years.[40]

In March 1810 Tapioi was given a passage on the ship *Canada*, which carried 121 convict women to Sydney. He was accompanied by his old *taio*, or customary Tahitian exchange-partner, Henry Bicknell, who had returned to England to plead for greater support for the mission, and collect women prepared to travel back to the Pacific with him to become missionary wives. (One had already agreed to marry him, preferring the certainty of the carpenter to a husband by ballot at the end of the voyage.) On arriving at Sydney's Port Jackson, the news from Tahiti was that rival chiefs were at war; Tapioi chose to stay in the colony until conditions improved. When Bicknell, with the women, travelled on to the island, Tapioi preferred to remain. He settled on a farm at Parramatta, declined several further opportunities to return to Tahiti, and sadly died of dysentery or some similar condition around April 1812. He was perhaps only thirty-five, perhaps somewhat older.[41]

* * *

Remarkable as Vason's history had been, Tapioi's was more extraordinary. His experience in Tonga, caught up in tribal conflicts that were essentially similar to yet more destructive and extreme than those of Tahiti, must have been suggestive if uncomfortable. He went on to visit many Pacific islands, east Asian and Atlantic ports, and innumerable places in between. He lived in England for more than two years, and in the colonial town of Sydney for a similar period. When he met up with Tahitians such as Toma in London, and perhaps others who passed through Port Jackson, they must have had a lot to talk about.

Frustratingly, of course, we have no access to these conversations, to Tapioi's perceptions of this range of experience, to this variety of meetings, with Islanders, Asians and Europeans. Vason's published memoir has its limitations, as an account of a particular person's cross-cultural experience – writing it, he no doubt felt he had to express himself apologetically, more apologetically than he probably felt. And, if the narrative is at times vivid, Vason was in no sense an experienced or professional writer: his accounts of circumstances, events and his own feelings tend to be somewhat superficial, to resort at times to cliché. But we are left nevertheless with a sense of how a cross-cultural passage, a chapter in a singular life, was experienced. We discern how a person who was not simply a 'European' but a particular Englishman – a young, evangelically-minded man from a lower-class, provincial background, with appetites and aspirations that made themselves apparent – responded to the Tongan environment, to Tongan society, to Tongan daily life. To have a sense of quite how Tapioi responded to Tongan society and Tongan life, to England and to English life, to the still new colony of New South Wales, and to the Aboriginal people it was swiftly and savagely displacing, would be intriguing. To view his long-lost drawings of any of these places would be remarkable.

Of course, historical sources are not simply 'one-sided' but partial, and always uninformative as well as informative. It is not true for the whole of Pacific history that indigenous voices and perceptions are unreported. And even when they are unreported, there are strategies that may be used to recover or reconstruct them. But these methods do not really help in this context. They work when one can associate a specific response with a general cultural precedent – an act of violence, for example, may have taken place because taboos or protocols were transgressed.[42] This sort of reasoning only illuminates our sense of a particular Islander in so far as he or she responds typically, as a member of that culture, that society, would or should have done. It gives no access to the idiosyncrasy, or the particularity, of an attitude or an imagination. Vason's story is arresting, because he was not like other missionaries. Maybe Tapioi, too, was not like other Tahitians. It is suggestive, in any event, that if he wanted to leave England, he did not in the end choose to return home. Like Kualelo, he found he would sooner settle elsewhere – there was more than one place he might belong.

* * *

In Tonga, Finau would remain the most powerful of the chiefs until his death in 1810.[43] He had no serious rival as ruler of the archipelago as a whole, though from time to time the chiefs of Tongatapu continued to assert their independence, and many prominent aristocrats left the islands, resettling temporarily or permanently with allies in Fiji or elsewhere. Soon after 1800 Palu, son of Mulikiha'amea, Vason's friend and protector, was among those who spent some years in Fiji. With his wife Fatafehi, he went on by ship from there to Sydney, and later visited Canton and Tahiti. They were Islander travellers of a new sort. With the exception of those who had sailed with Captain Cook, who were treated more or less as travelling informants, nearly all the many Hawaiians, Marquesans, Tahitians and Maori who joined ships during the 1790s and first decade of the nineteenth century were individual men, mainly of low status, who enlisted essentially as crew.

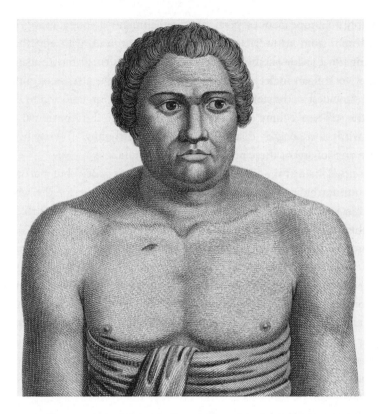

10 'Finau, chef des guerriers de Tongatabou', engraving from Labillardière, *Atlas pour servir à la relation du voyage à la Recherche de La Pérouse.*

Palu and Fatafehi were, to the contrary, aristocrats on tour. According to the missionaries, who met them on Tahiti, they were impressed by things European, they spoke English 'tolerably well', they wore European clothes, and allegedly denigrated Polynesian customs. 'They say that these Islanders are universal fools, and know nothing at all.'[44] Whatever was said was no doubt expressed rhetorically, to please the Europeans, and may well have been reported still more rhetorically, given that the missionaries had an interest in drawing attention to signs that Islanders might appreciate the merits of civilization, and might in due course convert.

When Palu and Fatafehi returned to Tonga in 1807, they told Finau about their experiences, conveying more ambivalent feelings about colonial society in Sydney. They had been invited to reside at the governor's house, but were expected to help sweep a courtyard and otherwise work like servants. 'In vain they endeavoured to explain, that in their own country they were chiefs, and, being accustomed to be waited on, were quite unused to such employments.' They were dismayed, too, by the necessity of money, the impossibility of obtaining it without work, and the measly amount that was given them, when they did work. Early in the course of their Australian sojourn, Palu was kicked out of a shop, not understanding that food was being sold rather than distributed. 'When he told them he was a chief, they gave him to understand that *money* made a man a chief.'[45] Yet, the Tongan couple only revisited their home in passing: soon after meeting with Finau, and apparently put off by the still-unsettled state of the islands, they returned to Sydney.

Over the first thirty or so years of encounter, many Islanders had been eager to acquire beads, iron, scissors, manufactured fabrics and other European things. From an early stage, too, in Tahiti the Pomares had expressed a deeper sort of interest, and imagined themselves as allies of Cook and King George III. To some extent they fetishized things British; 'Britain' was a sign of Cook, of exotic power, of a history that was already mythic. As other voyagers and beachcombers and then the missionaries appeared, this imagining was complemented by a more practical understanding of the diversity, indeed the poverty and weakness, of some who came from Britain, and elsewhere in Europe. By the early years of the new century, these attitudes were being enriched and extrapolated. The sense of European life was filled out by the experience of people such as Palu and Fatafehi. They gained an understanding of Europeans at home, as well as in the singularly male society of seafaring. Their responses were mixed. They appear to have developed a certain cultural versatility, behaving in a Europeanized way in dealings with Europeans that, needless to say, they dropped at other times.

* * *

The bulk of the LMS missionaries had, of course, settled at Tahiti, the island that, thanks to Cook and the *Bounty*, still loomed largest in the British, indeed the European sense of the Pacific. The seemingly warm welcome they initially received was quickly succeeded by more awkward dealings. While the source of Crook's difficulty was the Marquesan resistance to change, his brethren in Tahiti were made uncomfortably aware of how rapidly life and politics there had been affected – and affected deleteriously, they were in no doubt – by beachcombers, guns and trade. They were also rendered uncomfortable and insecure by patterns of conflict that had much deeper roots. Tu, or Pomare I, the great chief known to Cook, was being succeeded or rather displaced by his son, and fighting between their followers threatened to escalate.[46]

When the trader *Nautilus* visited Tahiti, just a year after the mission's estab-lishment, the missionaries compounded whatever suspicions their hosts already possessed by interfering in trade, attempting to prevent guns and powder being brought ashore. They also tried to round up five Hawaiians who had deserted, whose presence the Tahitians appear to have welcomed. Some missionaries trying to visit the high chief Pomare were harassed and stripped of their clothes; the incident, if minor in itself, aroused the anxieties of the party, and eleven of the eighteen, together with their wives, seized the oppor-tunity of the ship's visit to depart. When news of this withdrawal reached London, it was considered ridiculous. The *Oracle and Daily Advertiser* published 'An Otaheitan Impromptu':

> Wise Missionaries sent from above,
>   Sail o'er the briny flood;
> And hither come, with wond'rous love,
>   To teach us to be good.
>
> But when they find us bad – 'tis done,
>   They turn upon the toe;
> And so because we're BAD they COME,
>   Because we're BAD they GO![47]

The Tahitian mission was further weakened by the defection of two of the men, who took local wives and ceased to be involved in evangelizing, but it was then considerably reinforced by a second missionary party, which arrived in the *Royal Admiral* in mid-1801. Over the following few years, some at least of these missionaries acquired true fluency in Tahitian and a deeper grasp of the political complexities of the island. Tu died in September 1803, but the conflict between his party and his son's did not conclude so much as evolve, as Pomare II struggled to build on his foreign alliances – with European traders, but also with the resident Hawaiians the missionaries had failed to get rid of. Pomare told the evangelists he wanted them to remain on the island, but gave them little practical help, and still less spiritual encouragement. In 1804 one Tahitian told William Scott that he pitied him, because 'the people of Tahiti *never* would renounce their religion, and the customs of their fore-fathers . . . it would be better for the miss[ionaries] to *parahi noa* (sit down quiet) and let them alone.'[48]

CHAPTER TWO

✦

The Typees fought us to the last

During a December night in 1803 the whaling ship *Patterson*, which operated out of Rhode Island, New England, approached the island of Simbo, part of the New Georgia group of the western Solomon Islands. Early the next morning some thirty canoes, carrying around two hundred unarmed men, came alongside, and proceeded to engage in trade, pilfering when they could. The Islanders were well aware of the value of iron – they had been encountering ships for some fifteen years, albeit only occasionally – and sought knives, nails, pieces of hoop and glass bottles, for which they gave coconuts, plantains and 'trinkets', meaning presumably local artefacts, which sailors were souveniring. The captain considered them a 'hospitable ingenious people' but declined their invitations to venture ashore, despite what was interpreted as an offer of women.[1]

Simbo was, and still is, a small, hilly, densely forested island – but not an 'island society'. Its people were intimately connected with immediate and less immediate neighbours, their lives were truly archipelagic. They gardened and fished locally, but they also built and decorated great canoes, traded and raided around the islands and lagoons of the New Georgia group, and, directly or indirectly, further afield.

Their societies, their part of the world, remind us just how diverse transformations of human institutions have been. For more than a century, geographers and anthropologists characterized the people of Melanesia as less civilized than those of Polynesia. Whereas Polynesians – in Hawaii and Tonga most obviously – were ruled by kings, or at least chiefs, the peoples of the western Pacific were said to be basically egalitarian.[2] For many parts of Melanesia, this is misleading, profoundly so for the western Solomons, but not because there were 'kingdoms' that have been overlooked. There were, certainly, male leaders – magicians, warriors and chiefs, and there was a class of sorts, of men of rank. New Georgia societies were singular, however, for a kind of accelerated indigenous economic

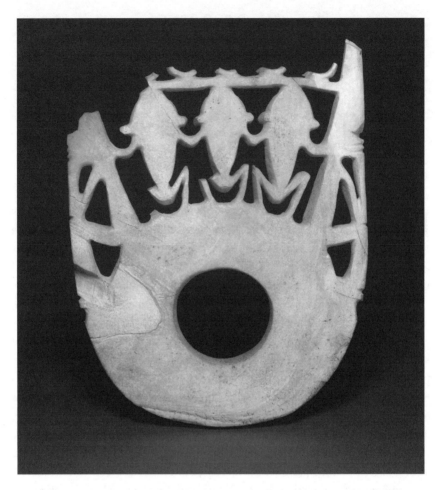

11 Bakiha, money-ring with figures, from Roviana in the western Solomon Islands.

development, centred upon shell money, magic, shrines, head-hunting and ceremonies.[3]

Although *bangara*, or chiefs, tended to inherit their titles, the last thing they could do was sit around and simply enjoy them. Their grandeur they had rather to constantly reinvent, through sponsoring the building of canoes, managing magic, staging feasts, undertaking raids to head-hunt or seize captives on neighbouring islands, and trafficking in captives or slaves. Captive women were ceremonially offered as prostitutes, their services paid for with shell money; shell money was used to purchase new magic, to commission great canoes and canoe houses; and canoes were not only expressions of grandeur in themselves, but the means by which further raids were carried out.

There was a world here of charms, taboos and rites of power that the crew of the *Patterson* had no inkling of. This meeting, and many others in the western Pacific in the early decades of the nineteenth century, was markedly constrained, mutual engagement being severely limited. In some cases, locals were unwilling to permit landing; when people did land, they were kept to the beach, and women were kept away. In this instance, caution came more from the other side: the sailors would not allow the Simbo men to come fully aboard the ship – trade took place across the rail – nor did they themselves venture ashore. Either or both sides wanted no more to traffic than traffic itself. The captain of the *Patterson* was no Cook, concerned to inform himself about a place's products or a people's temper, genius, manners and customs; nor was he, to any extent at all, an intervening evangelist, with a desire to remake the people he met. Meanwhile, if the Simbo men would possibly have welcomed the ship's men ashore, and might have included them in their meals, their diversions and their ceremonies, as the Tahitians had done, there was no scope for that on this occasion.

More than a century later, Simbo would remember – or 'remember' – the first white man's visit. Their ancestors had not wanted the tins of beef or biscuits that had been offered, but they accepted iron hoops, adzes and tomahawk blades. Half a dozen whites, it was understood, had remained on the island, and assisted the locals in a great raid. One white named Kurukuru had had children; his ship in due course returned, and 'Simbo men went with them to pilot them round' the neighbouring islands of Vella Lavella and Isabel. When the ship left, the white men who had remained departed on it, leaving goats, pigs and sheep.[4]

Events, in this telling, were no doubt conflated. It is not known when beachcombers first entered these communities, or when Simbo men first guided European ships, probably not for some years afterwards. Intriguingly, too, the man who conveyed this history to the anthropologist A.M. Hocart in 1908, said that the name of the captain of this first ship was Cook. In fact, Cook never went near Simbo; he perhaps figured in histories related by Islander mission teachers, who arrived on the island a few years before Hocart; for Hocart's informant, it made sense to connect a local and a global history in this way. A hundred years earlier, the *Patterson*'s visit in no sense resulted in this mingling of understandings or historical imaginations. Pieces of iron were received, they entered local use, they may well have been traded from island to island. New tools no doubt had a technical impact; certain ornaments, and certain kinds of shell money, were probably produced more easily. But the drama here was still locally scripted, it would remain so, and remain largely out of European view, for decades to come.

* * *

In 1813 David Porter was thirty-three, and Britain and America were at war. This intrepid and ambitious New Englander, whose naval experience had included a period as a captive in Tunisia, was engaged in the harassment of British shipping in the Pacific. With four prizes, he made his way in the *Essex* towards the Marquesas, where he thought he might obtain provisions, come upon other English ships, and perhaps make some discoveries. He considered also that his men needed 'relaxation and amusement', which meant – he made no effort to euphemize – sex. 'For the remainder of our passage they could talk and think of nothing but the beauties of the islands we were about visiting; every one imagined them Venus's and amply indulged themselves in fancied bliss.'[5]

After passing and calling briefly at the seldom-visited island of Ua Huka, Porter entered Nukuhiva's great harbour of Taiohae, and quickly encountered several beachcombers, including an Englishman named Wilson who had lived there for some years, was apparently fluent in Marquesan, and who subsequently served Porter as interpreter. The few days subsequent to the ships' arrival were chaotic: his men found the women accustomed to the desires of mariners; they indeed knew 'some few English words of the most indecent kind', and were as willing as the sailors had hoped. Porter's pride was stung, he was sufficiently candid to admit, when his own efforts to arouse the interest of a woman of high chiefly rank were rebuffed with coldness and hauteur, but he appears to have been alone in failing to find a ready partner. 'The ship was a perfect Bedlam', he wrote of their first night after mooring.

The chief, Keatonui had, at the time of Porter's arrival, been at a hill fort high above the beach. After Porter sent him a large pig he came out to his ship, but failed to impress. Nearing seventy in the American's judgement, his extensive tattoos made him appear entirely black, he was dressed in nothing beyond a simple cloth, he carried a staff, and he appeared stupified from kava drinking. He was pained rather than impressed when a cannon was fired in his honour, but he accepted the gift of a whale tooth – Porter had gathered that ivory in this form was here valued above all other trade – took a nap, and appeared somewhat more alert afterwards. He indicated he wanted to return to the beach, but said that they must first exchange names, to which the captain readily agreed – he was no doubt sufficiently familiar with voyage narratives to know that this was common, indeed de rigueur, in the management of contact. He also asked Porter to help him in ongoing conflict, as Taiohae people were at war with their neighbours, the Hapa'a. Porter said that if his allies were attacked, he would assist with the defence of the valley. Keatonui pressed him further, telling him that by virtue of their ritual contract, he was now implicated: the Hapa'a 'had cursed the bones of his mother, who had died but a short time since: that as we had exchanged names, she was now my mother, and I was bound to espouse her cause'.[6] Porter wrote that he felt that this 'sophistry' merited little by way of reply; but he would, however, be drawn into tribal warfare more deeply and swiftly than he could have anticipated.

The very next day Hapa'a raided the valley, destroying the breadfruit trees that constituted, as many visitors would note, the staff of Marquesan life. Those around Porter complained that he had failed to honour his undertaking, 'they believed we were cowards'. While busy establishing a shore base, he thought over the situation. 'Somewhat provoked', he found himself coming around to the idea that some exemplary punishment might 'frighten them out of their hostile notions'. He had a six-pound cannon landed and put it to Keatonui that it might be taken up to the hill fort, without believing that the Islanders would in fact be capable of carrying it even part of the way up the precipitous slopes that encircled the bay. He demonstrated the effects of guns, impressing those who witnessed them at first hand, but failing to daunt the Hapa'a. Porter now positively decided that 'the sooner they were convinced of their folly the better', especially since Taiohae people about the camp seemed inclined to believe the Hapa'a, who taunted the Americans, saying that they made threats but were too cowardly to act on them.

On 29 October Porter despatched one Lieutenant Downes with some thirty men, accompanied by locals carrying the guns and ammunition. When they reached the ridge occupied by the enemy, the initial engagement was unpromising. Downes was stunned by a stone, and another man speared through the neck. The Hapa'a 'scoffed at our men, exposed their posteriors to them, and treated them with the utmost contempt and derision'. Since their local allies now openly doubted the martial abilities of the visitors, it became 'absolutely necessary that the fort was taken at all hazards'. They rushed their opponents and killed some five almost immediately; the fort was promptly given up, and the Taiohae men pursued their advantage, descending upon a village, plundering it for 'drums, matts, calabashes' and pigs, among other things.

It was reported, whether quite accurately is uncertain, that the news of this victory astonished Keatonui. Supposedly, no former battle had seen so many killed. It was indeed true that the normal pattern of hostilities saw occasional skirmishing over weeks 'nay for months sometimes, without killing any on either side, though many are, in all their engagements, severely wounded'.[7] Like Tahitians, Marquesans engaged more in feuding than real warfare, though it does appear that not long before this, the chronic Hapa'a-Taiohae conflict had undergone some escalation: the Hapa'a assault on the breadfruit trees, on the subsistence base, seems to have been more characteristic of occasional all-out war than the antagonisms that always simmered.

In any event, the population was now in a state of exultation, or fear. Young warriors rejoiced over the bodies of their dead enemies; to drumming and chanting, the corpses were offered as sacrifices on the *me'ae* or sacred ritual ground, the equivalent of the Tahitian *marae*. Porter anxiously sought to establish whether the dead might be eaten, but was eventually reassured that cannibalism was not practised, though many he talked to claimed that it was, by their enemies or by unspecified individuals. Others, including the high-ranking women, were terrified by the violence and thought that Porter would now turn on them. He reassured them, insisting that the Hapa'a had provoked his action, that he sought only peace; he was visited by a Hapa'a envoy, and now set himself up as a conquering king, or, if his conduct is read generously, perhaps only allowed the Islanders to treat him as they felt was appropriate under the circumstances. Either way, the Americans were now the recipients of a steady flow of gifts of food. 'We rioted in luxuries', Porter wrote, though gifts of iron were widely distributed, and harpoons, presumably obtained from the whaling ships that the Americans had made prizes of, being most highly valued, were presented to many chiefs. Looting on one front thus helped consolidate conquest on the other.[8]

*   *   *

The Americans continued to riot in luxuries of the flesh as well as food. 'With the common sailors and their girls all was helter skelter . . . every girl the wife of every man in the mess, and frequently of every man in the ship.' He acknowledged he himself was 'rivetted' by 'some of the young girls' of a tribe they visited for the first time, just after the assault upon the Hapa'a.

Porter dignified this candid disclosure of his crew's licence with a rehearsal of what was, already, a hackneyed theme in Pacific travel narratives: the relative nature of ideas of virtue ('they attached no shame to a proceeding which they not only considered as natural, but as an innocent and harmless amusement', etc.).[9] He passed over a question that had preoccupied some earlier navigators: that of the introduction of venereal diseases among Islanders. Such infections were certainly by now endemic, and had already contributed to a deterioration of local well-being, but the rate of infection and reinfection can only have been dramatically accelerated by the presence of such large numbers of foreign men (the crews of the four prizes as well as those of Porter's own ship) who would, in due course, enjoy sexual contact with women from diverse parts of the island rather than just the vicinity of the usual port, over a period of months. The seeming frankness of Porter's narrative thus had its limits.

In the aftermath of conquest, Porter likewise passes over what seems to have been a sea-change in his thinking about the nature and purposes of his sojourn in the Marquesas. The shock of his military intervention had evidently been sufficient to provoke chiefs and people to mobilize, to accede to whatever the Americans requested, perhaps to outdo each other in servicing their demands. At any rate, early in November 1813 some four thousand Islanders were gathered at his camp, with materials for building, and he directed the construction of a new settlement, consisting of two houses, one for himself and one for officers, and other shelters for sails, coopers, the sick, a bakery and a guardhouse; these structures were some fifty feet in length, and were linked and protected by a series of walls. If not exactly a grand establishment, this gestured toward a colonial settlement. Porter soon took cannon ashore to defend it, and clearly thought he might act historically – to enlarge the possessions of the United States.

On 19 November he displayed the flag, fired a seventeen-gun salute, and read a wordy declaration, claiming that the chiefs of the island, now Madison's Island, had 'requested to be admitted into the great American family'. He considered that the 'pure republican policy' manifested in the comparatively

12 'Madisonville', from David Porter, *Journal of a Cruise*.

egalitarian Marquesan societies exhibited an essential kinship with the political ethos of the United States. He substantiated his claims, pointing to the conquest he had made, the considerable quantities of tribute with which he had been supplied, 'the village of Madison', with its 'appurtenances' that he had built, as well as the fort he had constructed.

The American supremacy would be short-lived. One of the island's most powerful groups, the Taipi (later renowned as Herman Melville's Typee) had long been hostile to the Taiohae tribes, and had no interest in rushing to conciliate either them or their new foreign allies. Porter had called on them to join other tribes in submitting to him, which entreaties they dismissed. The people he was friendly with complained of the insults they suffered, and prodded Porter to understand the Taipi as hostile not only to them, his allies, but to the American presence itself. While Porter later wrote tediously of his reluctance to be drawn into further conflict, he was quick to create expectations that he was then compelled to act upon. He sent messages to the Taipi stating that they would accept his peace or suffer its imposition. If this was a bluff, it was called, and as before, Porter's closer allies became – he at any rate understood – sceptical and troublesome when he failed to follow up his threats. And – here again, Porter was truly candid – they appear to have known how to needle the aspiring naval hero, calling his own courage into question.

Keatonui's son had returned from the Taipi, bringing not a message of conciliation but further insults: 'we were white lizards, mere dirt . . . the posteriors and privates of the Taeehs'. Mouina, the leader of Keatonui's warriors, boiled with rage and insisted on immediate hostilities. Porter felt his authority was being pre-empted and:

> told him, therefore, that I did not need his advice, and that I should go to war or make peace when I thought proper, without consulting him. . . . He walked off a few paces among the crowd, then turning round, coolly said, he believed I was a great coward. Forgetting that this was the observation of a mere Indian, I seized a musket and pursued him . . . on my approaching him and presenting the musket and threatening him with destruction, on a repetition of such expressions, terror was marked on his countenance.[10]

Porter perhaps thought he had reasserted his authority, but he then did precisely what Mouina had pressed him to do, which was to begin mobilizing a canoe fleet and other forces, with a view to mounting an assault on the Taipi.

On 28 November he took one of the ships and a considerable number of canoes to the east along Nukuhiva's southern coast, and into the bay, the deep and broad Taipi valley before them. Warriors to the number of around five thousand (Porter's probably very exaggerated figure) were massed on the ridges above, and the American force landed on the beach without opposition, but were then harassed by stones thrown from the bush. Porter and the warrior Mouina led a party of thirty or so of mainly Porter's own men into the valley. They advanced around a mile, gaining only fleeting glimpses of Taipi warriors, and Porter realized that he had entirely misunderstood the nature of the terrain and the kind of contest in which he was engaged. Suddenly, the small group was subjected to a shower of stones, and Lieutenant Downes, injured during the previous adventure, had his leg shattered. The Marquesans accompanying Porter's party began to slip away, and he did not know whether to press on with his diminished force or retreat.

They carried on a little further to a point where their route crossed the valley's main river, which here had steep and exposed banks. Porter's party fired into the brush on the other side, and then rushed across the stream. Once they did so, however, they realized they were up against a substantial earthwork, and here the Taipi made a stand. Porter himself was able to shelter behind a substantial tree, and could take potshots when warriors emerged from behind their defences to throw stones or spears. But his men had used most of their ammunition, all the Islanders other than Mouina had abandoned the venture, and once he sent a party back to the beach for more musket shells, he had only nineteen men, of whom three were injured and incapacitated.

Porter, sure that if they appeared weak, the Hapa'a, his former antagonists, would turn again upon his party, was desperate to secure some appearance of advantage from the situation. He retreated, then made a stand, and was able to shoot two of those Taipi who pursued him dead; he then retreated to the beach, 'with no contempible opinion of the enemy'. Here, however, the fact that two Taipi were dead counted for little. Among the Hapa'a and various other tribes in the vicinity ' "the Typees have driven the white men" was the constant topic of conversation'. Porter withdrew to Taiohae, with a sense of urgency.

The following day he assembled the largest force he could and tried an approach by land. Fortuitously the moon was full. Guided by locals, his parties ascended and crossed the high ridges that separated the Taiohaie and Taipi valleys. During the night they reached a position above Taipi villages, but were advised that they would need to wait on light before descending.

Porter's men were in any case exhausted, his plan frustrated by heavy rain; he was concerned that their guns would not fire, and in any case, as it became light, he realized that the route into the valley required them to find a way down or through cliffs, via steep slippery paths, that were perhaps negotiable by locals but not by his men. He again withdrew, on this occasion into the Hapa'a valley, where people vacated houses to accommodate his men but refused to provide food. Only when Porter threatened to shoot pigs and cut down trees, and went so far as to seize and break the weapons of a group of warriors, were the people sufficiently intimidated.

Here Porter's party rested for twenty-four hours, and the weather cleared. Then Porter again took his men over the ridge – pausing in his narrative to justify his action to the questioning reader, insisting that 'we must either attack them or be attacked'.[11] The Americans were exhausted merely by the descent from the mountain, and halted when they reached the valley, the

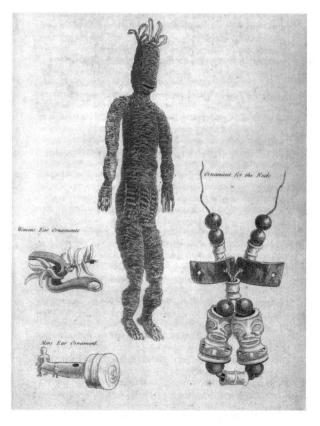

13 'Typee god', from David Porter, *Journal of a Cruise.*

trumpets and drums of the Taipi resonating. Porter regrouped and marched on the villages; his men were pelted with stones; but they were able to advance, killing a number of warriors; they took one settlement without much opposition, and moved on. The Taipi fought as they progressed, Porter set fire to houses as they proceeded, and in due course reached what he understood was the Taipi 'capital', a place that struck him as beautifully and regularly laid out, which however they laid waste to, destroying godly images, breaking and burning drums (which seem to have been associated particularly with temple sites, and were sacred objects in themselves), and 'several large and elegant new war canoes'.[12] The Typees fought us to the last, Porter afterwards wrote. His allies followed behind, plundering relentlessly, 'destroying bread-fruit and other trees and all the young plants they could find'. 'The whole presented a scene of desolation and horror.'

Exhausted, Porter's forces now withdrew to the beach: the Taipi continued to harry them, but, after he had returned to Taiohae, finally sued for peace a day or two later. Porter congratulated himself that, for the first time in the memory of any Islander, he had imposed a peace: 'They repeatedly expressed their astonishment and admiration that I should have been able to effect so much in so short a time.' He announced that he was shortly due to depart, but that he would return, and would punish any tribe that disrupted this new-found harmony.

Some ten days later Porter did depart, leaving three of the prizes at Taiohae, under Lieutenant John Gamble's command, with twenty-two men. Not long after leaving port, he was saddened, he wrote, by the loss of Tamaha, a Tahitian, who had been popular among the seamen, regularly entertaining them with both Polynesian dance and his own emulation of sailors' dances and drills. The man had 'received a blow from the boatswain's mate' that had distressed him to such an extent that he leapt overboard, an apparent suicide that led to 'a general dejection' among the men. In fact, Porter learned only after he returned to the United States, the Islander had swum or drifted the twenty or so miles back to Nukuhiva, and had been cared for by a Taipi man, despite the Tahitian's involvement in the recent aggression; he astonished the Americans by reappearing at Taiohae a few days later.

Porter planned to cruise further off the South American coast, seeking more prizes while sustaining the Marquesan base. He believed he had 'completely broken up the British navigation in the Pacific'. Towards the end of March, however, the *Essex* was intercepted at Valparaíso by the British frigate *Phoebe*. In the ensuing action almost two-thirds of Porter's crew of 250 were either killed or wounded before he saw fit to surrender. Gamble needless to say knew nothing of this, but the task Porter had left him, of sustaining the fledgling colony, was anyway proving challenging.

* * *

It was the rainy season. Gamble found that people around the valley were killing pigs which had been seized from the Taipi and were reserved for the use of the Americans. His protests to one chief or another were ignored. He put together the strongest force he could, took a few chiefs hostage on board one of the ships, and threatened to put them to death if the pigs were not replaced. The flow of provisions resumed, but then flagged again; people were openly hostile, or would only sell pigs for ivory. Gamble tried to conceal the weakness of his party by prohibiting Islanders, including women, from coming to the ships. His men resented and disobeyed this restriction. Rumours of mutiny were realized in early May. The greater part of the men seized one of the prizes, the *Seringapatam*, and sailed off. If the Marquesans had indeed feared and respected the Americans, in the immediate aftermath of Porter's violence, it was now evident that they were weak, they were unable to enforce any demand, nor indeed were they capable of resisting any attack. Gamble, who had already given up the shore base, and was badly wounded by one of the mutineers, prepared to depart.

Against his better judgement, a party ventured ashore to try to seize the beachcomber Wilson, the intruders' sometime interpreter who had turned against them and had stolen a good deal from Madisonville, Porter's 'village'. The attempt failed, and four men, as well as a beachcomber who remained friendly, were killed in an affray on the beach. Gamble then burned one of the prizes and made his escape in the last, with a crew of only eight consisting mainly of men who like himself were wounded, crippled, or unwell. They were lucky to reach Hawaii within two weeks, where they obtained provisions and recruited additional crew, but were perhaps luckier still to be captured, soon afterwards, by the British ship *Cherub*.[13]

* * *

This obscure and forgotten projection of American power might invite reading as a parable. Porter's shock-and-awe tactics, his convoluted self-justification, his exit without an exit strategy, are indeed resonant of more recent aggressions. But my concern here is with the local consequences of this extraordinary intrusion upon the lives of Marquesans. As people told Porter, his victories were unprecedented, unimaginable to them. Indeed, if local warfare was occasionally unrestrained, it simmered far more often than it ever exploded. The violence Porter inflicted was by Marquesan standards unprecedented, but it also gave those allied with him brief licence to revenge the grievances of generations. It is too late now to try to document the extent of Taipi trauma, but we can only suppose that what was by all accounts a populous, affluent, proud, indeed a defiant society was more or less shattered by the killing of warrior leaders, and the burning of villages, great canoes and sacred relics, as well as by the destruction of the bulk of the trees and the plants that people lived off. How all this affected people as individuals, and for how long its effects might be traced, is an unhappy enigma.[14]

In other respects, however, consequences of the American visit are well documented. Even those visiting mariners whose records were most cursory made some reference to what they gave and received in trade. Up to the time of Porter's visit, Marquesans exhibited little interest in guns: they instead sought iron, red feathers, or, as Porter noted, ivory. They were also notably unwilling to barter their pigs, unless visitors had goods that they specially wanted. But the spectacular violence they witnessed made a profound impression. Though this was based on the technology's capacity to kill, there was more to it than mere violence. Porter had acted like an invader-chief, something of a type in Marquesan, indeed in Polynesian myth. While the characterization of such figures – who might be rampantly destructive, and sometimes cannibalistic – was certainly ambivalent, they were heroes of a sort for their followers and dependants, who were the beneficiaries of conquests, as the looters who followed Porter through the Taipi valley had indeed been. The effects of Porter's campaign against the Taipi were thus magnified, because it was not a wholly foreign intrusion, but rather one that resonated with indigenous ideas, with local political and military tactics. That resonance prompted Islanders to join in, to seize the opportunity and run with it; but the parity that typically existed between indigenous antagonists was in this case upset, enabling a more absolute appropriation and humiliation of the defeated than is likely ever to have happened in earlier times.

The extraordinary nature of the events meant that they were well remembered for years afterwards. People also came, quite literally, to fetishize guns, to preserve them in houses or sacred sites, to associate them with Porter, to value them as heirlooms, well after they had ceased to work. In so doing they were treating them as they treated clubs and spears that had been used in famous conflicts. A weapon that had killed acquired a name, and was often tabooed and displayed, or consecrated on a ritual site, here and elsewhere in Polynesia. Even guns in poor condition retained at least their shock value, and were repaired by beachcombers, and in due course by Islanders who acquired the skills to maintain the weapons themselves.[15]

Given what guns meant, post-Porter, it is not surprising that Marquesans now wanted certain things above all others from ships, and that they wanted them desperately. Only three years after the American visit, one trader reported that 'Firearms & ammunition are the staple trade at the Islds'. The interest spread quickly from Nukuhiva to the other five inhabited islands of the group, and allusions to requests for guns and powder appear in the accounts of almost every visitor to the Marquesas from this time onward.

It may be assumed that this importation of arms was no good thing. This was true, but not quite for the obvious reasons. The numbers of weapons introduced was probably never vast, because traders charged a lot for them – ten to twelve pigs for one musket was the going rate, one reported. In this period, firearms were not in any case efficient; they were not ideal for the kind of fighting, in thickly vegetated rather than open places, that was typically engaged in; hence it is uncertain that Marquesan warriors with guns killed more people than Marquesan warriors with clubs and spears. Ships tended to resort to the same harbours, but not absolutely, so that even if some competing tribes had more firearms than others, no tribe appears to have managed to monopolize them, or used any such monopoly to gain an unprecedented dominance. The great victory of Porter and his Taiohae allies over the Taipi was a one-off, the unification of the island of Nukuhiva that it led to being no more than ephemeral. Taipi were embittered, certainly, but not subordinated; neither Keatonui nor his successors gained any enduring ascendancy.

The arms trade was indirectly more deleterious, because of the particular place that the Marquesas came to occupy in the emerging world of Pacific commerce. As was mentioned, the first initiatives, after Cook, involved cashing in on the high price of fur in the Asian markets. Early in the nineteenth century, sandalwood was discovered in Fiji, and subsequently in the Marquesas and Hawaii.[16] It, too, was highly valued in China, and fuelled an intensification of contact between traders and Islanders wherever it could be found; but the wasteful nature of its extraction – only the oil-bearing heartwood was valued – and the rapaciousness of the traders' interest meant that supplies were exhausted quickly, within, it is believed, only three years in the Marquesan case. Early in the nineteenth century, again for the Chinese market, a bêche-de-mer fishery developed.[17] Also known as trepang, the sea-slugs of various species were dried and used in soups, medicines and aphrodisiacs. Pearl-shell and tortoise-shell in due course became commodities too. In addition, ships including whalers sought provisions – pork, fish, yams, coconuts – as well as wood and water, wherever they called and could conveniently seek refreshment.

The Fijians who harvested bêche-de-mer in considerable quantities during the first decades of the nineteenth century had, from time to time, to divert the labour of substantial groups of men to diving for the creatures and to curing them on shore, but they were not surrendering any resource that was important to their own subsistence, or their own economy, other than their capacity to work. Given that village life, with its routines of gardening, fishing and occasional hunting, left many men with spare time, it could be said that the trade cost their communities little.

In the Marquesas, however, there were no reefs and hence no bêche-de-mer. The Marquesans had nothing to offer that could be traded on. Ships called, not in order to obtain goods, but to replenish their supplies. The problem was that pork and breadfruit were not peripheral to Marquesan subsistence, they were vital to it. They were vital, too, to the ceremonial feasts that tribes mounted, on great occasions, such as for the rites that marked the lives of chiefly children and chiefly people. Marquesans could therefore only engage in traffic by surrendering the stuff they lived on themselves. Before Porter, they had often refused to do so – what was offered by traders, they well understood, was worth less to them than their pigs. Afterwards, however, the scales were tipped, and pigs were traded, whenever the opportunity to get hold of guns arose. It should not be forgotten, it was not incidental, that the men of nearly all ships also sought sexual services. (A few vessels were owned or captained by pious New Englanders who could prevent women coming on board, if not prostitution ashore.) And many sailors bartered when they could for 'curiosities', for local artefacts, in many cases either sacred objects, heirlooms, or things that were otherwise costly, in local terms. If small things such as wire fish hooks might be obtained for coconuts, those who sought European things of higher value, but who possessed neither pigs nor artefacts they could spare, had little option other than offering sex, either personally or by prevailing on female relatives or dependants to trade favours on their behalf.

Marquesan engagement in trade, in other words, depleted local supplies of food and protein specifically, undermined the ceremonial economy by diverting elsewhere the pork central to feasting, entailed the loss of heirloom objects, and routinely exposed the population to venereal diseases (as well as other infections, such as strains of influenza, more likely to be passed on if foreign seamen and local women were in physical contact). Shortages of pork were such, around Taiohae, that in 1818 one French trader found that he was able to obtain sandalwood there in exchange for pigs he brought from Hiva Oa.[18] But the sandalwood was soon gone, and traders would call only to get pigs, not to bring them.

The sexually transmitted infections had an impact on maternal health and mortality; the incidence of infertility was increased; less to eat, and a poorer diet, diminished the abilities of people to work productively. There are no precise population statistics, needless to say no medical records, extant for these islands from the first half of the nineteenth century. It is hard to get a grip on a question as nebulous as a loss of morale, and hard to put figures to depopulation, or to identify the causes of particular stages of decline. But the broader picture can only be described as catastrophic. We do not know the baseline, but in 1800, a single island such as Tahuata was almost certainly occupied by seven to eight thousand people, perhaps nearer fifteen thousand. The number fell to no more than four thousand by the early 1830s, and was less than half that ten years later.[19]

* * *

In the early 1980s I was a doctoral student in history and anthropology. My topic was early Marquesan society and culture, and I spent some months on Ua Pou and Nukuhiva, reading in the archives of the Catholic mission, sitting with kids and others chatting on the shingle beaches, and taking long walks over the hills, activities that, strictly speaking, were not informative in any obvious way. Yet I wanted to get the feel of the land, to see for myself the valleys that had been visited and named by various Europeans, and intruded into with such violence by Porter. It was often hard to reconcile the sense I had acquired from seamens' journals and missionaries' letters, of these busy, energetic, intractable places, with the neglect and absence of people I witnessed. The Marquesan term for valley is *ka'avai*, and when people used the word it evoked not a topographic feature but an inhabited space, one full of gardens, paths, houses and other structures. A soundscape too, of footfalls, pigs grunting, raucous cocks, and people talking as they tended plants, the rhythm of barkcloth beaters, occasionally of drums and chanting on the marae, punctuating the afternoon.

By 1984 most people had moved to just a few settlements – many to Taiohae on Nukuhiva, which remained the principal harbour. Hence on all of the six Marquesan islands, many valleys had been deserted for decades. Old walls, paths and gardens were overgrown, essentially destroyed, by bushes and saplings. But it was evident everywhere that at one time there had been a dense and rich population. The Marquesans built their houses on massive stone platforms known as *paepae*. The platforms were often elevated, and on sloping ground the front was sometimes two or even three metres above the ground; many of the individual blocks of stone used were themselves huge; it is banal, but as with the iconic Rapa Nui figures, or European prehistoric megaliths, the visitor cannot help wondering how they were ever shifted and raised. The platforms were always stepped; the step was sometimes ornamented with red stones or carved figures; the raised rear third or so of each platform was the part on which steeply roofed thatch-and-leaf houses were themselves constructed. Today, in many parts of these islands, one can walk and walk through valleys, surrounded by these vestiges of a community, in deep shadow under great trees. In the stillness there is a kind of memorial.

CHAPTER THREE

✦

If King Georgey would send
him a vessel

For those who'd walked the shores of Matavai Bay in Tahiti, overshadowed by the great spines, the trailing clouds, of Mount Orohena, even for those who'd struggled across the ridges of Nukuhiva, the island of Hawaii can only have appeared a land on a new scale. Its cliffs and coasts are dramatic; its great domed mountains, Mauna Loa and Mauna Kea, approach fourteen thousand feet above sea level, and, outside New Guinea, are the only snow-covered peaks of the Pacific tropics. In many places the island exhibits the reptilian hide of new lava; elsewhere it is lush and intensively cultivated. If its pre-European population can never be accurately estimated, the numbers were certainly considerable, sufficient to bring out the tumultous throng witnessed by Cook in 1778, a gathering greater than he encountered at any place elsewhere in the Pacific. Its settlements, its *heiau*, or temple sites, and its agricultural systems were all on a grand scale. The Hawaiian archipelago as a whole must have been no less powerfully impressive, also for those Islanders who first colonized it, who came from the south – of the eight major islands four were bigger than Tahiti, and bigger than all but a couple of islands east or north of New Caledonia. Europeans encountered not only Polynesian islands writ large, but a noble variation upon the Polynesian societies they had encountered elsewhere. If travellers everywhere were prone to use the word 'king' loosely, here there seemed to be true kings: the *ali'i* were aristocrats who controlled and taxed great territories, indeed whole islands.

That politics was on a different scale here is manifest not least in art forms, above all in forms of regalia. Feathers, as we have seen, were highly valued across the Pacific. Never mere decorations, in much of Polynesia they were closely connected with divinity, sacredness and divine genealogies. In Tahiti the assumption of titles was intimately connected with the command of red and yellow feather sashes, and with god images: these artefacts were not 'emblems' of rank but its substance, they recalled the feathers that covered, in

14 'A View of Karakakooa, in Owhyee', Kealakekua Bay, Hawai'i, engraving after John Webber, from Cook and King, *A Voyage to the Pacific Ocean.*

various myths, the bodies of gods. In Hawaii, featherwork of all sorts was elaborated to a greater extent than anywhere else. Most strikingly, when kings went into battle, and on other occasions of ritual risk, they wore magnificent cloaks, woven of a mass of bright but tiny feathers into something like a varie-gated velvet. Like barkcloth and tattoo, an armour of images, these men bore an armature of divinity. The vibrant reds and yellows of cloaks remain striking today, even for observers jaded by a world crowded with dyed fabrics: in the early days of contact with Hawaii, when colouring agents were scarce and valuable, and introduced cloth and clothing were precious, these cloaks were eye-catching as no other fabrics or coverings could have been. They drew attention to sacred leaders and warriors, who were in any case often formi-dable and physically daunting personalities.[1]

What is however most telling about the cloaks is the sheer labour behind their production. The knotting and weaving entailed was formidable, but less so than the accumulation of the materials. The red and yellow feathers had to be extracted from various tiny birds, mainly found in remote uplands. Some could be snared and released, others had to be killed; the larger cloaks were made up from as many as half a million feathers, from seventy to eighty thou-sand birds. Each had to be pursued, caught and plucked. Nowhere in Oceania, apart from here in Hawaii, could chiefly men and women, even of the very highest status, mobilize the labour of common people and appropriate their products to anything like this extent. Relative to the gifts received by a

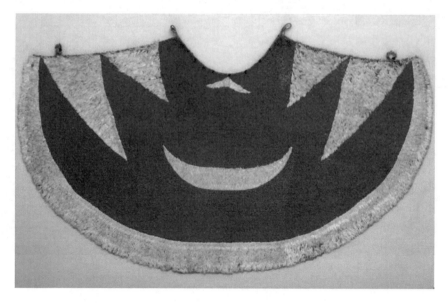

15 Hawaiian feather cape, late eighteenth or early nineteenth century.

Keatonui or even a Pomare, the cloaks suggest a system of corvée labour, on something nearer a Mayan or Egyptian scale.

The reader of Hawaiian history and anthropology encounters contradictory images of Hawaiian society. Some stress that this was a stratified state, implying the exploitation of the mass of common people. Others, and particularly native Hawaiian historians, present a great community bound by love for chiefs, who were like elder siblings to their junior commoners. If one image is Machiavellian and mechanistic, and the other at least a little romanticized, Hawaiian scholars such as Lilikala Kame'eleheiwa are surely right to stress that the relationships between the chiefs and the people were structured, as they were throughout the Pacific, by reciprocity.[2] People might garden, fish, fight and otherwise work for the *ali'i*, but those chiefs conducted rituals that kept the cosmos in order, that caused plants to grow, fish to be abundant, and otherwise secured the lives of everyone. A chief's opulence – his or her physical corpulence, for example – was not perceived to have been obtained at the expense of his or her subjects. Rather it was an expression of the plenitude that the community enjoyed, a condition of well-being that extended to everyone.

However, if Polynesians certainly did enjoy periods of peace and prosperity, chiefs were, in this understanding of society, under pressure to perform, to exhibit their greatness through largesse. Up to a point, they might create and sustain this appearance by drawing the contributions of their followers together, and redistributing them strategically or spectacularly. But they could be driven, also, to engage in war: battle could be a great theatre, in which divine *mana* might be made visible and demonstrated. For a victorious chief, it was additionally and as importantly a means to seize lands and other resources for redistribution among kin, loyal dependants and followers. If the use of terms such as 'feudal' in relation to Pacific societies is more often than not misleading, there was, in this respect, a real affinity between the conquering *ali'i* and the robber lords of medieval Europe and Asia. The religious underpinnings of these societies were very different, but a common political economy, based on expansion, conquest and gifting, drove them, with much unstable energy.[3]

* * *

T.T. Tucker, the commander of the *Cherub*, who had captured the miserable and still hobbling Lieutenant Gamble off Oahu, was back in Portsmouth by June 1815. His report to the Admiralty placed considerable emphasis on the assistance he had been given by Kamehameha, nephew of the great Kalaniopu'u, the ruler at the time of Cook's 1778–9 visit. Kamehameha had secured pre-eminence on the island of Hawaii by 1790, and then through a series of campaigns, which ran into the first years of the nineteenth century, extended his dominion to embrace the entire archipelago. Like other great chiefs, he had attracted beachcombers, but his were more than unreliable hangers-on. By the time of Tucker's visit, one John Young had been associated with Kamehameha for close to twenty-five years, and not only fought for him, as beachcombers did for their chiefs, but had become a friend and married into the family. He was truly what Vason had only ephemerally been, a *haole ali'i*, a white chief, and particularly an adviser who served, over the longer term, as a go-between and an interpreter. Tucker found that between them Kamehameha and Young made hospitable allies. The island of Hawaii itself was under a taboo at the time of the *Cherub*'s arrival, but arrangements were made to provision the ship from Maui, and over three weeks Tucker was well-supplied with pigs, food and fuel.

This generosity had a larger significance. Tucker reminded the officials at the Admiralty that the Hawaiian Islands were the vital point of rendezvous for American shipping between the north-west coast and China. In case of a

16 Kamehameha, lithograph after Louis Choris, from Choris, *Voyage pittoresque autour du monde.*

future war, a small squadron there 'would effectually annihilate that trade' and provide British ships with provisions, moreover rendering them independent of 'the Spanish Coast', meaning the ports of Chile and Peru, just in case Britain was at war with Spain too. For these reasons, he took the trouble to 'inform their Lordships that it is a national disposition among these people to expect a return for all they give'. More specifically, Kamehameha had, during the two days he spent on board the *Cherub*, asked frequently 'if King Georgey would send him a vessel, that he might visit his Islands in'; alternatively, would Tucker 'steal another American to give it to him'? The captain indeed regretted that he had already sent his two prizes to Valparaíso, since he could otherwise have presented one or the other to the king, but, the opportunity having been missed, he earnestly recommended that a ship be sent to Kamehameha. The Admiralty accepted this advice; Tucker, asked for clarification, suggested that 'a Vessel, about the size and rig of a Southampton or

Cowes Passage Boat, would be most acceptable'. 'I mention the rig,' he wrote, since it would be most appropriate if there were 'no occasion for a man to go aloft during the time he is onboard, as no one by their Laws is permitted to go above the King, and he only dispenses with it on board foreign vessels'. This specification was forwarded to the governor of New South Wales, so a ship, designed as it were to accommodate the Polynesian tapu system, could be built.[4]

Tucker's communications were slightly misleading, in that he neglected to make it clear that Kamehameha already had boats and ships, either European, or locally made on a European model. Otto von Kotzebue, who commanded a Russian exploratory voyage to the Pacific in 1816–18, was impressed in this and other respects by the 'progress' of the Hawaiian Islands. Kamehameha's home settlement, on Hawaii, included stone-built, European-style houses, and 'the mixed appearance of an European and an Owhyee village'; von Kotzebue and his officers were given wine to drink, offered mahogany chairs and seated around a mahogany table; many of the chiefs they encountered were uncomfortably attired in European garments, which were typically too small. Out for a walk, after their meal, the Russians were struck by the sight of a number of barges dragged up on the beach, 'sixty or seventy feet long, built quite in the European fashion [and] employed to convey provisions from one island to another'. Kamehameha, von Kotzebue noted, 'exerts himself' to bring European shipwrights to the islands and paid them well, to build boats and train Islanders in boat-building, he understood.[5] During the Russians' time in the islands they found that a dangerously strong local tobacco was popular; tobacco, vines, melons and rice were being grown, and cattle, oxen and horses kept. In Honolulu harbour they found Kamehameha's principal ships, a fast French-built brig, the *Queen Kaahumanu*, and the *Albatross*, which he was shortly to send on a trading voyage to China.[6] If, one might reasonably have thought, the juxtaposition of the ship and the canoe epitomizes the early European encounter in the Pacific, that image would convey a false sense of this history. Hawaiians in general had not made ships their own, but Kamehameha, and perhaps one or two other *ali'i*, certainly had.

How had Kamehameha been able to acquire such things? In part, the answer lies in the numbers of ships and the steady growth of trade from the 1790s on. Over this early period, Tahiti and most other Pacific islands and archipelagoes were still seldom visited, but Hawaii had become well established as the port of refreshment for the fur traders, and also for sundry whaleships and others. As Marshall Sahlins has pointed out, in his magisterial account of the period, Kamehameha was, until around 1810, supplying only the same stuff the Tahitians, Marquesans and others bartered with white men on ships – mainly pigs, vegetables and the sexual services of women. But the quasi-feudal nature of the Hawaiian kingdom, and the far greater extent of the islands' garden lands, made the king able to coordinate the supply of food in a way that was possible for no chief anywhere else in the Pacific.[7] If the Tongan rulers had, in theory, comparable levels of political power, they lacked the land area (Tongatapu was only a sixth of the size of Oahu), and at this time all the Tongan islands were in any case in a chaotic and impoverished state. Nor was Kamehameha simply tapping the rich fields and irrigation systems that already existed. As the trade grew, his warriors, who had not only invaded Oahu in 1795 but been subsequently resettled there, established new planta-tions, fishing ponds, storehouses and so forth. If diseases certainly had an adverse impact on the Hawaiian population as a whole over this period, it is possible that immigrant warriors, their dependants and a booming trade saw the population of Oahu grow over the first decade of the nineteenth century.

Trade had its ups and downs – Tucker's activities disrupted the engagement with American shipping during the war of 1812–15 – but grew exponen-tially when sandalwood began seriously to be cut for the Chinese market. Kamehameha never had been an 'ignorant native'; by the time Boston merchants began to focus on the wood, he was well advised by resident whites, and well aware of just how profitable cargoes were. Over the years he received tens of thousands, if not hundreds of thousands of the Spanish dollars that were then current, in cash or trade. He purchased lavishly – the mahogany furniture von Kotzebue sat at was just the tip of an iceberg of frip-pery and finery of every description – but he was also cautious, and was rumoured to possess a great hidden fortune. Ships, guns, clothes and luxuries, all needless to say accentuated his mana, in strictly Hawaiian terms, even as the context of those terms was shifting.[8]

* * *

The Tahitian Tapioi, we may recall, had been rescued from war-torn Tonga only to suffer shipwreck in Fiji. The reef upon which his ship, the *Plumo* or *El Plumier*, came to grief was in the opening of Bua Bay, on the western end of the great, elongated, irregular island of Vanua Levu, the second biggest of the Fiji Islands. For some months in the latter part of 1801, it appears between early September and late December, the *El Plumier* lay crippled in this vicinity. Whether it remained in one place, in Bua Bay, or limped about, is uncertain – its disastrous but fascinating voyage is documented, unfortunately, only through the most fleeting allusions in shipping registers and the Sydney press.

It is known, however, that while repairs were being undertaken, a beach-comber named Oliver Slater appeared and joined the vessel. He had sailed on the American trader, the *Argo*, which had a similarly obscure, but more cata-strophic voyage, ending in wreck on reefs east of the island of Lakeba, in the Lau group, under Tongan influence. Many of the crew survived the actual wreck, and made their way in boats to Tongatapu, according to one report, but were there caught up is ongoing warfare, and all but two or so killed. How Slater made his way, either from Tonga or some part of the Lau group to Vanua Levu, is obscure; but he, with the one other survivor, later picked up separately, were the first Europeans to have any sustained contact with Fijians. Slater perhaps possessed diplomatic skills that his fellow crew lacked, or was just lucky to be accepted by some set of locals, who evidently came from or had some reason to visit western Vanua Levu, where he was found sometime late the following year.[9]

With Tapioi and the rest of the *El Plumier*'s crew, Slater reached Guam, was imprisoned there, and in due course released, to proceed to Manila. The importance of all this lies in the fact that he had spent time in Canton earlier, knew the value of sandalwood to the China market, and around Bua Bay had his eyes open and discovered the trees in considerable numbers. It was not until mid-1804 that he sailed from Manila back to Sydney, but when he did he was less discreet than he might have been. The word got around that there was sandalwood as well as bêche-de-mer to be had in Fiji, a group of islands which up until this time was scarcely known to Europeans. In Tonga, in the 1770s, Cook had heard of the archipelago, and Captain Bligh among others had passed through it, but no contacts had been made with people who were rumoured to be intractably hostile, and such charts as had been produced were rudimentary, partial, and probably hard to come by.

Lucrative the trade might prove to be, but it was undoubtedly also hazardous. An American ship, the *Union*, sailed from Port Jackson, Sydney, intending to proceed to Fiji via Tongatapu, where however an attempt was made by some coalition of villainous beachcombers, which included a Malay and the Tongans, to capture the vessel. The captain and a boat's crew were killed; the survivors gave up the voyage and returned to Sydney, having rescued one Elizabeth Morey, herself a survivor of an earlier massacre – of the crew of the American ship, *Duke of Portland* – and one of very few female beachcombers of this period. She was on the island for almost exactly four months, living 'with the Chief's wife', and on the *Union*'s arrival was twice directed to go out to the ship, to encourage the officers to send boats and men ashore; when sent off a second time, Morey leapt into the sea and was picked up by the *Union*.[10] The brief record of her testimony conveys little sense of the nature of her stay on the island. The *Union* subsequently attempted a further voyage trading sandalwood, but disappeared with all hands and without trace – though a wreck on or near the island of Koro was later reported by Fijians to another trader, and very likely was that of this ship.

However, another vessel, the *Fair American*, did obtain a cargo of sandalwood from around Bua in Fiji. Slater feared that others would profit from his discovery, and teamed up with one James Aikin, a British subject involved in shipping on the New South Wales coast; they made voyages in Aikin's vessel, the *Marcia*, and the New England ship *Criterion* (which had brought the Tongans Palu and Fatafehi to Sydney); these ventures were so successful that Philip Gidley King, then governor of New South Wales, was troubled that Americans appeared to be gaining control of South Pacific commerce. He therefore supported at least two semi-official trading voyages by ships based in the colony in 1807–8.[11]

* * *

William Lockerby was born in 1782. He was a Scot from Dumfries, who had moved to Liverpool and had become a sailor. Soon after his marriage he had abruptly disappeared, press-ganged, as members of his family presumed. His movements are uncertain, but May 1807 found him in Boston, where he signed up as first officer on a trading ship named the *Jenny*, captained by one William Dorr. They sailed via the Indian Ocean to Port Jackson, Sydney, where Lockerby, by way of a 'private adventure' sold tobacco, which he had bought for a shilling per pound in Massachussetts, to the colonists for three dollars a pound. He happened to be in town when Governor Bligh was arrested by his own officers – the so-called 'rum rebellion' – and joined the celebrations. At Port Jackson, Dorr learned of Fijian sandalwood and decided to seek a cargo of it; they recruited additional men, guns and ammunition, and sailed for the islands. The ship was damaged in a storm near Tonga, where they met Islanders, engaged in barter and resisted an attempt to capture the vessel, firing grapeshot among the canoes and no doubt killing a number of men. They sailed via the Fijian islands of Vatoa and Koro and reached Bua, finally, on 21 May 1808.[12]

Here two other traders, both from Port Jackson, were anchored. The crew of the *Elizabeth*, owned apparently by a former convict, tried to run the *Jenny* ashore, while pretending to pilot them to a mooring; after some scuffles, rough enough to involve broken bones, they were ejected, and guns were fired toward both colonial ships to deter any further attack. Captain Dorr invited the Tui Bouwalu, the chief of the principal Bua settlement, aboard, and presented him with gifts. These included, most significantly, five whale's teeth. Sperm-whale teeth, known as *tabua* among Fijians, were supreme among local valuables: they were attached to sinnet cords, they became beautifully patinated, they were central to the ceremonial presentations at chiefly marriages, mortuary feasts and such occasions, and they were essential to any entreaty. If, for instance, a chief sought to solicit the support of a group in war, he could not approach their leader without the gift of a great kava root and one or more fine, heavy tabua. Teeth, in other words, were more than mere trinkets.

Dorr provided the Tui Bouwalu, too, with 'several saws and axes', but sandalwood around Bua itself was already exhausted, and Dorr's men had to send boats some forty miles up the coast to Wailea, where the Sydney ships were also active, and where fights frequently broke out between the crews over access to the wood.

On 29 June a boat appeared with the captain, two officers and two seamen from the *Eliza*, an American ship that had been wrecked off the island of Nairai, with some thirty thousand dollars aboard. Lockerby took two boats back to this area and recovered much of the money, but he was assaulted by locals trying to seize their boat, it appeared; they fought them off, killing a considerable number with a swivel gun. Such altercations were frequent. Lockerby gathered that the crew of a boat from the *Elizabeth* had foolishly fired on members of a canoe from the island of Tavea, who then reacted, killing the three white men and taking two Tahitians captive. Lockerby took the initiative, 'determined to recover them and the boat', and became involved in a tense standoff in which he held a local chief hostage in a boat while a man he referred to as his interpreter, probably the beachcomber Charles Savage, was held a counter-hostage on shore. In due course the Tahitians, badly beaten and disfigured by their captives, were given up, but a whale tooth was demanded in return for the boat, which Lockerby was unprepared to pay. He and his men, much 'exasperated' by the conduct of the Tavea people – and maybe angered specifically because they knew that the white sailors killed had been baked and eaten – then fired on the warriors ashore, and rowed briskly away, but they were chased by a group of canoes for more than twenty miles while the traders carried on firing at them, albeit probably ineffectively.[13]

Throughout July, Lockerby carried on the sandalwood trade at Wailea, but at the end of the month he learned to his 'utter astonishment' that the *Jenny* had sailed without him. He wrote later that it was claimed that the ship had been blown off in a storm and was unable to regain the coast; in another version of his memoir he related a different and incompatible story, suggesting that he had had a violent quarrel with Dorr, who then deliberately marooned him. Either way, he was appalled to find himself 'among a race of cannibals, far from every object that was near and dear to me, and possessing but very faint hopes of a vessel calling at such a simply dismal corner of the Globe that might carry me and my unfortunate comrades again into civilized society'. In fact, the *Elizabeth* was still at Bua, but dealings with the Port Jackson ship had not been easy. The contest over sandalwood aside, Lockerby comes across as a fractious and quick-tempered if certainly also an intelligent man. However awful the Fijians were, he preferred the idea of remaining with them to that of seeking a passage to Sydney on the colonial ship.[14]

* * *

Lockerby's situation initially was not uncomfortable. The Tui Bouwalu welcomed him into his house, he was well fed and kindly treated. He formed positive impressions – 'in peace their disposition is mild and generous towards their friends, and the affection they bear towards their relations is very seldom found among Europeans,' he wrote.[15] He wore nothing but the bark belt and loin cloth of local men; he permitted people to paint him black or red as the occasion demanded; he gained fluency in the dialect; and he learned something of local life, even of religion. He witnessed the practices of *kalou* – the word meant both spirits and priests – who were secluded in their own houses and fed offerings, and from time to time induced an ecstatic state. One old priest, who normally seemed barely to possess the energy to stand up, jumped, skipped, beat the ground, and twisted 'his limbs and his body to such a degree as to put himself into so great a perspiration, that induced me to think he was certainly mad', before announcing some prognostication that pleased the chief. As Lockerby understood, 'They have temporarily Callow [*kalou*] for almost everything, but they still believe in as many invisible ones, who they suppose have power over the winds, waters, fish, fowls, &c.: in short, in their opinion, everything has a Callow of its own species.'[16]

Lockerby got the men who had been marooned with him to work on enlarging one of their boats, with a view to making their escape by sail. At the same time, however, he understood that warriors from elsewhere in the archipelago were threatening the Bua people. The chief explained to Lockerby that others had pressed him to share the property he received from Europeans, that until this time he had done so, but he and his people were now fed up with these demands. They therefore constructed a fort, with a ditch and palisade, stores of food were prepared to resist a siege, priests were propitiated and ceremonies conducted. In the midst of all these preparations, in early October a ship appeared, the *Favorite*, another 'colonial' vessel out of Port Jackson. Lockerby was warmly greeted by its captain, William Campbell, and it was agreed that he would help procure their sandalwood, and then travel with the ship back to Canton and beyond.

Lockerby tried for sandalwood at Wailea, but the people everywhere had withdrawn into their fortified villages. On his way back, he was unfortunate enough to be intercepted by a great fleet of canoes from the powerful centre of Bau, off Viti Levu, among other places. They seized Lockerby and his companions, considered putting them to death, but decided, on the advice of one of their priests, that it would be better to keep them alive. Lockerby was compelled to accompany the war party, and proceeded in a fortified double canoe, capable of sailing, he reported, at twenty miles an hour. They reached Tavea and attacked people related to Lockerby's friends at Bua. They engaged canoes that came off shore and people on both sides were wounded; but some six hundred warriors on the island maintained an effective defence. Hostilities continued over several days, prisoners were taken, killed and consumed; white sailors with Lockerby ate part of one corpse 'involuntarily, mistaking it for pork, as it was cooked and resembled it very much,' he wrote.

On 15 October 1808 it appeared that Tavea had been evacuated, so the Bau force landed, seized pigs, fruit, vegetables, utensils, fishing nets and everything else of use, and burned or destroyed houses, plantations and trees. According to Lockerby's shocking, but oddly unsensational report, they then found some 350 people, too young, old, or unfit to escape: 'no sooner were they discovered than a general massacre took place,' he reported, and proceeds to describe, in plausible detail, the cleaning and cooking of the corpses.[17]

Such accounts have been questioned, indeed dismissed, as colonialist fantasy.[18] If, in many instances, reports of indigenous cannibalism are concoctions, the evidence in the Fijian case is simply too extensive and specific to dismiss. Lockerby's was a private memoir that remained unpublished for over a century, not a text trumped up for a commercial press. On virtually all points that can be cross-checked, he is historically accurate, and as geographically and ethnographically sound as can be expected of a text of this period, in his reports of Fijian places, people and practices. In any event, Lockerby's reports of cannibalism would be corroborated not only by similarly authentic historic documents but by many Fijians themselves, who, towards the end of the nineteenth century, were Christians, not proud of these reports of their former culture, but not so brainwashed either as to have colluded in their invention.

Like so much else in the Pacific, this seemingly stereotypic 'cannibal feast' belonged to a system of reciprocity. Warriors provided services to their chief; they were granted human flesh in return, as well, probably, as wives from junior chiefly lines. As in Hawaii, service and largesse, tribute and redistribution, flowed back and forth, perhaps uneasily, propelling expansion. Grandeur and generosity in one place demanded at least occasional aggression elsewhere. New sources of valuables would inevitably be contested. If the Tui Bouwalu resisted pressure from other peoples to redistribute such resources, those people would inevitably seek to impose redistribution – supposing that this was in fact the cause of the war, rather than the cause that the chief found easiest to explain to Lockerby.

Their victory accomplished, the Bauans and their allies made their way to Bua, where Lockerby offered or pretended to secure the help of the ships in the attack on his friend, the Tui Bouwalu, in exchange for a cargo of sandalwood. Lockerby and one Thomas Berry were kept hostage while a boat took the other whites to the *Favorite* to negotiate. Here, however, the two Fijian chiefs, local allies of the Bauans were seized. Lockerby persuaded those he was with to take him and Berry to the ship, so that they could be exchanged for the chiefs, which his captors agreed to try; they tied the two Europeans tightly to planks on one canoe, and set off, with a fleet of some thirty, toward the *Favorite*, singing and chanting as they proceeded. On board, Campbell thought that Lockerby and Berry were already dead, that this fleet was set on attacking him, and opened fire. Fearing that they would be swiftly put to death, Lockerby asked those in the canoe to tie him to the mast, so that he might be seen. When he was, he was sighted from the ship, and Campbell sent a boat, with 'a large present as our ransom', crewed by four men described as Lascars, evidently South Asians, since one spoke to Lockerby 'in the Bengalee language', disclosing the alarming news that the two chiefs had already been killed. The unknowing Fijians would have none of the 'large present' and insisted on their chiefs being returned. A subterfuge was then attempted, a boat being sent from the *Favorite* with 'two black men', their backs toward the shore, impersonating the chiefs who were already dead, while heavily armed men lay across the boards out of sight.[19]

As they came close, they fired. Lockerby succeeded in freeing himself and dived into the water, but remained entangled in a rope, which was used to haul him back into the canoe, where he was hit with a club 'on the lower part of my left jaw-bone, the effects of which I shall feel while I live'.[20] The shooting continued, many Fijians were killed, and Lockerby tried repeatedly to get overboard, but was dragged in again, finally escaping when a man swimming after him was shot dead. Half-drowned, Lockerby was hauled out of the water by his friends, who were able to rescue Berry also; they were chased toward the ship by many canoes, but once within cannon range several canoes were sunk and the others repelled. This reverse prompted the Bauans and their allies to abandon for the time being any assault on Bua, so the party dispersed and the warriors returned to their various *vanua*, their lands.

The traders – there were now three ships in the area – then hoped that sandalwood would again be cut, but conditions remained dangerous, efforts to negotiate proved unsuccessful, and the Europeans put it to the Tui Bouwalu that they could join forces to defeat not the Bauans who were too powerful, and at a considerable distance, but the hostile people of 'Tatalepo', properly Tacilevu, a settlement at the western end of Bua Bay. In November a force of some eighteen hundred warriors, supported by launches, swivels and cannon, made an assault on the well-fortified town. Though a considerable number of the warriors allied to the traders were killed, the party eventually succeeded in overrunning the settlement; again the massacre was great, and the dead enemies were consumed. It was now possible for the sandalwood trade to resume, and for a further five months Lockerby remained on the Vanua Levu coast, getting wood cut and on board, acting as agent for several different ships. Around the end of May 1809 he took his leave from the Tui Bouwalu, and those around him. 'I felt considerable pain on parting with them,' he wrote; 'from the good old King I had received kindnesses which I should remember while I live with gratitude.'[21] He left the islands on the *General Wellesley*, a Madras-owned trader, for Canton, New England, and eventually home without, one suspects, ever quite reconciling this sentimental attachment to the people he had lived among with the spectacular violence he had witnessed, and in part himself perpetrated.

Lockerby's reflections on the islands included a vindication of the characters of Fijian women. 'During the time I was amongst them, I never heard in a single instance that any of my companions had connexion with any of them, although the men are not inclined to jealousy.'[22] In support of the point, he related the story of a young woman who had agreed to spend a night on board with one of the officers from the *General Wellesley*, but asked him first to buy some sandalwood from her father; 'this request he could not well refuse, though she asked a whale's tooth for it, which would have purchased ten times the quantity at any other time'. She then took the officer around several other houses, taking advantage of his mounting desire and impatience to coax him 'out of articles which would have bought fifty tons of wood, without getting five'. Once his trade was exhausted, and just as the officer thought finally they were about to get into his boat to go off to the ship, the woman abruptly dashed off into the woods, leaving him less satisfied, but perhaps better informed, concerning the diversity of interests and expectations around sex, in the islands of the Pacific.

Even if we cannot be sure, and it may not have been categorically true, that there was no physical intimacy between any seaman and any local woman in Fiji during this period, there is no doubt that the enthusiastic trafficking in sex that was such a conspicuous element of the encounter almost throughout eastern Polynesia was not a feature of engagement here. This was so, but not for any straightforward or single reason. The notions that stimulated initial sexual traffic in Hawaii and Tahiti, such as the categorization of sailors as high-ranking, perhaps quasi-divine foreign chiefs, from whom commoner women especially would welcome insemination, were not present in Fiji. There, conversely, marriage was central to involved sequences of gifts, in effect to the creation and recreation of society, in a way that it was not in Tahiti or the Marquesas. This centrality, in the structuring of exchanges, in relations of mutual indebtedness that bound particular groups together over generations, does not mean there was no promiscuity, but it did nothing to make what amounted to a public market in sex positively attractive to women, especially when Fijian interest in European trinkets was restrained. All this, too, needs to be placed in the context of the overall pattern of inter- action, which was marked by a certain enthusiasm to engage, yet also by considerable caution, by tension, and frequent outright violence.

None of this was to change quickly. The contacts that came after are poorly documented, but they exhibit the same explosiveness. As Lockerby joined the *General Wellesley*, it seems that another mariner left her. Peter Dillon, later famous for his discovery (in 1826) of the wreck that had ended the great exploratory voyage of the French naval officer La Pérouse, and for solving the mystery of his ships' disappearance in 1788, had coincidentally been born in that same year, in Martinique, of Irish descent. Like Lockerby, he remained a few months in Fiji, procuring cargoes of sandalwood for various ships and learning the language.[23] Early in 1809 he returned to Sydney, joined a further voyage in trading sandalwood, visited New Zealand, and spent time in the Society Islands. In February 1813 he was back in Fiji, third mate of a Calcutta-based ship, the *Hunter*, captained by a James Robson. The aim was to obtain a cargo of sandalwood, and efforts were focussed on the Wailea area in which Lockerby had spent so much time, but cutting and trade were again frustrated by ongoing intertribal conflict. Working in consort with a second ship he owned, the *Elizabeth*, Robson expanded the venture to embrace bêche-de-mer and made Dillon responsible for the collection of a cargo of the sea slugs; to do this, Dillon relocated to the Kaba coast of the great island of Viti Levu to the south and remained there for over three months, employing locals to dive, while running boats back and forth, and curing the sea slugs in purpose-built smoke-houses on shore. This operation went smoothly, but over the same time little sandalwood was being obtained from Vanua Levu.[24]

Robson seems to have been a sharp trader, one who would avoid recipro-cating if he were able to do so. When the *Elizabeth* reached Viti Levu to collect Dillon and his cargo, it failed to bring goods to pay for the Fijians' labour. Hence Dillon returned to Vanua Levu with a considerable number of Bauan men, the latter presumably expecting their rewards when they reached the *Hunter*. At Wailea relations between Robson and the local chiefs had deterio-rated; the Bauans seem to have learned that they were planning an attack on Robson's ships, and they recommended that Robson launch a pre-emptive attack to destroy the Wailean canoe fleet.

On 6 September 1813 three boatloads of well-armed European sailors and a hundred or so Bauan warriors landed to conduct this operation, but they then decided that the tide was too low for it to be practical. They therefore marched towards the Wailean village instead, but then began to straggle and were sepa-rated into smaller groups, some of which had been attacked. Dillon was with the *Hunter*'s first officer, Norman, who was speared and killed. Stumbling across the body of one Terence Dunn – an Irish beachcomber resident in the area – they realized that there were far more hostile warriors in the area than they had thought, and that their retreat to the beach had been cut off. Dillon and a few desperate companions came upon 'a small steep rock that stood upon the plain' and swiftly decided that their best chance of survival lay in ascending and holding this position. With five men – the beachcombers Charles Savage, Martin Buchert and 'Luis a Chinaman', who had all resided at Bau, and two seamen from the *Hunter* – Dillon set about attempting to defend this place.[25] Fortuitously, the rock was difficult of access, they were too high to be stoned, and the wind rendered the Fijians' arrows inaccurate. Attempting to conserve ammunition, Dillon's men shot only at the warriors who actually attempted to climb the rock, but they cannot have felt comfortable: the Fijians below them dug earth-ovens, in preparation, they could only assume, for their bodies.

Since the rock was visible from the sea, Dillon and his companions hoped that Robson might rescue them, but there was no sign that he was preparing to do so. They began negotiating with the Fijians; Dillon drew attention to the fact that there were hostages on the *Hunter*; and one of the sailors was allowed

17 'Massacre at the Feejee Islands in Septr. 1813', lithograph frontispiece to Dillon, *Narrative and Successful Result of a Voyage to the South Seas* This imagining of the scene of barbarism was not based on any sketch or field drawing, but composed in England on the basis of Dillon's text.

safe passage to return to Robson, to propose an exchange. After he left, the Fijians insisted on their friendly intentions, which Dillon doubted, but Savage was more hopeful of. He insisted on making his way down the rock, and appeared to be mingling with people, without being harmed; 'the Chinaman', too, ventured down, and the warriors pressed Dillon to follow, pointing to the fact that the others were unhurt. When he refused to do so, however, they seized Savage and drowned him in a pond, and killed 'Luis' with a club-blow. If we are to believe Dillon's sensational (yet plausibly detailed) account, the bodies of the two men were promptly cut up and baked.[26]

Fighting then resumed, and the situation seemed desperate, especially when a boat from the *Hunter* landed, inexplicably releasing all of the hostages, together with the goods promised in exchange for Dillon's safe passage. A Fijian priest who had negotiated earlier then ventured up on to the rock and said that it had been agreed that Dillon and his remaining companions would give up their guns, and be allowed back to the boat. Dillon refused and instead held his pistol to the priest's head. 'I told him that I would shoot him dead if he attempted to run away, or if any of his companions offered to molest me. . . . I then directed him to proceed before me to the boat, threatening him with instant death in case of non-compliance.' The measure succeeded. The priest walked before Dillon and the other two survivors, calling on the people not to interfere. They then reached the shore, where the priest held back, refusing to go near the boat, and the Europeans backed gingerly into the water, continuing to level their weapons at the many warriors around the landing. As the Europeans dropped their guard to get into the boat, the warriors rushed forward and began slinging stones and firing arrows. The boat, however, got off safely, and Dillon lived to tell the tale, indeed he lived to dine out on it.[27]

It became evident that the operation against the Waileans had been ill-conceived. More than half the Bauan warriors had been killed, and many of the survivors horribly wounded. Apart from those killed near what would be called Dillon's Rock, at least five other seamen, several other European beach-combers and one Tahitian had also died. Even though both the *Hunter* and *Elizabeth* were in need of repairs, Robson decided to leave the islands without delay. He had on board, however, two Fijian women, apparently wives of beachcombers who had been killed, the surviving beachcomber, Martin Buchert, and his pregnant wife – and one 'Joe', a so-called Lascar, who had also resided at Bau. None of these people wished to go to Canton but neither could they safely have been put ashore on the Vanua Levu coast. Dillon was given command of the *Elizabeth* and directed to go via Bau, but weather conditions made it impossible there to launch a local canoe they carried on the ship's deck, and in the end both ships with their unwilling passengers made away towards China.

A week later, however, they passed the island of Tikopia, part of the Solomons archipelago but with a population of Polynesian descent, to be made famous in the twentieth century by the classic anthropological studies of Raymond Firth. Here, 'Joe', Buchert and his wife indicated that they wished to be settled. Canoes came off, and there were initial scuffles as Tikopians seized whatever iron they could lay their hands on; one of the Fijian women grasped one offender 'with the throat by one hand and the privates with the other', and Dillon thought she would have strangled him had he not interfered. In due course 'an elderly chief' ventured aboard and calmed people down, Dillon visited ashore and made presents, and despite the uncertain start, the three

18 Four inhabitants of Tikopia, and Martin Buchert, lithograph after Louis Auguste de Sainson, [Feb 1828] from J.S.C. Dumont d'Urville, *Voyage de la corvette l'Astrolabe. Atlas historique*. Buchert was still comfortably resident on Tikopia almost twenty years after having been left there by Dillon.

were pleased to be set ashore. The two Fijian women did not, however, wish to be left on the island, so they continued with Dillon to Sydney, while Robson sailed to Canton, to dispose of the bêche-de-mer and such sandalwood as he had succeeded in obtaining.[28]

* * *

If the sheer drama of Lockerby's and Dillon's experiences in Fiji remains striking, their narratives are nevertheless suggestive in manifold ways. While the two-sided model of cultural contact posits an engagement – whether marked by friendliness or antagonism – between Europeans and Islanders, strangers and natives in Greg Dening's terms, these confrontations cut across this opposition.[29] There were tensions, indeed violent altercations, between English and American vessels – the former including ships out of imperial ports such as Madras, Calcutta and Sydney, and the latter typically including British-born officers or crew, such as Lockerby. The violence in which they were caught up onshore was not simply with 'natives'. In 1808 the Tui Bouwalu and his people joined the Europeans in an assault on their neighbours and their neighbours' Bauan allies; in 1813 the Bauans joined the Europeans in an attack on Wailea.

The multicultural nature of these engagements is likewise extraordinary. In Lockerby's time the crews included Tahitians, Bengalis and, presumably Afro-Americans (the two 'black men' who impersonated the Fijian chiefs, already killed by the crew of the *Favorite*). One of Dillon's beachcomber companions was an unnamed Tahitian, one Chinese (Luis), and a third a 'Lascar' (Joe), presumably another South Asian. And among the consequences of these engagements was the resettlement of a beachcomber, his Fijian wife, and this same South Asian, on the island of Tikopia, which until this time was scarcely visited.

The two women who sailed to Sydney with Dillon spent ten months there, but they then travelled back to Fiji in August 1814 on the *Campbell Macquarie* with Captain Richard Siddons. He was accompanied by the man whose discovery had first sparked off the occasionally profitable but decidedly bloody sandalwood trade, the beachcomber Oliver Slater. Their decision to seek a further cargo of sandalwood is not easy to understand, given the virtual failure of Robson's attempt and the attendant disorder and violence. Moreover, Slater was also killed, while ashore overnight on the small island of Makogai, not far from Wailea and probably allied to it. It is not clear why the two women were with him, but it is likely that they died also; only a Hawaiian, one 'Bubbahae', perhaps Papahei, survived.[30]

* * *

With the growth of commerce in the Pacific, life had become cheap. Over the course of Captain Cook's three voyages between 1768 and 1779, which included visits to dozens of islands and sojourns of months at some, a total of about fifteen Islanders were killed as a result, up to the time of Cook's violent death. In the immediate aftermath of that event, however, more than thirty Hawaiians were massacred. In contrast, virtually every sandalwood expedition seems to have featured some fracas in which dozens of Islanders were shot. Yet these encounters were marked by deadly reciprocity. Lockerby was lucky to leave the islands with no greater injury than an ache in the jaw, albeit one that he thought he would feel for the rest of his life.

The extremity of this violence reflected the decentralization of power in Fiji. Islanders who had the opportunity seized boats, killed their crew and made off with whatever they could, or gave most survivors of wrecks short shrift. However, it is interesting that the personal qualities of certain beach-combers, the kindness of certain chiefs, or whatever other circumstances, made it possible for some outsiders to lead lives within, or on the margins of, Fijian communities. By contrast, in Hawaii the strategy of seizing ships was relatively short-lived. There had been a series of such incidents in the 1780s and 1790s, but by the early nineteenth century, King Kamehameha and his

19 Louis Choris, *Femme des Iles Sandwich* (portrait of Kaahumanu, 1816), watercolour.

subordinates took a longer view. They were already profiting from a more organized trade, which brought them the life of luxury, the degree of civilized opulence, that so astonished von Kotzebue among others. The trend – to embrace trade and traders, to adopt the trappings of western culture – would carry on. The faction dominated by Kaahumanu, Kamehameha's queen, pressed their advantage relentlessly, such that after the king's death the queen manipulated his successor, their son Liholiho, to abolish the *kapu*, the ancient taboos, and the cults that went with them. From the perspective of the New England missionaries who reached the islands in early 1820, all of this was miraculous:

> . . . the messengers have astonished and agitated our minds by repeating the unexpected information from the fishermen: – *that the aged king Tamahamaha is dead; that Reho-reho, his son, succeeds him; that the images of his gods are burned; that the men are all Inoahs, that is, they eat with the women, in all the islands; that one of the chiefs only was killed, in settling the affairs of government; and he for refusing to destroy his gods.*[31]

Yet they were not so naïve as to suppose that all was as it seemed. There was 'some reason to fear, that the government is not settled on the firmest basis'. Hawaiian society would possess a dangerous momentum that would harness the missionary enterprise, even as the missionaries attempted to manipulate and profit from it.

CHAPTER FOUR

✦

Not a vestige of idolatry was to be seen

During the first years of the nineteenth century, the LMS missionaries on Tahiti often played the role of itinerant preachers, walking up valleys, seeking out less-visited settlements, endeavouring to speak to people, to preach wherever even a few might be assembled. Men such as the former carpenter and wheelwright Henry Bicknell, friend of the Tahitian Tapioi, James Elder, a Scottish Presbyterian stonemaker, and Charles Wilson, who had been apprenticed to a baker before offering himself as a missionary and was also a Presbyterian and a Scot, walked around parts of the island, such as Tahiti Iti, 'little Tahiti'. The tribes of this peninsula, which protrudes to the east, were more often than not estranged from, or antagonistic toward, the chiefs and people of the north-west, those the missionaries knew best.

These excursions, following well-established paths among palms, breadfruit trees and shaded coastal plantations, relieved by breezes off the reef, might have verged on the idyllic, one might imagine, for men a world away from the harsh climates and hard labour of their homes. But there was a grim aspect to the evangelists' interactions with the people of these districts. The visitors were reproached, if not vigorously berated, virtually everywhere, by Islanders who drew attention to their own physical suffering. On one occasion, as the missionaries tried to address people, they had to compete with a counter-address from a man 'employed in enumerating the diseases the English have brought here . . . they were all dying, and but few left alive'. The visitors were often confronted by this sort of register of afflictions. 'They seldom fail wantonly to call on us to look on those who have broken backs, the ague, the venereal, &c. and ask if those will be healed by our *parrow*', that is, by the missionaries' words.[1]

If cross-cultural dealings are supposed to be plagued by chronic misunderstandings, the trouble, for these Europeans, was rather that their message was being clearly understood, but considered false. 'When they know that our business is to teach them the word of God, they generally laugh, ridicule, and tell us, that they have heard before, and still are not saved, but continue dying; desire us also to look at the crooked backs, scrophulous necks, and on those afflicted with the fever; and tell us, that these, with the venereal, flux, headache, palpitation of the heart, &c. have all come from England.' On occasion, too, the missionaries were made to listen to a fuller, historical account:

> They say, that Captain Cook brought the intermitting fever, the crooked backs, and the scrophula, which breaks out in their necks, breasts, groins, and armpits. That Vancouver brought a bloody flux, that in a few months killed a great number, and then abated; but is still among them. . . . According to the natives, the crooked back is an effect of the hotatte (and that after the back breaks the person recovers) which we see is the case. There are some of them dying of an intermittent fever, which has nearly the same appearance as in Europe; but there are others dying of a consumption; or, in other words, and perhaps more properly, of the scrophula, which breaks inwardly, and wastes them like a consumption.[2]

These grievances suggest that it was not in fact a dogged or unconsidered attachment to old gods or customs that predisposed Tahitians to resist Christianity, but rather their observations of new and dreadful circumstances, and a pretty reasonable assessment that the circumstances contradicted the missionaries' rhetoric.

It would not anyway be quite right to talk of 'old gods' in Tahiti. The cult of 'Oro had been imported from Raiatea during the eighteenth century; its introduction had occurred within the living memory of the oldest among those the missionaries met. Nor were the people in general much attached to 'Oro or associated figures. The commoners who lived away from the chiefly settlements surely revered immediate ancestors, to whom they made sacrifices at local shrines, but 'Oro was an enthusiasm of Pomare, of his rivals, and members of the arioi cult and subculture, not the population at large.[3]

Those who insisted that the missionaries acknowledge the illness that was everywhere, tended also to complain that Pomare was seeking out too many to sacrifice to his god.[4] Those sacrificed had generally committed some criminal offence, but the common folk among whom they lived may not have felt that they deserved to die, in order to raise the stakes of aristocratic ritual. These rites were moreover embedded within great ceremonies, which themselves made considerable demands on ordinary people. Over the period, insofar as it is possible to say, it seems that the scale and frequency of ritual events was stepped

20 Figure of the god 'Oro, early nineteenth century, Tahiti.

up, as the struggle between Pomare and the chiefs of Atehuru intensified. At a time when there was illness in every house, when the routines of fishing and gardening must have been disrupted, we can only suppose that commoners contributed to festivals of this kind less eagerly than they once had.

If Islanders were dispirited, the missionaries were too, in their case by the stand-off between the forces of darkness and light that just dragged on and on. But if, during the first decade of the nineteenth century, they saw little they could recognize as progress, they nevertheless witnessed rapid change. Some of them achieved real fluency in Tahitian, enabling a new level of mutual understanding, if not necessarily of agreement. Intelligible talk could go beyond the basics and extend even to theological questions. It is striking that as early as mid-1803, a missionary account of the afterlife might be clearly received, understood and contested by a Tahitian audience, who dismissed the notion that the dead might in future be resurrected. Their view was that 'They are rotten and become dirt; therefore they affirm it is impossible.' By way of riposte, locals presented a mythic history of human immortality – a possibility once offered by the goddess Hina, but declined by the first man, Ti'i – and their own understandings of afterlife, 'at death the soul leaves the body, and goes into the other world, and is eaten by one or other of the gods'. The missionaries Elder and Wilson transcribed these beliefs in terms broadly consistent with later, fuller reconstructions.[5]

* * *

If people were learning something of European religion, they were also learning a good deal about Europe. Yet Pomare's understanding derived not primarily from the missionaries. Among his entourage were a group of Hawaiians, considered by the missionaries 'a most daring hardened race', and much resented by them, for giving the chief many 'wicked' ideas. Among them was one who had been to England 'and who is constantly telling him something of what he saw there; so that his ideas of things are much enlarged'.[6] This 'enlargement' of ideas – of culture – indeed appears to have proceeded rapidly. Whalers and traders now arrived frequently. Every ship brought renewed contact, not only with Europeans but with people from elsewhere in the world – a Chinese sailor, for example, deserted from the *Myrtle* in July 1804 – and with Islanders, if not from Hawaii, from the Marquesas, the Tongan archipelago, New Zealand, or elsewhere. Many ships brought Tahitian crew back, either to return home, or to visit before voyaging again; on many vessels, too, one or more Islanders would be recruited for the first time.

The 'wickedness' that the missionaries attributed to Hawaiian influence included an interest in distillation. Spirits were beginning to be consumed, demanded in trade, or locally concocted, and Pomare, among other members of the elite, gained notoriety for excessive drinking, as however did some of the missionaries too. Apart from this, and European fabrics among other trade goods, Pomare and Tahitians generally were also acquiring a fuller sense not only of the European but the larger colonial world. In 1808, in a moment of danger, Pomare hoped he would recover his authority, but remarked that 'perhaps the people would cut off his head as the people of France had done with their king'.[7] A sense that, in other parts of the world, Europeans had appropriated produce or otherwise exploited people, lay behind opposition to the few petty commercial ventures attempted by missionaries or their associates. This became most evident a decade later, when in 1818 one Mr Gyles tried to produce sugar, but his scheme failed, 'in consequence of the king's jealousy, excited by false alarms insinuated into his mind by foreigners, that slavery and the culture of the cane were necessarily associated'. Even in 1803, however, a plan to gather turmeric for sale had been abandoned, the missionaries recognizing that Islanders' 'suspicions of our encroachment on their rights are easily raised'.[8]

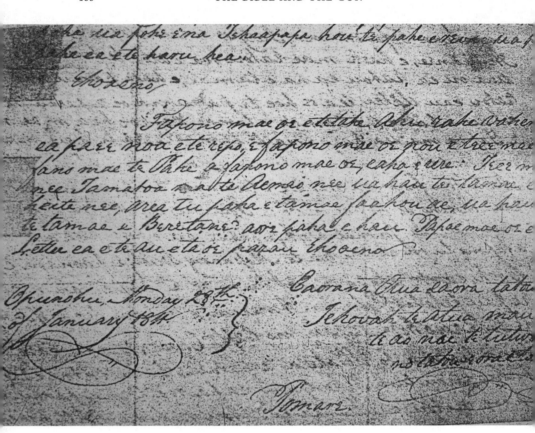

21 Part of an 1810 letter from Pomare II, with his signature. This was probably the earliest written document extant by any Pacific Islander, but the original is now missing from the collections of the School of Oriental and African Studies, London.

If Pomare quickly exhibited a thirst, it was for literacy as well as for liquor. He was intrigued by script, print and books. By late 1803 he had learned 'to make the letters of the English alphabet, to know their names, and to put them together so as to form sundry words and short sentences'. Around this time, the missionaries regularized a Tahitian alphabet, and only six months later, Pomare was said to be in the habit of writing short letters to the missionaries, which he began to do routinely.[9] He asked them to build a small house which might be set aside for him to write in, and in due course regularly kept a private journal. To remark on the high chief's near-obsession is risky. It would be easy to lapse into an imputation of naïve fetishism, the suggestion that these Polynesians attributed a magical power to writing. In fact, there is no evidence I am aware of that they did consider writing magical. But they certainly did consider it a practice charged with power.[10]

To some degree, this is not surprising. When Europeans first visited Tahiti, Islanders had observed them writing, and described writing as a form of tattooing.[11] Tatau was not so much an art of self-decoration – though beautification was certainly a part of it – as a technique for armouring the body, for safeguarding it from the unstable contagion and transference of taboo. Early on, writing would also have been an activity that Islanders associated particularly with Captain Cook, his scientists and his officers – those foreigners who seemed to be of the highest rank. Just as chiefs exchanged names with lieutenants and high chiefs exchanged names with captains, the practices peculiar to this odd, floating, prestige-encrusted European elite would carry prestige in themselves.

Yet this reasoning only takes us so far. Pomare was, if not a traveller in a literal sense, a cosmopolitan of the mind. If the efficacy of tatau contaminated his sense of script, he was not a prisoner of culture to the extent that he could not see the distinction between the two, or perceive that the letter was an instrument of action, a means of projecting one's will, most importantly perhaps of soliciting gifts or proposing transactions. His Hawaiians perhaps told him that King Kamehameha had written even to King George of England, to ask for a ship. For by now Pomare was well aware of the grandeur of Kamehameha's kingdom. Kamehameha had geographic and socio-economic advantages that no Tahitian high chief could aspire to – greater lands and a greater population, most obviously. But those did not prevent his regime from appearing a magnificent exemplar of what a Pacific kingdom might be. Historians and anthropologists have been quick to point out that European visitors were wrong to identify Pomare as a 'king', as opposed to a chief among many. But the European error was one that Pomare himself embraced with alacrity, creating a Polynesian truth, of sorts.

But his struggle to make an actuality out of misrepresentation would be prolonged. The first fifteen years of the nineteenth century saw a succession of assertions and counter-assertions of ritual precedence and sovereignty, outbreaks of violence, and (from Pomare's perspective) setbacks. While the chief was in a strong position in 1804, resistance thereafter stepped up, and he was forced to remove himself to Moorea in 1808. Over this insecure time, the bulk of the missionaries – perhaps mindful of their brethren who had died as a result of being unable to escape the Tongan strife – withdrew to Sydney, a few relocating to Huahine. By 1810, however, the reports reaching Australia suggested that overt conflict had diminished, and Pomare was earnestly seeking the missionaries' return. Over the latter months of 1811 and early 1812 the mission was effectively re-established, still on Moorea rather than Tahiti. Though peace prevailed, little had been accomplished toward what the evangelists described – disingenuously, given what they knew of the island's political history – as the 'restoration' of Pomare's government.[12]

* * *

In July 1812 Pomare told the missionaries that he was ready 'to cast away his false gods'. What the missionaries had 'long, long wished for' now gained momentum. In mid-1813 Bicknell visited Tahiti – still considered unsettled and essentially off-limits – and reported that 'some natives' there had likewise 'renounced their former heathen practices, observed the Sabbath, and worshipped the true God'.[13] Islanders evidently took these steps independently, in the absence of direct missionary encouragement. Over the weeks and months that followed, people around the missionaries on Moorea, and Islanders visiting from Huahine and elsewhere began to participate regularly in worship. But Islanders who had no direct connection with either Pomare or the mission continued to 'convert' autonomously. In July 1814, for example, a man named Auna visited Moorea from Tahiti. 'He had been sometime a worshipper of the true God and had acted as a sort of Teacher among a few people at Tautira in Taiarapu.'[14]

Taiarapu was the part of the island that Elder, Bicknell and others had toured several times, some ten years earlier, where they had been confronted with the awfulness of European-introduced illness and angrily rebuffed. Whatever had changed did not include much diminution in the impact of disease. The worst phase of depopulation occurred probably before the missionaries arrived, but the subsequent trajectory saw the population of the whole island fall from over 16,000 in 1797 to about 8,000 in the early 1820s, according to the missionary estimates which are the most accurate for this period. The rapid increase in shipping during the first years of the nineteenth century meant continuing sexual traffic and continuing infection or re-infection, poorer general health and greater vulnerability.[15]

It is clear enough that Pomare's own conversion was politically motivated. If he was putting his money more unambiguously on an association and alliance, at once symbolic and practical, with Europe generally, the British particularly, and the missionaries in person, Polynesians in more out-of-the-way communities stood less obviously to gain. True, they might establish relationships with the missions, but trade gifts were anyway mostly monopolized by chiefs. Their conversions may oddly have been 'truer', perhaps precisely because they were in fact consistent with the complaints they had addressed to the missionaries a decade earlier.

These Islanders had, of course, been right to identify European contact as the source of disease and malaise. But by 1814 it had become abundantly clear that their own gods and cults – which had always centred on prosperity and well-being – had lost their efficacy. There was, by now, surely a deep exhaustion, an acute demoralization, in Tahitian culture and belief. Fragmented evidence suggests that formal Tahitian ritual – such as took place at marae, led by 'official' tribal priests – was in decline. Another class of priests, *taura*, or shamans, the loose cannons of the religious world, were in their place increasingly prominent – a mark of the destabilization of belief.[16]

The adoption of Jehovah in place of 'Oro would have been facilitated, too, by fortuitous resonances between Christian and local cosmologies. Among the missionaries' favourite juxtapositions was that between darkness and light. As it happened, similar divisions between epochs of dark and light, coexisting realms of death and life, and worlds of the spirits and of the living, were pervasive in Polynesian myth and thought. Varied other notions and metaphors – of botanical and agricultural fertility, for example, as well as a rhetoric of truth and power – were also loosely congruent.

Historians and anthropologists who take cultural differences to be deeply seated, and who presume that different peoples bear profoundly different world-views, have been committed to an understanding of conversion to Christianity as just 'conversion', an appearance rather than a reality, something less than it was made out to be. Up to a point, this view is a valid one. 'Conversions' like Pomare's were strategic, and as new religions were embraced by wider populations, they were locally adapted, and assimilated to pre-existing beliefs. The apparent rupture of 'conversion' might indeed seem less significant than underlying continuities of symbolism or belief, hence the emergence of locally distinctive Christianities in many parts of the Pacific or Africa.[17]

Tahitian history suggests, however, that this perspective might easily exaggerate continuing cultural integrity. Conversion was not a new, or inherently anomalous, feature of Polynesian religion. The cult of 'Oro had been recently embraced, and no doubt the gods he displaced had earlier displaced others. There was a tension anyway between priests' rites and shamans' cults, that is, there were already competing approaches to divine power.

More importantly, however, both ordinary and aristocratic Tahitians did grasp the distinctiveness of Christian belief and practice at general and particular levels. It is worth hazarding that Islanders embraced some things, practices or institutions, not because they could be readily assimilated but because they could not – because they did in fact bring or promise unprecedented change.

* * *

Christianity's ascendancy became decisive in November 1815. Pomare and many of those who had years earlier been forced to retreat with him to Moorea had taken advantage of disarray among the Atehuru and their allies, to re-establish themselves, and ceremonies of reconciliation 'to reinstate them in a formal manner in their old possessions' were anticipated. But, according to John Davies, missionary, linguist and historian of the mission, when Pomare and his people were assembled to worship on Sunday 12 November, the Atehuru ventured 'a furious, sudden and unexpected assault'. Or not so unexpected: the missionaries took credit for warning Pomare 'of the probability of such a Stratagem', hence many of those now called the 'praying people' were discreetly armed. Soon after fighting commenced, one Upufara, described by Davies as the 'principal leader in this final battle of the idolaters', was killed, and Pomare's party quickly overwhelmed their opponents.[18]

The new era was marked by the fact that the vanquished were spared, and the hitherto customary practice of plunder was refrained from. Or so we are told. In any event, the mission, and Pomare, now entered a triumphant phase. By early 1816 the profession of Christianity was said to have 'become national' in both Tahiti and Moorea, and was swiftly becoming so in the remainder of the Society Islands. Pomare despatched his own 'family idols' to the missionaries, giving them the option of destroying them or sending them to England. They chose to do the latter, where the woven and sculpted gods were published as barbaric trophies in the popular magazine, *Missionary Sketches*, and later treated as star exhibits at the LMS's Missionary Museum. By 1817, when the Reverend William Ellis arrived with a printing press, Pomare and the missionaries were securely established, and were already discussing the promulgation of a code of laws.[19]

There would be no swift transition to a missionary state. The Polynesian polity was too fluid and Pomare (from the missionaries' perspective) too inconstant an ally to effect that. But the people who had embraced 'Oro in the eighteenth century and Jehovah in the nineteenth were engaging this time in a process of conversion that would have far-reaching ramifications. In one sense, the process was one of substitution. Chapels and great churches were constructed, often on or near marae sites, which provided convenient sources of stone. Traditional ceremonies, in which chiefs were central, were replaced by great Christian services, which again reflected glory on the principal chiefly actors.

But there was pressure to transform virtually every area of life. Architecture, work, adornment, dress, food, and needless to say sex all fell within the missionary remit. In some cases local chiefs and teachers became highly zealous in their policing of offences, fining those guilty of fornication or bad language. The most enthusiastic converts went to the trouble of constructing and whitewashing wattle-and-daub houses; new crops were planted, in part for trade and church subscriptions; and new garments appeared, marking Christian from heathen. In the first half of the nineteenth century, these often took a European form, but were made of customary materials. Missionaries on tour remarked with pleasure on seeing hats and bonnets woven out of pandanus, emblems of Christian affiliation that women still wear to church in Tahiti and elsewhere today.

* * *

William Crook had begun a voyage back to the mission field as early as 1803, but settled for thirteen years in Australia before, at the age of forty, taking his wife and seven children to Tahiti. He was among the more senior missionaries and made the most of opportunities to correct and expand his 'Account of the Marquesas Islands', composed half a life earlier. He seems to have enjoyed some intimacy with Pomare. One day late in June 1820, the chief:

> asked me to point out to him Lima in the map that hung up, and he pointed out Cape Horn as a place he knew well, and the River Amazonia under the Line. He amused himself by looking over the West India Islands, and Jamaica, in particular, from whence Mr. Gyles came. He said he was going to send some Sandwich Islanders to Teturoa to make salt, as they had learned to make it in their own country.[20]

It is not clear whether these were the same Hawaiians whose arrival and intrusions had so vexed the missionaries twenty-two years earlier. Yet it is evident that the chief, charged so often with inconstancy by his evangelical friends, had over so many years taken note of Hawaiian enterprise and had Hawaiians about to help him emulate it. A year and a half later, however, he was dead.

* * *

In 1824 Otto von Kotzebue, the Russian who had already visited the Pacific in command of his own first expedition of 1816–18, and earlier during the first Russian circumnavigation, commanded by Adam Jean von Krusenstern (1803–6), returned to the islands. Though he was, like most European navigators of the period, an ardent fan of Captain Cook, he saw nothing to applaud in the work of Cook's compatriots and successors, the English missionaries in Tahiti. His ship arrived, as it happened, on the Tahitian Sabbath, and he was immediately and unfavourably struck by the 'stillness of death' that prevailed. Everyone was indoors, engaged in loud prayer; there was something inhumane in a regime that prohibited 'even the children' enjoying the beauty of the tropical morning.[21]

Von Kotzebue may have reflected on these observations over the course of his expedition. When his *New Voyage round the World* appeared in 1828, the Tahitian section of the narrative took the form of a sustained polemic against the London Missionary Society. He began by remarking on the 'unlimited influence' the missionaries exerted over the population as a whole, and proceeded to narrate the history of conversion, claiming that opponents of the Church had been massacred in great numbers. 'Streams of blood flowed – whole races were exterminated; many resolutely met the death they preferred to the renunciation of their ancient faith.' The new order was notable mainly for 'bigotry, hypocrisy, and a hatred and contempt of all other modes of faith, which was once foreign to the open and benevolent character of the Tahaitian.'[22] When the book was published in English in 1830, it was reviewed favourably and at length in the *Westminster Review*, the radical journal associated with Jeremy Bentham and James Mill (the father of John Stuart Mill). For the LMS, that charges of this severity might be made in a Russian or German book was unwelcome. When they were reproduced and cited with approval in English, the mission had to react.

William Ellis spent some seven years in the Society Islands and Hawaii, but was by this time well established back in London, and had set himself up as something of a mission historian, indeed as the author of the most compendious of the early anthropological treatises on the islands.[23] But he set his Polynesian researches aside to bring out, in 1831, a *Vindication of the South Sea Missions from the Misrepresentations of Otto von Kotzebue*. He cannot have found it difficult to prepare this defence. The Russian had got his history of conversion thoroughly scrambled, misidentifying the chiefs, tribes, events and places involved. Nor did any report substantiate his charge that depopulation reflected the mass killing of defiant heathens. Von Kotzebue's text remains important, not so much as a valid exposé but as a reminder that even during its ascendancy the missionary effort was ambivalently regarded, and sometimes vigorously castigated.

Many voyagers joined von Kotzebue in lamenting the inappropriateness of introduced dress – the point that European garments were unflattering, shapeless and unsuited to the climate was to become a cliché in commentary on the colonial Pacific. And many remarked, too, that missionary morality was sustained only under missionary eyes. The sexual traffic for which Tahiti had long been notorious was carried on, only a little more discreetly.

If these observations were already commonplace, von Kotzebue struck also at the heart of the endeavour. In Russia, those who engaged in Christian instruction had studied long and hard at schools and universities. The London Missionary Society was more easily satisfied, the critic contended. It suited the LMS to send out 'a half savage, confused by the dogmas of an uneducated sailor'.[24] He was referring to a native teacher who had been himself trained by one of the white missionaries, said by the Russian to have been a former seaman. In fact, virtually none of the LMS missionaries had any sort of maritime background, though their prior occupations embraced every conceivable trade and artisanal activity, from carpentry to printing. If their class backgrounds were not those of ordinary seamen, and if many had in fact received instruction at a missionary academy or similar institution, these 'itinerant preachers' certainly did not rank as gentlemen.

This question, however, paled into insignificance next to that of the so-called 'half savage' who, it appeared, was in fact integral to missionary work. Von Kotzebue's racist language highlighted something extraordinary: that Islanders were being converted (in whatever sense) to Christianity not by white missionaries, but *by themselves*. Given that it was more or less axiomatic among the missionaries that civilization (or 'true civilization') and Christianity were inseparable, this moreover implied that Islanders might similarly civilize themselves. For von Kotzebue, this simply signalled the absurdity of the enterprise. White missionaries were not themselves in agreement about the roles that their local counterparts could play, and usually did not refer to them as 'missionaries'. In his *Vindication*, Ellis opted to do so, passed over any uncertainties, and baldly declared that, despite their obvious lack of university training, Islander teachers were up to the task of instruction in 'reading, writing and arithmetic, and mechanical arts . . . and of teaching the plain and essential principles of religion'. Not only were they capable of doing so in principle, he cited navigators such as John Byron and Frederick William Beechey who had reported that islands with considerable populations had rejected idolatry as a result of 'the labours of these native Missionaries'. Some thirty islands were at the time, he claimed, 'under their instruction, advancing in knowledge and religion'.

The benefits were not merely spiritual. Ellis called on his readers to remember incidents of violence that had taken place when Europeans had arrived among heathen islanders. The death of Cook at Hawaii, the assault upon La Pérouse's crew in Samoa and many similar hostilities marked the epoch prior to missionary influence. There was a sheer unreasonableness in von Kotzebue's assault, Ellis protested, given that his own very security, and the security of his ship, his crew and his property, was in fact now assured on islands such as Tahiti as a result of the Christian presence, adding that 'The change in the behaviour of the islanders, among whom only native teachers are settled, is not less decisive.'[25] While anti-colonial critics would later charge missions with paving the way for trade and formal colonization, Ellis and others would have acknowledged and affirmed precisely such a complicit relation. To prove their broader usefulness, they hurried to declare that they were making the Pacific safe for navigation and commerce, even as they were conscious of the dangers of trade, in weapons, spirits and sex, for example.

* * *

Islanders were what we might call spiritual activists from the earliest stages of the process of conversion on Tahiti and the neighbouring islands. But their involvement gained greater momentum only around the time of von Kotzebue's observations, with the encouragement of the man who would, until David Livingstone, be perhaps the most famous of all British missionaries. The initial chapters of John Williams's story are wholly typical of missionary biography. He was born into a large family just off the high street in Tottenham, then as now a less prosperous quarter of north London. After basic schooling he was apprenticed to an ironmonger, whose wife persuaded him one evening to attend a service at Moorfield's Tabernacle, a chapel with strong Methodist connections off Old Street, near the City. The occasion provided the catalyst for spiritual rebirth: Williams discovered a fervent commitment, and engaged enthusiastically in activities around the Tabernacle, which happened to be the base for an auxiliary society linked with the London Missionary Society. He in due course applied to the LMS itself to serve as a missionary and was examined and interviewed. The committee's minutes noted that his responses to questions 'evinced the want of further instruction' but that he 'showed considerable talent and appeared to have taken a most decided resolution to devote himself to the Missionary Work.'[26]

This early assessment is consistent with a curiously frank characterization of Williams published years later, after his death. The biographer emphasized his strength of character, but remarked that 'On nearly all subjects, except that of missions, his views were narrow and superficial.' There was worse. 'He was decidedly a man of genius – of great genius – but of genius wholly mechanical. He was also strongly marked by the chief intellectual infirmity of men of that class. His judgment, although sound, was neither strong, comprehensive, nor exact.'[27] These decidedly back-handed compliments were accompanied by the extraordinary imputation that Williams's features and manner suggested a sort of racial degeneracy:

> Few men, skilled in the physiognomical attributes of nations, would have pronounced him an Englishman: most would have found it difficult to determine whether he was of Welsh or of Scottish extraction. . . . The Welsh and Scotch, in several points, closely resemble each other; they are both generally of a dark complexion, of hard features, of a somewhat heavy and rustic appearance, with but little of that airy, elegant, lofty, and not seldom reserved deportment, which are the chief characteristics of the English.[28]

If these remarks in all likelihood stemmed from some resentment over the preeminence among missionaries that Williams had by then assumed – the writer, John Campbell, would have seen his own literary eminence eclipsed – they were probably provoked too by an obduracy and single-mindedness that was indeed characteristic.

The examining committee required that the would-be missionary receive further tuition. Before departing for the Pacific, Williams joined forces with one Mary Chawner, also a member of Moorfield's Tabernacle, and who may have possessed similar strength of character. It is at any rate unusual to find her referred to in the LMS records as embarking, not only as Williams's wife, but explicitly 'in the capacity of Missionary to Otaheite', that is, as a missionary in her own right. There is, however, nothing to suggest that, once in the Society Islands – the couple arrived on Moorea in November 1817 – her status was any different to that of other missionary wives. De facto missionaries these women certainly were. Their responsibilities, most obviously in the areas of girls' education and women's work and craft, were considerable, but they were never salaried, nor did they attend the committee and circuit meetings that dealt with local business and issues of policy.

A year later the Williams moved to Raiatea, which was to be their main base until 1830. John Williams's 'mechanic' background had predisposed him to an interest in craft and industry, but there was a larger imagining behind his effort to get Islanders engaged in everything from house- and boat-building through new kinds of agriculture to needlework and bonnet-making, the latter areas in which Mary no doubt took the lead. While his brethren had tried several times to persuade the LMS to purchase a ship, Williams simply went ahead and bought one. The vessel, the *Endeavour*, was to be co-owned by the chiefs of Raiatea and partly funded by an advance on the profits of trade. The notion was that it could both finance missionary work and undertake regular cruises around new mission stations. When profits failed to materialize, the ship had to be sold a few years later, but it had already exemplified the capaciousness of Williams's vision. Mission activity would no longer restrict itself to Tahiti and the adjacent islands, but could expand without limit throughout the islands of the Pacific. The vision 'of great extent and importance' behind the first voyage of the *Duff* was recovered, though Williams went further, to cast himself in the role of the heroic explorer, a seeker of peoples as yet untouched by civilization or Christianity. As he would also aspire personally to the status of a man of business, multiple movements, across geographic, social and religious gulfs, were eagerly anticipated here. When he later wrote a book, Williams entitled it *Missionary Enterprises in the South Sea Islands*. Enterprise: he could not have picked a more aptly expansive, suggestively commercial word.[29]

The project hinged absolutely on the participation of Islander missionaries. Williams, from his reading of mission history, or on his arrival in Polynesia, quickly realized that much of what had already been accomplished had depended absolutely upon their only superficially subordinate participation and support. In any event, it was obvious that British missionaries in the islands would number, at best, in the dozens rather than the hundreds. (The LMS fielded a total of only about 125 missionaries in the South Seas between 1797 and 1860; the figure includes some twenty who, like Vason, defected or served for less than two years.) Despite the evangelicals' strength at home, few were prepared to commit their lives to work in distant mission fields, nor in any case could the Society afford to send out many more. Yet there were clearly many, many islands, some in the western Pacific densely populated and on almost a continental scale, where people might be prepared to receive the Gospel. And, in the highly charged rhetoric of the time, it was plain that those people ought not to be surrendered to heathenism, deprived of the light, and the chance of eternal life.

* * *

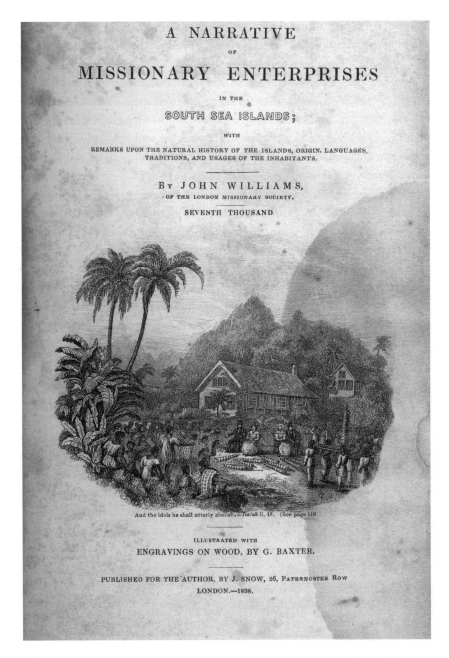

A NARRATIVE

OF

MISSIONARY ENTERPRISES

IN THE

SOUTH SEA ISLANDS;

WITH

REMARKS UPON THE NATURAL HISTORY OF THE ISLANDS, ORIGIN, LANGUAGES,
TRADITIONS, AND USAGES OF THE INHABITANTS.

By JOHN WILLIAMS,
OF THE LONDON MISSIONARY SOCIETY.

SEVENTH THOUSAND.

And the idols he shall utterly abolish.—*Isaiah* ii. 18.   (See page 116)

ILLUSTRATED WITH
ENGRAVINGS ON WOOD, BY G. BAXTER.

PUBLISHED FOR THE AUTHOR, BY J. SNOW, 26, PATERNOSTER ROW
LONDON.—1838.

22 Title page, John Williams, *A Narrative of Missionary Enterprises in the South Sea Islands.*

'The year 1821 was fraught with important events', Williams would write. 'It was, in fact, a year of great things.'[30] The dramatic and unanticipated repudiation of idolatry on the part of the whole population of Rurutu was one. Another was the formal establishment of a native missionary society. Williams, in the course of a passage to Sydney, dropped two Raiateans, Papehia and Vahapatu, off on Aitutaki in the Cook Islands. He received letters from them the following year calling for more workers, and news that there were people there who had embraced Christianity, who came from another island named Rarotonga. This island – the largest of the Cook archipelago – was known to the missionaries only through references in the 'legendary tales' of the Society Islanders. Here, then, was at once an exploratory and an evangelical challenge.

A vessel was hired and new Islander missionaries recruited. At Aitutaki it was learned that the Raiatean teachers had already obtained dramatic results – marae had been burned, god images destroyed or surrendered to the missionaries, and a chapel some 200 feet in length already erected. They proceeded in search of Rarotonga, which they were unable to locate, but called at Mangaia and the smaller islands of Mitiaro, Mauke and Atiu, where teachers were deposited. At Atiu, one of the high chiefs, Rongomatane, volunteered to direct them to Rarotonga. At first perplexed by the apparent inconsistency of his navigational instructions, Williams then understood that 'the natives, in making their voyages, do not leave from any part of an island, as we do, but, invariably, have what may be called starting-points'. He fully acknowledged the dependence of this chapter of his enterprise on local guidance. 'At these places, they have certain land-marks, by which they steer, until the stars become visible; and they generally contrive to set sail so as to get sight of their heavenly guides by the time their land-marks disappear ... we determined to adopt the native plan, and steered our vessel round to the "starting-point." '[31]

They in due course arrived at Rarotonga and met with a 'king', Makea, who welcomed them in principle. But the Raiatean teachers, who remained on the island overnight, were treated badly, the women particularly having been abused, and were unwilling to remain. Papehia, exemplifying for Williams true devotion, volunteered to stay on his own, only on the condition that another Islander would be sent in due course to work with him. Within a year reports were positive. Robert Bourne, the first white missionary to visit, was staggered by the contrast with the experience on Tahiti, where it had taken a considerable group of white missionaries fifteen years 'before the least fruit appeared'. Here, as he unfortunately put it, 'Two native teachers, not particularly distinguished among their own countrymen for intelligence, have been the instrument for effecting this wonderful change, and that before a single [European] missionary has set his foot upon the island.'[32]

In fact, Papehia appears to have been both canny and tireless. He intervened directly in ritual life, attending marae ceremonies, interjecting and criticizing the rites of priests. He also adopted nuanced strategies to secure the adherence of particular chiefs, convincing the ariki in one district, who had long been subject to depredations from more powerful neighbours, that they would recover lands and prosperity under the peace that would follow conversion to Christianity.[33]

One missionary later wrote that he considered Islanders 'qualified for commencing the work' but only 'indifferently qualified for carrying it on', and it was perhaps this thinking that led to a white mission establishment on Rarotonga.[34] Williams, too, planned a sojourn there, intended to be of only a few months, but extended because no ship appeared. Over the period he was meditating upon the larger possibilities that the Pacific offered, and resolved to construct a vessel himself. He later minutely described his own ingenuity, by improvising a wind-pump in lieu of a pair of bellows, and in making much use of local substitute materials, pandanus mats for sails, and so forth. With a cheap and enthusiastic labour force he was able to complete a 60-foot boat in some fifteen weeks, and then to revisit Aitutaki and in due course sail back to Raiatea and Tahiti, leaving his colleagues Charles Pitman and Aaron Buzacott to oversee the work of a still-growing number of teachers from one part of the Society Islands or another.[35]

As early as 1826 Williams had written, 'it may almost be said, We came, we saw, we conquered'. He had long thought that the work ought to be extended to Samoa, and undertook a voyage there in 1830. In this case, it seemed that he would have no local go-between, but was fortuitously able to pick up an expatriate chief, Fauea, in Tonga, who gave him advance warning that the high priest and chief Tamafaiga could be expected to be a trenchant opponent of any change. Remarkably, however, they learned on their arrival that this individual had been assassinated just fifteen days earlier. Malietoa, the chief contender in a battle under way for pre-eminence, welcomed them and appeared pleased that the inauguration of his own regime might coincide with the introduction of a new religion. Indeed, prophecies were reported, foreshadowing the arrival of new gods.[36]

Fauea made speeches explaining the purpose of the visit. The ship was a 'Pahi-lotu, a praying ship'. Many other islands, from Tahiti to parts of Tonga, had embraced the lotu, and:

they are all much better since they embraced Christianity. Wars have ceased among them. Ships visited them without fear and anchored in their harbours and brought them an abundance of Property. And you can see he observed that their god is superior to ours. They are clothed from their head down to their feet and we are naked. They have got large ships and we have only got these little canoes. On hearing Faaueas speech they all exclaimed It would be good to lotu too.[37]

Given that Williams did not understand Samoan, and that Samoan was not closely related to the Polynesian languages with which he was familiar, this cannot be a precise rendering of what was said. Yet it is unlikely to have been a complete concoction either. When missionary writers put words into the mouths of former heathens, they more usually emphasized spiritual revelation – a discovery that old gods were false or evil. To draw attention to great material things, to cite them as expressions of spiritual power and truth, would in fact have been consistent with a pervasive Polynesian interest in efficacy. More specifically, fabrics, in the form of beaten barkcloth or of woven mats, were of fundamental importance across the Pacific, as vehicles of sanctity and status. There is a good chance, in other words, that Fauea did draw attention, in a rhetorical way (Samoans were certainly not naked), to the contrast between local and missionary dress, citing it as an expression of the power and truth of the new cult that the visitors brought.

* * *

The appeal of Fauea's message, as Williams renders it, does not in itself explain quite how or why the Samoans, too, would embrace Christianity rapidly. Though most Polynesians were nominally Christian by the 1840s, the histories were as strikingly different as Bourne had noticed. In the Society Islands the process had indeed been protracted. This was the case, too, in the Marquesas. William Crook revisited and tried to establish Islander teachers, who failed to impress the locals. Stations involving white missionaries were set up both in the southern part of the group and (by Americans based in Hawaii) on Nukuhiva in the 1830s, but they were abandoned within a few years. The bulk of the population was eventually won over by Catholics, of the Congregation of the Sacred Hearts, who worked on Tahuata in 1838, and in due course had resident fathers throughout the group.[38] In contrast, as we have seen, in various parts of the Austral and Cook Islands, as well as in Samoa, the arrival of Islander missionaries and in some cases brief visits by their white brethren resulted very rapidly in the destruction of idols, the construction of churches, and the adoption of Christian dress and ritual.

The most important factor that in the end prompted Tahitians to adopt Jehovah was the collapse of customary belief following depopulation and malaise over many years. This would not have been salient elsewhere. In the Cook Islands, for example, contacts with Europeans were very limited prior to missionary arrivals. Introduced disease may well have had some impact, but epidemics are thought only to date from 1830, some years after conversion. More positively, in the Cooks mission ships were among the earliest to arrive, hence iron, cloth, and similarly prestigious novelties were closely identified with Christianity and with missionaries, whether Europeans or Islanders.[39] By contrast, in Tahiti people had decades of experience with mariners who were not missionaries, so the latter were not fully or necessarily embraced by the aura of prestige attached to Cook, King George and things European. Indeed, the missionaries were compared adversely to visiting mariners who had more in the way of trade to offer.

There can be little doubt that the rapid pace of change in the Cook Islands and Samoa owed a great deal to Islander go-betweens. Williams arrived at a number of islands with people of the place, such as Fauea, who they had picked up en route and were repatriating. Yet the case of the Marquesas, and that of eastern Fiji, make it clear that Islander teachers might be as prone to failure as white missionaries. In the Marquesas local resistance was no doubt due to the fact that people believed, with justification, that Society Islanders who adopted Christianity had at the same time become subject to Pomare. They had no interest in accepting any such subordination in a new Polynesian empire. The people of the Cooks, who were closer to Tahiti, may have been unconcerned by this prospect because they were better informed. It is doubtful whether Pomare or his successors ever really had the capacity to exercise meaningful sovereignty over more remote island groups such as the Cooks or Marquesas.

* * *

In a candid appendix to a manuscript journal from his second Samoan visit, in 1832 John Williams made it clear that he was not naïve about either the complexities that underlay apparently dramatic spiritual change or the heady mix of motivations at issue in Islander interests in Christianity. 'I by no means affirm that any are truly converted to God,' he wrote of Samoa. 'All I affirm is that the religion of the Gospel is highly esteemed by all classes of people.' He went on:

Some no doubt think that by embracing Christianity vessels will be induced to visit them & by that means their country will be enriched. Others think that it will give them a name among their country men. Some think by becoming Christians they will be protected from the effects of the anger of their gods. Others hope by the same means to prolong their lives. Some hope that by the introduction of Christianity war will be entirely abolished. Some are undoubtedly convinced of the folly of their former system of religious worship. Others now have an indistinct notion of the salvation of the soul after death. The Christian cause received a great addition lately from a purely political motive.[40]

This decidedly mixed bag did not loom large, one suspects, in the rousing accounts of missionary progress that Williams delivered while back in England from 1834 to 1838. He hit the campaign trail hard, speaking at meetings across the country, and fundraising to establish a training institution for native pastors at Rarotonga, and again to buy a missionary ship. He prepared and published his *Missionary Enterprises*, which was something of a bestseller: more than seven thousand copies were sold within two years of publication. Though something of a hodge-podge of scientific observation, ethnographic description and missionary narrative, the book must have delighted every evangelically-inclined reader of its time. It conveyed missionary triumph unambiguously and unapologetically, was finely illustrated, rich in its affecting details and anecdotes, full in its tabulation of the practical and social as well as spiritual acquisitions of Christian Islanders, and resounding in its conclusions.

Missionary Enterprises, which Williams ventured to dedicate to King, William IV, was no less a vindication of its author. Its preface declared that he had travelled a hundred thousand miles in the course of promoting the Gospel over eighteen years. His boat-building project on Rarotonga was recounted as the effort of an evangelical Robinson Crusoe. His departure, to return to his Pacific stations, was a major occasion. A set of verses 'Printed for Gratuitous Distribution, on April 11, 1838' underscored the concluding point of his book, that his mission was most importantly, but not only, a religious one. Or rather, its civilizing dimensions, and not least its national character, were accorded the same sacred dignity:

Well has thine errand sped. And now again
Thou leav'st for that vast and shoreless main;
No exile, but an envoy, charged to bear
Britain's best gifts to those who wait thee there.[41]

Williams returned to Samoa and lost little time before attempting a further voyage of missionary colonization westward. His venture was into the archipelago named the New Hebrides by Cook, today the nation of Vanuatu. Here he was entering a region that had been settled a good deal longer than the islands he knew well, in which entirely different cultures had emerged, that had hierarchies, yet not hierarchies organized around the familiar institution of chieftainship. Whereas, in eastern Oceania, the propensity had been, long before the arrival of Europeans, to celebrate and incorporate the foreign – hence the many 'immigrant' chiefs of aristocratic genealogies – in these islands, to be autochthonous was to be legitimate, and that status was trenchantly defended. Here, too, Williams's knowledge of Polynesian languages would not help, but instead associated him with (he could not have known) Islanders from the east who had made regular incursions, who had indeed colonized parts of the archipelago, in living memory. As if these circumstances did not make an approach already inauspicious, on this voyage Williams lacked guides who had any connection with the people among whom he was landing. The native missionaries he conveyed and hoped to establish were, for ni-Vanuatu, as foreign as he was himself.

En route to these islands, Williams very likely reread Cook's *Voyages*. If he did so, he would not have been surprised that the people on the island of Tanna were cautiously friendly. Of those Cook had visited in the archipelago, the Tannese were the least hostile, and though the visit there was marred by tension and violence, they were the only ni-Vanuatu who had, in the 1770s, permitted the Europeans to venture inland, beyond the limits of a beach. Yet Williams would also have known that at the neighbouring island of Erromango, Cook had been unable to land. Worse, an effort had been made to lure the landing party ashore, apparently with treacherous intent. As soon as Cook declined to have his boat pulled up onto the beach, the men on shore had attempted to seize it, and let loose a volley of arrows, spears and stones. Erromango was, in fact, one of only two places out of the dozens in the Pacific that Cook visited over the course of his three voyages, at which his attempt to land was repelled.[42] The record from subsequent visits was no more auspicious. Around 1829–30, ships seeking sandalwood found the inhabitants more unsettled and difficult than any other population in the archipelago. Although some Tongan labourers who had been recruited to cut wood got on reasonably well with locals for a period, relations then deteriorated, and Hawaiians who had mounted a trading voyage of their own to the area were drawn into violence.[43]

There were no published narratives of these voyages in trading sandal-wood, but Williams would have known of them through shipping gossip. He certainly knew that these Islanders had in the past been hostile and that what had occurred recently would have been more likely to exacerbate than amelio-rate their dispositions. He, and the men who accompanied him on shore on 20 November 1839, were both foolish and brave. In Williams's own case, there is a real possibility that his was a particular kind of courage, that he was, in fact, seeking out martyrdom. Though it is no doubt pointless to speculate, his knowledge of Pacific encounters was certainly sufficient for him to under-stand that what he was doing carried risk which was singular and acute, risk beyond any that he had run before.

* * *

The captain of the *Camden*, Robert Morgan, reported that as their boat approached the beach in Dillon's Bay, some men on shore 'made signs for us to go away'. The Europeans threw some beads ashore, and induced a man to fill one of their buckets with fresh water from a nearby stream. The men on the beach 'were still extremely shy'. Those in the boat were clearly in two minds as to whether to venture ashore. Williams, encouraged by the presence of some boys playing, chose to do so, remarking 'you know we like to take possession of the land', which he presumably intended in some figurative sense. 'If we can only leave good impressions on the minds of the natives, we can come again and leave teachers.' So he, the missionary John Harris, and Cunningham, vice consul in Sydney, stepped ashore and walked along the beach for perhaps a hundred yards. Cunningham, aware that Williams was counting in Samoan with a boy, began to examine some shells that were new to him, but then heard a yell, and as he wrote 'instantly perceived it was run or die'. Though ashore only a few minutes, the men had become separated; Harris and Williams were separately pursued, and Harris beaten to the ground first. Cunningham ran towards the boat and reached safety. Williams, he was perplexed to record, ran rather straight to the sea's edge, thinking perhaps of making an escape by swimming off, but somehow fell backwards as he reached the water and he, too, was clubbed. The boat pulled away, it clearly being too late to attempt any rescue. Despite guns being fired, Erromangan men soon carried the bodies off into the bush, precluding the possibility of their recovery.[44]

* * *

In England, the notice given to the news of the deaths of Bowell, Gaulton and Harper in Tonga in 1799 had been negligible. The contrast with the treatment of Williams's killing in 1839 was extraordinary. The news was reported in Sydney, Bengal, London and provincial newspapers. Books such as *The Martyr of Erramanga* appeared and were swiftly reprinted. The event was visually commemorated in a pair of prints by George Baxter, inventer of a colour-printing method. One represented the missionary's arrival on the island of Tanna, bearing gifts such as a mirror and pieces of fabric, where he is being welcomed in a dignified manner by Islanders. The second captured the drama of his death. Bernard Smith drew attention to reworking of a preparatory sketch for this print. Whereas the watercolour depicted the Erromangans according to the convention of the noble savage, as heroic, classicized warriors, the print as it was produced made them considerably thicker and squatter, essentially bestialized figures. A long-standing propensity to represent the peoples of western Oceania as less civilized than those of the east was, for a wide public, now given a racial, indeed a racist, foundation.[45]

The scene was also, Smith pointed out, closely modelled on John Webber's famous image of the death of Captain Cook, as the Tannese landing was highly reminiscent of a series of engravings after Cook's second-voyage artist, William Hodges, depicting the landings on various islands, which had been

23 A commemorative image: A. T. Agate, 'View of the mission chapel at Apia, Upolu, with the graves of Williams, Barnden and Harris', 1841, pencil and wash.

24 George Baxter, *The massacre of the lamented missionary the Rev. J. Williams and Mr Harris*, Baxter print, 1841. Baxter pioneered a popular early colour printing technique, and this scene was one marketed vigorously among the evangelically-minded.

included in the official publication, *A Voyage toward the South Pole*. Both clearly displayed the attributes of history paintings: they presented monumental events that were full of significance, significance that was not at all ambiguous for the evangelically minded public of the time.

Although Williams actually engaged in little that can strictly be described as exploration, he was widely perceived – like Livingstone subsequently – as an explorer as much as, or more than, a missionary. With the ascendancy of evangelical values, he could even seem a more appropriate hero than Cook, who had been a tolerant witness to, not an activist against, heathen barbarism. The argument did not need to be made explicitly. Williams's life, great achievements and martyrdom would be told and retold. They would become part of the staple diet of the Christian mind, in Britain and in many parts of the Pacific too.

Potent as this colonial myth-making was, it is important to add that the news of Williams's death made a considerable impact not only in Europe but in Christian communities in the Pacific – which had by now existed for a generation – though it is needless to say hard to know whether the missionary was genuinely held in affection by Polynesians. Cook Islanders among others erected memorials, and the event entered the mission-dominated public history of these islands. Even today, in Protestant milieux, many Cook Islanders and Samoans are well aware of Williams and his story.

* * *

David Cargill was a younger contemporary of John Williams and more or less the first of a new generation of highly educated missionaries. After studying classical languages at the University of Aberdeen, he put himself forward to the Wesleyan Methodist Missionary Society in early 1832. This body had been formed soon after the LMS and had a presence in Australia, but did not attempt work in the Pacific until around 1820. It then did so with the encouragement of Samuel Marsden, the influential churchman and colonist of New South Wales, who advocated a division of the Pacific into spheres to be evangelized by the LMS, the WMMS and the Church Missionary Society.

With his wife Margaret, Cargill left London for the south Pacific in October 1832. The intention was that he would reinforce a mission that had been established in Tonga in 1826. Though the mission was initially unsuccessful, some converts had been won over, and there were great hopes for the missions's future. Owing to Margaret's poor health and pregnancy, they remained in Sydney for much of 1833, and on their departure for Tonga, Joseph Orton, the superintendent of the mission, wrote to the brethren in Tonga to prepare them for Cargill's arrival. He readily conceded that the young man had talent and 'a fine imagination' but warned his colleagues that he was also vain, imprudent, divisive and totally inexperienced. 'He has caused me sleepless nights, & great anxiety and almost discourages me as to future efforts', Orton admitted.[46]

As it happened, however, Cargill's years in Vavau, Tonga, passed without major contention. Though the 'king', or Tui Kanokupolu, Joseph Tupou, had already embraced Christianity, Cargill arrived in time to witness and support a great wave of emotionally intense conversions. In March 1834 he wrote of a meeting at which successive teachers spoke of their religious feelings. One 'rose to speak of the love of God to him, but could not, for tears of joy choked his utterance. He stood for a minute or two & made several efforts to speak, but his tears still prevented him. . . . His emotion excited a deep interest and feeling throughout the crowd . . .'[47] These 'drops' became 'a copious shower' a few months later. In the village of Utui a local preacher inspired mass worship, weeping and crying out. Chapels were crowded early in the day, prayer meetings were held at all hours, work was left aside, thousands joined the church, and the numbers of villages building chapels multiplied.

In passing, Cargill mentioned that walking sticks made from spears, from former weapons of war, were 'very common'. A 'before–after' story was always

25 'Revd. David Cargill, M.A., missionary to the Feegee and Friendly Islands', c.1840.

central to the mission's public propaganda, but notions of transformation must
have loomed large in times like these in local imaginations too. The singular artefacts that are referred to suggest that if the missionaries were preoccupied above
all with the repudiation of idolatry, it may well have been the promise of an end
to warfare that had greatest local appeal. Yet it has to be acknowledged that the
nature and intensity of the wave of religious passion that Cargill and his brethren
found themselves in the midst of is not easy to characterize or account for today.

Success throughout the Tongan archipelago emboldened the Wesleyans,
and it was decided that the work should be extended to Samoa (where local
rivalries were evolving into a split between adherents of the LMS and the lotu
Tonga, that is Methodism) and to the Fijian archipelago. The latter prospect
must have been daunting. Reports such as Peter Dillon's had set the tone for
western perceptions of the Fijians, now routinely characterized by mariners

and others as intractably savage and addicted to cannibalism. Though the projected station would be on Lakeba, an eastern island marked by strong Tongan influence, Cargill was clearly troubled by the prospect. 'I feel considerable exercise of mind with regards to Fiji,' he wrote, shortly before he and his older colleague William Cross, together with their families, made the short voyage westward to the island.

Cargill was to remain at Lakeba for almost four years. He would see nothing like the dramatic turn to Christianity that had occurred in Tonga. Though the Lakeba chief conceded the power of the introduced religion – 'muskets and gunpowder are true, & your religion must be true,' he once remarked – he and others seemed to be waiting on more powerful chiefs to turn first.[48] Cargill and Cross preached a good deal to the Tongans on the island and converted a handful of Fijians, but were frustrated, aware that Tanoa, the aging leader of the *matanitu*, or confederacy, based on the small island of Bau, off south-eastern Viti Levu, was a pre-eminent player. They wrote repeatedly to London begging for additional men, sensing there was little they could accomplish unless they could take their campaign from the periphery to the centre of this turbulent world. In the meantime Cargill carried on with his linguistic studies, preparing a Fijian dictionary and grammar, translating catechisms and Gospels. Late in 1838 the mission was reinforced, not least with a printing press, which was soon busy, and various texts being read 'with ease and delight'.[49]

Around this time, however, it became apparent that Cargill had a serious drinking problem. From time to time one or other of his brethren found him insensible, while meetings of the newly established Fijian district committee were marked increasingly by contention, in part around matters of policy, but it seems entailing personal animosities. Cargill and his family relocated to Rewa, the closest practical base to the small island of Bau, the enclave of the paramount chiefs, and began tentatively to build relationships with powerful figures such as Tanoa. But during late May, and at the beginning of June, 1840, Cargill was shattered by the illness and death of his wife Margaret, to whom he was clearly profoundly attached. 'Grief lacerated my soul, and my heart began to bleed at every pore,' he wrote, as it became apparent that she would not survive.[50]

In the aftermath it was resolved that Cargill should take his children back to England. He reached there about April 1841 and published *The Memoirs of Mrs. Margaret Cargill*, no doubt written as a means of coming to terms with his loss, and a William Ellis-style tract defending the missionaries against charges similar to those made by von Kotzebue. In this case the author was Peter Dillon, who had gained fame for his discovery in 1826 of the long-lost wreckage of La Pérouse's ships, and returned to the South Seas trade. The copious title of his now-obscure pamphlet indicates its scope and tone: *A Letter to Richard More O'Farrell, Esq., M.P., Secretary to the Admiralty, Whitehall, London, from Chevalier Dillon, late French Consul to the Islands of the South Seas, on the defeat of His Majesty's Ship, Favourite, and Death of her Commander, Captain Croker, at Tongataboo, one of the Friendly Islands, where he volunteered his services to the Wesleyan Missionaries to massacre the innocent and inoffending natives, whose only crime was, that they would not embrace a religion that has already caused more bloodshed and cruelty than any other event on record connected with the Friendly Islands.*[51] While Cargill's response was vigorous, the question was considerably murkier than it had been in Tahiti: conflict on Tonga in 1837 had in fact pitted Christians against non-Christians, and the missionaries were implicated.

Towards the end of the year, Cargill remarried and began making arrangements to return to the Pacific. The general secretaries of the WMMS were aware that the Fiji district had been racked by contention, and determined to send Cargill back to Tonga rather than to his last station at Rewa, ostensibly on the grounds that he was best placed to complete the important task of translating the New Testament there. He reached his old station of Vavau, with high hopes of experiencing again the dramatic exhibition of new faith of 1834. But the moment had emphatically passed. Almost a decade on, Christianity remained in place, but it seems had little emotional or intellectual hold. Cargill's state of mind declined and he lapsed, in part as a result of a bout of dengue fever, into acute depression. On 25 April 1843 he drafted a letter, distilling his impressions of the people, lamenting the 'apathetic spirit', 'stiff formality' and 'cold indifference' of their religious feeling. Those who continued to profess did so in a manner that he considered contemptibly vacuous. There was, moreover, a great decrease in church membership, and there were hundreds if not thousands of 'Apostates or backsliders'. Those who had written well a few years earlier had lost the ability. Chapels and houses were, he considered, filthy; 'They manifest little desire to imitate the manners and enjoy the comforts of a civilized life. Such desire a few years ago appeared ardent and general.'[52]

This same afternoon Cargill continued to write and drink brandy, presumably becoming drunk, since at some point the second Mrs Cargill 'reproved' him. In an agitated state he walked to the other end of the house, where medicines were kept, poured out a quantity of laudanum into a glass and drained it. His wife then gave him an emetic and Cargill vomited profusely, but evidently failed to rid his system of the opiate. Though he appeared to recover, and resumed his writing, he became drowsy during the evening and despite desperate efforts on the part of a fellow missionary, George Kevern, and his wife, died about midnight. Little credence was given to the suggestion that Cargill had perhaps confused the medications. The conclusion, that he had committed suicide, could only have been a profoundly shocking one for his evangelically minded family and colleagues; the letters and minutes reporting the event are replete with ellipses and phrases scored out. Though the event occasioned genuine trauma, it was a case of little love lost, and there would be no published eulogies or efforts to account for the tragic circumstance. Over subsequent years, Cargill's linguistic researches were credited to other missionaries, and his name was quietly dropped from the histories and hagiographies.[53]

About the time Cargill died on Vavau, Ebenezer Prout published his *Life of the Rev. John Williams, Missionary to Polynesia* back in London. Williams was clearly not prone to his Methodist colleague's depression and pessimism, but he had conceded, in his private writings, that few Islanders were in any strict sense 'converted', and that their reasons for embracing the Gospel were diverse and worldly. Yet this practical understanding of the messiness of change in the islands was bleached out of his own triumphal narrative of missionary enterprises. Prout's biography further inflated the triumph, which was now capped with the awful glory of martyrdom. Williams's death thus did much to reinforce a myth. Cargill's death sparked no story, no myth. It was, rather, an effect of a reality, of ordinary, universal inconstancy, of the banal imperfection of Christian life in the Pacific, a reality that for this man was in the end intolerable, unbearable.

CHAPTER FIVE

✦

Haunted by the example of Cook

Genealogies bound Pacific societies together. Ancestors empowered and challenged the living. Their names and acts were the sources of one's rights and one's debts. The manifold qualities of these relationships often eluded the understandings of Europeans, though they had their genealogies too. Notoriously, William Bligh, hoping to be acknowledged as a bearer of the great navigator's mana, had told Tahitians that he was Captain Cook's son. Aside from that literal, if concocted, descent, explorers were daunted and haunted by great ancestors, and were linked with them by myth and oral history. They were linked, too, in practice. Just as an Islander might tend the gardens of his ancestors, or fight their battles, seamen sailed the same ships or ships that bore the same names. They sailed with the men who had sailed with eminent predecessors, they revisited ports, and were inhibited by custom.

John Gore accompanied both John Byron and Samuel Wallis on their voyages to the Pacific before he joined Cook's first expedition in 1768–71. He sailed again with Cook on the third voyage in 1776–9. Charles Clerke sailed with Byron and on all three of Cook's voyages. As young lieutenants, George Vancouver and Bligh sailed with Cook. Matthew Flinders sailed with Bligh. John Franklin, famous rather as an Arctic than a Pacific explorer, sailed with Flinders. Frederick William Beechey, who took HMS *Blossom* to the Pacific in the 1820s, had sailed with Franklin. Edward Belcher sailed with Beechey and in turn commanded the *Sulphur* in the 1830s. Similarly, Otto von Kotzebue and Fabien Gottlieb von Bellingshausen had both participated in the first Russian circumnavigation, led by Adam Johann von Krusenstern. A succession of overlapping experiences likewise linked the French voyages of Nicolas Baudin, Louis de Freycinet, Louis-Isidore Duperrey and Dumont d'Urville. These voyages were all published, and their narratives were opulent and often extensive. But their connectedness in men's experience, and the talk and rancour that bridged one voyage with the next, constitute scarcely discernible undercurrents in the written record.

* * *

In the last quarter of the eighteenth century the Europeans who had met Islanders and had brought an idea of Europe to them, along with opportunities to travel and a host of objects, were primarily explorers. By the end of that century, whalers and traders were visiting more places, usually for brief visits, that tend to be only cursorily documented. And as we have seen, beachcombers and missionaries became increasingly consequential. Yet it would be wrong to see the baton of encounter being passed from one class of Europeans to another. Rather, all these sorts of intrusions carried on, often in mutual tension. Though whites or Europeans were no doubt lumped together, as Europeans lumped Islanders together, locals became increasingly aware that naval men, traders and beachcombers all had different social stations and behaved differently. In missionaries they encountered not only white men (almost no naval officers, and few traders, were accompanied by wives or children) but families, oddly displaced expressions of European domesticity.

Yet these distinctions between classes of visitors, or would-be settlers, should not be understood schematically. Traders engaged, some inadvertently, in discovery. A few missionaries such as John Williams assumed the mantle of the explorer, others like George Vason became beachcombers or traders. Many beachcombers were escaped convicts from New South Wales, but others were marooned seamen, some considered decent by missionaries, some even engaged in a quirky independent evangelism. In several cases the first generation of missionary children went into trade. Hence in manifold ways the European presence in the Pacific became more heterogeneous; it engendered its own genealogies. Through all this, the business of official naval exploration was sustained and extended, above all by Britain and France, but also by Russia, the United States and (more episodically) various other nations.

Fifty years after Cook's, voyages the Pacific was known and not known. The islands had of course always been known to inhabitants and their neighbours, as well as, in some cases, to Islanders at a considerable distance who had travelled and traded certain sea paths for generations. Europeans knew and had charted more or less all the major islands, though many archipelagoes were incompletely mapped, and many particular coastlines and reefs would remain unsurveyed until much later in the nineteenth century, in some areas until the twentieth.

In a human sense the picture was considerably more complex. Certain Tahitians, Hawaiians and Maori were well known as individuals to European readers of voyages and missionary tracts. Polynesian ways of life had been described, pretty richly, in some respects even precisely, if defectively from the perspective of twentieth-century ethnography. Johann Reinhold Forster's extraordinary 1778 opus, *Observations made during a voyage round the world*, was followed up by beachcomber books – the best was William Mariner's *Tongan Islands* of 1818 – and William Ellis's *Polynesian Researches* of 1829. Though composed nearly thirty years after William Crook's manuscript account of the Marquesas Islands, Ellis's was the first of many published missionary treatises on Pacific custom, folklore and history. Inevitably interlaced with the usual evangelical rhetoric, books of this kind nevertheless reflected much serious enquiry into rites and traditions. Their insights were patchy but they did reflect the genuine curiosity of a minority of missionaries, among the contradictions in their commitment to lives half a world away from home.[1]

The emerging knowledge of Oceania was, however, geographically lopsided and spectacularly so. It was lopsided within Polynesia. Some islands were far more frequently visited than others. While John Williams had exaggerated his accomplishments as an explorer, it was quite correct that little was known about the Cook archipelago prior to the 1820s. Rapa Nui (Easter Island) had been described in some detail by Cook and La Pérouse among other eighteenth-century visitors, but relatively few ships called there during the early decades of the nineteenth century and familiarity lapsed. This was probably because Cook and others had reported that provisions were sparse. Those who did visit tended to stop for hours rather than days, and were hence hardly in a position to add information of any consequence to that already published. Likewise the basic geography of many atolls, let alone particulars of social or cultural life, lay beyond European awareness until decades later. But it can be said that by 1830 Europeans had a broad familiarity with Polynesia and the Polynesians.

In contrast, the understanding of western Pacific peoples at the time was superficial, indeed negligible. Dealings with the populations of many islands went scarcely beyond the kinds of uninformed transactions that had been reported by the commander of the *Patterson* off Simbo in 1803. While whalers and other ships might obtain provisions, they often did so by dealing with men in canoes, without themselves landing or even coming to anchor. Along some coasts, such as those of Malaita in the Solomons, the locals were said not to understand trade, indicating presumably that they had no wish to be involved in it. Samuel Henry, who tried to establish a sandalwood trading base on Erramanga in 1829 found the inhabitants at first avoided all dealings with his party, and then violently resisted the intruders. Scarcely anywhere in New Guinea, the Solomon Islands, Vanuatu or New Caledonia was any voyager or would-be colonist permitted to enter into the life of a community, as Cook and many others had around Tahiti and elsewhere. Nowhere in Melanesia had Europeans gained the kinds of insights they typically had in Polynesia into local society – into broad organization as well as into the alliances and rivalries that shaped political life. Neither, it is almost superfluous to add, had any European ventured much beyond the beaches of the larger islands, or in any sense studied the upland interiors of such considerable landmasses as New Caledonia's Grand Terre, Guadalcanal, Malaita or New Guinea itself.

The reluctance of most Island Melanesians to engage with visitors was compounded by linguistic heterogeneity. Whereas, in Polynesia, an understanding of Hawaiian or Tahitian would enable basic communication or quick adaptation to dialects in the Tuamotus, the Marquesas and elsewhere, Melanesian languages were far more diverse. Other than a few beachcombers, outsiders did not learn local languages at this time, but even if they had, a knowledge of one would have been unlikely to have helped them, even ten miles up or down a coast.

It was inevitable, however, that missionaries and traders would turn their attention to the region, the former seeking openings among the heathen, the latter new sources of sandalwood or bêche-de-mer. And explorers remained anxious to attach their names to new discoveries, or at least to surveys that surpassed those of their predecessors. They would compete to penetrate the Antarctic, but turn also to the seas to the north and east of New Guinea.

* * *

Jules Sébastien César Dumont d'Urville, born of minor nobility in Normandy, joined the French navy in 1807. He was a rapacious reader of geography, exploration and natural history, painfully ambitious, and unlucky to enter the service when he did. No major French exploratory voyage was mounted between that of Baudin (1800–4) and Freycinet (1816–19). D'Urville had earnestly applied to join Freycinet – who would take the *Uranie* to parts of Micronesia, Hawaii and western Australia – but was rejected. He participated instead in a minor mission in the Mediterranean and was fortuitously involved in the 'discovery' (actually made by a local farmer) of the marble that became known as the Venus de Milo. Though the piece was procured for France by the ambassador to Constantinople, it was Dumont d'Urville who had alerted the ambassador to it, and he gained considerable renown for his role in its acquisition. He secured a position in the cartographic office, and was closely involved in the planning of the first major Pacific voyage after Freycinet's, which would be led by his friend Louis-Isidore Duperrey. Though the endeavour was ostensibly scientific, it was certainly also motivated by revived French colonial aspirations. Consideration was being given to the establishment of a penal colony in western Australia (which at that time had not yet been annexed by the British) or New Zealand.[2]

D'Urville's relationship with Duperrey cooled during the three-year voyage (1822–5), and he subsequently censured his commander's unadventurous approach to surveying. Certainly the *Coquille* visited places that for the most part were already well and truly on the map. The first Pacific port of call was Tahiti, where officers and seamen were stunned to discover, not the island of easy sensuality that their reading of Bougainville had led them to anticipate, but a church-going people, seemingly under firm missionary control. Though it transpired that sexual services could still be procured, the French were profoundly and unfavourably impressed by the impact of recent history – there were two Tahitis, d'Urville would later write, one of the epoch of discovery, the other of the present, the latter a degenerate product of evangelical fanaticism.

Duperrey cruised subsequently through the Samoan and Tongan archipelagoes and in due course past the northern coast of New Guinea, but attempted no landings. He then sailed around the west and south of Australia to Sydney and on to New Zealand, repatriating two Maori who had spent time at Samuel Marsden's missionary school. Here, in the Bay of Islands, d'Urville encountered Hongi Hika who was busy strategizing and accumulating gunpowder. D'Urville was intrigued by the Maori travellers and impressed by Hongi and, like Cook, by what he took to be the rugged nobility of Maori warriors. Efforts to restock were however largely unsuccessful – little was available and Maori sought high prices for what they did offer – and the *Coquille* soon proceeded north, calling at several islands in Micronesia, before turning west.

Only at Dore Bay (also called Dorey and Dorei), on the so-called Bird's Head that forms the north-western extremity of New Guinea, did the ship anchor for a period, and trafficked with locals. These people were not, however, an isolated tribal group. They were subject to a minor Moluccan sultan, who in turn was under Dutch control. By way of tribute to the sultan they sent turtleshell, slaves and birds of paradise; some of which probably at length reached European markets. And they had been described, albeit superficially, by Thomas Forrest, who had visited the area in the 1770s, on an exploratory mission for the East India Company.[3]

The *Coquille* had encountered a great social interface – between an island Melanesia shaped by exchange systems, and an insular south-east Asian sphere of commerce, kingdoms and empire. It was a fuzzy border and cultural affinities of all sorts stretched across it. But the 'East Indies' – which from a

26 Chiefs (left) and ordinary people (right) of Dorei, West Papua, as seen by participants in d'Urville's expedition.

Pacific vantage point lay to the west – did not represent a domain in which navigators might 'discover' new peoples or propose new colonies. However notionally, they belonged already to Europe.

* * *

Duperrey's voyage was praised for the quality of meteorological, geological and botanical observations and specimens, by scientists no less eminent than Alexander von Humboldt. But d'Urville rejected his commander's proposal that they co-author the official account of the voyage. It was not only a snub to a sometime friend, but an intriguing decision. Such publications, typically consisting of several volumes of narrative, scientific findings, finely repro-duced illustrations, and charts, had represented, since Cook's day, the supreme expression of a voyager's accomplishments, indeed a monument in book form to them. It is a mark of d'Urville's unrestrained ambition and self-confidence that he declined to be involved, and instead made haste on a scheme of his own. He submitted a proposal for a new voyage to the French ministry and then the king, advocating a closer investigation of the coasts of

New Guinea among other islands. The official documents also signalled that there might be scope for identifying territories that France could annex, potentially, it was imagined, as naval bases that could provide staging-points for attacks upon 'the enemy's settlements'. Which enemy, which settlements, were unspecified, but there can be no doubt that the Parisian strategists had England and the colony of New South Wales in mind.[4]

D'Urville's project was endorsed, he was allocated the *Coquille*, which was renamed the *Astrolabe* after one of La Pérouse's ships – genealogy at work again – and after the usual drawn-out preparations, he departed the Mediterranean port of Toulon in late April 1826. In October of the same year they reached King George's Sound, a harbour on the south-western Australian coast called at before by Baudin among others. Here they made observations of the Aboriginal people of the vicinity and encountered a group of men who had probably deserted from a colonial sealing ship. (They claimed they had been abandoned by it.) They had lived for some time on a small coastal island with a few Aboriginal women. Some officers believed that these women had been abducted, not from the communities of the immediate vicinity, but from Tasmania or the eastern Australian coast, en route. The men subsisted in part from fishing, in part from the hunting and gathering these women engaged in.

Though d'Urville was under the initial impression that they were all English, one of three who accepted his offer of a passage to Sydney turned out to be a Maori from Kerikeri (in the Bay of Islands) who had been 'attached for nearly eight years from a very early age to the miserable lot of these vagabonds'. We have no way of testing d'Urville's understanding that the young man had almost 'completely forgotten' his homeland.[5] A few days later the ship picked up more castaways or runaways, including a black American named Richard Simons. Even on this remote coastline, a curiously multicultural mix was to be found, the upshot of long and no doubt strange voyages.

They proceeded to Sydney. The white population of the colony by now approached fifty thousand. The well-established state of the place accentuated d'Urville's sense that France lacked any comparable Pacific settlement, and there was much rumour-mongering among settlers, and awkward conversation with the governor, as to how directly connected the voyage was with any proposed act of annexation on the part of France. The *Astrolabe* had in fact crossed paths with a brig headed for western Australia to establish a settlement there and eliminate any ambiguity as to whether Britain's territorial claims embraced the whole continent, or only its eastern portion. By default, then, the question of where a future French colony might be sited focussed now on New Zealand, a place about which d'Urville and Samuel Marsden, the veteran missionary and passionate advocate of civilizing ventures among the Maori, had a friendly discussion. He also encountered Richard Siddons, who, more than a decade earlier had sailed with Oliver Slater, instigator and in due course casualty of the sandalwood trade to Fiji. Siddons, now working as a pilot in and out of Sydney harbour, had undertaken one or two further voyages to Fiji, and gave d'Urville a good deal of advice about the hazardous reefs of the archipelago, 'and the customs and language of the islanders'.[6]

The *Astrolabe* then sailed to New Zealand, at first coasting the western side of the South Island, which Dumont d'Urville hoped to survey with a view to superceding Cook's charts: he later acknowledged that he had long been 'haunted by the example of Cook'. They survived a tricky passage through the strait and proceeded up the east coast of the North Island, dealing with Maori at a number of points. In Tolaga Bay he was pleased to anchor in the same spot as Cook had in the *Endeavour*. On 12 March 1827 they reached the Bay of Islands, on this occasion resuming the anchorage of the *Coquille* there in 1824. They encountered a landscape and communities scarred by protracted warfare, though the vicinity was at the time safe enough to undertake excursions into neighbouring forest and settlements. Some local men addressed Dumont d'Urville as 'Marion', perhaps assuming he was son of, or otherwise related to, Marion du Fresne, who had been killed in the area fifty-five years earlier. Despite the violence and uncertainty of the time, the navigator romanticized the Maori and imagined a magnificent future for a civilized society in the islands. Intriguingly, he anticipated that this might emerge either under European tutelage or through some self-advancement on the part of Maori themselves:

> there can be no question that its inhabitants will make rapid progress towards a civilized life as soon as Europeans or Australians are willing to assume responsibility for the job, or perhaps from the moment that there emerges from among these people themselves an extraordinary genius capable of becoming lawgiver to his fellows and of uniting them into one nation. Then these shores, at present uninhabited except for a few isolated *pas*, will be alive with flourishing cities; these silent bays, crossed occasionally by frail canoes, will be shipping lanes for all types of ships.[7]

Dumont d'Urville went further, to anticipate the kinds of arguments that local intellectuals, members of a future 'Academy of New Zealand', might engage in, regarding the accuracy of early accounts of the wilderness of the country, which in time would seem incredible.

In an age pervaded by deeply colonialist ideologies, it is striking that Dumont d'Urville might imagine that Maori would be advanced by an exceptional leader from among their own. But it is interesting also that the navigator cites this as an abstract possibility, when he had, just a few years earlier, met the man who aspired precisely to unite Maori 'into one nation'. Hongi Hika had exhibited what was indeed 'an extraordinary genius' in cultivating, winning over and manipulating individual Europeans, in reorganizing Maori agriculture toward trade, and in reinventing Maori warfare. If the accelerated engagement of Maori with modernity was a civilizing process, he was driving it forward with all the imagination and alacrity that d'Urville could have wished for. Yet the emblem of the time was the musket. And whereas Marquesans, enamoured of guns after David Porter, were mostly the recipients of poor or ineffective weapons, Hongi Hika and his associates knew the difference, and systematically imported 'good' guns in great numbers. The level of fatalities over a series of campaigns of the 1820s, though impossible to determine with any precision, was on a scale way beyond that of customary fighting.[8] It possibly crossed d'Urville's mind that future members of the Academy of New Zealand would have many historical issues to reflect upon, among them troubling and bloody ones.

If d'Urville must have had Hongi Hika in mind, in evoking this notion that an emergent Maori king might civilize his people, yet avoided directly referring to the chief, it is a sign that the larger idea, the rhetorical possibility, was more appealing than the disorder and entanglement of cross-cultural history. This had already been a feature of the European response to the region. The figure of the noble savage, the image of islands of love, the triumphant tale of conversion – all these evocations and stories were in one way or another seductive, they meant something, in a way that the flotsam and jetsam of the Pacific, the mess of happenings, mishaps and moral uncertainties did not.

* * *

On 16 April 1827 the *Astrolabe* entered Tongan waters, and, carrying charts published by Cook and Burni d'Entrecasteaux, d'Urville hoped to find a passage into the anchorage at Tongatapu without difficulty. A lack of wind and adverse currents made the situation at first difficult and then critical. The ship struck the reef and was held away from disaster only by the most tenuous cables, and by anchors that were lost one after the other. Many canoes appeared, and d'Urville became anxious about the fate of survivors if the ship was lost.

Over a number of days the ship was moved, but again struck the reef; the position changed but became more rather than less desperate. Everyone expected the *Astrolabe* to be wrecked, and Tongans appeared poised to launch an attack. The commander attempted to forstall this by inviting three chiefs, Palu, Taufa and Lavaka, on board, feting them in his cabin, and attempting to persuade them – through William Singleton, a beachcomber who had been on the island for twenty-one years and who acted as interpreter – that they would be rewarded by the French king for treating them well and punished severely if they did otherwise. It was d'Urville's understanding that they offered their friendship, but it is notable that no mention is made of any exchange of names, which was how such alliances were routinely expressed and formalized.[9]

Just as the apparent agreement was reached, it became clear that the ship had floated off the reef. All was well. Gifts were presented to the Tongans and they in return were generous with supplies of food. For two weeks the mariners were feasted and were able to make repairs. They also collected extensively, acquiring beautifully carved Tongan weapons, some of which

27 Palu receiving the officers of the *Astrolabe*.

later found their way into the French ethnological museums. D'Urville witnessed healing rites and visited the sacred mortuary place of Mafanga. He met the Methodist missionary John Thomas; he was warned about chief Taufa by a Christian chief, Langi, who had sailed on English ships, and willingly provided much information concerning reefs, islands and place names in Fiji. He made observations of all sorts and was in general impressed by the people.

But some of his own people had decided that they liked Tonga rather more than they liked the *Astrolabe*. Desertion was a fact of life on most voyages, though d'Urville had a reputation for coldness and hauteur, which for the ordinary seaman may have exacerbated the essentially oppressive character of life on a naval ship. On 15 May, as a load of sand was being collected in order to scrub the decks immediately prior to the ship's intended departure, Islanders attacked the boat and appeared to capture its crew. D'Urville responded by sending a party ashore who recovered the boat, without either its contents or any of the men. A further party landed, burnt some houses, and brought two officers back. It was discovered that the sailor Charles Simonet had somehow conspired with Taufa to desert. It was unclear whether some or all of the other men were part of the intrigue, or accidentally involved. Further raids were made ashore, and a number of Tongans as well as Richard, a corporal of marines, were killed. Though Tongan warriors were using firearms, it was strongly suspected that an officer grazed by a bullet had been shot at by Simonet.

D'Urville then threatened to bombard the sacred site of Mafanga, contrary to the advice of his beachcomber-interpreter, who with the help of a prominent woman, secured the release of one captive and encouraged prudence. Of the chiefs d'Urville had hosted it appeared that only Taufa was involved, and he had been persuaded by the others to hand over those Europeans who wished to leave. D'Urville was inflexible, insisting that all the seamen ashore were returned to the ship. He acted on his threat, firing many cannonballs toward the site, which landed ineffectively on the beach or in a protective sand rampart. The stand-off continued for some days. Taufa in the end agreed to return everyone, though Simonet and one other remained on the island. D'Urville was relieved: either executing the ringleader or not executing him would have raised profound problems for the future management of the expedition.[10]

* * *

Just a couple of days out of Tonga, d'Urville sighted islands in the southern Lau group, and picked up some men from a canoe who wished to be taken to Lakeba, the island that had long hosted visiting Tongans, and that as a result

LA CORVETTE L'ASTROLABE
embossée devant le village de Mafanga
(Tonga-Tabou)

28 The *Astrolabe's* bombardment of Mafanga, Tongatapu.

later gave David Cargill, among other Methodist missionaries, their first Fijian base. One of these men, named Mouki, claimed to be a chief and to have sailed on British ships to New Zealand and Sydney. Another, Mediola, was a Chamorro who recalled Freycinet's 1819 visit to Guam and recognized two of the naturalists, Jean-René-Constant Quoy and Joseph Paul Gaimard, who had been on the *Uranie* and were now members of d'Urville's expedition. He claimed to have been abandoned in Fiji by a Spanish sandalwood trader, and appealed to d'Urville to help him get home. D'Urville was pleased to recruit a man who he hoped might also act as an interpreter among the Fijians. In due course at Lakeba they picked up three Spanish sailors, off the same ship as Mediola, who as it transpired had few opportunities to interpret.

An effort to traffic for a lost anchor on a nearby island failed because people were hostile. Attempts to survey Kadavu among other islands to the south of Viti Levu, the largest island of the group, were also largely unsuccessful, owing to adverse weather. The *Astrolabe* turned back to the north-west and followed the Viti Levu coast, and here people came off from the coastal villages, and twenty or thirty spent the better part of a day on board, but poor conditions again precluded an anchorage or any visit to the shore itself. Clubs among other weapons were offered in trade and d'Urville considered those here finer artistically, though very similar in form, to those of the Tongans. After eighteen frustrating days, the ship left the group, without having been able to make a proper landing on any of the many islands sighted. D'Urville had, however, seen enough of the Fijians to have had his anthropological, or rather his racial, curiosity provoked. The darkness of their skin relative to that of the Tongans led him to see them as the easternmost residue of a black Oceanian population, which had, he presumed, resisted an invasion of lighter-skinned Polynesians from the east and reached some accommodation with them.[11]

D'Urville proceeded to survey the Loyalty Islands which had been only partially charted and that lay to the east of New Caledonia. Here again his thoughts were dominated by the explorers who had come before – d'Entrecasteaux's ship, the *Espérance*, had come close to destruction on reefs near the Beaupré Isles. After the voyage d'Urville would write of d'Entrecasteaux's lieutenant, who had effectively become leader of the voyage after his commander's death, that 'Dear old M. de Rossel . . . could not look without a shudder at that part of our chart of the Loyalty Islands'. Rossel, who himself died soon afterwards, held one of the most senior positions in the French admiralty, and it is not surprising that d'Urville should have acceded to his request, to reproduce the track of d'Entrecasteaux's ships on his new chart of this archipelago.

On to New Ireland where some ten days were spent in Carteret harbour, where locals were sketched but little in the way of barter or any other sort of engagement took place. Gaimard tried to persuade people to show him their village, but was refused. The lack of friendly local advice proved costly – some men who cut down palms and ate the pulp, not understanding that it was toxic without extensive processing, suffered hideous pain and one died. A set of sketches were, however, made, augmenting the atlas of human types that d'Urville had in mind.

From here they proceeded along the north coast of New Guinea, and d'Urville was able to redress, to some extent, what he considered the timidity of Duperrey. A course nearer the coast was followed, and numerous features were named, mainly after luminaries of the French naval world. However, what had been the case since Tonga remained the case – for whatever reasons, it was difficult to find anchorages or land, Islanders were seldom sighted, and when they were sighted contacts were fleeting and uninformative. Not until they revisited the Bird's Head did any real interaction with local people take place.

The *Astrolabe* spent a further full year cruising first around the south of Australia, calling at Van Dieman's Land (Tasmania) and then Vanikoro in the south-eastern Solomons. Peter Dillon's discoveries of remains of the wreck of La Pérouse's ships were followed up – here again d'Urville was haunted by the history of navigation in the Pacific. His men managed to bring up an anchor, heavily rusted and covered in coral, a cannon similarly encrusted, some brass guns, some fragments of china and miscellaneous other relics. They erected a monument to La Pérouse and his companions, proceeded to Guam with many ill, and from there made a course back through the East Indies, across the Indian Ocean to Cape Town, and from there home to France.

* * *

On his return to Paris in 1829, d'Urville was rewarded with promotion, but he sat uneasily among the divided scientific and political elites of the time. Though the voyage gained the approval of those at the highest levels, and publication on a grand scale was authorized, d'Urville felt slighted and, after being heavily defeated in a ballot for the presidency of the geographical section of the Institut de France, a learned academy, he withdrew to write.[12] He would, however, be unusual in becoming a highly energetic and prolific yet always an awkward writer, prone to stilted and somewhat rambling expression. In due course the *Voyage de la corvette l'Astrolabe exécuté par ordre du Roi* appeared in five volumes of narrative, prepared by d'Urville but including extracts from officers' journals, eight additional volumes dedicated to supplementary scientific reports, and four atlases. Though commensurate with the enormous trawl of natural specimens, which had overwhelmed the curators of the natural history museum, this scale of publication exceeded anything of the kind that had appeared before in the history of exploration.

The natural historical collections were unambiguously of major importance. The observations of the people of the Pacific made over the course of the voyage possessed less certain value. In one sense the range of places d'Urville had visited was extraordinary. Yet, as we have seen, his engagements were with populations who were already pretty well known to Europeans – such as the Maori – while contacts elsewhere were fleeting. His presentation employed a well-established convention of scientific travel writing, which was to alternate the narrative of events with descriptive syntheses concerning particular places and peoples. The latter, however, relied, not so much on his own observations as on the literature that had already been published.

The section on Tonga, for example, drew heavily on Cook's *Voyages*, and on the beachcomber memoir of William Mariner, who had survived the massacre of the crew of the *Port-au-Prince* in December 1806. Back in Britain, he had been extensively interviewed by John Martin, an Edinburgh surgeon, who had written up a lively narrative of Mariner's experience, but one enriched by his own, ethno-graphically minded questioning. Undoubtedly one of the best and most sympa-thetic accounts of a Pacific culture of its time, it is not at all surprising that d'Urville should have drawn on it. What is notable is that he had his own survivor of the *Port-au-Prince* to hand in the person of his interpreter, William Singleton, who had never left the island, and who presumably could have added much to the Mariner-Martin picture, not least through some account of the political turbulence of the years that succeeded Mariner's departure. Singleton was helpful, entirely settled among the people, and had the confidence of men of rank. D'Urville was no doubt preoccupied by the desertion of Simonet and others, and the conflict with the locals it engendered, but he surely missed an opportunity to interview a potentially remarkable informant.

* * *

Among the books d'Urville knew well was Charles de Brosses's *Histoire des navigations aux terres australes*, published in 1756. De Brosses's charter for the discovery of a great southern continent was somewhat out of date by the 1820s. Its advocacy of colonial establishments in the Pacific had renewed and indeed poignant salience, as the French could only stand by and witness the ascendancy of British influence in the region. Yet the *Histoire des navigations* remained vital as a source-book for a range of earlier voyages, and moreover for the first sustained synthesis of information concerning the peoples of the Pacific, that attempted a national-cum-racial classification. De Brosses's sources were mainly the unreliable accounts of various early visitors, but out of them he extracted the understanding that the inhabitants of the tropics were light-skinned and quick-witted, and that inhabitants of the lands further to the south were physically distinct, resembling the 'negroes' of Africa rather than other Oceanic peoples, and were moreover brutes: his language was bestializing.

This contrast, informed or rather misinformed by William Dampier's early denigration of indigenous Australians, was not directly reproduced in the narratives or reflections of the late eighteenth-century or early nineteenth-century voyagers. Indeed, this sort of ambitious anthropological synthesis was not much taken up, though Johann Reinhold Forster, the senior naturalist on Cook's second voyage of 1772–5 had observed that there were 'two great varieties of people in the South Seas: the one more fair, well-limbed, athletic, of a fine size, and a kind of benevolent temper; the other blacker, the hair just beginning to become crisp, the body more slender and low, and their temper, if possible more brisk, though somewhat mistrustful'.[13] This discrimination was the departure point for an involved, qualified and extended set of reflections on the influence of climate, education, religion and society on shaping human bodies and temperaments. Forster's discussion rested on the environmentalism of the period, but was loose rather than deterministic, and saw successive migrations, among other complicating factors, as shaping the characters of particular peoples in particular places. These discussions occupied the better part of his six-hundred-page book, *Observations made during a voyage round the world* (1778), which had sunk without much impact in England, but was incorporated in translation into the main editions of Cook's voyages in France, and had undoubtedly been read by d'Urville.

The navigator had certainly been mulling over the issues, at least since having been struck by the physical differences between Fijians and Tongans. Soon after the *Astrolabe* returned to France, he presented a paper to the Société de Géographie that boldly redrew the human map of the Pacific. It divided the region up, racially and geographically, in a fashion that owed a good deal to des Brosses and Forster but was more rigorous, speaking not vaguely on 'great varieties' but concretely of 'races'. More importantly, d'Urville went as far as to draw lines on a map, marking out the boundaries occupied by the several populations.

Drawing on des Brosses, he used more or less the terms that became standard – Polynesia, Melanesia and 'Malasie' – and emphasized that Polynesians were unified by their developed arts, civilization, regular government, castes, laws, etiquette and so forth, as well as traits such as kava drinking and the observance of *tapu*, or taboo. Although this description was not as celebratory as Forster's had been, it was considerably more so than his evocation of Melanesians. Whereas Forster did consider the peoples of the western Pacific less refined than those of the east, he made no claims concerning their mental capacity. D'Urville's characterization was damning on every point. They were black, their women were 'hideous', their languages were diverse and fragmented, their political organization was attenuated. 'More degraded towards the state of barbarism than the Polynesians or Micronesians, one encounters neither a form of government nor laws nor established religious ceremonies among them. All

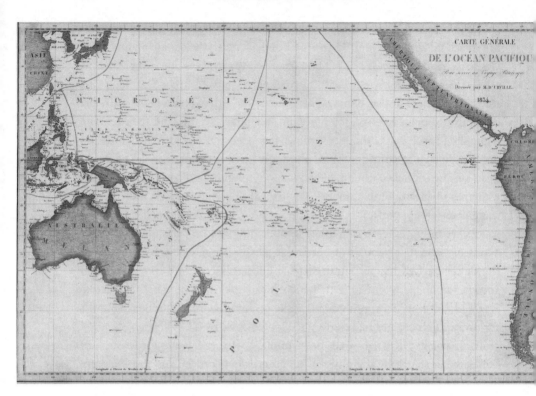

29 D'Urville's 'Carte générale de l'Océan Pacifique'.

their institutions appear still to be in their infancy; their dispositions and their intelligence are generally inferior to those of the tan race.'[14]

If d'Urville had indeed sighted Melanesians, he actually knew next to nothing of their lives. If it is not surprising that thinkers of the time were struck by the marked physical distinctions between Islanders of the west and the east – they were and are indeed darker and lighter-skinned respectively – this contrast does not map onto the others that he cites. Although all Polynesian societies did have chiefs of some sort, in some cases their authority was pretty slight; and in many parts of Melanesia chieftainship and similar institutions of hierarchy were in fact well developed, although they often took forms that were not immediately recognized by European observers. Kava drinking was common in Melanesia; tapu, or similar religious restrictions, were observed in one form or another everywhere. The major points of d'Urville's contrast were thus credible to those who heard or read his lecture, only because they were so profoundly ignorant about the lives of Melanesians.

Today it is understood that human biological variation in the Pacific does not map the pattern of cultural affinities, which is however reflected in language. Juxtaposing 'Polynesians' with 'Melanesians' was to make a category error, like opposing the people of Norfolk with the English. If all such terms are inventions, and often contentious ones, it would have been more sound to understand Polynesians as a sub-group of an Oceanic population, which also included Island Melanesians. What underpinned d'Urville's distinction was not a serious comparative anthropology but a racist aesthetic, a response to colour, augmented by an aesthetic of political form, which privileged what appeared to be centralized government over more localized forms of leadership.

An essay such as 'Sur les îles du Grand Océan' could easily have lapsed into obscurity – there were many such treatises in the synthetically minded nineteenth century. But d'Urville's would have a lasting impact in both scientific and popular understandings. His classification, though not faithfully followed, was broadly appropriated by one Grégoire-Louis Domeny de Rienzi, an intriguing character who claimed to have visited the Pacific five times, but probably never went there at all. His three-volume encyclopaedic work, *Océanie*, of 1836–7, was promptly translated into German, Spanish and Italian.[15] Its rich illustrations – ostensibly original but in fact ransacked and freely adapted from a host of earlier voyage books – no doubt ensured its popularity. His text was similarly derivative, but the introduction of the term 'Micronesia' for the islands of northern and western Oceania was effectively incorporated in d'Urville's classification as it was handed down.

The scheme was assured of circulation among anglophone readers through its adoption by James Cowles Prichard in his *Researches into the Physical History of Mankind* (1836–47), a work of foundational importance for nineteenth-century physical anthropology. It was picked up, too, by Horatio Hale, in *Ethnography and Philology* (1845), one of the reports of the United States Exploring Expedition, led by Charles Wilkes, the most influential American scientific venture into the Pacific in the mid-nineteenth century. It featured, too, in materials aimed at the broadest of publics. In Victor Levasseur's *Atlas Universel*, a popular reference work often reprinted through the nineteenth century, the boundaries between Melanesia, Polynesia and the other Oceanic regions were accentuated by hand-coloured lines. An invidious and nebulous set of distinctions, made out of uncertain observations and accidental happenings, acquired the reality, the physical certainty, of a coastline. The map's illustrated surround incidentally also placed d'Urville's portrait among romanticized images of Islanders, and, more suggestively, a swarthy sailor, perhaps supposed to be a half-caste of some sort, smoking as he leans against a couple of crates of cargo on a dock.[16]

* * *

In 1834 d'Urville would also publish his *Voyage pittoresque autour de monde*, a semi-fictional synthesis of previous voyages, which was reprinted four times within the decade as well as subsequently. He tried his hand, too, at novel-writing, producing a romance of New Zealand life, which has only been published in recent years and has not in any way enhanced his reputation.[17] Whether he would always be 'haunted' by Cook's example, who knows, but d'Urville would be given the command of a further Pacific voyage in the 1830s, which, after his death in a railway accident in 1842, would be written up and published on a still grander scale than that of 1826–9, in a total of thirty volumes.

For d'Urville it can be said that he appears genuinely to have admired Islanders such as Maori; despite the pejorative slant of his Melanesia-Polynesia juxtaposition, he was also impressed by Fijians among others. More importantly, he was careful to avoid violence in his dealings with local people: with the exception of the unfortunate bombardment at Tongatapu – which had at least the virtue of being ineffective – he seldom had his men use guns against them. Yet if this behaviour mattered more at the time, and more to people locally, who had no knowledge or interest in alien notions disseminated in one way or another in Europe, it is not what has endured. What endured was the harshness of his language, and the persuasive simplicity of a racial map. The subsequent influence on European perceptions of the Pacific was broad and broadly pernicious.

* * *

From the beginning of the nineteenth century onward, the United States became increasingly engaged in the Pacific, though not in any official way. David Porter's aggressive, if finally shambolic attempt to colonize the island of Nukuhiva was exceptional. Aside from this, there were virtually no American naval ventures that impinged in any way on the lives of Islanders during the first decades of the century. Yet New England mariners were energetic. Dozens of whalers, sealers and traders seeking sandalwood, bêche-de-mer and pearl-shell, among other commodities, left ports such as Nantucket, New Bedford and Salem to range widely in the Pacific, from Guam to Hawaii in the north, and from the Solomons to New Zealand and Rapa Nui in the south. During the 1830s traders such as John Eagleston, Benjamin Vanderford and

30 Frontispiece, from Dumont d'Urville, *Voyage Pittoresque autour du monde*.

Benjamin Wallis returned regularly to Fiji, gaining fluency in Fijian, and becoming unavoidably, if peripherally, involved in the turbulence of political rivalry and violence there.

Over these decades, in fits and starts, American politicians, scientists and naval men had debated the desirability and the feasibility of the United States launching a major exploratory expedition, comparable to those undertaken from Britain, France and Russia. Among the bodies lobbying in favour was the East India Marine Society of Salem representing some of the most active ship-owners, which in 1834 had prepared a petition, drawing attention to the extent of commerce then being undertaken in Fiji and the risks traders ran, which arose from inadequate charts and the hostile Islanders. Finally, in the latter part of the 1830s, a commitment was made to the project, and in April 1838 Lieutenant Charles Wilkes was appointed commander. Wilkes, somewhat like Dumont d'Urville, was highly ambitious, intellectually accomplished, and a capable surveyor. But he lacked experience, not having participated in, let alone commanded, any extended voyage of remote exploration, and he would prove an unhappily divisive leader.[18]

If the Americans came late to the business of grand exploratory voyaging, they made up for it by despatching something of an armada. In addition to the flagship, the *Vincennes*, a 127-foot sloop-of-war, the squadron consisted of a second, slightly shorter sloop, the *Peacock*, the storeship *Relief*, the brig *Porpoise*, and the schooners *Flying Fish* and *Sea Gull*, both of some 70 feet – a veritable fleet manned by over five hundred men. The aims were expressed in terms that were by now familiar – primarily the 'promotion of the great inter-ests of commerce and navigation' and secondly 'to extend the bounds of science and promote the acquisition of knowledge'.[19] To these ends the ships carried seven naturalists and two artists. Given that the islands of the Pacific were now, it was considered, charted to a degree that made it unlikely Wilkes could make major discoveries in tropical or temperate latitudes, grand plans were made to approach and survey the Antarctic continent, and to investigate the mouth of the Columbia river on the American north-west coast. Yet if no major archipelago was likely to remain undiscovered, many islands in the Pacific remained to be precisely charted. A detailed survey of the Fijian group was certainly a subordinate aim of the voyage, no doubt reflecting the level of American engagement and the Salem petition, and one of the Salem traders who already had a detailed knowledge of islands, Benjamin Vanderford, was signed on as a pilot. While British surveying voyages from those of the *Beagle* (which carried Charles Darwin) onwards had directed their attention, first to Tierra del Fuego at the southernest tip of the Americas and then to the seas

around Australia, Wilkes anticipated dedicating weeks if not months to Fiji's
hazardous seas.

Among the crewmen was one 'Tuati', generally known as John Sac, a Maori,
described as having been 'a petty New Zealand chief at the Bay of Islands', who
had lived for some years in Tahiti before moving to New York, where he had
been exhibited, and from where he had joined a voyage to the South Shetland
islands. Though he was not to be much noticed in the voyage narratives, he
played a prominent role in the expedition's very first landfall in the islands of the
Pacific. In the Tuamotu archipelago Wilkes considered he might test the expedition's surveying techniques and charted the small atoll of Reao, sighted on
August 13, 1839. Only after the ships had investigated the various reefs, and
several boats had been sent toward the shores, did a group of some seventeen
islanders gather on a beach, which Wilkes proceeded to approach, with a view
to making contact. Tuati addressed them and found he was understood, but
'The only answer he could get from them was, several of them crying out at the
same time, "Go to your own land; this belongs to us, and we do not want to have
any thing to do with you." '[20] Wilkes threw gifts toward them that were eagerly
received, but did not in any way ameliorate their hostility. Tuati, supposedly
angered, proceeded to engage in a tournament of defiance and oratory with the
apparent leader among those on the beach. 'Half-naked as he was, his tattooing
conspicuous, he stood in the bow of the boat brandishing his boat-hook like a
spear with the dexterity of a savage. It was difficult to recognise the sailor in
the fierce, majestic-looking warrior before us . . . John's animated attitudes and
gestures were the admiration of all', Wilkes reported, though worrying that Sac
was exacerbating rather than smoothing over the situation.

Yet no other approach fared any better. A couple of officers reached the
edge of the shore, were threatened with spears – though not actually speared –
and saw prudence in withdrawal. Though Wilkes had, in the days prior to
approaching the archipelago, circulated a set of orders emphasizing the paramount importance of 'courtesy and kindness towards the natives' and the need
to leave favourable impressions, he swiftly revised this policy, judging now that
he ought not let the Islanders think they had succeeded in driving him off.
While avoiding the bloodshed attendant on a forced landing, he thought it
desirable to fire on the men on the beach, at first with blanks, then with shot,
but 'according to John Sac, they hooted at these arms, calling us cowards, and
daring us to come on shore'.

Just as Tupaia, who had travelled with Cook in the *Endeavour*, played a key
role in the early meetings with Maori in 1769 and 1770, here Sac/Tuati must
have appeared less a go-between than the leader of the strange party that

approached these Tuamotuans. And he lent the meeting, not the character of some dignified arrival of civilization in a savage place, which Wilkes no doubt would have wished exemplified, but that of a confrontation between Polynesians. Just a common sailor, this Maori nevertheless, for a short while, eclipsed the character of the great expedition, simply by behaving as he felt the occasion required.

From here the ships passed by other Tuamotuan islands, and encountered entirely different circumstances at Raraka, where the Tahitian flag introduced by the missionaries was seen to wave, and where Wilkes indeed felt 'as though we had issued out of darkness into light'. People were sociable, a Tahitian missionary was modest and quiet, the women wore either the pareu, 'consisting of three or four yards of cotton', or 'a loose gown', presumably the type of dress known as a 'Mother Hubbard', already notorious among detractors of missions. The Sabbath was rigorously observed, meaning no one would collect specimens for the naturalists, but a day was spent ashore before the ships moved on.[21]

* * *

The 'Ex. Ex.', as the expedition became known, passed via Tahiti and Moorea to Samoa. In each of these places Wilkes, like von Kotzebue, Duperrey and d'Urville before him, encountered a converted Polynesia, a place reordered in various ways by mission influence, yet unlike his predecessors he tended to celebrate rather than denigrate the evangelists' accomplishments. This mind, this mission, was at a greater remove than any of the European voyagers had been, from the dispositions of Bougainville, or from the romantic affirmation of cultural diversity that writers such as Forster had stimulated. While Wilkes would go to some pains to describe manners and customs wherever he could, he was a stranger to nostalgia – it seemed no great shame that Tahiti's luxurious civilization was a thing of the past.

After an Antarctic cruise and two visits to Sydney, the ships made their way to Fiji, which they reached in May 1840, some twenty-one months into the voyage. They called first at the island of Ovalau, where there was a small beachcomber settlement; by this date, too, David Cargill among other Methodists were based at a number of stations in various parts of the group. Yet the many wrecks and tales of cannibalism had predisposed the voyagers to consider the Fijians savage to an extreme degree. Indeed one of Wilkes's tasks was to hunt down the prominent chief Veidovi, who was considered responsible for the killing and allegedly the eating of ten crew from the *Charles Doggett* of Salem, who at the time had been processing bêche-de-mer on shore.

Captain William Hudson, in command of the *Porpoise*, was sent to Rewa – a powerful settlement on the south-eastern coast of Viti Levu, near the mouth of the great river of the same name – to seek the agreement of the chief there to a set of port regulations that Wilkes hoped would be generally adopted. They sought out Ro Cokanauto, known by the Americans as Phillips, an English-speaking chief who had long acted as pilot for the New England trader, John Eagleston. They spent time ashore, were welcomed by the high chief, the Roko Tui Dreketi; Cargill carefully interpreted the document Wilkes wanted signed, which in due course the Fijians agreed to do. Gifts were distributed, fireworks were let off, and then a kava ceremony and feast were provided by the chief. Hudson stayed overnight in the chief's huge and finely constructed house; breakfast came with more kava, and cigars. The naturalists went off on excursions and were struck by the density of irrigated cultivation. The town itself consisted of some six hundred houses. The delta was among the most intensively cultivated and inhabited parts of the precolonial South Pacific.[22]

Hudson gave out word that he had gifts for Veidovi, and understood that he was likely to visit the ship with other chiefs on 21 May. The others did come, but Veidovi did not, and Hudson resorted to telling those they did have, that they would be kept as hostages until Veidovi was brought on board. This resulted in trauma; the queen feared that they were to be put to death; Cokanauto, despite his experience of Europeans, was so shocked and frightened 'that he was unable to light a cigar that was given him, and could not speak distinctly'.[23] In due course, however, it was agreed that the the king's brother, Qaraniqio, should go ashore with another man and try to take Veidovi by surprise. Hudson was sufficiently well advised, probably by Benjamin Vanderford or by Cargill, that he understood there was enmity between Qaraniqio and Veidovi. They were not full- but half-brothers, and conflict in Fiji came down largely to power-struggles between half-brothers and their factions, who sought control of chiefly towns such as Rewa and Bau, and the *matanitu*, the confederations, that they led.

With Qaraniqio away on his mission, the Roko Tui Dreketi and the other Fijians confined on board were to some degree reassured; kava was made; the sailors entertained them with theatricals; it was noted that while some Tongans aboard studied their books quietly, the Fijians were pretty raucous. Cokanauto, however, provided a couple of the scientists and officers with a history of Rewa, Bau and the struggles among various chiefs. In the morning Qaraniqio returned with Ro Veidovi – it was said that he came of his own free will, simply on being told that the king was on the ship and had called for

31 'Veidovi', from Wilkes, *Narrative of the United States Exploring Expedition.*

him – who was subjected to a formal examination by Hudson in the presence
of his officers. He acknowledged responsibility for the killing of the men and
indeed to having held the mate while another man clubbed him (though some
information indicates that the responsibility was, at least, shared with other
chiefs with whom the Americans were friendly). All the hostages were now
released. Veidovi was put in irons and kept on board the ship, and there were
emotional partings with his servants and even the chiefs who had been
complicit in his capture. He was allowed to be accompanied by only one man,
a Hawaiian barber known variously as Oahu Sam or Oahu Jack, who had
resided with the Roko Tui Dreketi for some years.

* * *

The American ships split up to survey various parts of the group of islands. On the southern coast of Vanua Levu, Wilkes felt obliged to mount a punitive raid after a boat was taken, though the crew were not harmed and the launch itself was returned, but without the clothing and equipment it contained. He assembled a strong party that landed and marched on the village of Solevu, burning the settlement to the ground. Fortunately, its inhabitants had withdrawn on the Americans' approach, and so there were no casualties on either side. But just a couple of weeks later, on a beach on the small island of Malolo, part of the Yasawa group off the western coast of Viti Levu, tensions led to fatal violence.

A few men had been ashore, engaged in drawn-out negotiations to purchase a couple of pigs. One Fijian, apparently the son of a chief, had agreed to remain in the boat, just offshore in shallow water, as a hostage. As time passed, however, he had become uneasy, and then suddenly leapt out of the vessel and made his escape. One of the men fired a shot after him, and an affray then broke out. Some subsequently believed that there had been a conspiracy – that the man's escape was planned, that it would give a signal to the warriors on shore to attack. Others thought that it was the shot that provoked the Fijians. The chief cried out that his son was killed, another man tried to seize a musket from one of the sailors, in any case fighting broke out. Some ten Fijians were stabbed or shot, but two officers, Joseph Underwood and Wilkes Henry, Wilkes's own nephew, were also killed and stripped of their clothes by warriors who then retreated. Another officer, Joseph Clark, was badly mauled but still alive, in shock, when a boat that had been further away reached the scene. On realizing that one Fijian was injured but still alive at the scene, the incensed seamen revenged themselves furiously, repeatedly shooting and stabbing, and in the end decapitating the man.[24]

Before taking retaliatory action, Wilkes had both his officers buried on an isolated islet, where he was confident the bodies would remain undisturbed. No doubt aware, from his wide reading of voyage narratives, of how violence ashore might tarnish a navigator's reputation, he was concerned, he claimed in the published *Narrative of the United States Exploring Expedition*, to avoid an excessive or indiscriminate response. Officers who left journals, however, record a general declaration of war on the island, and orders given that women and children only were to be spared. On 26 July, two groups of seamen armed with rockets as well as guns, were landed, one to attack the village nearest the beach where the killings had taken place, the other to deal with the people of the other main settlement on the island, who were thought to be to some degree complicit. Two launches cruised offshore, so as to be able to attack any who tried to escape. These boats indeed did come upon several canoes, which were fired upon with blunderbusses; most of the men they carried, and probably also some women and children, were killed.[25]

A party under Lieutenant Cadwallader Ringgold surrounded the village of 'Sualib'; the people there were denounced as a set of pirates 'at war with every body . . . the terror of all their neighbours'.[26] This demonization no doubt helped license the all-out assault that followed, but was certainly disproportionate to the actual events, better described as a fatal brawl or skirmish than a massacre. If a massacre had taken place, the Fijians, of whom ten had been killed, were more obviously the victims than the Americans. Though vigorous in defence, the Malolo warriors were not a match for men who could shoot accurately. Many were killed by shot, smoke or flames – within fifteen minutes or so the rockets had landed on houses, the fire was intense, and the smell of burning flesh conspicuous. The second village, of Aro, had been abandoned and was burned also. Towards the end of the day Lieutenant Emmons, in one of the launches, met with five canoes containing some forty Fijians, virtually all of whom were killed. Oahu Sam, or Jack, was an effective man with a hatchet, it was recorded; many of the American seamen were equally enthusiastic with whatever weapons they could lay their hands on.

The following day Wilkes required that the survivors surrender in a customary Fijian manner, with a vast presentation of food and property, and labour for the Americans by filling water-casks. He delivered a speech chastising them and warning them that if any further action was ventured against whites, he would return and exterminate them.

Notwithstanding the lack of clarity as to what actually triggered the violence, the considered view, even among some of the more thoughtful officers, was that what had taken place was an expression merely of this people's extreme savagery, hence that the punitive assault had been fully justified. At Tahiti, Midshipman William Reynolds had expressed himself relativistically – 'What man can say, this people shall be my standard, by them I will judge all others?' – but he aired no uncertainties when he came to pass judgement on Fijians. 'They presented a spectacle of mingled hideousness and ferocity,' he wrote. 'May they be smitten from the Earth!'[27]

Even after the voyage, in the calm of the study, this anathema might be reiterated. Horatio Hale's treatise on the peoples of the Pacific, heavily indebted to d'Urville, mulled over what the author considered to be a 'general debasement' of the Fijians, which was unambiguous but also oddly difficult to specify. 'Their evil qualities do not lie merely on the surface of their character, but have their roots deep in their moral organization,' he wrote. 'The Feejeean may be said to differ from the Polynesian as the wolf from the dog; both, when wild, are perhaps equally fierce, but the ferocity of the one may be easily subdued, while that of the other is deep-seated and untameable.'[28]

* * *

One man who played no part in the Malolo tragedy but who nevertheless suffered the depth of American anger at the time was Ro Veidovi. He was transferred from the *Porpoise* to the *Vincennes*, where Wilkes had his great head of hair shaved off. Hair, for a Fijian chiefly man of the time, was no mere matter of vanity, it was an expression, almost the substance of, status, power and identity; from Veidovi's perspective, this would have been a gratuitous and barbaric assault. The chief was kept in irons for many months, but eventually permitted, when the expedition reached the north-west American coast, to walk around on deck and even on shore. He spent a good deal of time, in particular, conversing with Vanderford, and was shattered when the trader died on the passage home. Veidovi himself died, just a day after the ship reached New York; his head was swiftly removed and the skull prepared for anthropological analysis. It was for a time kept at the Smithsonian and then transferred to the US Army Medical Museum, now incorporated into the National Museum of Health and Medicine in Washington.

* * *

From the 1820s onwards, the Royal Navy mounted a succession of surveying expeditions, all of which were extended, indeed circuitous ventures, that carried accomplished naturalists, and made considerable and diverse collections. From 1826 to 1830 the *Adventure* and *Beagle* investigated the South American coasts of Patagonia and Tierra del Fuego, under the command of Philip Parker King. From 1831 to 1836 the *Beagle* returned to the region under Robert FitzRoy, who had served with King on the first voyage. The second voyage would, of course, become famous as that which took Charles Darwin to the Galapagos Islands and elsewhere. The focus of investigation then shifted to Australia and the islands of the Pacific south-west. John Lort Stokes commanded the *Beagle* on a third voyage of six years, which built on Matthew Flinders's charts of the northern Australian coast. From 1842 to 1846 Francis Pine Blackwood in the *Fly* investigated north-eastern Australia and Torres Strait. This venture was followed up by others involving the *Rattlesnake*, the *Havannah* and the *Herald* through the 1850s and early 1860s.[29]

From the perspective of maritime history the voyage of HMS *Fly* was notable for surveys of the Torres Strait between northern Australia and New Guinea. But it was more remarkable for early meetings with the people of lowland Papua. In April and May 1845 Blackwood was exploring the waters of the northern part of the strait, near the mainland of New Guinea, the outlines of which had been known to Europeans for centuries. 'On approaching the coast of New Guinea', the geologist Joseph Beete Jukes, author of the expedition narrative, would write, 'the sea quite loses the deep and transparent blue it preserves among the islands and coral reefs of the Great Barrier, and acquires a dirty green colour, like that of the sea in the English Channel. This river water, however, was of a brown mud colour.'[30] The crew of the *Fly* had happened upon the entrance to one of the great waterways of the Papuan south coast. Even some miles offshore, over a muddy bank, the water was 'only slightly brackish'.

A couple of boats that had been sent out to survey some of the shoals and islets were lost to view, and from 10 May onwards Blackwood made several forays in different directions, to try to locate them. Two of these took him into the mouth of the great river. On the first of these excursions, a group of about a dozen men were sighted on the shore. Blackwood called out to them, using words from the language of Erub, the nearest place with which they had any familiarity, but these evidently meant nothing to these men, 'and they shouted words back, which were equally incomprehensible to us'. In due course some six or eight of these men came off in their canoe, to within about ten yards of the British, at which point the Papuan men simply stopped and stared, 'as if,' Jukes wrote, 'we were something inexpressibly fearful and disgusting to behold'. The next day they ventured further upstream, the river branching out into many channels, 'little narrow winding creeks and canals struck off into the jungle here and there in every direction, full of soft mud at low tide . . .'. Here, for those mariners who thought they knew the Pacific, was a new environment, the edge of a vast river basin, a watery land on a different scale to anything they had encountered before.[31]

Jukes, who had food only for three days, was about to turn back when they sighted several canoes. When the men in them let off a couple of arrows in their direction, Blackwood had warning shots fired, and the canoes then retreated. The British followed them upriver a short distance and were astonished to come in view of a great longhouse. They 'were greatly surprised at its size and structure. It looked like an immense barn, one gable of which projected towards the river, but the roof stretched so far back as to leave the other end completely hidden in the woods. . . . The end of the house that was visible was far larger than any barn I ever saw.'[32] A further but again unintelligible 'conversation' took place with one man who approached the intruders alone. At this point Blackwood considered that it would be unwise to remain so near a strong and potentially hostile party, and they dropped down the river on a strong ebbing tide.

Just over a fortnight later, without yet having traced his boats, Blackwood took two other boats, one armed with six-pound cannons, up another broad channel. They passed one settlement and saw 'the roofs of four or five immensely long houses' as well as a number of canoes; at this point the river was some two miles wide and around twenty feet deep. As it became dark, they were approached by several canoes, one with as many as twenty-five men with whom they again tried to talk. On this occasion Erub words seemed to be recognized; the men gave a general shout, but nevertheless discharged a couple of arrows in their direction. Blackwood, who had decided to react with force to any sign of aggression, gave an order to fire, and several of his men, without orders, reloaded and continued to fire. In a footnote, Jukes discloses that 'The men were just at this time become exasperated, with the loss of their messmates in the boats, and expressed great hatred against the blacks.' He estimated that 'ten or a dozen savages were struck, of whom several were no doubt killed'.[33] Insofar as this was an act of vengeance for the presumed massacre of the men of the missing boats, it was not only premature but, it would transpire, unfounded: the vessels had in fact proceeded in the opposite direction, toward Port Essington to the west, and the crew had in no way suffered from Islander hostility in this place or elsewhere.

A careful watch was maintained overnight, but the volley of fire prompted no retaliatory attack. The next morning the boats drifted upriver, passing further longhouses and settlements. They would go no further, but had a six-hour wait for the tide to turn. Blackwood felt they ought to land and take a look at one of the great houses. The cannon was fired before and during their landing. They approached the house, Jukes fully expecting 'a flight of arrows' from 'the savages' who might have 'made a very pretty stand of it here' – but the locals, perhaps anticipating that the intrusion would only be a fleeting one, had simply abandoned the settlement.[34]

The party proceeded to enter the house, which was about 30 feet in width and more than 300 long. It was an awesome sight: like a great tunnel, it was subdivided by cabins along every inner wall, each of which contained beds, mats, bows and arrows, baskets, axes and drums. But between these rows of sleeping-places, in the forward third of the longhouse, was a clear space, forming what Jukes called 'a noble covered promenade'. To a central roof-post they found attached a sort of framework covered with skulls, 'very curiously ornamented' with red and white seeds gummed into the eye sockets and

32 'New Guinea House', from Joseph Beete Jukes, *Narrative of the Surveying Voyage of HMS Fly.*

around the mouth, and a piece of wood that constituted a sort of elongated nose. Four of these they took away, two of which Blackwood later deposited with the College of Surgeons in London. Jukes too obtained a bow, arrow, knife, club and stone axe, which he later gave to the Museum of Practical Geology, at the time a new institution, just off Piccadilly. 'We nowhere saw any sign or fragment of European articles or workmanship,' he reported, which indicated that these people were not yet part of that history of travel and empire, to which so many Islanders had been, by now, long exposed.[35]

Jukes wrote self-consciously of this visit. They returned to the boats with their 'spoils'. Two pigs, which they had shot ashore, were swiftly cooked and consumed. 'It was not indeed until they were all gone that the reflection occurred to me that we had in fact *stolen them*,' he acknowledged – but went on to admit that such was their appetite for fresh provisions, he would happily have stolen more. As they departed, the locals returned and were seen looking around as if to establish what damage had been done. 'I am afraid they must have thought us a shocking set of buccaneering savages,' Jukes wrote.[36] There was a jocular quality to the admission, as though the sense of outrage he imputed to the Papuans was more an expression of primitive naivety than reasonable anger over actual theft. Of course, we have no sense of what these people really thought. They were consistent in their caution, and seemed alarmed or even disgusted by the European visitors, who quite possibly were considered spirits, perhaps malevolent ones, as their own dead, or their enemies' dead returned.

The visitors' responses to what they had seen were somewhat confounded. On the one hand, their reaction to the people was like that of d'Urville to the Islanders of the western Pacific in general. Blacker meant baser, it implied hideousness of feature. Jukes does not demonize those he observed, but they are remote from him; there is not much signalling of any common humanity. On the other hand, however, he and his companions were frankly astonished by the houses they encountered. Their grandeur seemed utterly incommensurate with a savage state. Their spectacular character Jukes wonders at, but does not attempt to resolve. Was this, if not a civilization of a sort nineteenth-century Europeans could acknowledge a society that was complex in ways they could not yet recognize?

For the moment, for Jukes, the mystery and wonder was not human, or social, but geographic. The tentative ventures into these rivers drew attention to a world that remained to be investigated. 'Unknown New Guinea' would become a cliché, indeed it remains one, but Jukes had the merit of originality, at this time, in articulating it:

> I know of no part of the world, the exploration of which is so flattering to the imagination, so likely to be fruitful in interesting results, whether to the naturalist, the ethnologist, or the geographer, and altogether so well calculated to gratify the enlightened curiosity of an adventurous explorer, as the interior of New Guinea. New Guinea! the very mention of being taken into the interior of New Guinea sounds like being allowed to visit some of the enchanted regions of the 'Arabian Nights', so dim an atmosphere of obscurity rests at present on the wonders it probably conceals.[37]

PART TWO

✦

THE TRIBE AND THE ARMY
Labour, Land, Sovereignty

CHAPTER SIX

✦

The smell of burning flesh is not nice

From the sixteenth century onward many Europeans had taken possession of many islands in the Pacific. In most cases these claims were without substance or effect. A mariner might bestow a name, or raise a flag, and write a line or two in a journal, but such assertions often passed unreported, of scant interest to authorities at home. When reported, they were occasionally ridiculed. For their part, native people often never knew that claims had been made upon their land or their loyalties. Among such acts in the Pacific in the early decades of the nineteenth century, David Porter's was performed with greater determination. It was given a degree of architectural substance in the form of a fort, and backed by violence on a scale that was then unusual in Polynesia. Yet the American presence on Nukuhiva fell in on itself so rapidly that Porter seems in hindsight to have suffered a hallucination, so detached was he from the realities of the place in which he found himself.

Colonial ventures in the islands continued for decades to be possessed by fantastic misapprehension in this sense. The contrast, in particular, between the imagination of those in Europe who sponsored missionary enterprise and the practicality of engaging with locals was often stark. Bishop Jean-Baptiste Epalle, attempting to establish one of the first Marist missions in Melanesia, was at once profoundly ignorant about the environment he entered and supremely confident of his own capacity to pacify apparently hostile Islanders. In Astrolabe Harbour on San Cristoval, on 2 December 1845, he walked forthrightly toward a group of men who bore weapons, expecting to win them over with a few gifts. But their hostility, probably aroused by the fact that a neighbouring group, their own local enemies, had already had friendly dealings with the French, was real, not apparent. Within moments an affray broke out: Epalle was wounded in the head by axe blows and died subsequently, others were less severely injured. Though some of the bishop's brethren stayed on, to establish a station at Makira Harbour nearby, they struggled to obtain sufficient food, with malaria, and with the local language. Here, too, the Catholics became embroiled in intertribal enmities. Two tried to cross the island but were advised that neighbouring people might well be hostile. They ignored the advice and were killed. The San Cristoval mission was abandoned in under two years.[1]

Yet where missionaries overcame the initial obstacles and were able to gain some competence in local languages – far more challenging in the western Pacific because of the region's linguistic heterogeneity – sheer tenacity tended to result, eventually, in the 'conversion' of communities. However partial this process might have been, at the level of deeper beliefs and commitments, it was marked by a reorganization of local life, at least by adherence to the routines and forms of Christian worship. Colonies that had uncertain or even farcical beginnings might similarly, in the longer term, change local people's lives and local societies in profound ways.

In the wake of Dumont d'Urville's voyages, the French remained concerned to establish some presence in the Pacific. A settlement was founded at Akaroa, on the coast of the South Island of New Zealand, near the present city of Christchurch. Consisting of some three hundred settlers, supported for a few years by a warship stationed continually in its harbour, this could conceivably have provided a base for a more ambitious colony of settlement – a French New Zealand – had it not been overtaken by the 1840 Treaty of Waitangi, and associated claims and negotiations, that led to the whole of New Zealand being ceded to the British Crown. The British push, most importantly, already had momentum because of the proximity of Sydney, and the long-standing engagement of Sydney-based traders, missionaries and settlers, with and among Maori.[2]

French interest then shifted, improbably, to the Marquesas Islands. Abel Aubert Dupetit-Thouars was Dumont d'Urville's successor in politically minded Pacific navigation. On a third voyage in 1842, he negotiated with the chief he knew from previous visits, Iotete of Tahuata, who initially acquiesced in annexation, but became dismayed as the French transformed his valley of Vaitahu into a military base, with a blockhouse, roads, ditches and walls. Here some two hundred soldiers were stationed. The inhabitants of the valley were themselves depleted to around two hundred and could not sustain the demands for food, labour and sexual services that the occupying force made. They simply evacuated the valley. In due course the lieutenant in charge of the garrison launched an attack in which both he and his deputy were almost immediately killed. Further fighting was succeeded by an uneasy peace, or rather by segregation. The people left, or were excluded from the valley of Vaitahu, which the French occupied; for their part the French seldom ventured elsewhere.[3]

The island of Nukuhiva was annexed at the same time and there the occupation similarly, though less immediately, provoked tension, conflict among the Marquesan chiefs, and violence. In order to uphold the status of 'king' Temoana, the French resident illegally executed his rival, Pakoko, and had one Oko, a sorcerer who was considered troublesome, shot too. The hopes that these islands would soon become major ports for French Pacific traders evaporated almost immediately: they were not environmentally suited to sustain plantations, there were no minerals to be mined, there were not even reefs that might have made pearl-fishing profitable. Attention shifted to Tahiti which Dupetit-Thouars had likewise annexed, and where armed conflict also broke out before a more stable order was established. A few years later the occupying forces in the Marquesas were withdrawn, and the governance of the possessions left to the Catholic missions. Though an official presence was re-established within a few years, it was for decades a token one.[4] These were colonies without colonization.

* * *

By the late 1840s the intermittent but long-standing French interest in forestalling British dominance in the Pacific acquired a different rationale, however. There was a crisis of overcrowding in French prisons and consideration was given to the establishment of a penal colony. Existing possessions such as Algeria were ruled out for one reason or another, and the decision was taken to annex New Caledonia for the purpose. Marist missionaries had been active on and off since 1843; they had begun to establish themselves, and learn something of the Melanesian worlds they inhabited. A naval expedition from Tahiti was despatched, a ceremony was conducted and possession declared on 24 September 1853. From 1854 the colony's capital was established at Noumea, on the south-eastern extremity of the main island that would become known as the Grande Terre. Despite an aspiration to attract free settlers and commerce, to establish a bustling colonial port city comparable to Sydney, Noumea remained for many years essentially a penal-military establishment.

Kanak (indigenous Melanesion) society would subsequently be studied with sympathy and imagination, most notably by the missionary-ethnographer Maurice Leenhardt, whose writings from the first half of the twentieth century have been more recently appreciated and employed by Kanak leaders such as Jean-Marie Tjibaou.[5] Out of the observations from the first decades of the French colony, those of missionaries provided the richest insights into the kinds of people with whom the French would inevitably interact. Settlers were more proximate to, in more sustained contact with, Islanders than any explorer or trader had been, yet there is a sense that they saw less, and were less curious, or thought only in terms of a savagery that would be superseded by their own presence.

A few years earlier the Rarotongan mission teacher Ta'unga had been stationed on Mare in the Loyalty Islands, on the Isle of Pines, to the south of the Grande Terre, and on the Grande Terre itself, on the south-eastern coast. He prepared notes on the customs of the people for Charles Pitman, his missionary mentor back in Rarotonga. Ta'unga's evocation was in one sense rich – he refers to diverse rites in preparation for war, observances at the time of birth, marriage and death, forms of sorcery, medicines, agricultural rites and so forth. Yet his account more conspicuously suggests that this Islander had fully embraced the missionary repugnance toward 'heathen' ways of life. A Cook Islander, he was of course remote culturally from the peoples of southern Melanesia. We should not expect him to have any greater natural understanding of or empathy for them than a white missionary might. But even so there is something numbing in his recitation of the many facets of Kanak violence. He understands the people of southern New Caledonia and the Isle of Pines – whom he describes somewhat generically – as addicted to vengeance. 'Their very natures are truly vindictive. That is why all forms of evil are widespread here', he writes, describing fighting, cannibalism, and the participation of women in assorted atrocities in stark detail.[6]

Beyond all these visions, there were real societies. Like many Melanesian peoples prior to colonial pacification, Kanak did fight regularly, but typically in a limited, even deliberately restrained fashion.[7] Feuding was the negative side of a cycle of reciprocity that constituted society, that reproduced life. There was, in any case, much more to Kanak life than warfare. The symbolism of the remarkable beehive-like houses, the sacredness of the environment and geography, and the power and drama of the great feasts known as *pilou pilou* were documented somewhat later, and most eloquently and engagingly in Leenhardt's writings, which were based on experience and enquiries in districts around Houailou on the east coast. Like most systematic descriptions of Pacific cultures, his and those of earlier missionaries such as Père Lambert were particular to specific regions, and put together from observations made well after communities had suffered depopulation and disruption. Yet these evocations of a world of masks and spirits, and a dramatic ceremonial and political life, is nevertheless suggestive for Kanak society in general, and for what must have existed on the eve of the initial French settlement.

In their outlines Kanak communities were typically Melanesian – like those of the Solomons and Vanuatu, major rites and ceremonies centred upon ancestors and agriculture. Paths of kinship and relatedness were marked by exchanges of food and valuables. Status was associated with rank and specialist knowledge. In New Caledonia, unlike most parts of Vanuatu and the Solomons, local communities were led by hereditary chiefs, and they were central to ritual life, their genealogies marked in art and architecture. In some regions, too, these local chiefdoms formed larger confederations, like those of Fiji. Yet visitors and colonists frequently misrecognized chieftainship, imputing straightforward secular authority when the men concerned possessed less power in this crude sense, and more ritual precedence.

There was one sense in which New Caledonia differed notably from the neighbouring archipelagoes. Environmental rather than social, this was that its formation was not recent in geological terms, but truly ancient: the Grande Terre, like Australia, is a remnant of the Gondwanaland continent. Broadly speaking, the landscape was heavily eroded, and the soils less rich than the more recent volcanic-derived formations that sustained Melanesian life elsewhere. The larger land mass was also more prone to drought than many Pacific environments. Islanders had consequently developed some of the most complex and intensive agricultural systems in Oceania, growing taro in networks of irrigated ponds. Though populations probably declined considerably during the first half of the nineteenth century, as a result of epidemic diseases introduced by mariners from Cook onwards, pressure upon the fundamental resource of the land was nevertheless considerable. This was a predictable but vital feature of the conflict that simmered as the white colony expanded during the 1860s and 1870s.

Despite their marginalization Kanak were incorporated into colonial society, widely employed as stockmen, in other farm or urban labouring roles. Some entered into these relationships because they had been forced to work – local officials were entitled to requisition labour from chiefs – but Kanak who gained experience might go on, for example, to become native policemen in town or elsewhere. Many settler families were allocated convicts who served as domestic or agricultural labourers, some Kanak were domestics, and indentured Islanders, primarily from Vanuatu, worked on plantations or as servants also. Settlers included French sugar planters from La Réunion in the Indian Ocean, who brought with them South Asian labourers, so-called 'coolies', originally from the Malabar coast. The convicts included ordinary criminals (recidivists were sentenced to transportation and hard labour), but many were political prisoners. Some of those deported were Kabyles from Algeria who had rebelled against French rule in 1871. They wore Arab dress and appeared 'highly interesting and poetic-looking individuals', thought the Australian journalist Stanley James, while complaining that those in Noumea hung about the streets attempting to interest convict women.[8] After the suppression of the 1871 Paris Commune, some four thousand Communards were shipped to the colony. The bulk were exiled to the Isle of Pines; around a quarter were sent to a loosely supervised settlement on the Ducos peninsula, which forms one side of Noumea harbour; others were permitted to reside in town.[9]

Noumea was utterly unlike any other settlement in the Pacific Islands. The emerging port towns of Honolulu, Kororareka, Levuka and Papeete had begun as missionary or beachcomber settlements; they were sites of interaction in which local chiefs or their agents and offsiders might also live, or keep houses, and were as prominent as any whites. Noumea was not this kind of beach community; it had not grown untidily and organically. It was more a brutal imposition, and one that had a distinctly military character, though its barracks and prison were not designed to subordinate the native people but to contain and police convicts. Little thought had been given as to how the Kanak population was to be dealt with. Official and settler opinion embraced various harshly racist and more philanthropic attitudes, but the situation in practice was that little by little Kanak were displaced. As was typical of settler colonies, the administration took steps to defend and preserve Kanak tenure, by surveying tribal reserves, while actively pursuing other policies – most obviously the encouragement of settlement – that made the reserves unsustainable.

The pressure intensified, especially when the settlers began to introduce livestock. Given the affinities between the environment of the Grande Terre and that of parts of Australia, and the fact that Australians loomed large among the free immigrants to New Caledonia, it is not surprising that the settler economy acquired something of an Australian character. Crops were tried but were not generally successful, mining was risky but potentially lucrative, and cattle were imported from Australia on a large scale from as early as 1859, along with Australian terminology: the words 'paddocks', 'bush' and 'stockmen' appear a good deal in French accounts of the period.[10] Within a few years there were tens of thousands of cattle. As in Australia, herds had a catastrophic impact on local life. Kanak had not kept pigs and had not designed agricultural systems from which beasts needed to be excluded. Water sources were polluted, and produce eaten or trampled. Above all, the demand for extensive grazing lands propelled one set of appropriations after another.

If many Islanders had, at one time or another, resisted strangers who landed upon their shores, because they feared some threat to their land and livelihood, it was inevitable that actual and extensive intrusions would be resisted. From the 1850s onward, there were protests and outbreaks of violence. Some were isolated events – the killing of an individual settler – born of personal anger or desperation. Others were more carefully planned, wider assaults. In most such cases the administration responded, not only by executing the warriors considered responsible, but by dispossessing the entire tribe. Antagonism, violence and expropriation thus came to provoke each other in turn, constituting a vicious circle.

Notwithstanding intermittent violence around European outposts, Noumea became the enclave for an introverted settler society, with a routine of balls and concerts, and in which an effort was made to keep up with Parisian fashion, insofar as distance permitted. Little thought was given to the Kanak people, to what might become of them. As Lieutenant Henri Rivière put it, '. . . I had always believed that they did not exist, or that they no longer existed'.[11] This was in one sense a nonsense: Kanak were everywhere in the colonial economy. Yet in another it manifested a real myopia, an inability, particularly in the insulated urban milieux, to acknowledge who inhabited the colony and what tensions its existence inevitably engendered.

* * *

Events in mid-1878 would turn this complacency to trauma. Rivière would be a protagonist in perhaps the bloodiest colonial war in the Pacific, excluding only the long series of conflicts in New Zealand.[12] I can do no more than sample an involved succession of conflicts here, and moreover sample them obliquely, via interested, indeed in part fanciful narrations of white observers.

Among Rivière's routine duties were tours of inspection. On Tuesday, 25 June 1878 his vessel, the *Vire*, entered the pass of Uaraï on the west coast and made for the military post on the islet of Teremba. The sea was flat, oily and heavy, he would later write, portentously. Across the water the settlement of Uaraï could be seen. It featured the fine house of the head of the *arrondissement* – as the colony's districts were called – a church, stores and various other buildings. Here, too, was the mouth of the La Foa river. No sooner had Rivière's boat anchored than he was brought a note from the local administrator. That very morning the gendarmes at their post at La Foa, some eight miles upstream, had been massacred. He showed the message to his deputy, who remarked, simply, 'C'est bizarre'.[13] The sense initially was of disbelief. Yet as they were rowed ashore by Kanak crewmen, Rivière sensed embarrassment and unease. It was an odd thing, he reflected, that the French in New Caledonia who lived, essentially, with Kanak workers or servants never entertained doubts as to their docility – they might never do so, up to the moment they received a blow with an axe. His thought exemplified the kind of colonial understanding that Ta'unga had shared, which attributed viciousness and treachery to a Kanak 'mentality'. Yet it also acknowledged a fatal obliviousness in a settler 'mentality', that had attributed a pathetic quiescence to the dispossessed locals, that had neglected to be cognizant of them at all.

On reaching the shore, Rivière could see a brickworks burning. Yet otherwise there was silence, the land was uncannily empty. He was met by a local lieutenant who had returned from a reconnaissance, who understood that colonists throughout the region had been assaulted, and reported that some were in disorderly flight. In due course they saw approaching a long column of people who had evacuated interior settlements, who carried improvised arms such as pitchforks, who brought their cattle, and two carts, one carrying the wounded, the other the dead, their bodies carelessly hacked about. Deeply shocked by the sight of their injuries, Rivière imputed a lust for cruelty to their killers. Most alarmingly, this was not a case of a single massacre but a coordinated set of attacks. The word was that Kanak were continuing to work their way around the district, attacking settlers and their dependants, and burning their homesteads. At this time it was believed that around one hundred had been killed.[14]

That afternoon one François, a Kanak corporal among Rivière's detachment, deserted, abruptly sprinting away from a boat he had been attending to, and disappearing among the mangroves. The other five Kanak soldiers were perhaps not their enemies, Rivière considered, 'but they no longer had the air of servants'. Since they feigned ignorance, when he sought to understand why François had left, he had them confined in the station's prison. That night, Rivière and various officers ate together with some of the survivors and their families in the grand dining room of the resident's house. They spoke of the horrors of the day. Emotion, he maintained, rendered them hungry. At any rate they had a good meal with wine and dessert. Around nine in the evening a storm broke. The rain was torrential, the night pitch black, but intermittently shattered by lightning.[15]

By the following morning the weather had cleared. A boat arrived with a company of marines. The colony's military commander, Colonel Galli-Passebosc, accompanied them. Rivière found him more put out than genuinely disturbed by the insurrection. Galli-Passebosc was due to return to France within a month and did not like the thought that a major conflict would detain him. 'Are you afraid of the Kanak?' he asked Rivière, rhetorically, and was taken aback when the officer replied that indeed he was.[16]

The news that came with this boat was to some extent reassuring. The rebellion was confined, at any rate thus far, to the Ourail district. The important and powerful tribes of Canala on the east coast gave greatest cause for concern. They were fully aware of what had happened and appeared to be engaged in deliberations. The evening brought news too that Kanak had been

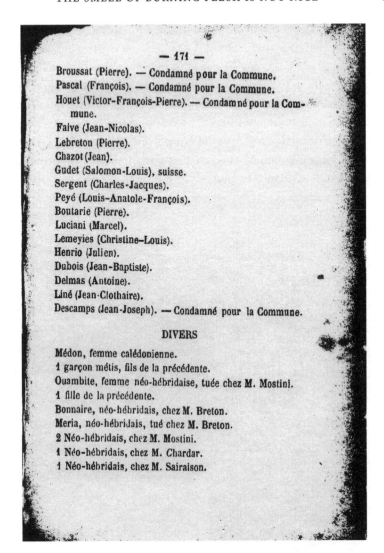

— 171 —

Broussat (Pierre). — Condamné pour la Commune.
Pascal (François). — Condamné pour la Commune.
Houet (Victor-François-Pierre). — Condamné pour la Commune.
Faive (Jean-Nicolas).
Lebreton (Pierre).
Chazot (Jean).
Gudet (Salomon-Louis), suisse.
Sergent (Charles-Jacques).
Peyé (Louis–Anatole-François).
Boutarie (Pierre).
Luciani (Marcel).
Lemeyies (Christine–Louis).
Henrio (Julien).
Dubois (Jean-Baptiste).
Delmas (Antoine).
Liné (Jean-Clothaire).
Descamps (Jean-Joseph). — Condamné pour la Commune.

DIVERS

Médon, femme calédonienne.
1 garçon métis, fils de la précédente.
Ouambite, femme néo-hébridaise, tuée chez M. Mostini.
1 fille de la précédente.
Bonnaire, néo-hébridais, chez M. Breton.
Meria, néo-hébridais, tué chez M. Breton.
2 Néo-hébridais, chez M. Mostini.
1 Néo-hébridais, chez M. Chardar.
1 Néo-hébridais, chez M. Sairaison.

33 Extract from the list of victims of the Kanak insurrection, including ni-Vanuatu (New Hebridean) indentured workers, from C. Amouroux and H. Place, *L'administration et les Maristes en Nouvelle-Calédonie*.

active in the nearby Bouloupari area, massacring colonists and burning and pillaging their houses. A telegraph operator, Riou, was killed just as he sent a message through to Noumea raising the alarm. Over the next few days Galli-Passebosc undertook various sorties. He came back appalled by what he had seen. Consistently, white observers were shocked. Of Bouloupari a prospective settler from Queensland who happened to be in the area wrote: 'What a sight! Unburied corpses of women and children, hacked in pieces, and the birds, dogs, and even pigs feasting on the dreadful debris. There lay what was left of the bodies of Madame Rondel, her three little girls, Augustine, 7 years old; Louise, 2 years old; and Tricottee, 2 months old, with her little brother Vincent, 5 years old.'[17] Typically, families such as this were killed by Kanak known to them, who entered houses on the pretext of an errand or enquiry and then attacked suddenly and ruthlessly.

The Kanak campaign was, it could be said, one of terror. This term has long been used judgementally, to suggest that particular acts of armed violence directed against civilians are arbitrary and indiscriminate, that they lack any

VII

LE LIEUTENANT DE VAISSEAU
SERVAN ET LES CANAQUES
DE CANALA. — HÉROISME DE
SERVAN. — PREMIERS MOU-
VEMENTS EN AVANT. — LA
MORT DU COLONEL GALLI-
PASSEBOSC.

34 Vignette from Henri Rivière, *Souvenirs de la Nouvelle Calédonie: l'insurrection canaque.*

conceivable legitimacy. It goes without saying that terrorists belong always to the other side. My interest here is not in adjudicating the legitimacy or illegitimacy of Kanak tactics. Rather those of us struggling to understand the attacks of 25 and 26 June 1878 from a twenty-first-century vantage point may gain some insight by considering them as effective, as successful, acts of terror.

These acts targeted not the gendarmes' post, the settler family, or even the particular settlement. The target was rather the French presence itself. Even though the insurrection was not that of the Kanak population as a whole, it was a war for land and autonomy fought by particular tribes; the coordinated, sudden and excessive violence was intended to traumatize the whole settler population. The evidence suggests that it did so. All reports of the time indicate that many of the French were in a state of panic. There was probably no likelihood that Noumea or the colony itself could ever have been seriously threatened, but the confused state of news in the early days permitted rumours of all sorts to circulate. 'A spasm of fear seized every one,' wrote Stanley James, 'to be succeeded by hysterical shrieks for vengeance.'[18]

Alarm and anxiety were compounded in early July by the death of Galli-Passebosc. He was leading an assault party toward Bouloupari along a narrow path that proceeded through the bush. Just two shots were fired, he called out 'Bien touché!', and his aide thought that an enemy must have been hit. But Galli-Passebosc was referring to a wound he himself had received in the stomach. He stood upright momentarily then collapsed and was carried away, to die after protracted suffering the following day.

Rivière, back at the Teremba base, noted how carefully the commander had been targeted – no fire had been directed at any of his men, and the Kanak made no attempt to broaden the attack, vanishing immediately into the scrub. Among 'savages', Rivière remarked, the death of a chief generally meant the end of the war.[19] That was not the case in this instance, but the impact on French morale was certainly considerable. Even two Communards who wrote a history and polemic concerning the conflict felt the commander's loss keenly, and incorporated a lengthy eulogy into their narrative, noting the officer's evident talent, rapid promotion and extensive experience in various European and African campaigns.[20] That their sense was widely shared is attested to by settlers' photo albums of the period, which include images of the site of the fatal shooting. The event entered the public memory of the colonists, and no doubt too that of the colonized, in terms that cannot now be reconstructed – but were certainly different.

35 Said to be the last photograph of Colonel Galli-Passebosc, before his death in a Kanak ambush.

One of the heroic tales in Rivière's self-aggrandizing, novelistic account of the uprising was that of his subordinate Servan, who went alone to make contact with the Canala chiefs, thought to be veering toward joining the revolt. Servan reputedly astonished them by taking the risk of venturing among potentially hostile people alone, travelling through the night with them to conferences among petty chiefs and asserting considerable force of personality, in the end simply directing them to fight for him. The chief warrior Nondo and other prominent Canala men no doubt had their own reasons for taking the side they did. But from this point onwards, the military balance was unfavourable to the rebels, who at no time are likely to have fielded more than two hundred or so fighters. Canala warriors alone numbered some three to five hundred. The French had some twenty-five hundred soldiers in the colony, and they were quickly reinforced by irregulars – Communards among others were eager to play their part – and later by reinforcements from overseas.

If this overwhelming superiority of numbers might have been expected to ensure a quick French victory, this was far from so. The Kanak employed guerrilla tactics, appearing from time to time to burn buildings and cut telegraph wires, but then melted away into rocky uplands and thick bush that French troops were poorly equipped to navigate or penetrate. As Stanley James wrote jocularly:

> it was high noon under a blazing sun. We had just finished the brilliant attack on the native village, near Tia, in which we proudly distinguished ourselves by destroying acres of bananas and yams. Under the shade of a cocoanut tree we reposed after our toil, and breakfasted heartily, recking little of the skulls of massacred convicts which lay around. My companions, Captain Rathouis and Lieutenant Maréchal, who had charge of the expedition, were hardy warriors, who jested at the signs of mortality. After all, it was not our fault that we did not meet the enemy. We meant fighting, and if the foe disappointed us, we had to revenge ourselves on the innocent vegetation.[21]

After Galli-Passebosc's death, Rivière led the counter-campaign. He reoccupied the areas that had been terrorized and looted in the initial days of the uprising, and established a secure network of bases. He made short excursions, burning, in the manner described, dozens of Kanak villages and destroying plantations. It was a hectic campaign but he found time, on at least one evening, to borrow James Fenimore Cooper's *Satanstoe* dealing with Indian wars in North America. For two months the French continued to destroy villages and gardens, an effort that no doubt caused wider, long-term suffering to the Kanak population but failed to strike at the insurgents directly.

Ineffective as these engagements were, there was a certain savagery to the campaign of counter-insurrection. At La Foa in the latter part of August, James expected to witness a court martial, at which locals accused of failing to warn settlers were likely to be sentenced to deportation. But after a vague report came in that a courier had been shot at, Rivière decided that more exemplary punishment was appropriate. According to James, who may have distorted or even concocted events, five of the prisoners were to be taken to a nearby place where one Brière, a liberated convict, had earlier fallen victim to unidentified rebels.

A party was formed and they marched to the site. 'For six miles we toiled through the blazing sun. It was hard work; and it seemed to me cruel to drag these poor wretches out thus far to kill them.' They arrived at the thatched hut that had been Brière's. His bones were still visible in the remnants of a fire. The fact that his house and outbuildings had not been burned suggested, James considered, that he had been murdered out of an act of individual vengeance, which perhaps had little to do with the wider insurrection. The four adult men, and a boy of thirteen, were required to sit while convicts pulled broken fence posts and other pieces of timber together for a fire. Varnauld, the officer in charge, addressed the Kanak, citing the outrages perpetrated by rebel chiefs, and stating that they were therefore 'condemned passer par les armes', a locution that James presumed the men did not understand.

They were given a few minutes to talk among themselves. Their calmness disconcerted the journalist, who could not judge whether they understood their fate or not, and they were then taken to a stand of niaouli, the paper-barks common in the colony. One after another they were unchained and tied to a tree. 'The last,' wrote James, 'was my handsome friend.' (He had exchanged looks with the man, earlier in the day, silently communicating sympathy, he would have us understand.) 'Released from his fellow, he remained for a couple of minutes perfectly free and unshackled, and again looked at me with those wistful eyes. Why did he not make one effort for life and freedom?' *The Last of the Mohicans* sprang to the journalist's mind. Varnauld gave the orders, and firing squads, six for each prisoner, were assembled and readied. Of the victims, 'four stood up erect, with chests inflated, and every nerve and muscle strung, ready to die like warriors. The boy alone had his head sunk on his breast.'

James had seen, he claimed, thousands of corpses, but 'never immediately after death a naked one'. He was shocked by the flabbiness and 'quivery appearance' of the bodies as they were dragged across the ground to the pile of wood. 'The smell of burning flesh is not nice,' he reported, retreating from the scene 'to smoke and moralize'. These deaths, unlike that of Galli-Passebosc, did not enter the public memory of the colony, indeed they appear otherwise to have been unrecorded.[22] This may be so if the incident was invented by James, though if it was, not dissimilar punitive killings certainly did take place.

* * *

The attrition approach resulted only in a stand-off. Rivière became frustrated and changed strategy, locating a hand-picked assault force in a new fort at La Foa, in the centre of the most hostile territory. The new base was attacked on 24 August, but only after its defences were completed. Though the Kanak were said to number several hundred, they were repelled, and may have suffered extensive casualties – their losses were not easily determined, since they carried their dead and wounded away. But information obtained later suggested that one of the Kanak leaders, Moraï, later died of injuries sustained during the assault which was, therefore, a damaging reversal for the Ouraïl rebels. Rivière could now go on the offensive. His men fought side by side with Canala warriors and to some extent emulated their methods. They now avoided the cross-country paths which had been so easily watched and ambushed. By creeping through the scrub, they found they were able to surprise and engage Kanak fighters.

On 1 September a force of some 110 French soldiers and 200 Canala warriors made a sweep through the La Foa valley, which, it transpired, would be the most effective action from the colonial side of the entire war. Some sixteen or seventeen Kanak fighters were killed, mostly by the Canala, and decapitated. They included the rebel chiefs Atai and Baptiste, the former considered the single most influential instigator of the revolt. Some sixty women and children were taken captive, prizes for the Canala. Rivière's success lay, essentially, in assimilating his own campaign to an intertribal war. It had been agreed that Kanak allies would receive captives and could loot as extensively as they wished. The Canala were thus fighting very much in their own interest, not because they had been cowed into assisting in the defence of the colonial order.[23]

Though substantially won, in colonial eyes, the war in Ouraïl carried on in a less intense fashion for months. The continuing operations were largely led, independently of French supervision and involvement, by the Canala warrior chief Nondo, who killed Naïna, the last hostile leader in the Ouraïl area, in January 1879. Late in 1878 the French, exhausted by the campaign, reluctantly accepted that the pursuit of small remaining groups of hostile fighters might continue indefinitely. Groups were encouraged to surrender and accept exile from their lands. In the end the remaining thirty-five or so Ouraïl fighters gave up, together with women and children. They were exiled and their lands alienated. In other regions such as Koné and Bourail intense fighting carried on, well into the following year, but resistance in these regions too was eventually put down, the people generally dispossessed. What had once been a Kanak landscape – of great houses, ceremonial grounds and taro gardens – would sustain Kanak life and Kanak meanings no longer.[24]

* * *

Reflections on the part of the French on the causes of the war did little to mask what were all too evidently its origins in the fundamental conflict that French settlement had engendered. Colonization could not proceed without dispossession, and as in New Zealand, and for that matter in settler colonies elsewhere in the world, there was a contradiction of interest between colonizers and natives that would inevitably give rise to violence. The official inquiry, which submitted its report, perhaps a little prematurely, in February 1879, acknowledged that Kanak lands had been appropriated on a massive scale, and in an effectively unrestrained way. It cited also the 'invasion' of livestock; the ill-feeling that arose from the recruitment of Kanak for public works, from settler logging, and from the disturbance of Kanak cemeteries. It noted, too, that the propensity of bush settlers to take Kanak wives, *popinées* in the derogatory New Caledonian French of the period, engendered local resent-ment – though it was claimed that the women preferred life with white men to arduous customary roles.

The report also considered that the administration should never have established a 'police indigène'. This force had been occupied largely in tracking down fugitive convicts. Young and strong Kanak men were thus given the opportunity to engage in 'a sort of hunt of white men', and even allowed to use arms such as clubs while doing so. They frequently took such convicts by surprise, beat them, tied them up, and brought them back to Noumea, where they would be rewarded with a fifty-franc bounty. Neither this nor the fact that, in Noumea, Kanak police might frequently see, and have to arrest, drunken soldiers, were conducive, the authors of the report consid-ered, to an appropriate level of respect for the white race. The point of conclu-sion was an acknowledgement, moreover, that the administration, and indeed the settler population, had been blind.[25] The inquiry quoted from a report of Rivière's; the sentences were reproduced in his memoirs, published a couple of years later. I have already quoted in translation the same words from the memoirs; most recent commentators have quoted them too, in French or English. This text amounts to a monument of a sort, to the shocking chain of events, of 1878–79.

... j'avais toujours cru que les Canaques n'existaient pas ou n'existaient plus.

* * *

In their polemic the Communards Charles Amouroux and Henri Place vigor-ously denounced the dispossession of the Kanak. There was a strong anti-clerical strand to their analysis: they found that the Marists had done more than their share of land-grabbing, and suggested that both the future of the colony and the honour of the republic called for a full inquiry into the circum-stances of their acquisitions.[26] But in fact the missionaries had intermittently advocated Kanak rights, while Amouroux had put himself forward, the leader of a group of Communards who wished to join the official forces in the

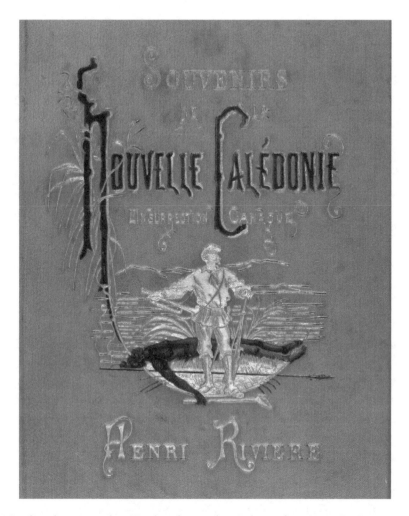

36 Binding depicting a slain Kanak and triumphant colonist, from Henri Rivière, *Souvenirs de la Nouvelle Calédonie: l'insurrection canaque.*

defence of the colony. Their diagnosis of the causes of the conflict was critical of the administration, but their revolutionary project failed to extend to, or embrace, the anti-colonial cause.

Only Louise Michel, anarchist, poet and teacher, had expressed support for the Kanak side during the insurrection. She was alone among the Communards, too, in exhibiting any particular curiosity about Kanak culture. Among her prolific writings was a volume of *Légendes et chants de gestes canaques* (1885), in fact a mix of memoir, vocabulary and short retellings

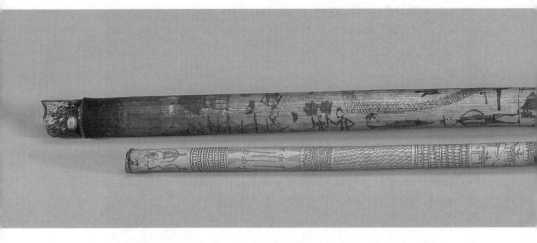

37 Kanak engraved bamboo, second half of the century.

of folk tales.[27] While exceptional in its context, the book attests really to the shallowness of her familiarity with Kanak languages, individuals and cultures. For all their overt prejudice, many missionaries knew a great deal more, and even sympathetically documented much more, of the beliefs, institutions and narratives that they were working tirelessly to relegate to the past.

* * *

If Rivière was right and the French had failed to 'see' the Kanak, the Kanak certainly did not fail to see the French, or – it should be said – the settlers, many of whom were from Australia or elsewhere. There is a remarkable and unique genre of Kanak art that offers an entirely different perspective on culture and conflict in the colony to that of documentary history. The works I have in mind do not offer an alternative telling, a competing story that can be set against that of Rivière, James, or the archive more generally. Rather they suggest an ironical indigenous vision, and a deeper understanding of a world turned upside down.

Travellers of the time refer occasionally to 'Carved bamboo combs, staffs of bamboo, with representations of men, animals, stars, &c' that in their view amounted to 'the limited works of art manufactured by the native'. Somehow these 'observers' did not know or did not see the spectacular houses and their bold door posts.[28] Though seldom at this time described in detail, the bamboo 'staffs' appear to have been made in considerable numbers, in part for

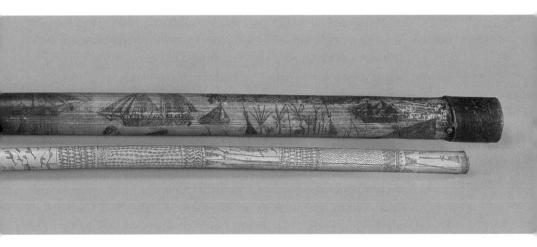

personal use, in part for sale to foreigners, an early form of tourist art. They were visible enough for the missionary ethnographer Lambert to ask rhetorically: 'Who, among travellers to New Caledonia, does not know the engraved bamboo?'[29]

Prior to European contact, bamboos were decorated in various ways across the Pacific, and used as smoking pipes, flutes, lime containers (for betel chewing), and for a host of other purposes. Designs were most often geometric or curvilinear, but sometimes included figures, and artists from a good many communities experimented with figures, having been stimulated by exposure perhaps to European printed engravings, perhaps to the popular arts of sailors such as scrimshaw (engraved ivory). Only among Kanak, however, did new styles of bamboo engraving become an established art form. Frustratingly little is known about exactly when pictorial imagery appeared or became dominant (assuming that pre-European styles were not pictorial, which cannot be known for sure), or such basic matters as where, when and by whom were made the some hundreds of bamboos that ended up in museum collections. Yet it is at least clear that the bulk date from the second half of the nineteenth century, and are products of the epoch in which the conditions of Kanak life were changed forever.[30]

The bamboos could be flippantly characterized as a cross between the comic book and the tribal carving. They are salient here because they incorporate a lively and surely satiric sense of colonial life. But it should at first be acknowledged that they are remarkably heterogeneous. What they have in common is that they are trimmed lengths of bamboo in which designs have been scratched or etched. They have been rubbed with some blackening agent in order to bring out their designs, and sometimes polished with oil, or perhaps just extensively handled. In some cases they have been decorated with considerable compositional skill and bear groups of figures that are carefully defined and ordered in one sense or another. Some bamboos, if imagined 'unrolled', bear a scene that is as structured as any altarpiece. Others have been treated like a piece of paper, a space to be filled with a variety of images that do not necessarily go together in any meaningful or narrative sense. In some cases men and women are deftly portrayed or caricatured, in others the figures are stick-like.

On some bamboos the conspicuous motifs represented the irrigation channels, fields and crops that were so fundamental to Kanak life. Great tribal houses, ceremonies, feasts, funerals and sacred creatures such as turtles were similarly often depicted. Yet the corpus is also a chronicle of curiosity. Colonial ships, houses and guns feature extensively. The representation of individual colonists is particularly striking. Gents in suits smoke a pipe and strike a pose. Others look to be drinking liberally. There is an interest in sheer oddity, in a one-legged man, in the same-sex antics of sailors. On the other hand, the graphic depictions of the sexual coupling of white men with Kanak women could be taken as a form of ethnographic erotica. These bamboos may well have been created with the tastes of tourists or soldiers in mind, but they spoke surely also to the tensions and resentments around interracial sex, which were said to loom so large among Kanak grievances.

The most remarkable of all extant bamboos is one that entered the collections of the Museum für Völkerkunde in Berlin near the end of the nineteenth century. It is a metre and a half long and is divided into two sections by the natural node. Half bears a set of related images that are to be viewed horizontally. They depict three moments in an engagement between indigenous warriors. The most inclusive of the three drawings describes the initial stage of fighting. Two parties of warriors face each other. One is advancing upon the tribal houses and ceremonial ground of the other. Fighting is already taking place in the ground between the houses. An injured or dead man is being carried away. One warrior is climbing up the roof of one of the houses. The second scene is immediately below this. Fighting continues and the second great house is burning. In the third image the climbing man has reached the top of the unburnt house and presumably seized the ancestral carving from its apex.

Though the figures are delineated schematically, their weapons and accoutrements are clearly identified. They all bear Kanak clubs and axes, and customary hats. None wear European clothes, nor do any carry guns. The conflict is firmly situated in a precolonial epoch, a time of struggle between

38 Scenes from a Kanak bamboo, showing (above) an indigenous military engagement, culminating in the destruction by fire of a clan house, and (below) part of the French military hierarchy. Second half of the nineteenth century.

Kanak tribes. A carefully drawn crayfish, shown much larger than any of the human figures, is the odd image out, depicted perhaps because it was of some totemic or ritual significance, perhaps simply because the artist wished to draw a shellfish.

The other half of the bamboo is to be seen vertically and is entirely different. It bears scenes associated with colonization and specifically with the French military hierarchy. It represents not a narrative but a static hierarchy, with ordinary soldiers at the bottom, those of intermediate rank in the middle, and officers with elaborate uniforms and decorations at the top. There is no apparent narrative element in this section of the work, but it is rich in anecdotal observation. Soldiers with a dog are shooting birds in trees. Local women with baskets and babies are seemingly in attendance. A *militaire*, or soldier, examines a document. Another is giving orders to a man who salutes. One is being gripped around the throat and threatened by a man with some sort of sword or rapier.

The simplicity of the juxtaposition between the horizontal and the vertical underscores the profundity of other contrasts – between the local and the foreign, the customary and the alien, and the past and the present. There is humour in the imagery on this bamboo but – however hard it is to speculate concerning the artist's intentions – the overall intent was surely not comic. Rather there is something grave, matter-of-fact and poignant that can be read off the sheer contrast between the drama of traditional war and the social relations that structure an occupying force, which have a space, it appears, for Kanak women but not for Kanak men.

This book has emphasized the cosmopolitanism of the Pacific during the nineteenth century. Even in the 1790s, we have seen, Hawaiians, Maori, Tahitians and others mixed and exchanged ideas. As each began to suffer, deal with and understand Europeans of various sorts, experiences of travel led to new contacts among Islanders, and between them and East Asians, black Americans, Aboriginal Australians, and a host of other native and non-native peoples. By the 1850s a second or third generation had witnessed and partic-ipated in voyaging, trade and evangelization, and encountered the violence of settlement. In New Caledonia, Kanak had to deal with Polynesian, French and British missionaries, French, Australian, Irish and other settlers, Kabyle and French deportees, ni-Vanuatu indentured labourers, and immigrant workers from south and south-east Asia. And some Kanak were working with the French and fighting others.

Yet in the imagining of the artist who engraved this particular bamboo, this diversity collapsed into polarity. Here, what was going on was not merely an unstable mixing. The mixing that did take place was underpinned by a more powerful contradiction. The reality was that there were many worlds here, but the seeming profundity of the conflict between the French and the Kanak prompted this particular artist to juxtapose two worlds, two that faced each other, the one threatening to banish the other to the past.

✦

CHAPTER SEVEN

A new phase of piracy

Easter Island, known now to Polynesians as Rapa Nui, has fascinated Europeans, indeed fascinated the world, in many ways over the last few hundred years. The 'mystery' of its statues has been rehashed in an extraordinary succession of pseudo-scientific and popular books and films. Thor Heyerdahl's mission to identify native Americans as the authors of the monumental figures, among other features of the Islanders' art and culture, has been seen, for decades now, to lack any scholarly credibility whatsoever, but his and similar theories have continued to intrigue that sector of the public with a taste for such supposed historical–mythological conundra. More recently, as archaeological understandings have been dramatically refined, and the historical archive has been more carefully examined, the story of the island has been re-popularized. Jared Diamond and others have argued that, before European contact, the Polynesian inhabitants had a catastrophic impact on the environment, leading to a dramatic reduction in bird species and plant life, turning the island into something approaching a treeless waste. Islanders had, in effect, destroyed their own conditions of existence; Rapa Nui becomes irresistible, as a microcosm of the planet, its story pointing toward the kind of catastrophe that might take place on a global scale.[1]

Unwelcome as this rhetoric is, among those prone to romanticize indigenous relationships with nature, the accumulating archaeological and geographic evidence points clearly toward marked change, and decidedly deleterious change. The island was probably settled around 400 AD and by 1500 a relatively stable kingship had developed, the kings being the persons commemorated by the famous statues. In this period, the population was high, perhaps as high as seven thousand. Yet relatively thin volcanic soils were being eroded, and the capacity of the land to support these numbers overstretched. Trees became increasingly sparse, to the point that none existed large enough to supply the

39 William Hodges' dramatic view of the monuments of Easter Island, painted during Cook's second voyage.

timber from which canoes could be made. Such watercraft as were constructed were more like rafts, assembled from smaller pieces of wood that were tied together. Even these were scarce, visitors often reporting that they saw no more than two or three.

To be without a canoe, on an island of this kind, was to suffer deprivation. When I lived on Ua Pou in the Marquesas in the 1980s, young men took small canoes through the surf and out to sea almost daily, and almost daily brought back game fish such as bonito and tuna, of a size that fed a family. For Rapa Nui this had become impossible. The archaeological record indicates a proliferation of spear points in the later stages of the island's history, material evidence that complements oral traditions, recording internecine warfare. If fighting employed the same methods it did elsewhere, enemies' gardens would frequently have been raided or destroyed, thus exacerbating the conditions that caused conflict in the first place. Any stable chieftainship collapsed, new cults arose, and the population declined.

Pacific cultures and histories have frequently been imagined via spectacular instances rather than contextualized histories. The story of Rapa Nui is indeed spectacular but is emphatically not unique. Across the Pacific, environmental change occurred on every island, in the wake of first settlement by Islanders, and change continued, as populations grew and agricultural techniques evolved. Various species of birds – or in the case of New Caledonia, larger mammals – were hunted to extinction. Swidden (slash and burn) agriculture caused erosion. In some cases soils lost to uplands accumulated on lowlands, particularly where lagoons had existed. In parts of Hawaii and Tahiti these shallows were filled in, resulting paradoxically in an enhanced environment, with fertile garden lands that had not previously been there. Elsewhere, such as in the Marquesas and Rapa Nui, there were no extensive reefs, soils simply disappeared into deep water, and the natural resource was depleted for good.[2] Many islands, too, were subject to famine and to other catastrophes such as tsunami.

Political changes, which entailed a transformation or decline of the power of customary chiefs, were also a feature of the histories of many islands. In Tonga and Fiji, in recent centuries, sacred and secular aspects of kingship were distributed between different people, and the executive rulers tended to eclipse those with purely ritual status. Elsewhere shamans and warrior leaders assumed the prominence that chiefs had once enjoyed. The paucity of resources, the crisis of intertribal conflict, and the decline of population prior to European contact on Rapa Nui were more extreme than the vicissitudes suffered by other Islanders, but the processes that drove them were similar in kind.

The Rapa Nui experience of contact over the first half of the nineteenth century was likewise similar, yet refracted by the singularity of the Rapa Nui environment and the island's sheer isolation. There was a hiatus of almost fifty years after Jacob Roggeveen's 1722 visit, which marked the European 'discovery' of the island, before the Spanish explorer Felipe Gonzalez called in 1770, followed by Cook in 1774, and La Pérouse in 1786. The Islanders' inability to provide significant quantities of food for trade meant that these visits were typically very brief. Naturalists and others from Cook's *Resolution* spent the better part of one day on the island, and landed again only for a short second visit. A larger party off La Pérouse's *Astrolabe* and *Recherche* were on shore for one day only.

Cook's collected *Voyages* were often reprinted, and represented the handbook to the Pacific that mariners were still referring to decades later. The navigator had reported that 'Here is no safe anchorage; no wood for fuel; nor

40 Rapa Nui gorget.

any fresh water worth taking on board. Nature has been exceedingly sparing of her favours to this spot.'[3] Given that he went on to note that garden produce was limited, and few fish were to be caught, it is not surprising that the island was never as extensively called at as islands in the Societies, the Marquesas, or the Hawaiian group. There are records of visits by only about fifty ships to Rapa Nui between the 1780s and 1860s. Many visits by whaleships or trading vessels were no doubt unrecorded, but it is likely that the archives capture a quarter, probably more, of all visits, meaning that there were contacts with perhaps two hundred ships between 1790 and 1860.[4] In the Marquesas around five visits a year are typical of the 1810s, around ten a year of the 1820s, and as many as twenty-five ships a year called during the 1830s.[5] Even if a comparison is between an estimate for Rapa Nui and the documented visits for the Marquesas, it would seem that more ships visited the latter group in a single decade than called at Rapa Nui in more than half a century.

This relative sparseness of contacts suggests why Rapa Nui people were clearly excited by the arrival of visitors, at a time when ships and trade had become more like day-to-day business in what had become true ports of call, such as Papeete and Honolulu. Observers including the British naval captain Frederick William Beechey, who visited Rapa Nui in 1825, describe a great hubbub, a disorderly enthusiasm on the part of Islanders, an almost indiscriminate eagerness for whatever European goods they could catch at. Unusually for Polynesia, for the period, it was reported that the people had evidently had 'so little communication with Europeans . . . that we did not perceive any European cloth among them'.[6] There were no beachcombers, no resident Europeans to mediate contact. No white missionary from any denomination sought to establish himself on the island before the 1860s. Nor even did the London Missionary Society try to send Tahitian teachers, probably because ships that might enable them to be landed and from time to time visited were not known to be calling at the island. Certainly, a few Rapa Nui joined whaleships and travelled. One man, 'Henry Easter', even reached London around the same time as Tapioi, and was baptized at Rotherhithe church.[7] By mid-century a good number of others must have done so, though of these just a few are likely to have returned. Whereas Tahitians and Hawaiians who travelled could return to their homes relatively easily if they wished to do so, because Papeete and Honolulu were intended destinations for many ships, those vessels that stopped at Rapa Nui did so as often by accident as by design.

By the 1850s Islanders in various parts of the Pacific were being not only contacted, in some cases converted, but also, in a more profound and damaging sense, colonized. In New Zealand, New Caledonia and the Society Islands their sovereignty had been eclipsed by formal annexation. In Hawaii and elsewhere their lands were rapidly being alienated, and in many places their labour was sought. Even in the scattered islands of the Tuamotus, a cross-cultural economy of occasional barter was giving way to a regular business in pearls and pearlshell. But Rapa Nui had no lands suitable for coconut plantations, no sandalwood, nothing to mine, and no reefs, hence no pearls and no bêche-de-mer. Sexual contacts were inaugurated early on, venereal and other infections had been introduced, and the population had certainly declined, to some extent, though probably to nothing like the extent witnessed in the Societies or the Marquesas. Rapa Nui was 'neglected' in the sense that it was insulated from much of what Islanders elsewhere had suffered. But such insulation as had sheltered these Islanders was to be punctured, suddenly and catastrophically.

* * *

The Spanish colony of Peru gained its independence in 1824. The settler economy depended on plantations and the plantations depended on labour – the labour, until 1854, of slaves of African descent. Bonded labourers from China were trafficked into the country and their contracts auctioned, but it quickly became apparent that they were treated essentially as slaves, and the system was prohibited, only to be reintroduced in 1861, after pressure from politically influential plantation owners. But so discredited had the Asian indenture system become, both in Peru and east Asia itself, that the flow of new workers was insufficient to sustain what was then a rapidly growing economy.[8]

J.C. Byrne was a colonial speculator of Irish origin. He had twenty years' experience in launching almost invariably unsuccessful ventures, involving both the emigration of white settlers and the importation of native labour, to a number of colonies. His schemes had embraced the southern hemisphere, from Natal to Australia via Mauritius, and from New Caledonia to Brazil, via the then New Hebrides, where he tried to act as a broker in the establishment of a Belgian colony. He was a man of his time: quick to see opportunities, quick to act upon them, unconcerned that he might lack expertise in the business at hand. He was frequently unable to pay his debts, and hence compelled to move on, but must at times have been persuasive. When he reached Lima he quickly recognized the urgency of the labour question, and proposed the importation of workers from the western Pacific. He claimed that he had considerable experience in recruiting in the region, signing up natives from Vanuatu to work in New Caledonia, and that the Islanders were eager to work and easily recruited. In fact, he had never set foot on any island in Vanuatu, nor on New Caledonian soil, but the plan was music to the ears of the Peruvian administrators who saw nothing but a minefield in further attempts to bring immigrant workers from Asia. Though ill, Byrne, together with one B.D. Clark, an American who shared his experience of bankruptcy proceedings, was given permission to introduce 'colonists', as the workers were euphemistically described, from the south-western Pacific. The partners moved quickly, perhaps suspecting that support for their scheme might not remain in place for long.[9]

They proceeded to charter a ship named the *Adelante* to undertake a trial voyage. Having spent time in Australia, Byrne was well aware of the characterizations of Melanesians current at the time – the killers of John Williams, and the perpetrators of various other outrages, they were perceived as savage and intractable. The ship was fitted out, not in a fashion consistent with a complement of willing passengers, but on the assumption that those recruited might be detained or put down by force. The hold was divided by iron gratings and swivel guns were mounted, so that men on the deck could be mown down if need be. Four extra crew members were signed on specifically as guards, and the ship carried an abundance of weaponry that would not have been out of place on a man-o'-war.

En route to the south-western Pacific, the ship called at the Marquesas and then at Tongareva in the northern Cook Islands. Quite what bloodshed would have ensued, had the *Adelante* ever reached Vanuatu, is unpleasant to imagine, but Byrne, from his perspective fortuitously, came upon an island where Polynesians happened to be starving – atoll environments were fragile at the best of times, and on Tongareva coconut palms had been affected by a blight, resulting in widespread desperation among the people. Unsuspecting mission teachers encouraged Islanders to join the ship, and some 250 men, women and children were soon signed up. The ship returned to Lima and soon sold them (or, formally, their contracts) off, some as domestic workers, some as agricultural labourers. The profit from the venture has been estimated at twenty to thirty thousand US dollars, an extraordinary sum at the time. Byrne had died on the voyage back, but other merchants around the port of Callao outside Lima rushed to enter the business: they had little notion of what they were getting into, and certainly no understanding that this first group of willing 'colonists' had been recruited in exceptional circumstances.[10]

Within three weeks of the *Adelante*'s return some seven ships had been swiftly refitted and sent out on recruiting voyages. The *Adelante* itself returned to Tongareva and collected most of those who remained, leaving only forty in one village, where the mission teacher feared for what might become of them, and dissauded his people from joining the ship. Another forty-eight, who were mainly infants or the elderly, also remained on the island. The upshot of the two visits was that, of a population of around seven hundred prior to these visits, some two-thirds were removed to Peru. Over the period from September 1862 to April 1863 about thirty-two ships attempted to recruit 'colonists' in the Islands. Several made more than one trip, hence at least thirty-seven voyages were undertaken. About half of these were 'successes' from the perspective of the speculators who financed them. Yet on only two islands did any number of people join a ship willingly. The first of these islands was Tongareva. The second was Rapa Nui.

Beginning in October 1862, three Chilean ships called at Rapa Nui in quick succession, shipping 154, 115 and 238 Islanders who, observers such as the British Consul in Callao considered, appeared to have joined freely.[11] This is not inherently implausible. From the 1790s onward, Islanders from Hawaii and Tahiti in particular were often willing to join ships, and typically, several Islanders might be among the crew of any particular vessel. They were often allowed to depart from ships at islands when they wished to do so, or at any rate had no difficulty in deserting if necessary. In other words, they did not face departing permanently from Polynesian milieux, they perhaps escaped tensions or oppressions in their home community, and they might gain special status as immigrants in other island communities, as the Hawaiians certainly did on Tahiti. Or, if they returned home, they had the chance of capitalizing in whatever ways on their experience elsewhere. More simply, Islanders were often outward-looking.

Yet it was one thing for a few men to join a ship and another for a community to embrace mass emigration, or to tolerate the emigration of many people – though this too was not unprecedented. During periods of famine, in the Marquesas for example, it was known that whole families or groups of families might load their belongings, and even domestic animals, into seagoing canoes and depart in search of new homes.[12] The Rapanui appear not, in late 1862, to have been suffering the effects of any specific famine, but life was certainly harder for them than for most Pacific communities of the period. The island was from time to time affected by drought, garden food was never abundant, and there was a good deal of conflict. In addition, it appears from traditions recorded later, gods and rituals were perceived to be failing, as they had been in the Society Islands fifty years earlier. The situation was not as desperate as it was at Tongareva, but it is understandable that mass emigration might have appeared desirable to the five hundred-odd Islanders who joined the *Bella Margarita*, the *General Prim* and the *Eliza Mason* in late 1862.

Of these merchants, Captain Sasuategui of the *Eliza Mason* at least went through the form of securing the consent of those Rapanui he recruited. Contracts stipulated that each Islander would be provided food, passage, a blanket, cash, medical care and clothing, in return for an agreement to work for eight years. These documents were interpreted and signed, or rather marked, by both the worker and the interpreter. The interpreter would probably have been a Marquesan or Tahitian who would not have spoken Rapanui but could have made himself crudely understood. Yet whatever mutual understanding there may have been could not have prepared these Islanders for the environment into which they would be transported. Such contact as they had had with foreigners in no way enabled them to grasp the realities of continental lands, plantations, or colonial cities. Nor would conversations they might have had with Islander crew from passing ships, or from the two or three Rapanui who had travelled and returned, have prepared them in any way for the long, rigid hours and routine servitude of farm or domestic labour. In other words, even those who the British consul happily thought had 'come of their own free will' were remote from an understanding of what they acquiesced in. In today's jargon, there could be nothing approaching 'informed consent' from these people at this time.

* * *

H.E. Maude's careful calculations suggest that the population of Rapa Nui on the eve of these events was just over four thousand. Out of this number, some five hundred were evidently keen, or at least willing, to embrace the opportunity to leave. But when a further group of labour-recruiting ships arrived, it became apparent that those who remained felt differently about the prospect of emigration. Some eight ships had left Callao in Peru around the same time in early December 1862. They took only a fortnight to reach Rapa Nui, and those which arrived first quickly established that there was little interest among Islanders in coming aboard. On the evening of 22 December the captains met together and plotted to work in concert, to seize as many people as they could.

Early the following morning some eighty crewmen off what had become a slave-raiding fleet were marshalled on the shore and given orders by Captain Marutani, the commander of the largest of the ships, the *Rosa*, who had assumed leadership of the operation. Some of the men were to disperse and wander nonchalantly about, like any other seamen enjoying shore leave, while others laid out curiosities and trade goods, which Islanders soon congregated around. Many were seated or on their knees, examining what was on offer. Marutani abruptly fired his pistol into the air, a signal to the sailors, all of whom were armed, to join in a volley intended to terrorize the locals, which it effectively did – not least because about ten Islanders were shot dead in the course of what was supposed to be fire into the air. People ran in all directions, shouting and screaming, some into the sea, some heading inland to the shelter of gullies and rocks. Sailors seized and bound anyone they could lay their hands on, and having captured as many as they could in the vicinity of the beach, moved inland and scoured the area for those who had hidden.

Notoriously, one Aguirre, the captain of the smallest of the ships, the *Cora*, cornered two Islanders in a tight gully, but was unable to persuade them, or force them at gunpoint, to surrender themselves to him. Frustrated, he shot them dead, a witness would later testify before an inquiry conducted at Papeete.[13]

A follow-up raid was undertaken the next day, but on this occasion people were prepared, as they were for a further attempt on Christmas Day 1862. Islanders fired brush near the shore and withdrew to the interior. The ships abandoned the effort to kidnap further Islanders and withdrew, having seized 349 Rapanui. Of these, one elderly woman was thrown overboard, far from land, by a supercargo who considered her too old to sell.

Over January and February further ships out of Callao made new assaults on the island. Not all were successful, but both the *Rosalia* and the *Teresa* each brought around two hundred men, women and children back to Callao. How the *Rosalia* obtained her 'colonists' is unknown, but it appears that those captured by the *Teresa* ventured on board to trade. As soon as the decks were crowded, the ship abruptly made sail. In all likelihood, those on board were restrained or confined until the vessel was well away from the island. In March two ships acted in concert, employing the methods of the December raid, threatening and shooting people ashore, and seized around a hundred more Islanders. At the end of April – the activities of the Peru-based traders at Rapa Nui and elsewhere having become known and thoroughly discredited – the authorities in Lima prohibited all operations to import Pacific Islanders. Two ships that at this time were already at sea returned later, however, with a further fifty-four captives from Rapa Nui between them.

* * *

The documented total of all Rapanui 'freely' recruited or kidnapped is, 1407. This actual figure of those removed from the island is likely to be higher, because the count is based in part on numbers of those who reached Callao, and does not include those who died during the voyage. In any event, more than a third of the population of the island either left or were abducted, over a period of just six months.

Peruvian slaving ships were active over the same period in many other parts of the Pacific – in the Marquesas, the Tuamotus, the Austral and Cook Islands, Niue, Samoa, and the atolls of the Tokalaus and Gilberts. In some cases their efforts were happily incompetent. On Mangareva they were blocked by the formidable and autocratic Catholic priest, Honoré Laval. In the Tuamotus the *Mercedes* succeeded in recruiting some 150 men from various islands (who were used to travelling for pearl-diving and similar work), but the ship in this case made the error of working in the French Oceanic territories and was intercepted by a French steamer, taken to Papeete and impounded. The Tuamotuans were subsequently freed.

On a couple of islands in the northern Cooks, however, over a hundred people were induced on board, and in May 1863 the *Dolores Carolina* left the atoll of Nukulaelae, part of the Tuvalu group, with 250 Islanders. These people, who had converted to Christianity, more or less on their own initiative, and in the absence of any white or Islander missionary, were anxiously awaiting a pastor, and were persuaded to join the ship, being told that they would merely be taken to a nearby island for six months, during which time they would work making coconut oil, while being given Christian instruction. At the end of the period they would be repatriated with Christian teachers and a considerable quantity of property. For these people the lotu evidently had the cultish appeal that it had, always only ephemerally, at one time or another in many parts of the Pacific. Their eagerness to engage with or appropriate the cult was such that they fell for the deception, and the small island's population was depleted by almost 80 percent. On a number of islands this sort of deception, rather than forcible entrapment, brought recruits on board.

Of the eight ships that had participated in the Rapa Nui raid, two took the bulk of those seized back to Callao and the others proceeded to the west, seeking further captives. They planned to rendezvous at Rapa, the most remote of the Austral Islands, some thousand kilometres south of Tahiti, which no doubt appealed to their seamen as a suitably obscure theatre for their overtly piratical methods. But the Rapans knew more than the Rapanui had done of the worst aspect of European intrusion. Very likely the extraordinary tale of Fletcher Christian's invasion of neighbouring Tupuai and effort to establish a colony for the *Bounty* mutineers there had entered local tradition. There had been beachcombers on the island, who naturally shared stories with their hosts, and were not usually the sort of men concerned to whitewash white civilization or its empires. In any event they were suspicious and easily eluded the Peruvians, who soon departed.

The smallest of the ships, Aguirre's *Cora*, was however running behind the fleet and only arrived after the others had left. Among this ship's crew was a Samoan, who told a local man that one Rapa Nui boy was imprisoned aboard. The local man, named Mairoto, had served in French forces and received a medal for his part in helping deal with an earlier disorder on Tahiti. He acted quickly, convening a meeting of the island's chiefs. They determined that they would take the ship, and deliver it to the authorities on Tahiti. Captain Aguirre, the man who had casually shot at least a couple of Rapanui, was in no way prepared for such a bold initiative on the part of any natives. Islanders with concealed weapons came on board the ship, took him and his crew by surprise, and had the vessel secured without difficulty. Some crew, either disgusted by what they had been involved in, or unwilling to be implicated, assisted the Rapans or at any rate did nothing to resist them. The bulk of the crew remained on the island while a few helped Mairoto and other Rapans take the ship and captain to Tahiti. It arrived on 17 February shortly before the proceedings against the captain and officers of the *Mercedes* were due to commence. The concatenation of events was, needless to say, the talk of the town; they aroused great interest among both Society Islanders and colonists, and were in due course reported in Australia and elsewhere.[14]

* * *

A succession of inquiries and trials ensued, and though Captain Aguirre and others off the *Cora* did their best to conceal and deny the facts of the Rapa Nui raid, George Nichols, the American carpenter of the *Guillermo*, who appears genuinely to have been disgusted by the venture, and who had deserted at Rapa, gave a fairly full narrative. It was he who had seen Aguirre shoot the two Islanders who would not surrender themselves, and he who had witnessed the supercargo on his own ship, 'after deliberation' with the captain, throwing the old woman overboard. Much of his account was corroborated by one Robert Fletcher, apparently a Scot, and cook on the same ship. Other witnesses including the Rapan Tamatamihi spoke of what took place when the fleet reached his own island:

A. I was on the beach with a black man [a beachcomber] who lives on our island and who speaks Spanish. They asked him if there were many inhabitants on our island, he said yes, but they lived elsewhere. These men asked me to go and get them, as they wished to give everyone a big dinner on board. Knowing that people on other islands had been seized, and being suspicious, I refused. Suddenly two men jumped on me and tried to get me into one of the boats, but the black called out that the bush was full of armed Islanders. The sailors were frightened and they let me go. The five ships left two or three days later, and after that the Cora arrived.

Q. Did the crew of the Cora commit acts of violence on shore?

A. No. They just wanted to get people to leave, to work in another land. But no-one agreed to do so.[15]

The investigations into the activities of the *Mercedes* revealed that the plan had been to take the Tuamotuans to Chincha Island off the Peruvian coast to mine guano there. It was known in Tahiti that work conditions on these islands were horrific, that the Chinese indentured workers were kept in irons, and that no small numbers had killed themselves, throwing themselves over cliffs, unable to face struggling on. This information stunned and shocked the Tuamotuans, some of whom were present at the hearings in Papeete. For once, the French were able to play the part of humanitarians, acting decisively to suppress these outrages, and at the same time affirm their status as the responsible European power, in eastern Polynesia.

* * *

The entrepreneurs behind the *Mercedes*'s voyage certainly intended to take the Islanders they recruited to Chincha. But they were prevented from doing so, the people were freed, and the ship and its effects sold off by the authorities in Tahiti. Aguirre and one or two of his accomplices were permitted to slip away on an American trader, and he never faced any sort of justice for the murders he was alleged to have committed or for his part in the December raids at Rapa Nui.

The publicity given to the case of the *Mercedes* engendered a widespread misunderstanding, which has persisted up to the present, that the recruited and kidnapped Polynesians were in general made to work as slaves in the Chincha group. In fact, all those who reached Peru were sold as domestic or agricultural workers. The only firm evidence that Islanders worked in the guano diggings remains the find, on one of the islands, of what is indisputably a Rapa Nui carving. The figure, which passed through various hands before it was donated to the British Museum in 1872, could have reached the guano diggings in various ways at various times, but it is most likely that some Islander or Islanders contracted to work on plantations on the mainland nearby, were sold on, or having escaped, were rounded up and taken to the island some time in 1863 or soon afterwards.[16] The find suggests too that at least one Rapa Nui man or perhaps woman – presumably one from the first wave of 'voluntary' recruits, rather than those who were kidnapped during the raids, who could hardly have had much in the way of personal possessions with them – chose to carry what was presumably a treasured ancestral figure, and carried it to this hellish and poisonous place, in all likelihood the end of his or her journey.

If all but a few Rapanui, if the Polynesian labourers generally, were spared the horrific conditions of the Chincha Islands, they nevertheless coped as poorly as might be expected, in Peru. Byrnes's rhetoric – his claim that the Islanders would be docile and would be excellent workers – was utterly false. Those in domestic service suffered isolation, since they were split up one from the other. If the environment, dominant language and diet were alien, and the work arduous and demoralizing, they were moreover exposed to new diseases and infections. It may be relevant in this context that most of those who reached Peru were from more or less isolated islands, not, say, the Societies or Hawaii. If the vulnerability of various Pacific populations to various infections over time is hard to gauge, Tongarevans and Rapanui had been far less visited than the inhabitants of the better-known islands, and can only have been at greater risk. In any event the ramifications were catastrophic. Suffering from fevers and various gut and lung infections – dysentery, tuberculosis and notably smallpox – the Islanders died by the score.[17]

Plantation owners made no effort to train Islanders or ease them into farm work, but instead pressed them into the routine previously imposed on slaves – a twelve-hour day – leading to acute demoralization and swiftly to mass fatalities. A tour of inspection made by an agent of the French Embassy in Lima, accompanied by a Marquesan interpreter, reported that in one case a group of thirteen workers had all died, and that in another, out of thirty-two, just two survived. Beatings had, it appeared, been routine, living conditions were appalling, medical help non-existent. It was not known that a single Islander worker had survived in Peru for more than six months.

Liberal opinion and the liberal press in Peru swiftly turned against a trade that had clearly been profoundly misrepresented. By mid-1863 the Peruvian authorities accepted that those Islanders still alive should be repatriated. But Lima was in the grip of a smallpox epidemic and those awaiting transport were crowded together in an unhealthy warehouse. On 20 July one ship, the *Diamant*, took twenty-nine Islanders to Taiohae, Nukuhiva. Their arrival resulted tragically in an epidemic that would kill nearly a thousand on that island as well as six hundred on neighbouring Ua Pou. The main ship charged with repatriating captives, the *Barbara Gomez*, suffered acute losses from the same disease prior to even leaving Callao. Of 470 intended passengers only 318 survived at the time of departure. Out of about a hundred people from Rapa Nui, only fifteen were still alive by the time the ship reached that island. No consideration appears to have been given to quarantining them elsewhere, though uninhabited islands in this part of the Pacific, such as Juan Fernandez, were well known to mariners. Once landed in Rapa Nui, they inevitably made contact with friends and kin, and smallpox swiftly killed around a thousand of those who had remained on the island after the raids. Between the raids and the epidemic, it appears that a population of roughly 4,200 had been reduced to about 1,750 within a year.

The *Barbara Gomez* proceeded westward, with a view to repatriating those Islanders still aboard. This ship's voyage must surely have been the most dreadful the Pacific had known. In due course the vessel reached Rapa. Four hundred and thirty-nine of the original four hundred and seventy passengers were dead, the bulk thrown overboard en route. The remaining sixteen, who were all ill, were originally from various islands in the northern Cooks and elsewhere, but were left at Rapa, where locals cared for them but became infected themselves. Here the infection led to the loss of some 240, or two-thirds of the small population of this island. In due course what is presumed to have been dysentery was carried elsewhere, resulting in many further deaths in various parts of the Austral and Society Islands.

* * *

Among Islanders the raids were recalled and mourned for generations after-wards. Just a handful of Islanders who returned survived the impact of subse-quent disease. In no case were their stories recorded in any full way, or in their own words. The recollections of Taole, a Niuean, were however written down by John Lupo, a Samoan mission teacher, resident on Niue from the 1860s onward. He wrote a history of Niue which included a section entitled 'The Man-Stealing Ships'. This recorded that the second of the Callao vessels that raided the island targeted the village of Avatele, where forty men were seized. Among them was Taole, son of Hengotule, the blind chief of the village. Once on board the men, who had ventured to the ship to trade, 'were thrust down into the dark hold and the hatches were fastened . . . the prisoners became wild with fear'. Some broke out onto the deck and fought with some of the sailors, and some were able to jump overboard and swim ashore. 'The loud cries of the bereaved ones ashore rose in the villages. As for the prisoners down in the dark hold of the slave ship, they wept and wailed aloud when they found that they were carried off, and lamented with streaming tears their lost home.' The ship raided further, in the Tokelau islands, and by the time it even-tually reached Callao many had died, their bodies thrown overboard:

> At Callao, Taole and his brother and all the other men were sold to the people on shore, who set them to work, some at digging out guano on the islands. They worked every day, every day. They got no pay. They were worked till they nearly died. Guards watched them continually. Taole and his brother were set to work in Callao. They worked near the roadway.[18]

In town, and presumably not far from the port, an opportunity to escape arose. An American whaler crewed by Hawaiians called in, Taole spoke with them, and persuaded the captain to take him away. At the appointed time he mingled with a group of the seamen, who had brought a set of sailor's clothes which he hastily changed into, and walked off past his inattentive guards. As he reached the beach, the guards discovered his absence and rushed in pursuit, but too late – he was in a boat, and once he was on board, the ship swiftly made way – or so the story goes. On board this ship, Taole subsequently travelled into Arctic waters, suffered the extreme cold, and then to Honolulu, where he left the vessel. He then 'shipped for one of Mr Arundel's guano islands, where other Niuean men were at work'. This was possibly Starbuck, an uninhabited island in the Line group; John Arundel was the son of an LMS missionary who had established himself in Pacific commerce. In due course Taole returned from this island to Niue, the only one of some 109 'stolen people' ever to reach home.

* * *

Eugène Eyraud, a Catholic missionary acting individually, landed on Rapa Nui early in 1864, and an official mission followed in 1866. The latter establishment included several teachers from Honoré Laval's station at Mangareva, who, like the 'native missionaries' of the LMS, more easily communicated and built rapport with the locals. The fathers reported to their superiors on the state of the population in the aftermath of the smallpox epidemic. Yet there is really no account that enables an understanding of how the events of 1862–3 were seen and felt by the Islanders. Though it is hard to say what more detailed observations, what interviews even, could possibly add. If the facts of these events could be baldly described, the experience of them, and the psychological consequences of that experience, could surely not. Rapanui were no strangers to hardship. The population had suffered the distress of conflict, disease and famine during the first half of the nineteenth century and before. But the sudden violence of the raids, the void left by those taken away, and the awful attrition of life that followed were surely incomprehensible. It has often been stated that the events killed off the island's culture, that they marked the 'final annihilation' of the old society.[19] Yet as had been the case elsewhere, surviving Islanders faced the most awful of circumstances with a certain resilience, and a community was gradually rebuilt, that as it were faced this history.

The mission made, from the Catholic perspective, considerable 'progress' – within a few years virtually all Rapanui became adherents – but was no match for unscrupulous settlers who arrived soon afterwards, bought up lands, made war on those who refused to relinquish their property, and preyed upon local girls. In June 1871 the station was abandoned and, according to reports at the time, the entire indigenous population would have been happy to leave with the Catholics. Only about 275 could be accommodated on the ship, more than half settled on Mangareva, others went on to Tahiti, and still others followed them subsequently. The day of emigration has been considered 'one of the saddest' in Rapa Nui's history, leaving the place 'a ghost isle'.[20] Which is perhaps to miss a point fundamental to the whole of Pacific history. From the earliest human ventures east from New Guinea into unknown waters, through the sophisticated navigations between the great Polynesian archipelagoes, to the anxious departures of those facing famine, voyaging could mean gain, not just loss. If it certainly entailed risk, it offered a path toward survival, toward new lands, new homes and new lives.

* * *

By the time of the exodus, no more than about five hundred Rapanui survived, meaning that close to 90 percent of the population had gone in less than a decade. Those who died included elders, priests and experts, and much cultural knowledge must have been lost. Yet those travellers and ethnologists who later engaged in patient, sympathetic and systematic enquiries were able to record a surprisingly rich range of traditions, and to reconstruct areas of the ancient culture in some detail – even if some of the information gathered, in the early twentieth century especially, reflected interaction with other Islanders, a partial rejuvenation of Rapanui culture stimulated by experience elsewhere.[21]

Notwithstanding a surprising resilience in local knowledge, scientists and others were seduced by the notion that Easter Island was 'mysterious'. Back in the eighteenth century, Cook and his companions had correctly grasped that the Rapanui were closely related to other Polynesians they had encountered – the affinities of language were unmistakable, and they recognized other commonalities such as tattooing that, astonishingly, linked these people with Tahitians, Tongans and Maori, half an ocean away. These early visitors were struck by the great statues, but understood that they represented deceased chiefs. Their sensible if unavoidably superficial observations did not, however, set the tone for later interest in the island. Some nonsensical speculation invoked a lost continent, but ostensibly serious inquiry searched out implausible cultural affinities with whichever ancient civilization most appealed. There was never any true 'mystery' about the *ahu moai*, which are remarkable elaborations, but elaborations none the less, of closely related stone sculptures commemorating potent ancestors, that in one form or another are found across eastern Polynesia, and that have counterparts too in many cultures right across the Pacific.

41 *Rongorongo* board, Rapa Nui, late nineteenth century.

There was, however, another mystery, a genuine mystery in Rapa Nui culture, that concerned certain rongorongo boards. It was one that seized the imagination of a host of interested outsiders, before lapsing into arcane academic obscurity. Shortly after his first visit to the island in 1864, Eyraud had reported in detail to his superiors back in Paris. Though he was mainly concerned to drum up support for a formal mission establishment, he dedicated one paragraph to a singular discovery. In 'all' of the houses, he wrote, he had found 'wooden tablets or staffs covered with sorts of hieroglyphic characters'. He was unsure of the meaning of the characters but considered that they amounted to a 'script'. His report found its way into the major missionary journal, the *Annales de la Propagation de la Foi*, and (presumably because it provided one of the first detailed descriptions of the island since the eighteenth century) was translated in *Globus*, the German geographical journal, in the same year, 1866. By the early 1870s further reports, and tracings of boards of the sort he had referred to, that had been sent to Santiago, had reached Europe. The news was considered sensational in anthropological circles. Announcements were made at meetings of bodies such as the Ethnological Society in London, and Adolf Bastian, director of the Museum für Völkerkunde in Berlin, and the most influential German anthropologist of the time, was among those captivated.[22]

In *Moby Dick* Herman Melville had evoked the tattoos of Queequeg, his Polynesian sailor-traveller, his Oceanic Odysseus, 'the work of a departed prophet and seer of his island, who by those hieroglyphic marks, had written out on his body a complete theory of the heavens and the earth, and a mystical treatise on the art of attaining truth; so that Queequeg in his own proper person was a riddle to unfold, a wondrous work in one volume, but whose mysteries not even himself could read'.[23] An esoteric writing system, an ancient cryptography, seems to have been an object of excessive fascination – more fascinating, in fact, than any text that could be read, more intriguing than the Polynesian myths that were beginning to be documented, by more literate and anthropologically minded missionaries in various parts of the Pacific. Bastian and others were also, like most scientific intellectuals of the period, profoundly influenced by evolutionary ideas. The rongorongo boards, or 'wooden tablets', were captivating not only because their script was cryptic, but also because it surely represented an 'early' or 'primitive' writing system, which nevertheless suggested a higher order of culture and civilization than had otherwise been known to exist in the Pacific. Hence the boards also represented a rich field for philology, for a comparative tracking of motifs and meanings, that might enable a researcher to trace hitherto unsuspected ancient migrations.

The treasure was there to be unlocked. But the tragedy was that the key appeared to have been lost. Right from the start, Eyraud suspected that the Rapanui he had encountered in 1864 no longer had the capacity to 'read' the rongorongo. Bishop Jaussen in Tahiti, one of a number of ethnologically minded Catholics in Polynesia in the period, struggled to induce Rapanui in his household and who he otherwise knew to help him decipher the script, but his best informant freely acknowledged that he did not know the motifs' significance. What he could do, and what he did, was to perform: he held the board and chanted, as he understood experts in the old days had done. This was perhaps the first, but certainly not the last, time that these sorts of scenes were played out. Rapa Nui men, who no doubt valued their ancient traditions, tried to help interested Europeans, and volunteered versions of rongorongo meanings, which turned out to be inconsistent. What they did, it seemed, was recite something appropriate from the script, rather than read it.

In 1886 the USS *Mohican* was despatched to undertake scientific investigations on Easter Island. The Paymaster, William Thomson, had experience in the investigation of antiquities, and though the ship could remain at the island for just thirteen days, he was tirelessly, indeed relentlessly, inquisitive for the duration of that short period. His report ranged over a host of topics, but he was most exercised by the rongorongo question, and despite being told initially that no inscribed boards remained on the island, he learned of two, which 'were finally purchased after a great deal of trouble and expense'.[24] He established also that:

> Hotu-Matua, the first king, possessed the knowledge of this written language, and brought with him to the island sixty-seven tablets containing allegories, traditions, genealogical tables, and proverbs relating to the land from which he had migrated. A knowledge of the written characters was confined to the royal family, the chiefs of the six districts into which the island was divided, sons of those chiefs, and certain priests or teachers, but the people were assembled at Anekena Bay once each year to hear all of the tablets read. The feast of the tablets was regarded as their most important fête day . . .[25]

Thomson then embarked on a hunt. He wanted the tablets he had obtained deciphered. At first the quest appeared hopeless. But he then established that an old man named Ure Va'e Iko possessed knowledge dating back to the eve of the slave raids. Ure, however, exhibited great reluctance to assist the Americans, and declined various offers of payment, claiming among other things that the revelation of information had been 'forbidden by the priests', referring, presumably to the old local priests, rather than the Catholic fathers who had left and were never to re-establish their mission. Ure rejected gifts, ran away, and clearly aimed to keep his distance from the visitors for the remainder of their stay. But one evening a storm broke and he returned to his house. Thomson, who would not take no for an answer, found him at home asleep, woke the poor fellow, and again tried to cajole him into playing informant. 'When he found escape impossible he became sullen, and refused to look at or touch a tablet.'[26] Eventually, not having any choice, Ure acquiesced, and an all-night session of recitation ensued. Thomson, however, was suspicious: he considered that the Islander was not actually reading from the rongorongo, and at the conclusion of the chant told the old man that he considered him a fraud.

Ure protested, and Thomson subjected him to an examination, finding that though he claimed 'that the characters were all understood', 'he could not give the significance of hieroglyphs copied indiscriminately'. The man was, it seems, challenged further, and in due course explained 'that the actual value and significance of the symbols had been forgotten, but the tablets were recognized by unmistakable features and the interpretation of them was beyond question; just as a person might recognize a book in a foreign language and be perfectly sure of the contents without being able to actually read it.'[27] What on Thomson's own account was plainly a coercive inquisition hardly constituted an ideal occasion for the revelation of old and sacred knowledge. The fact that strong drink was offered as an inducement, and consumed pretty liberally not only by Ure himself but by those asking him questions and taking down his chants and answers, compounds the sense that the night had more the character of a wartime interrogation than an ethnographic interview, yet the most painstaking and exhaustive of recent investigations of rongorongo considers Ure's texts to be more suggestive than any other recorded rendering of the script, indeed as the key to their decipherment.

* * *

The rongorongo boards excited missionaries, travellers and ethnologists in part because they knew of nothing else like them, in any other area of the Pacific. Though a variety of mnemonic devices, such as knotted strings, are reported, and though rock engravings (which on Rapa Nui shared motifs with rongorongo) had in some cases a pictorial, storytelling aspect, nothing approaching a script was otherwise documented.

Those who sought to decode the script, in the late nineteenth century and subsequently, almost all presumed that the writing system was an ancient one, brought perhaps by the first Polynesian settlers of the island, or some other earlier or intermixing immigrant population, the identity of which, needless to say, was a favourite topic for pseudo-scientific speculation. What none of these investigators did, however, was closely read the earliest voyage records, such as those from Cook's and La Pérouse's visits. These sojourns were not extended, but the Europeans did spend many hours ashore, touring the island, examining gardens, houses and the *ahu moai*. The visits were also, relatively speaking, peaceful; naturalists and sailors engaged a good deal with Islanders, artists made sketches, gifts were exchanged, and there were sexual contacts.

These observers were interested in local arts and crafts; this was one of the topics they would remark on wherever they visited, but no mention whatsoever was made of anything like a rongorongo board, though other well-known genres of Rapanui art were described and collected. The artefacts acquired included sacred images, ancestral figures and the like, hence there is no evidence that Rapanui willingly bartered certain things but held back others. It is worth mentioning here that however sacred objects were in Polynesia, they were never secret, as was the case in New Guinea and Aboriginal Australia. To the contrary, divine images were paraded, they exemplified and displayed power, and it was consistently the case, across Polynesia during the late eighteenth century, and over the first half of the nineteenth, that an extraordinary array of highly valued objects of religious significance were revealed to visitors, and indeed traded with them. So it is perplexing that important objects might have existed, that considerable numbers of them might have existed, yet were never seen by these visitors. All the more so, because the parties consisted not only of ordinary sailors and officers but naturalists, who were passionately interested in anthropological topics, and alert to languages, to what was then called comparative philology. If George and Johann Reinhold Forster, who accompanied Cook, had sighted any form of indigenous script, they would without doubt have described such artefacts and inscriptions at length, and no doubt speculated themselves, about the origins and significance of such discoveries.

The mariners who visited Rapa Nui during the nineteenth century lacked, for the most part, the anthropologically minded curiosity of the Spanish, Cook and La Pérouse, and their accounts are typically also much briefer. Yet there is an artefactual record of their visits as well as a documentary one. Many trafficked for curiosities – Rapa Nui people had little else to trade – and it is notable that rongorongo are not only not mentioned, prior to Eyraud's 1864 report, but that none are attributable to any collections made before that date.

Negative evidence, needless to say, can never be definitive, but there are strong grounds for considering that rongorongo were not observed earlier because they did not exist earlier, they were in fact not part of Rapa Nui's customary, pre-European culture.[28] Late nineteenth- and early twentieth-century ethnologists were quick to claim that an indigenous culture was dying or dead, but failed to recognize that contact with Europeans was not always just corrosive or destructive, that it might positively stimulate innovative cultural forms.

It is well known that Rapa Nui ritual was changing dramatically over the century or so that followed Roggeveen's 1722 visit. When he made his observations, the bulk of the moai were still standing and it is presumed that the ancient chiefly system prevailed. It was over the fifty or so subsequent years that warfare appears to have intensified, with the result that by the time of Cook's visit many of the great statues had been overturned. None of the explorers spent long enough on the island to gain any sense of what sorts of rituals, performances and leadership loomed large in Islanders' lives, but there is broad agreement that a novel cult had emerged. This centered on the *tangata manu*, or birdman, the winner of a race to obtain the first frigate-bird egg of the season from the rocky offshore islets where the birds nested. Though superficially unlike other Polynesian rites, this was not unrelated to ceremonies around first fruits and harvests, which often celebrated reproduction, life and fertility. Conditions were turbulent, beliefs were changing rapidly. It would not be at all surprising, indeed it would be absolutely consistent with better-documented histories of other Polynesian islands, if new cults – and new artefacts – were emerging, perhaps to be embraced and then abandoned in succession.

Nor would it be at all surprising if a new form of script loosely emulated European writing. We have seen that excitement around literacy loomed large in Tahiti, most notably from the time the missionaries arrived. An intense interest in reading, writing and the possession of books was among the motivations that loomed largest, in driving chiefs such as Pomare, and Tahitians more generally, first to associate themselves with the mission and subsequently to formally convert. Similar enthusiasm for literacy is broadly attested to elsewhere in Polynesia, though in many cases Islanders were clearly attracted by a package of Western things and technologies of which scripts, books and teachers were part. In Samoa those who lacked access to Islander or white missionaries frequently invented or embraced cults of their own and recruited any available beachcomber, who might perform the missionary role, teaching reading if he were able, and sea shanties if he knew no hymns. Christianity seems often to have attracted Islanders because it represented a route to literacy, rather than vice versa.

When Islanders had the opportunity to appropriate European artefacts, customs, or technologies, they often did so. They bartered for guns, they drank alcohol and they worked diligently with white missionaries or Islanders who were already literate to learn to read and write. But when it was not possible for them to acquire or reproduce the powerful and prestigious foreign forms that interested them, they often created their own versions, for example by carving wooden clubs in the shapes of European swords and knives (in Tonga and Samoa), and by creating structures out of stones or trees, which mimicked ships (in Samoa and on Rapa Nui). Emulation of the form, evidently, was seen to tap some of the prestige, some of the mana, that they had seen demonstrated in European practice.[29]

Like other Polynesians, Rapanui had had sufficient contact with Europeans to become excited by the foreign and keen to capture aspects of it, to make sense and make use of, on their own terms. But unlike others they had little awareness of or access to missionaries, or even beachcombers. They lay beyond the orbit of the London Missionary Society, the contagious enthusiasm that surrounded Christianity, which led even those who were less visited, such as Austral Islanders, Tuamotuans and Tuvaluans to seek teachers. The ripples from the splash perhaps reached them, but Rapanui had no way of tapping this energy. Their response was therefore one of emulation, the invention of forms that for a time empowered and captivated the Islanders themselves, and that would subsequently captivate Europeans.

From the Dutch visit onward, the Rapanui certainly witnessed European officers and naturalists in the acts of writing and sketching, and very likely also saw them consulting books and charts. Islanders were predisposed to be impressed by paper – which appeared to be a fine form of *tapa*, a sacred material – and were also typically engaged or awed by pictorial images such as portraits that they saw drawn, and when they realised that European script incorporated meaning and knowledge. The particular circumstances that may have aroused Rapanui interest in the form cannot now be reconstructed. Interest may have stemmed from what was witnessed on ships off Rapa Nui, from what Europeans were doing on the island, or from books that were sighted or pilfered. It is possible, too, that Rapanui who had visited Tahiti and become caught up in writing and Christian teaching there, started some kind of cult in which forms that mimicked books were central.

It is less likely that this happened early on. Had rongorongo been invented in the 1770s, the form would surely have been remarked upon, and examples would surely have been collected, some time over the decades prior to 1864.[30] And had the cult been established as early as the late eighteenth century, it is unlikely that it would still have been going strong as late as the mid-nineteenth century. Better-documented cases elsewhere suggest that new beliefs typically flourished and withered, or were transformed, in quick succession – a leader might die, or disenchantment set in.[31] Hence some experience in Tahiti or else-where, in perhaps the 1840s or early 1850s, represents the most likely stimulus for the creation of these extraordinary objects. There is no direct evidence for any Rapa Nui man, men, woman, or women travelling away from and returning to the island in this period. But, again going on better-documented histories, it is very likely that some did so, that catechisms, letters, books, prayers, or some-thing else caught the imagination of just one Islander, who probably came back, was sufficiently charismatic to excite others and instructed carvers toward an unprecedented form.

If the specifics of this story are likely always to elude understanding, the balance of probabilities lies very heavily on the side of rongorongo being a post-contact innovation. If this is so, the fascination of the ethnologists in the form exhibits great irony. For Bastian and others, the boards were remarkable, because they instanced an ancient, indeed a primordial script. Rongorongo were indeed remarkable, not as antiquities but as expressions of Polynesian modernity.

CHAPTER EIGHT

✦

Man-o'-war all same old woman!

In the south-western Pacific, Islanders began to work for Europeans from the first years of the nineteenth century. The traders who sought bêche-de-mer and sandalwood neither had the sea slugs gathered, nor the wood cut, by their own crews. In Fiji the captain of a trading ship, or an agent such as William Lockerby, dealt with a chief and it was the chief who was paid, in trade goods rather than cash. The common men who did the actual work were not entering into any sort of labour contract with the white man themselves; they were simply performing work on a collective basis for their chief, as they might at other times have laboured to build a canoe, fortify a village, or gather garden food or fish for a feast. The work they did was no doubt hard but it was short-term and irregular, and it was reciprocated with chiefly largesse. Those who worked would have been offered a feast, as those who work for chiefs, or on communal or church projects, still are in villages across Fiji today.

Traders such as New England men like John Eagleston and Benjamin Vanderford, who visited and revisited Fiji, and spoke Fijian, certainly had an impact, but it was an impact commensurate with the fact that they came and went. Their presence was intermittent, and in many ways Fijian societies and economies carried on as they had. Those who could do so capitalized on new foreign trade, chiefly ambitions were enhanced, and conflict accelerated, but the conception of work, and the place of work in the life of a Fijian man or woman, cannot have been changed profoundly.

One James Paddon, a native of Portsmouth, around thirty years old in the early 1840s, was responsible for the transformation of relations of this type, for a shift of gear in the nature and pace of colonial engagement. He had started out, it is believed, in the Royal Navy, but soon became engaged in one of the largest drug-trafficking operations in world history – the officially sanctioned trade in opium between India and China. It is a sign of the hetero-geneity of life in a colonial world that he commanded a ship owned by one

Heerjeebhoy Rustomjee, a Parsee merchant based in Canton. Paddon happened to witness a cargo of sandalwood being unloaded, and went to the trouble of finding out where the wood came from, and what was paid for it. His interest was aroused, and he aroused Heerjeebhoy's. Their innovation lay not in partic-ipating in the business on what had become the established model, but in an adventurous notion, that they might set up permanent trading bases in the Pacific archipelagoes themselves.[1]

There were, of course, already settlements, and well-established ones, in Honolulu, Papeete and elsewhere. But all of these were in parts of Polynesia where contacts with Islanders had been frequent for fifty years, and where missionaries were well established. It was a novel notion in Melanesia, where it was widely known that Islanders typically resisted prospective intruders. But Paddon was wholly committed to the project. He went to New Zealand, publi-cized his plans, and recruited would-be settlers. Several men who had had offi-cial positions of one sort or another joined him, as did some thirty white men who were described as 'sawyers and woodcutters', and six Maori. Together with sixteen Chinese, whom he had presumably brought from Canton, this group embarked for the then New Hebrides, as Vanuatu was then known, but stopped at Mare in the Loyalty Islands. They arrived on 5 November 1843, and spent a couple of days trading, apparently amicably, with locals, but then both the ship and the party ashore were suddenly attacked. On board, nine of Paddon's men were killed almost immediately, others were injured, and it was only after an extended struggle that the Islanders were forced off the ship. Three of the men who had been ashore were picked up, but the remainder were killed and, Paddon understood, eaten. It was unclear whether the assault was a reaction against some offensive or injurious behaviour on the part of one among Paddon's party, or whether the Mare men simply thought they might seize the ship and its effects.

The would-be colonist was not, however, to be cowed. After briefly visiting Australia he proceeded as he had planned, and arrived at Aneityum in southern Vanuatu in January 1844. Here Paddon was more fortunate. He came upon an uninhabited islet in Anelgauhat harbour which was at once ideally suited to his purposes and considered haunted by the local people, who were happy to sell the place and were not inconvenienced by any alien-ation of lands they used themselves.[2] After an uncertain start – like so many colonial ventures his was under-capitalized – Paddon's began to thrive. He sent loads of sandalwood to China, recruited additional settlers, including even a few families, provisioned whalers and other sandalwood ships, and set up further stations, on the Isle of Pines and elsewhere. Other entrepreneurs, notably Robert Towns, a Sydney settler and capitalist, quickly entered the field, and by the mid-1850s there were a number of rival stations in various parts of Vanuatu, the Loyalties and New Caledonia. The establishment of the French colony in New Caledonia meant greater potential profits, and Paddon was quick to respond, obtaining official contracts to provide supplies for Noumea and subsequently working as an immigration agent, encouraging white settlement from Australia.

What all this led to, which was also novel, was the recruitment of Islander labour. Both Paddon and various itinerant traders called at Tanna to pick up workers, typically wood-cutting parties of twenty or so men. While Hawaiians, Tahitians and others had long been maritime workers, men from southern Vanuatu, the Loyalties and the Isle of Pines made themselves available to an increasing degree as ships' crew. It became common for smaller trading vessels to be crewed largely by Islanders, who might be supervised by just two or three white officers. At the same time, Islanders became involved in these new, shore-based trading operations not only as labourers but as go-betweens, agents and managers. In the early 1860s Paddon's sometime employee, then trader-colonist in his own right, Andrew Henry, worked with one Toriki Rangi, 'a Polynesian of unknown origin' resident on Erramanga, who had greater success than any European in obtaining sandalwood. Over the years stands of the trees dwindled. Toriki worked with one Jonas, possibly another Islander, and between them they organized parties of local woodcutters or bought the wood and sold it on to Henry, for cash on delivery, rather than trade goods. On at least one occasion, Henry owed Toriki something in the order of £300, and was struggling to commission, and have delivered, a small trading boat that the Islander wanted. Toriki was discerning, when it came to vessels, and he had plans to expand his sphere of operations.[3]

Though information on migrant work at this time is sketchy, it is clear that the arrangements involved relatively small groups of men, who were relocated short distances – to neighbouring islands, islands that they already knew or knew of – for periods of a few months. Missionaries were often opposed to recruitment because it undermined their efforts to build and maintain congregations – and it may be that some of those men who were more outward-looking, and interested in what the Church had to offer, also found the prospect of travel and temporary work elsewhere appealing. But their interest aside, these departures and engagements appear not to have caused profound disruption either in the communities men came from or those they entered. Work such as cutting sandalwood was demanding but perhaps not that different to the clearing of new garden land; perhaps it was similarly punctuated by a good deal of rest and conversation, its rhythm like that of activities to which Islanders were accustomed.

It was no doubt well known among Sydney entrepreneurs that arrangements of this kind had worked well for some years, and perhaps only a matter of time before some thought that they might deal with labour shortages in the Australian colonies by bringing Melanesians in significant numbers. Benjamin Boyd was a prominent settler and grazier who thought he paid white men too much to work as 'shepherds' on his farms. In 1847 he sent one ship, the *Royal Sovereign*, in search of labourers, but it was wrecked on Efate in northern Vanuatu and the bulk of the crew were killed. A second vessel, the *Velocity*, was however successful in recruiting some sixty-five men from Tanna, Aneityum and Lifou. These men no doubt assumed that they were agreeing to work of the kind they were familiar with, and when they arrived at Boyd Town – near present-day Eden on the south coast of New South Wales – and discovered that they were expected to walk some hundreds of miles inland to one of Boyd's massive pastoral properties, many simply refused. A good many of those who completed the trek and reached the remote station quickly decided that neither the vast Australian outback, nor the work expected of them, was to their liking, and promptly walked a further four hundred miles to Sydney.[4]

The Islanders' arrival in town provoked anger from diverse points of view. Some charged Boyd with kidnapping or slave-trading. Others were appalled by the presence of people they considered savages in the colony. And still others were angered by what was, after all, an undisguised effort to undercut the wages earned by white men. In the meantime the *Velocity* made a further voyage and collected over forty men from Uvea before sailing toward Tuvalu and Kiribati via Rotuma in search of further recruits. This cruise proved to be drawn out and, for the Islanders, tedious. When the ship called at Rotuma for a second time on the voyage south, the Uveans deserted. Boyd's captain, one Edward Kirsopp, became embroiled in efforts to secure their return, with the result that a local chief who was possibly sheltering the Islanders was shot dead.[5] Subsequent enquiries established that the prospective recruits thought that they were being taken to Sydney simply to see the place, which was not implausible, given that by this time many Islanders ranging from Christian teachers to chiefs had been given passages, or had worked passages, without there being any expectation that they would be required to remain and work in New South Wales, for any extended period.

Although there is no evidence (nor any reason to believe) that Boyd's recruiting ventures entailed the violent seizure of Islanders, those who joined ships were misled. If they were unwelcome in Australia, Australia was in no way attractive to them. Whether acting mainly on philanthropic or racist grounds, or some mix of the two, the colonial authorities quickly made arrangements for the Melanesians to be repatriated. Boyd's ambitious scheme collapsed within months of its inauguration, but had after-effects on the imaginations of many Islanders and the lives of a few.

John Elphinstone Erskine was commander of the *Havannah*, which undertook a surveying voyage in the south-western Pacific in 1849. At Lifu, among the Islanders who came on board the ship were a number 'returned from their forced visit to New South Wales'. 'Their experience had apparently excited the curiosity of their countrymen, although the recollection of the treatment they had met with, left no desire to return in their own persons.' However one boy of fourteen or fifteen insisted that he wished to travel to Sydney, despite being told 'Too much work at Sydney, too little eat!' by one of those who had been there. 'George Havannah', as the boy was called, did in fact sail with Erskine, and in Sydney:

> met a fellow-countrymen, a domestic servant at Balmain, a suburb of Sydney, who induced him to leave the ship and take a similar arrangement. Having ascertained that the boy was in good hands and perfectly contented, I took no steps to induce him to return, and a year afterwards I was accosted by him in the street, in the dress and with the appearance of a smart footman.[6]

During the 1850s and 1860s local recruiting within Vanuatu carried on, and Islander workers were regularly sought for New Caledonia also. In the early 1860s, however, the demand for labour escalated, both in Fiji and in Queensland. The American Civil War of 1861–5 disrupted supplies of cotton to England. Settlers and planters in the colonies were quick to respond, and the scale of colonial engagement in Fiji escalated. Before 1860 the white presence was limited to beachcomber and missionary settlements, but thousands of would-be planters entered the islands during the decade. The bubble quickly burst, but most settlers stayed on, trying maize and other crops. There was little to attract Fijians to plantation work, so those settlers who did more than simply subsist needed to look elsewhere. In Queensland, on a much larger scale, cotton and later sugar cane would be planted. Indigenous Australian peoples had been driven off their lands, decimated by disease, and had never customarily engaged in agricultural work. Again, there was considerable pressure to import labourers.

In this period the practice was virtually unregulated. Outside of New Caledonia and the Loyalties no island group in the south-western Pacific was considered to fall within the jurisdiction of any European power. Indeed apart from Guam, the French Polynesian territories, New Caledonia and New Zealand, which were Spanish, French and British respectively, the islands were informally rather than formally colonized. While contacts were limited to occasional visits by whaleships or other traders, which might or might not involve violence, distant governments could afford to take little interest in what went on. But an epoch of colonial 'contact' was being succeeded by one of greater, more disruptive, and more sustained exploitation. What escalated was not neutral 'interaction', shore-to-ship provisioning of the sort that had gone on for decades, which might entail tension and indeed violence but might also be conducted pretty amicably. Recruiters were seeking, not baskets of yams and coconuts, a pig or two, or a few curiosities that might in due course end up in the drawing rooms or studies of antiquaries. They sought people themselves, who might be willing but who were often not, hence the stage was set for confrontations that could only be explosive.

But the stage was set, too, for the confrontations that did take place to be widely publicized. Colonial violence was nothing new. In the first decades of the nineteenth century, in Fiji for example, traders convinced of the absolute savagery of Islanders killed indiscriminately, and participated in massacres by Fijians of other Fijians. But by the 1860s the environment in the islands was entirely different. Missionaries not only occupied influential positions in many Christian Polynesian societies, but had also established many stations in Vanuatu and New Caledonia, where Presbyterians and the LMS (at first through Islanders such as the missionary Taunga) were active from around 1840 on. In the Solomon Islands the Melanesian Mission had tried its own method, of encouraging individuals to travel to Mission schools in New Zealand and on Norfolk Island. Once considered as converts, and to some degree trained, these Islanders were repatriated in the hope that they might evangelize their own communities, but typically with little or no success. Yet the regular visits the Anglicans made to many communities came to be welcomed, if only for the trade goods that arrived, and if the activity was yet to bear fruit, in the form of a new Christian community, it had quickly created a missionary intelligence-gathering network.[7]

Missionaries were predisposed to be critical of traders and sailors who were seldom known for their temperance, and who sought sexual services, when-ever they could be bought, from local women or from men who appeared to control local women. From the start, also, evangelical missionaries had at least

SOUTH SEA ISLANDERS.

FURTHER CORRESPONDENCE

RESPECTING

THE DEPORTATION OF SOUTH SEA ISLANDERS.

In Continuation of Correspondence presented to Parliament.
[C. 399—1871.] FOREIGN OFFICE PAPERS.

Presented to both Houses of Parliament by Command of Her Majesty,
FEBRUARY, 1872.

LONDON:
PRINTED BY WILLIAM CLOWES & SONS, STAMFORD STREET & CHARING CROSS,
FOR HER MAJESTY'S STATIONERY OFFICE.

1872.
[C. 496.] *Price* 1s. 6d.

42 Title page, *Further Correspondence Respecting the Deportation of South Sea Islanders.*

aspired to be middle class, by the 1860s many genuinely were, and they looked down upon those they considered maritime ruffians, on the grounds of social status as well as morality. When it came to the issue of labour recruiting, missionary minds moreover bore the legacy of the great anti-slavery campaigns. The movement, the high point in every sense of evangelical activism, had, like the Civil Rights campaigns of the 1960s, resonances for decades afterwards. Hence missionaries would not be slow to denounce any form of slavery in the South Seas. Anything that looked like slaving would not only offend them on humanitarian grounds, it also provided a resonant vindication of the missionary presence and the missionary endeavour.

* * *

If these circumstances inflamed debate around recruiting from the 1860s onward, the events that were debated were real, and indeed outrageous by any relevant standards. Like the Callao-based ships a few years earlier, those active first in Vanuatu in the 1860s and the Solomon Islands from around 1870 engaged in both deception and outright kidnapping. Cases of actual abduction were more likely to be reported and followed up, but were not necessarily any less common than those involving the misrepresentation of the labour contract. The ships involved frequently employed as agents 'old Sandalwooders who have acquired a smattering of some of the New Hebrides languages'.

One such was Charles Hyde, 'a native of New York, rather below the middle size, about thirty-five years of age, peering eyes, sallow countenance, sufficiently sunburnt, bloated face, and very emaciated, certainly no great temptation to cannibals, and yet the deceived Erromangans are threatening him to try him in the oven should he fortunately fall into their hands. . . . He remained on this island four or five years, shifting from place to place as circumstances required, for he made himself very odious to the natives by running off with other men's wives, stealing fowls and pigs, and having a hand in killing,' wrote James McNair, the resident Presbyterian on the island of Erramanga. On 6 October 1868 'Charley' had encouraged nine Erramangan men to visit a vessel by telling them that one Captain Joe, a trader known to them and liked, was on board. He was not, and when they boarded they were quickly forced below decks, and the hatches secured.[8]

These people's relatives alerted the missionary to the events and he encouraged the Islanders to seize a boat belonging to the vessel. When George Smith, the captain of the *Latona*, the ship in question, came ashore to recover the boat, he and the missionary argued, Smith denying that anyone had joined him unwillingly, but eventually signing a note undertaking to send the Erramangans ashore, though he did not do so and presumably never intended to do so.

As a result of letters sent to Sydney by McNair, enquiries were made of the Immigration Office in Brisbane. The agent there, John McDonnell, was carefully dismissive of McNair's report. He had visited the *Latona* on its arrival and dealt with the paperwork relating to some seventy-five Melanesians from Mare, Lifu, Tanna and Erramanga. Although the names of individuals had been inconsistently transcribed, it was clear that several of those he registered were the men whose alleged abduction had been reported to McNair. Yet when he had asked them, 'using signs and words', whether the captain 'had stolen or run away with them ... they replied as well as they could in the negative'. McDonnell commented upon the cleanliness of the ship, the abundance of food, and the good character of the owner. The men, he said, 'were in good health, condition, and spirits', and he had no qualms about releasing them for hire. They were promptly hired, to work 'in agricultural occupations' around Logan and Nerang, south of Brisbane, and Maryborough to the north.[9]

Among the Islanders aboard were men 'who had been employed in the colony before', one of whom 'could make himself understood by the Erramangan men'; 'he spoke and made signs in such a way that I could understand him as well'. Not quite a year later, in Britain, the case was the subject of some correspondence between ministers, MPs, and others interested. One, admittedly of the missionary party, asked whether a conversation partly or largely in sign language could really have clarified 'the amount of voluntariness' that the Erramangan men had brought to the original engagement. It was a partisan observation, and one clumsily expressed, but the point was sound. McDonnell's inquiry had proceeded more or less by gesture, and was simply not of a nature that could have enabled him to establish the truth, neither of this nor of any similar case.

A naval vessel that visited Erramanga in mid-1869 reported the testimony of a woman, Walapo, who was both daughter of the local chief and widow of the Polynesian go-between, or entrepreneur, Toriki Rangi. Her connection with Rangi associated her as much with the traders as with the locals, and she had in fact been on board the *Latona* at the time of the disputed incident. 'Charlie seduced on board nine Erramangans, telling them he had plenty of pigs on board for their coming feast, very fat ones; likewise plenty of tobacco. He took them off to the vessel in his own boat, and when they wanted to return to the shore they were put down below under the hatches. They cried a good deal', she recalled. By this time, too, there were reports of several other abductions, all involving different ships, by the same agent, Charles Hyde, and similar inducements of trade in tobacco or pork.[10]

This evidence vindicated McNair, but a point mentioned in passing by McDonnell is significant for how the labour trade is to be understood. The *Latona* carried not only the Erramangans but also Islanders from Mare, Tanna and elsewhere. Some – from which island is unclear – 'had been employed in the colony before, and were returning for further service'.[11] Even at this early stage of recruitment to Queensland, and despite evidently widespread deception and violence at the moment of engagement or abduction, recruits adapted to and endured three years' work, and returned home, but were evidently prepared to sign on again. If the labour was hard, they considered it had compensations, though whether the compensations consisted primarily in the pay and in the trade goods they acquired, or in other aspects of life in Queensland, is unclear. Indeed, whether they were not so much attracted as propelled away from home communities by the stress of routine responsibilities, or by other hardships or oppressions, is likewise uncertain. Their motivations may have been obscure, even at the time, even to themselves. An ethnographic report from Papua New Guinea, on Highlands tribesmen who sought work in town in the early 1970s, found that the individuals concerned were certainly drawn to urban milieux, but were unforthcoming when asked about their motivations, unable even to give a clear account of the circumstances of their travelling to town. It was as if they had a language that valued any number of accomplishments at home but that had no words or reasons for departure, for engagement elsewhere.[12] Those observations may or may not be relevant to the lives of Melanesians a century earlier, but they do remind us that a decision to migrate temporarily or permanently, or to acquiesce in and accept deportation, is always ambivalent and awkward; it suspends and calls into question the most important of one's identifications and attachments, balancing like against unlike, against nebulous but perhaps powerful inducements. Today it is taken for granted that ambivalences like these constitute the predicament of the migrant or refugee in general, but issues of the same sort must have been equally salient for Islanders 140 years ago, whose minds and feelings are inaccessible to us.

* * *

Among the stories that were coming to light, that of the *Latona* was typical, representative of business more or less as usual. Other reports were considerably more shocking. About the same time as the *Latona* was at Erramanga, a Sydney vessel called the *Young Australian* was cruising in search of labour in north Vanuatu. The master was one Albert Hovell; he was assisted by Toriki Rangi, several French seamen, perhaps picked up in Papeete or Noumea, and several Rotumans. One of the French mates, Robert Lennie, had induced three men to come off from the small island of Paama, south of Ambrym, but of these one refused to board the ship when they reached it, rather jumping overboard and swimming away. According to 'Mummy', one of the Rotuman sailors, the boat pursued him, on Lennie's orders, and another Rotuman identified as 'Sam' 'took a boat-hook and hooked the swimming man in the face, making a hole through his cheek. They got him into the boat and flung him down on his back.' Once secured on board, the men were given mats and put down into the hold, but received a hostile reception from men from Efate, Tanna and Rotuma, who had already been recruited. 'The wounded man demanded to be put on shore, and tried to get on deck, but was flung back again; he tried again to get up, but was again flung back.' A fight then broke out, arrows were shot about, and recruits and seamen alike were injured.[13]

Hovell made some attempt to calm the Paama men, but it was unclear what was going on below, and none of the crew were prepared actually to venture into the hold to try and pacify or secure them. For half an hour or so they became quieter, but it then appeared that some in the hold were husking coconuts in order to light a fire, surely a tactic employed only out of absolute desperation. Hovell then ordered the six or so crew who had rifles to shoot the Paama men in the legs, it was subsequently claimed, but two were in fact shot dead, and a third who was seriously wounded was then killed by one of the Tannese with his club. The bodies were promptly thrown overboard. Though the ship proceeded to Fiji and sold on contracts for some 230 workers at Levuka, reports leaked out and both Hovell and Rangi were arrested in Sydney, and in due course tried and convicted of murder. Intriguingly, it was the opinion of the judge that Hovell 'lost his head', was shocked and bewildered, and in fact only intended to wound and subdue the Islanders, while Rangi was 'the most guilty of the two'. Whether this was apt or fair is anyone's guess, but were there to be any substance to the characterization it would imply that Rangi was more knowing and calculating, perhaps the de facto 'master' of the mission, while Hovell was completely unprepared for the intractability of these Islanders. Another report suggested that both Hovell and Rangi played rather more subordinate roles, the orders to shoot having come from the supercargo, Levinger.

The case aroused much controversy in Sydney. Some took a philanthropic view and were disgusted that Islanders might be shot *'fighting for their liberty on board of an English vessel'*.[14] Others were astonished that a white man might even be brought before a court for having killed a native of the Pacific. Hovell's lawyer argued that the evidence of one of the witnesses, Josiah, a Rotuman, ought not to have been admitted. It was suggested that there was a lack of 'positive and complete evidence that he understood the nature and obligation of an oath'. In fact, the man was a Christian, had sworn on the Bible, and explained that he 'believed that if he kissed the book and told lies he would go to hell'. The appeal was not accepted, but does reflect real argument at the time as to whether a native witness could count as a witness at all. However, the sentences were commuted to life and subsequently waived, probably because Hovell had well-placed friends. Rangi was fortunate that the venture had not been his alone, since he would almost certainly have been hung, but he was anyway killed soon afterwards, in an unrelated revenge attack by a chief of Efate.[15]

The case of the *Young Australian* paled into insignificance a couple of years later when events during the cruise of the *Carl* came to light. This ship, part-owned by one Dr James Patrick Murray, left Melbourne in June 1871. Its methods had been widely employed. A crew member was sent ashore dressed up as a missionary to lull any local suspicions. When Islanders came off to trade, lumps of pig-iron attached to chains were dropped into their canoes, to capsize or break up the vessels, and Islanders were then seized from the water. Islander crew were said to play an active role in securing the captives, by clubbing them in the water, or by slinging stones. These assaults were not casual, but carefully planned, 'each man had his appointed duty and place', Murray acknowledged, in a statement he later volunteered, as Queen's evidence, in return for immunity from prosecution. Some eighty men were seized and shut into the hold, but they became increasingly discontented, and on the night of 13 September the crew inferred from what they could hear that the men were breaking apart the bunks, using the splintered wood as spears, and were vigorously attacking the main hatch. It was considered, too, that some fight was going on within the hold itself 'between the quiet natives and the wild ones'.[16]

The crew began to fire into the crowded space below decks. 'Every one on board was more or less engaged in the firing into the hold', Murray would acknowledge subsequently. The shooting, directed in part with the aid of torches that were dropped into the hold, carried on for more than eight hours, through the night. As it became light, one crew member tried the hatch, but was immediately wounded by a makeshift spear. The shooting was then started again, and when it was properly daylight the hatches were opened, and about five men who were unhurt came out. It transpired that of the remainder 'eight or nine' were lightly wounded, sixteen were badly wounded, and at least fifty had been killed. Not only were the dead thrown overboard, but so were most of the wounded. Some were conscious, and some had their hands or legs tied, even though there was no land in sight and no hope that any might survive. Of about eighty men who had been in the hold on 13 September, it seems that seventy were dead the following day.

While two men were later tried and sentenced to death for their subordinate roles in this affair, their convictions were commuted to long prison sentences. Albert Markham, captain of the naval ship *Rosario*, then attempting to police the labour trade, considered it extraordinary that Murray had been permitted to turn evidence. One seaman had reported that the doctor, at the time he was firing into the hold, had been singing 'Marching through Georgia', the popular Civil War song, and that subsequently he 'coolly picked out the ten who were least wounded to take on in the ship, the remainder being thrown overboard'.[17]

* * *

As if a massacre on this scale was not horrifying enough, it was reported in early 1872 that recruiters had begun to engage in head-hunting in the Solomon Islands. 'The chief of one of the tribes or islands enters into an agreement with the master of a ship, that if he will supply him with so many heads of his enemies, which they keep as trophies, he will give him an equivalent in men, to be sent away for labour.' Off the island of Florida, it was reported, a canoe had come out to one ship. As it came behind the vessel, the stern boat was abruptly dropped on top of the locals, who were then quickly captured, 'but directly they were seized their heads were cut off over the gunwale of the boat with long knives'.[18]

Although head-hunting was well established in the western Solomons, the report is not entirely plausible, since it is unclear why the ship seeking labour should not merely have taken away those who were abducted, rather than have gone to the trouble of killing them and then trying the surely dangerous venture of exchanging their heads for recruits elsewhere. But there were a number of reports of this kind, perhaps all distorted versions of one or more incidents. Charles Brook, of the Melanesian Mission, had been on the island of Florida in August 1871, and he was told of a broadly similar attack that took place some four miles from where he was staying. Two canoes were upset. One man, Brook's witness, was able to conceal himself behind the ship's stern, and subsequently swim to shore. He saw a boat appear from the other side of the ship. Four white men in it then killed his companions: 'They were at first beaten with oars, and then beheaded with tomahawks, &c. The heads were taken on board.'[19] Brook wondered whether the men were in fact white, or were perhaps lighter-skinned Islanders (he perhaps had Rotumans, who often worked as crew, in mind). But in either case, the ship must have been commanded by a white man, hence there was little doubt of the extraordinary and appalling fact that some white merchant had aided and abetted whoever may have been the killers.

'A large black brig', perhaps the same, or a different ship, arrived a couple of weeks later, while Brook was still on Florida, on an occasion when he was together with locals on a beach, from which people could see their kin in canoes approaching the sinister vessel. Two of the ship's boats then appeared, apparently again from a concealed position behind the ship itself, and converged on the canoes. The missionary claimed that he personally was too horrified to watch what took place, but he believed the people around him who did, who saw the men in the canoes assaulted, and reported that the people were killed, 'the heads taken as before'. Again, this is a somewhat curious report. The missionary puts himself in the position of being an eyewitness – and missionaries were generally anxious to document any abuses of people they ministered to – yet describes himself as overcome, and he exempts himself from having to swear to what precisely took place.[20] It is moreover, difficult to square the specific description with the 'mile and a half' that, according to Brook, separated the ship from the shore. At such a distance, say 2,000 to 2,500 metres, it is hard to imagine that, without a telescope, anyone could have seen much at all, were they standing on the beach, at water level. From a higher point, perhaps, it would have been apparent that some violent assault was taking place, but unless part of the story is missing – did a witness escape, or were the decapitated bodies washed up on shore? – none of those on the beach or nearby could have known what was said to have occurred.

One Richard Elliott, of the 'Detective Office' in Sydney, made enquiries among seamen, attempting to establish what truth may have lain behind these reports. Walter Oates, employed on ships that had, he frankly acknowledged, kidnapped many Islanders from Kiribati (the Gilbert Islands), the Marshall Islands and the Solomons, to work in Tahiti rather than either Queensland or Fiji, offered more precise, albeit hearsay evidence. So far as he knew, no white seaman had ever actually taken a head. But he did understand that some ships seeking tortoiseshell 'or other produce' in 'the north-west' Solomons – presumably the New Georgia group, home to the most active and feared head-hunting Islanders of the archipelago – conveyed warriors to the south specifically so that they could take heads, and then transported the warriors home again. This ferrying presumably got warriors further, more quickly and easily, than they would have travelled in their own canoes; it also associated them with the power of Europeans, and at least initially provided cover. This assistance, Oates reported, was provided by way of part payment for tortoiseshell, or whatever else it may have been that the Europeans were seeking.

Hence Brook's report appears to have contained a truth, albeit probably a distorted one. If the missionary was mistaken in supposing a direct link with the labour trade, an indirect link there certainly was. The 'large black brig' that had been sighted, it was considered, could only have been one ship. The innocently named *Water Lily* was owned and captained by 'Bully' Hayes, a notoriously violent swindler, bigamist and blackbirder (a slaver in the Pacific parlance of the period), born in Ohio in 1829, but active in Australia and the Pacific from the 1850s onward. If Hayes was, in all likelihood, at this time 'financing' a tortoiseshell operation in this grisly manner, he had before, and he would afterwards, abduct Islanders to be sold as slave labourers. As Detective Elliott observed, the man was 'considered capable of any atrocity'.[21]

* * *

It is not surprising that these circumstances created something of a crisis in government circles, and among the educated public of the period. A sector of that public was pro-imperialist, yet philanthropic, or considered the promotion of Christianity a duty, and a project closely linked with the promotion of commerce and civilization. Here the promotion of commerce was conspicuous, yet men who had once belonged to civilized society were practising a peculiar, it must have seemed a gratuitous, savagery. Head-hunting was not simply something savages did, it was like cannibalism; exemplifying savagery in its most extreme form, it demanded extirpation. Yet here white men were not only condoning, but actively assisting, perhaps even themselves practising, this devilish form of warfare. Not only missionaries, but liberals and humanitarians among the naval officers, who were certainly revolted by the behaviour of the slavers, who were perhaps genuinely anguished by the killing of men trying only to secure their own legitimate liberty, on the decks of English ships, seem to have been strangely entranced by the figure of the white head-hunter. If, behind the figure, there were genuine atrocities, there also appears to have been much rumour-mongering, a propensity to craft an anti-ideal, a pure sinner, an exemplar of the maelstrom of greed and lawlessness into which colonial enterprise could so easily and vigorously enter.

* * *

In 1858 the authorities in Queensland had passed 'An Act to Regulate and Control the Introduction and Treatment of Polynesian Labourers' (so-called, as was the practice in the period, even though nearly all recruited workers were from Melanesia, not Polynesia, as the terms have been otherwise understood). The bill provided for the licensing of recruiters, who were obliged to conform to a variety of regulations, to report, to supply clothing and provisions including tobacco 'during good behaviour', and to pay at standard rates.

These rules may have improved conditions aboard ships and on plantations, once labourers reached the latter, but these conditions had never particularly troubled those who objected to the trade. If plantation work was certainly hard, it seemed in fact that Islander men who had the chance to adapt to it, did so and did not on balance mind doing it. The focus of criticism, criticism that had been abundantly documented and justified, was rather the moment of engagement, and the act contained nothing that ensured that those who joined labour ships in fact did so willingly. Or rather, it did specify that labourers signed, or rather marked, agreements, and that it was part of the duty of the Queensland-based immigration agent to enquire and confirm that the Melanesians understood the contracts and had voluntarily entered into them. In other words, agreements were verified only at the point that Islanders arrived in Queensland, by men such as McDonnell, who could only judge on the basis of 'signs and words' the feelings of men (and occasionally women) who might well have been recruited involuntarily but in the course of the voyage had reconciled themselves to work.

Not surprisingly, public opinion in Queensland was in favour of the trade, but in the southern Australian states, and in Britain itself, various cases were widely publicized and following pressure from London, much more rigorous regulations were introduced by the Queensland legislature from December 1870; a similar act was introduced in Fiji, once it became a Crown colony in 1874. The single most important change was the requirement that all recruiting ships carried a government agent, soon known in the trade as 'the G.A.', who was required to ensure that Islanders were genuinely willing to embark, and that food, clothing and so forth was provided to the prescribed standards. Most importantly, agents were not permitted merely to oversee recruitment from the ship, but had to be in the recruiting boat, or in one of the boats, that went onto the beach to bring men (and the minority of women interested in recruiting) off.[22]

Government agents may in many cases have been incompetent, lackadaisical, or unprepared to stand up to tough and experienced captains. Irregularities of various kinds – the recruitment of under-age workers, for example – continued to be reported for many years. Yet outright kidnapping virtually ceased to be perpetrated by those seeking workers for Queensland or Fiji. Though recruitment to New Caledonia and Samoa, among other places, continued to be less regulated, cases of blatant, mass abduction became less common not least because the frequency of shipping of all kinds increased, and plantations and missionary stations became more numerous. Hence acts that were recognized as criminal were unlikely to pass unreported, and the trader risked the attention of the police and the courts, in some colonial settlement or another.

More importantly, kidnapping became unnecessary. By the early 1870s cohorts of Islanders who had worked three-year terms were returning home at the conclusion of their contracts – repatriation was strictly required by the legislation, and the agents were charged with ensuring that people were taken back to the precise location from which they had been recruited. However hard their work had been, however difficult the adjustment, those who returned were often, it appears, more or less affirmative about their experiences and adventures. The proof of the effort was also there to be displayed, in the heavy chests, packed with goods ranging from rifles through metal cooking pots, axes and knives to clothes that each returning worker brought home. No doubt, some Melanesians found indenture an ordeal, but the balance of opinion was in favour, to the extent that by about 1910, when the trade was coming to an end, some 100,000 Islanders from various parts of New Ireland, Vanuatu and the Solomons had left their homes for work in Queensland, New Caledonia, Fiji and Samoa.

The fact that labour recruitment became a regular and well-established practice, engaged in by dozens of ships, did not however mean that dealings

43 J.W. Lindt, 'Recruiting, Pangkumu, Mallicolo [Malakula]', albumen print, c.1890.

between Islanders and recruiters became straightforward and amicable. William Wawn, whose 1893 memoir provides one of the most vivid and informative, if certainly partisan, accounts of the business, conveys a sense of how recruiting was normally conducted in Vanuatu in the early 1870s.

He would send two boats ashore, but also deployed a third that lay offshore to provide 'cover', in the event of violence. Each boat carried a 'lug-sail, the handiest rig with an island crew', and was rowed by four Islanders – often Loyalty Islanders or Rotumans – all armed with 'a smooth-bore musket, cut short so as to lie fore and aft on the boat's thwarts under the gunwale, to which was nailed a long strip of canvas, painted, and hanging down to protect the arms from the salt spray'. The white men – the recruiter in one boat and the mate and G.A. in the other – carried revolvers and Snider rifles, which in due course were replaced by Winchesters.[23] The presumption of these engagements was, in other words, one of profound distrust. Islanders were not labelled 'natives', as they generally were by explorers and missionaries; for Wawn and his contemporaries they were emphatically 'savages', constitutionally bloodthirsty, and predisposed to treachery. If missionary writers often paraded some paternalistic affection for particular Islander men and women, such feelings were seldom exhibited or acknowledged by the white men who participated in, and wrote about, the labour trade.

Each recruiting boat carried a trade box containing tobacco, pipes, gunpowder, beads, fabrics, knives and a range of other goods, all of which were intended as gifts to the relatives of men recruiting, who had to be compensated for the departure of young men and the occasional young woman. 'To take a recruit in the presence of his friends without "paying" for him, however willing to go he might be himself, would be, at any rate, extremely dangerous', Wawn noted.[24] He was at pains to make it explicit that these presentations were a form of compensation, emphatically not of purchase. He certainly had an axe to grind and his book returned again and again to ways in which the stigma of the slave trade attached to labour recruiting was unjustified. But on this specific point his analysis was reasonable: neither young men nor women were owned by those to whom gifts were presented, the prospective workers were not being sold by chiefs or relatives, there was rather an economy of redistribution in play.

As well as the varied goods and trifles, the boats carried a bag of Brown Bess muskets. 'Good serviceable weapons, despite their age', Wawn claimed. They perhaps had to be, since unlike Islanders at the beginning of the nineteenth century, Tannese men especially could tell good firearms from bad, and were 'very particular about the guns having "TOWER" on their locks'.[25]

44 'Recruiting, N.H. [New Hebrides, Vanuatu]', albumen print, *c*.1890.

The boats would be not be pulled up onto the beach, but rather backed up to the shore, the stern or keel just touching the ground, poised for a quick escape in the event of tension. Locals would typically crowd around, to see what was on offer, which ship had called, who the captain was, and which port he was recruiting for. In general, Queensland destinations such as Maryborough were preferred, because wages were known to be better, and conditions considered better, than in Fiji. Some food might be offered and some barter take place: ships were always seeking supplies as well as recruits. In due course a recruiter might see a 'boy', meaning a young man, 'quietly slip off all his bead and shell ornaments, and part from them', and then some telegraphic conversation in the pidgin language would ensue. One man might say 'Boy he like go' to the recruiter. 'The intending recruit comes close to the boat for inspection, a friend carefully guarding him on each side, not so much to prevent kidnapping as to stop him from getting into the boat before he is "paid" for.'[26] If the man and goods changed places, the recruiting boat would then back out to the covering boat, to transfer the recruit before returning to the shore to try for others. A recruiting cruise would involve working around the coasts of a succession of islands, repatriating returning workers, and taking on new men and women, until either the number the ship was permitted to carry was met or the captain gave up. If the ship, captain, or destination was unpopular, if a community's potential recruits had already been taken, or if people were at that time diverted by other activities, recruiting efforts might and often did fail.

At the best of times these transactions appear to have been tense. Violence was not uncommon. It was a truism of the trade that a ship might be attacked because of some offence perpetrated by a previous recruiter. Locals might be angry because men and women who had left some time earlier had, they learned, died while on plantations, or never returned for whatever other reason. In one case reported by Wawn, some seventy men from Gala, a small island off Florida, went through the form of joining the Dancing Wave, but then massacred the entire crew, with the exception of one white man and nine or ten recent recruits. Distrustful of the recruits, the surviving seaman departed from the ship in a small boat during a storm, and was able to reach the station of a trader on the island of Savo, not far distant. He later returned to Australia and told his tale to the authorities, who despatched a naval vessel to undertake a punitive raid.

Wawn, who later spoke to some of the Gala men, understood that the assault had occurred because men from the island had worked in Queensland for a planter whose business failed, and whose station and assets were repossessed. 'Although such a proceeding was certain to result in outrage and murder, they were actually sent home by the ministry of the day without receiving a farthing of their hard-earned wages.' If the trader considered this unjust, he was disgusted that the naval vessel left the area without inflicting any punishment, indeed he felt that missionary and what was referred to as 'Exeter Hall' influence – that of broader philanthropic opinion – led naval officers in general to hold back from responding vigorously to violence perpetrated by Islanders. Islanders learned, he feared, that whatever they did they would get off 'scot-free', as he put it; they tended to laugh and jeer if threats of naval intervention were made by traders. ' "Man-o'-war all same old woman!" said they.'[27]

Royal Navy ships that formed part of the so-called 'Australian station' made an increasing number of cruises through the islands of the south-west Pacific, in part to check abuses on the part of recruiters and in part to investigate and respond to 'outrages' committed by Islanders. But although they did bombard villages and engage in a range of other punitive actions, the misdirected or ineffective nature of their efforts highlights the extent to which archipelagoes such as the Solomons were not colonized, and not subject to government, at this time. It is important to recall that islands such as Guadalcanal and Malaita were not atolls but mountainous and heavily forested land masses. Europeans, it is clear, felt quite insecure even on their beaches. With the possible exception of one or two beachcombers, no whites had yet attempted to venture any distance into their interiors, emphatically a no-go zone.

It is true that over the last few decades of the nineteenth century, thousands of Islanders were recruited from their communities and returned to them

45 'Recruiters and boats crew, New Hebrides, Queensland Labor Traffic', *c.*1895.

46 Indentured Melanesian workers on a Fijian plantation, c.1875.

without major outbreaks of violence. Certain recruiting captains, such as
Wawn, worked in the trade for twenty or so years, commanding, in his case,
twenty-five cruises. He and his ships were often shot at, and shot back. He
experienced many minor incidents of casual fire between ship and shore that
in all likelihood resulted in no injury on either side. On one voyage his G.A.
was killed, but perhaps because he himself was prudent Wawn otherwise
escaped any truly serious assault. Yet many ships' masters were imprudent.
More importantly and fundamentally, the labour trade engendered confrontation; it was inherently explosive.

   During the 1870s and 1880s recruiters resorted increasingly to the
Solomon Islands. The demand for labour continued to rise, and though men
and women from Vanuatu continued to join ships, they did not do so to the
degree that met growing demand. At the time the trade got under way in the
Solomons, the depth and range of contact was far more limited than it had
been in Vanuatu. Ni-Vanuatu had hosted missionaries and traders such as
James Paddon for decades, and had considerable experience of local labour

migration even before recruitment to Queensland, New Caledonia, Fiji and Samoa had begun. The zone of contact had, in other words, moved beyond the beach; there were ongoing engagements and forms of accommodation. In the Solomons, despite decades of occasional exchanges with ships, cross-cultural dealings had not reached even this tentatively settled stage. If recruiting encounters in Vanuatu were always dangerous – witness Wawn's precautions – they were still more unpredictable in the archipelago to the north.

The *Young Dick* left Maryborough in Queensland in April 1886. The ship was under the command of Captain John Hugh Rogers, the part-owner. Its G.A. rejoiced in the name of Mr. Home Popham Popham, the first mate was Charles Marr, and the second mate and recruiter, John Hornidge. The remaining crew were mixed, some Europeans, some Islanders. During the last week of April the boats 'worked' the Guadalcanal coast with some success. At the beginning of May the *Young Dick* sailed across to Malaita and began recruiting on the east coast of that island. Eight Islanders having joined the ship, Hornidge reported that 'a lot of bush natives' had come down to the coast, presumably with the intention of signing on, and he went ashore in search of them. On the beach he met an old man, and one Rady, 'a boy who had done service in Fiji'. They invited him to a nearby village, but as they walked through thick brush towards the settlement, suddenly attacked him with their tomahawks. The mate, knocked down twice and badly hurt, was nevertheless able to keep running and gained the beach, where he was picked up. The *Young Dick* then moved to Port Adams, encountering another trader, the *Meg Merilees*. Hornidge was fortunate that the G.A. on this ship had some medical training; he was ministered to and survived.

Two or three days later, the naval ship HMS *Opal* arrived. Its commander, Lieutenant Wright, made enquiries, went back to Mabo, the place the incident occurred, issued demands for the culprits and then a warning that he would bombard the village. The result of him firing nineteen shells was, it was reported, the destruction of a single coconut tree. 'In the meantime the natives, who had received through the missionary ample time to clear out their families and goods, were conspicuous on the beach a mile further up, enjoying immensely the fun of the bombardment.'[28] This characterization of utterly ineffective punitive action may well have been distorted, greater damage may have been done, and locals may have considered that they had suffered. Yet in any event this type of action did not result in pacification and instead may well have motivated further violence.

The *Young Dick* resumed recruiting but less than a week later was attacked again. As one boat was passing a rocky point part way along a beach, 'a shower of arrows was fired from ambush', injuring a man from Efate named 'Bust', or elsewhere and more probably, 'Bush'. 'Me belong Government boat on "Young Dick". Me savvie arrow strike me long a arm lon Malayta. Two fellow arrow shoot at me when me pull um boat', he would testify, on his return to Queensland. Nine days later, on 20 May, the ship had adopted a position in Sinerago Bay from which Captain Rogers had taken two boats, to try recruiting further down the coast. In his absence a canoe approached from the beach, asking people to come ashore to pick up a 'boy' who wanted to go to Queensland. Popham, the agent, was unwell, and told the Islanders to bring the boy out to the ship so that the deal could be done there. Half an hour later the canoe returned with half a dozen men, including one referred to as 'the king' – though these societies had prominent priests and warriors and nothing like chiefs or kings. This man was ostensibly to receive trade to permit the 'boy' to leave; while the 'king' was within a cabin, examining what was on offer, some dozens of local men approached from the shore, swimming or in canoes, swiftly boarding the ship, some offering food, many (it was later claimed) carrying concealed weapons. The 'king' insisted on more in the way of trade.

What precisely then occurred was later disputed, but Marr refused, either gently (one story) or aggressively (the other) and shut the trade-room door. 'The king', it was said, then 'gave the signal for attack', at any rate, the Islanders did attack. The cook, carpenter and government agent were quickly despatched. The sailmaker, Lagerblom, put up a desperate struggle but suffered repeated blows. An able seaman, Thomas Crittenden, who had been asleep in the forecastle, woke, and was able to seize a rifle, a good deal of ammunition, and climb to the topsail yard. In the government agent Douglas Rannie's 'Boy's-Own' narration, 'he coolly sat down and opened fire on the seething, screeching mob of brutal devils who were rushing hither and thither on the deck below'.[29] He shot a considerable number of the Malaitans, who in due course abandoned the ship. He found then that the mate Marr, who had also been firing on Islanders from within the trade store, was still alive, as was Lagerblom, who died an hour later, 'feebly expressing some wish that his watch should be given to his mother'. The other whites and one 'friendly' recruit who had become caught up in the fighting had all been killed. Before long Captain Rogers returned with his boats, having had only friendly dealings with the people further down the coast, and was horrified to discover the carnage; 'The scuppers were literally running with blood'. He is said to have cried out 'Oh my God!' and gone to the ship's side to throw up.[30]

Back at Maryborough the following month, June 1886, an inquiry was held. Marr, Crittenden, Rogers and several Islander crew testified, though on his first appearance Marr had to be dismissed because he was drunk. Rogers asserted that he understood that the motivation had simply been plunder. The papers were in due course referred to the Royal Navy. Arthur T. Brooke, captain of the *Opal*, which had bombarded the Malaita coast after the first of the three incidents, stated it was highly unlikely that that incident had triggered the killings. Different tribes were involved, they were mutually hostile, and there would have been no rationale for the perpetrators of the massacre to react to the punitive shelling. Brooke went on to note 'a circumstance to my mind that wants more fully clearing up', or rather to insinuate that Marr had provoked the 'chief' who then let out a yell, or 'gave the signal' to attack. The ambiguity, if it did not fundamentally alter the understanding of what had taken place, raised the question of whether the *Young Dick*'s cruise had not been characterized by a certain carelessness, given that, as Brooke also stressed, the Malaitans had, in general, the reputation of being 'the most treacherous and least to be trusted' of any Solomon Islanders.

The naval officer went on to doubt whether an inquiry, let alone a punitive venture, would be practical or advisable. 'During the time of the south-east trade it would be unfavourable for taking action on the coast of Malayta, and also it would be necessary for some one cognizant of the exact spot to be able to point it out as there are so many small villages dotted along the coast, and a good number not visible from deck of ship on account of thick bush and trees.'[31]

Brooke's letter was commented upon by Rear Admiral Tryon, commander-in-chief of the Australian Station, who took the view that 'an opportunity was rashly and most imprudently offered to men of the same race' as those who had already and very recently 'treacherously assaulted' members of the crew. Tryon's overall assessment was unsupportive of the labour recruiters: 'On the one hand, in the islands we have missionaries who are gradually establishing free and safe communication with the natives; on the other, we have men in pursuit of trade forcing themselves on natives.' He went on to spell out something of a philosophy of colonial intervention, as it applied to the time and place. Were a punitive mission to take place, it would require white men to venture inland, into the bush, clearly a hazardous undertaking, not to be embarked upon 'without strong reason'. 'Does it exist in this case,' he pondered, given that the violence arose from the 'rashness and incaution' of 'white men in pursuit of gain'? If the implicit answer was clearly no, the labour trade was, he conceded, 'not unlawful', so men 'employed in what is lawful' ought to be protected – or, he went so far as to say 'allowed to take the law into their own hands', but immediately stopped himself short. 'This latter is quite inadmissible; the argument cannot apply beyond certain limits.' On balance the rear admiral's view was clearly that 'more harm than good' would arise from pursuing the matter.[32]

These documents tacked between frankness and pomposity, insight and circumlocution. What they reflected was a full acknowledgement of the extent to which Melanesians, and Melanesians of the Solomon Islands especially, lay beyond the reach of even the crudest instruments of colonial governance. The nature of the geography, the sheer lack of visibility of local populations, and the apparently fragmented character of local society, all mitigated against even the sound identification of those responsible for a particular attack. As to the natures of the people themselves, these reports are laced with racist language, and the view that the Islanders were intractably treacherous as well as probably bloodthirsty is repeatedly aired. Yet, in partial contradiction to these imputations, local violence was consistently blamed on provocation, and missionaries were considered capable of creating milieux that might be or might become peaceful and safe.

* * *

Many of these incidents of violence were long remembered locally. If Europeans such as Rannie, Brooke and Tryon, among others, retold the tale and burdened it with the causes and moral values that variously made sense to them, Islanders did much the same thing. In the 1960s, some eighty years after the events, Kwaio (Malaitan) elders told the anthropologist Roger Keesing a number of versions that, so far as the bare facts were concerned, were broadly consistent with the European documentary record, though they do much to fill out a picture of the motivations behind the assault and the individuals involved.

The story from the local perspective began some years earlier. One Boosui, son of a prominent man, Taafana'au or Tafa'au, had been kidnapped, taken to Queensland, and died. Tafa'au was angry and wanted the death revenged. In keeping with the practice of the place, he offered a bounty consisting of pigs or valuables. This was accepted, and warriors raised pigs for sacrifice, to assure the success of their venture. The strongman 'Arumae consecrated and offered pigs, then saw one day that the ship, the *Young Dick*, was there, but that its boats had gone away. That was his opportunity. He took twenty warriors out to the ship, boarded it, seized the white men and killed them. But one white man eluded them, got hold of his gun, and shot 'Arumae's uncle, 'Ala'otana, and his son Fa'auta, as well as another relative, Fi'oi. Angered, 'Arumae seized Tafa'au, the man whose bounty had motivated the attack, and he too was killed (whether at the time, on the ship, or later on shore is unclear). His 'thinking went like this: "You, Tafa'au, put up blood money for a ship to be taken to avenge your son Boosui, and now Fa'auta has been killed and his body abandoned because of it", explained Talaunga'i, a man of about fifty-five in 1966.[33]

A contrast was drawn with earlier assaults, which had been carried out more successfully, with fewer lost on the Islander side:

> It was Maeasuaa who attacked the two ships before. The first one was at Leri. I never heard much about that one. Maeasuaa sacrificed first in purification. He killed the crews – every man. The ship I heard about burned for three full days. Maeasuaa sacrificed, then performed magic, then attacked and killed everyone, to satisfy his ancestors. But 'Arumae didn't sacrifice properly for *his* ancestors; he just consecrated the pigs, and then attacked. That's why it went badly for him. (Fa'atalo, 75 in 1969).[34]

In the light of these narratives, what was perceived by Europeans as an unprovoked massacre, motivated by an ignoble appetite for plunder, comes into view in an entirely different way. The action was a customary one, which followed from the loss of a son, from conventional modes of reward and reciprocity. Brooke's suspicion that the violence was triggered by Marr's aggression was wrong: the attack was indeed premeditated and planned. What the pro-recruitment whites saw as a barbaric assault, which ought to have been further punished, was considered a failure, a botched attempt, by at least some locals. One fuller narrative noted that even the initial motivation rested upon a misconception. 'It turned out that Boosui hadn't died. He was just working there. People had lied,' said Lounga, a younger man who knew a version of the history that took the form of an epic chant. He dramatized the violence on board the *Young Dick* in the following terms:

> 'Arumae [sic] was stepping on the captain's boot, and they were shouting angrily at one another. 'Arumae wasn't intimidated. He hit the white man in the face with his axe. Ongeamae hit the second white man with his axe. And Lamoka killed the third one. . . . But there was another white man aboard they didn't know about, the one who sewed up the sails. . . . He dashed out with the gun. . . . He climbed up and up. He loaded and cocked the gun . . . [and called out to each warrior as he shot him] 'This is yours, Gwalaa'. . . . He fell dead. . . . 'This is yours, Talange'enia.' And he shot him. . . . The sailmaker took five more cartridges from the pouch. 'This one is for you, A'ala, from Fonfonaile.' And it knocked him dead.[35]

This strangely intimate succession of killings substitutes, for a reader's sense of a mass of 'brutal devils', a listener's sense of a group of kin instead, who were from a cluster of hamlets, who were bold and almost successful, in their own violent terms – but who ultimately failed, on account of a failure of ritual.

If, from the Malaitan perspective, a venture which was misconceived and ill-prepared brought misfortune upon its perpetrators, Europeans believed in different terms that those who sailed in the *Young Dick* were fated. In the aftermath of the June 1886 inquiry the ship swiftly embarked on a further recruiting voyage. It was never seen again, but thought lost on a reef in the Torres Strait. Around the time a coastal steamer sighted a good deal of wreckage in the water, and the corpse of a red-headed man that 'answered the description of Captain Rogers'.[36]

* * *

Recollections of the Kwaio of Malaita, bear out the sense that their islands lay beyond any domain of European control at this time. The stories suggest a set of actions and reactions that followed from European intrusion, but were in no way influenced by or responsive to either the philanthropic projects of missionaries, the commercial agendas of traders, or the naval officers' efforts to police 'outrages' of whichever kind. The world that the warriors inhabited was not one that perceived or understood, still less acknowledged or respected, European distinctions between civility and savagery, between just and unjust action.

Yet it was a world that was changing rapidly and irreversibly. Change was marked by the emergence of a language that has already been alluded to, and here and there quoted, in this chapter. From as early as the late eighteenth century, Islanders had begun to employ a sort of jargon, made-up words picked up from traders and others. In Polynesia a good deal of interaction took place through local languages, since many mariners, such as those active in Fiji, considered it worth the trouble to learn languages that were useful to them, despite variant dialects, right around an archipelago. This was not the case anywhere in Melanesia, however, where distinct languages were far more numerous. Though beachcombers and some missionaries identified themselves with particular communities, cross-cultural interaction proceeded overwhelm-ingly through what Europeans called 'broken English', which in fact even before 1850 was developing into a properly structured language. That language, known in Vanuatu as Bislama (after bêche-de-mer) and elsewhere as pidgin, drew its vocabulary primarily from English but was based grammatically on the forms common to Oceanic languages. It featured and features, for example, the dual pronouns that exist in addition to singular and plural, 'they two' or 'us two', and the basic distinction, which gives everyday talk its texture in so many Pacific languages, between 'we' (including the person addressed), and 'we' (excluding them). *Yumitufela*, you-me-two-fellow, is 'us two', 'you and I'.

It will never be possible to quantify how many Islander sailors worked on European ships in, say, 1840, 1850 and 1860. Yet given the increasing incidence of trade, and the greater engagement of Europeans in the south-western Pacific, especially following the establishment of the French colony in New Caledonia, more Islanders were more routinely mobile, more inhabited the singular transcultural space of the merchant ship, than had ever been the case before. To the Hawaiians, Tahitians and Maori who had sailed on whalers and traders from the late eighteenth century onward, were added many, many others, Rotumans, Tannese and Loyalty Islanders among them. This multicultural maritime milieu was certainly conducive to the development of pidgin languages. But it was the labour trade that propelled pidgin, from a somewhat specialized argot associated with ships' decks to a plantation language spoken by tens of thousands of Melanesians, from Queensland to Fiji and beyond.[37]

If pidgin was most obviously a lingua franca that enabled Europeans and Islanders to communicate, its more profound importance was that it enabled Islanders from across Melanesia and beyond to communicate with each other. Though Tannese, Malaitans and others clubbed together on labour ships and on plantations, and were often said to be mutually antagonistic, a culture of common experience and exchange also emerged that had as its medium the common language. Although much of the activity and belief that organized and drove local life at home was suspended in Queensland, there is some evidence that novel forms of sacrifice, and novel cult groups, drew men from different islands and archipelagoes together. Oral traditions telling of gifts of rites and exchanges between labourers were recounted decades afterwards: ni-Vanuatu knew of 'Solomons magic' and Solomon Islanders knew of 'New Hebrides magic'.[38]

Colonizers had long been struck by the highly localized nature of Melanesian identities – or, more judgementally, they lamented what appeared as divisiveness, mutual hostility and fragmentation, ignoring the rich and diverse exchange networks that had linked communities, indeed drawn them together, for centuries. In any event, what was indeed a locally heterogeneous world was not exactly displaced by a novel, common Melanesian culture; rather it was reframed. Local identifications remained strong and profound, and they remain so today, but a sense of affinity among the populations of islands, regions and archipelagoes emerged. It was in the nature of the hard, profoundly hierarchical, and racialized social relations of plantations that the distinctions between white Australians and Melanesian workers would be underscored, every minute of every day, and the upshot could only be a sense of a common predicament, a common sufferance of ordinary oppression.

* * *

After the federation of the Australian states, early in the twentieth century, the white Australia policy resulted in the end of recruiting and the deportation of the thousands of Islanders who had, by the early twentieth century, established viable communities up and down the Queensland coast. If the bringing of Islanders to Queensland had entailed widespread savagery, especially in the earliest phases of recruiting, this repatriation proceeded with little overt physical violence, but was perhaps still more savage, in a different way, in the disruption and trauma it engendered for people who had inhabited a country for a generation. The plans were vigorously protested, and a Royal Commission was established. The hardship that deportation meant was recognized up to a point, and grounds for exemption were clarified. Henry Diamuir Tongoa, who was about thirty years old, born in Vanuatu but resident in Queensland from the age of four, was literate and articulate, the proprietor of a boarding house. He formed and led an association that opposed the proposals, and put it to one of the Royal Commissioners that 'If the boys have to go back then the white men will have to leave the islands.'[39] Though concessions were made, over 7,000 Islanders were repatriated between 1904 and 1908, and only 1,654 were permitted to remain, with official exemptions.

Most of those forced to return to their island had been away for a decade or longer. They had absorbed experiences and understandings remote from those of kin at home. Some would not be welcome, some would not choose to rejoin their communities. Many had affiliated themselves with missions that had been established specifically to work among the Queensland 'Kanakas'. On returning, they often claimed or appropriated lands distinct from those of their communities of origin and established new Christian settlements. In diverse other ways repatriation had profound ramifications. Those who were repatriated took a much deeper understanding of colonial society back to the islands than that possessed by Islanders in situ, who had responded in some cases to missionaries but otherwise dealt only occasionally with men off boats. Returned labourers and their families were more canny, in their sense of finance and fair dealing. On Gela in the Solomons, men who had come back from Queensland convinced the Melanesian Mission teachers that they were miserably paid, organized a strike, and otherwise boycotted and disrupted the paternalistic regimes of many mission stations. In manifold ways, which cannot now be fully reconstructed, cosmopolitan experience was diffused among communities, and it changed them. The Solomon Islands had become a British protectorate in 1893, efforts had been made to pacify the head-hunting peoples of New Georgia in 1897–8, and in the years that followed a colonial administration was gradually put in place. The islands of Vanuatu became the Anglo-French condominium of the New Hebrides from 1906 onwards. Over the decades that followed, indeed until independence in 1978 and 1980 respectively, Islanders in both colonies would struggle against the diverse oppressions of their rulers. To no small degree, they had been equipped to do so by the experience of the labour trade, by the great window it had opened onto the workings of world economies and the inequalities that energized them.

CHAPTER NINE

✦

The whites would serve the natives

Towards the end of the 1860s, Frederick Moss, who intended to join the small army of white Australasians setting themselves up as planters in Fiji, was making a preliminary tour of the islands. He naturally spent a day on Bau, the tiny island off the south-eastern coast of Fiji's main island of Viti Levu, one that had had such a disproportionate impact on the history of the archipelago as a whole, from perhaps the mid-eighteenth century onwards. There were, in one sense, as many histories of Fiji as there were tribes, but the history of modern Fiji that would come to be written and taught would be the history of Bau's ascendancy. In fits and starts, and with notable reverses, the influence of the little island's polity indeed expanded over the course of the nineteenth century. Cakobau, its war chief, or Vunivalu, was considered 'King of Fiji' as early as the 1840s by Europeans, and his precedence was more or less grudgingly acknowledged by many, though never by all Fijians.

Moss remarked on what was to be found in Cakobau's house. 'A double-barrelled fowling piece, a Snider rifle, and a couple of swords hung against one of the great upright posts on which the ridge-pole lay. On the only table there is usually a huge Bible, and at its side I noticed another sword, a revolver in a holster, a glass candlestick, and a broken stereoscope. . . . Art is represented by likenesses of the Princess Royal of England and King George of Hanover, by some highly coloured daubs of ships, and by other smaller pictures and coloured cuttings from the Illustrated London News.'[1]

By this time there was nothing novel about a collection of this kind. At the beginning of the nineteenth century, the principal Pacific chiefs such as Kamehameha and Pomare were liberally supplied with European curiosities of diverse sorts. They were also well aware of European kings and were anxious to class themselves with them. They were given or they sought portraits of them, and they would display those images, not out of some naïve awe or subservience, but in order to assert that some kinship, some alliance existed. This kind of effort would persist right through the century, and beyond: a fondness for British monarchs in particular was marked, even among lesser leaders on many islands, and the assertion of alliance or affinity would prove a well-tried technique of chiefly self-aggrandizement.

For Cakobau, however, the relationship with the Crown had ceased to be a matter of symbolic appropriation. If he was an effective strategist he was everywhere overstretched, and the reciprocal relationships and affirmations of rank that were the stuff of Fijian politics were always provisional and mutable. Cakobau's pre-eminence had been acknowledged by the paramount chief of Cakaudrove, the dominant confederation in the north-eastern part of the

47 Portrait of Cakobau.

archipelago, as early as 1841, and he had dedicated the remainder of the 1840s to a campaign against Rewa, nearby on the Viti Levu mainland, that was considered by missionary observers to be uniquely ferocious. Several polities – Bau, Rewa and Verata – had at one time or another held sway over the Rewa river delta, which supported extensive irrigated taro fields and was among the most agriculturally productive regions of the Pacific. Chiefly families in all these polities were intermarried, and long-standing rivalries periodically erupted into skirmishes, essentially theatrical outbreaks of fighting that were the mode, in many parts of the Pacific. But, as in Tonga at the end of the eighteenth and start of the nineteenth century, warfare was from time to time prosecuted with deadlier intensity, and Cakobau was unrelenting. The Bau-Rewa war was pursued to the point of extirpation, and in due course the chiefly town was burnt and the Roko Tui Dreketi, the reigning chief, executed. In Fiji, however, no victory was permanent, no relationship would remain settled. From time to time during the 1850s, old enemies who had sent tribute would cease to do so; they would hazard alliances among themselves, and cultivate potential defectors within Bau itself.[2]

Having been closely courted by the Methodists for many years, Cakobau turned to the Church in 1854, perhaps because he was half persuaded by the missionaries that customs such as feasting upon defeated warriors were indeed evil and might anger a god more powerful than any his ancestors had known. Yet in any event his conversion had, like Pomare's some forty years earlier, been carefully timed. The increasing level of European engagement in the islands meant that a missionary's or a naval officer's understanding of who was king, and of the extent of a king's dominions, was beginning to mean much more than it once had. If it had certainly been advantageous for Cakobau to remain heathen while brutal military campaigns were being undertaken, it made still more sense for him, at a moment of eminence, to firm up the level of European support he enjoyed, to freeze – to the extent possible – the power relations of the instant.[3]

The would-be king was behind two offers of cession to Britain in the late 1850s. These were given serious consideration, and the Colonial Office despatched Colonel W.T. Smythe to investigate the proposed acquisition. Berthold Seemann, the distinguished botanist who participated in the mission, was excited above all by the prospects for a cotton-planting colony, but Smythe's assessments of Fiji and the Fijians were unfavourable. The climate was unhealthy, the Islanders lacked unity and discipline, the European settlers were mainly former sailors who had done 'nothing to civilize or improve the natives'.[4] Indigenous institutions were inimical to commerce.

'The general habits and sentiments of the Fijians are opposed to the acquisition of property by individuals. The chief seizes anything belonging to the people that takes his fancy, and as readily gives it away, and the people are equally ready to beg and to give', the colonel lamented.[5]

Though a third of Fijians had adopted Christianity, Smythe argued further that the majority remained wedded to 'frightful' customs, among them cannibalism, the strangling of widows and infanticide. An obvious disadvantage of taking on the government of the islands would be an immediate need to suppress such practices – Smythe was not explicit, but implied that it would surely be necessary to impose Christianity, by force, upon the archipelago as a whole. To this expensive military undertaking would be added the cost of an administrative establishment, which he calculated at some £7,000 a year. Given the subsistence orientation of Fijian life, taxes could only be raised in kind, and it would be many years before the colony could be expected to cover its costs. His conclusion clothed this expediency in philanthropy. 'Judging from the present state of the Sandwich Islands . . . the resources of the Pacific Islands can be best developed, and the welfare of their inhabitants secured, by a native government aided by the counsels of respectable Europeans.'[6] At the time he wrote, however, the bulk of the Hawaiian population had been cruelly dispossessed of their lands for more than a decade, by the settler-dominated monarchy.

In the wake of London's rejection of the offer, Cakobau's position was perilous. He was threatened, in particular, by the high-ranking Tongan chief Ma'afu, who had acted as a general, directing a campaign to expand long-established Tongan influence in eastern Fiji, and as governor of the *vanua*, the lands that had deferred to him. Ma'afu was physically impressive, considered astute, and widely experienced. Twenty years earlier he had played a prominent role in a Tahitian-sponsored sandalwood voyage to northern Vanuatu, he knew a wider Pacific world, and a world of colonial commerce. When Cakobau wrote to Taufa'ahau, Ma'afu's master and the most powerful Tongan ruler of the time, seeking an agreement that each would allow the other to rule his islands in peace, he was mocked. Many important parts of Fiji that Cakobau claimed he ruled, Taufa'ahau pointed out, had been conquered by Tonga or had themselves sought Tongan protection. If it was wrong for Tonga to control Fijian lands, 'then it is wrong', wrote the Tongan, 'for England to rule over India & New Zealand – and for France to rule over Tahiti.' Get real, this was to say – we live in a colonial world.[7]

* * *

By the mid-1860s the Methodists had been active in Fiji for thirty years. For much of that period Fijians had identified the lotu – Christianity – with European power, with efficacy, and therefore with 'truth'. Yet as in Tahiti and elsewhere, mass conversions would only follow the conversions of chiefs, and chiefs weighed commitments to ancestors and ancestral ways against the advantages to be gained from new foreign gods and technologies. Some of those technologies, such as guns, could of course be had without Christianity, and a shift closer to or away from the Church had, at any time, a host of cross-cutting consequences. These might diminish or strengthen a chief's position, on the one hand among 'the people of the land', his Fijian subjects or followers, and on the other those Europeans who both supported him with trade goods but also made demands for land or payment that might be difficult to meet.

Following the conversion of Cakobau himself, many subordinate chiefs and their people embraced the lotu in various parts of the archipelago. Yet for a good many Fijians, the close identification of the high chiefs with the Wesleyans would not encourage conversion, but to the contrary it reinforced their identification with ancestral gods and ways. Fiji was far from being as culturally heterogeneous as Vanuatu, but it was considerably more so than, say, the Tongan archipelago. In particular, the people of the interior of the main island of Viti Levu belonged to societies that were organized differently to those of the hierarchical confederacies of the coasts and smaller islands. It has long been a cliché of the anthropological literature that the Viti Levu interior was 'Melanesian' in character, as opposed to the 'Polynesian' coastal kingdoms, and though the observation often underpinned nonsensical theories of racial mixing, it did reflect real social and cultural differences. Viti Levu societies were localized and structured around reciprocal exchanges. Their ritual life celebrated warriors' rites and male initiations rather than ceremonies of deference to high chiefs. Whereas coastal peoples frequently celebrated the immigrant origins of high chiefs – whose usurpation spoke power and prestige – a counter-ideology identified authority and authenticity with autochthonous origins.

There was more to all this than contrasts between one region and another. It could be said that all Fijian societies incorporated a tension between reciprocity and hierarchy. On the one hand there was a binary sociality, based on giving between groups that intermarried, that as it were faced each other, that took turns to present each other with feasts and valuables, that acknowledged prior gifts of women, who made reproduction and the continuation of life itself possible. On the other hand certain groups had elevated themselves, such that they extracted tribute and service, they from time to time feasted

48 The Viti Levu interior, watercolour by Constance F. Gordon Cumming, *c*.1876–7.

those who served, but in the context of an unambiguously hierarchical relationship. Whereas much of coastal and eastern Fiji was Tongan-influenced,
overlain by decidedly hierarchical social forms, in the Viti Levu interior the
reverse was the case, and the relationship between the independent tribes of
the hills and the *matanitu*, the confederations of the coast, was not merely one
of difference, but antagonism. Coastal Fijians had long considered kai Colo,
people of the interior, as brutish or backward; indeed, 'kai Colo' was and is still
a term of abuse in Fijian, not a term of ethnic identification that interior
people themselves use.

   As of the mid-1860s no attempt had been made to capitalize on the conversion of coastal peoples and evangelize the interior. In July 1867 the missionary
Thomas Baker had ventured up the Rewa river, the great watercourse that
extended inland from a rich delta on the south-eastern coast, near Rewa and
Bau. He was determined to reinforce Islander teachers who had recently been
sent to villages in the area. But contrary to advice he was given at every point
on his journey, he pressed on beyond the villages they worked in, into Navosa

which at the time had been scarcely visited by whites. He had no notion that a chief much nearer to his lowland residence, probably provoked by Baker's effort to evangelize the chief's own people, had in effect offered a bounty. A *tabua*, a fine whale's tooth, the supreme valuable of Fijian gift exchange, had been sent ahead of the missionary, with the request that Baker might be killed.

As the often-told story goes, each tribe who received the tabua demurred and gifted it on, preferring not to bring upon themselves the anger and retribution of Europeans or of the missionaries' powerful Fijian allies. But when Baker reached the village of Nabutautau, in almost the centre of Viti Levu, he committed a grave error of judgement. The chief there had casually picked up Baker's comb and inserted it into his own hair, an instance of petty but customary appropriation. By associating the object with his own person, and with the most sacred part of his body, he was rendering it tabu and inalienable. Baker, who had been in Fiji some years and should have known better, was angered and snatched the comb back. He was not indulged, as an ignorant foreigner might possibly have been among coastal people more accustomed to whites. The Nabutautau men promptly decided that the tabua would be accepted, whereupon a warrior followed the missionary out of the village and swiftly despatched him with an axe. While this is the substance of the story repeated in most Fijian histories and travelogues, and one still well known among Fijians today, it is likely that there was a more political layer to the assassination. Just as Marquesans and others in eastern Polynesia rightly suspected Christianity to be a vehicle for Pomare's empire-building, the Navosa people very likely considered Baker and the lotu as agents of Bauan-European domination.[8]

The ramifications of the killing – including the consumption of Baker's body – were enduring. Baker was the first, and would be the only, missionary ever to be killed in Fiji, and it is not surprising that his death should be singled out as a defining moment in the struggle between darkness and light in the islands. Profoundly racist white settlers, who already considered the 'hill tribes' to be more savage and primitive than the coastal people, literally demonized the inhabitants of the 'devil country'. Aristocratic and Christian Fijians, who subscribed to a sort of racism of their own, would stigmatize the people of the interior and never let the culpable tribe, in particular, forget their offence. Navatusila people have, in their own eyes, suffered misfortune ever since. As recently as 2003 they offered a major ceremony of atonement, when they sought forgiveness from, among others, the then prime minister of Fiji. Yet even subsequently, the villages of the district have lacked proper road access and otherwise suffered neglect and poverty.[9] The sins of the fathers have indeed been visited upon the children.

In the short term, the white settlers pressed Cakobau to lead a retaliatory operation. While the Europeans presumed that such an assault would be uncomplicated, and assumed the hill warriors were at bottom cowardly brutes, Cakobau was less inclined to underestimate them, and was aware of the formidable challenges that would confront an invasive party. He stalled for the better part of a year, but in April 1868 finally made an effort to marshall a substantial force of some thousands of warriors, which was divided into two main parties. One followed Baker's route up the Rewa river, and the other approached from the Ra coast of northern Viti Levu. Despite their considerable size, these armies suffered, within a few weeks, an ignominious defeat. Although a number of undefended hostile villages were taken en route to Korokula, the hill stronghold of the Dawarau warriors, the perpetrators of Baker's killing, the locals had the advantage of an intimate knowledge of their own terrain, and carried off surprise attacks on several of Cakobau's parties. Before the Korokula fort, fifty-nine of the would-be invaders were killed during a single forty-minute engagement, and many others, including many chiefs allied to Cakobau, lost their lives before the Bauan troops beat a retreat.[10]

The failure of the operation was seen to disastrously embolden the 'hill tribes', but some of the 'outrages' of subsequent years, such as the massacre of Ba planter William Burnes, his family and eighteen workers from Tanna, were perpetrated by people other than those who had killed Baker and repulsed Cakobau's men. The two distinct groups were not even allied, and the assault on Burnes's plantation was believed to have revenged the murder of one or more Fijians by some of his labourers: there was more than a single cycle of violence that linked settler society in Fiji and the Viti Levu tribes, but planter opinion passed over this, and the complicating presence of the Melanesian indentured workers, who in some cases mixed pretty comfortably with Fijians, but in others were drawn into battles of their own that the whites of the time could neither understand nor control. Small wonder that instead they traced trouble in the colony to an undifferentiated set of cannibalistic demons.

* * *

In June 1871 what became known as the 'Cakobau government' was established at Levuka, the beachcomber settlement that had become a petty colonial capital. It was on a Westminster model; certain high chiefs constituted a kind of House of Lords, but government business was in the hands of mostly European ministers, who however liaised with Cakobau; and Cakobau appears to have been genuinely influential. His kingship was recognized and the power of Bau extended. Chiefs, in some cases Bauan chiefs, were appointed governors of provinces, of *vanua* that had not consistently acknowledged Bauan supremacy. Yet at the same time there were multiple tensions. Europeans disagreed vigorously, most settlers wanted to be allowed to purchase lands without restraint, and some chiefs were only too pleased to 'sell' lands that they might at one time have seized but had never really owned. Some of the European ministers, notably John Bates Thurston, who was later governor, were broadly supportive of the Fijian chiefly hierarchy, but the majority were bitterly opposed to the customary order, and the pages of the *Fiji Times*, the journal of white opinion that had been established in 1869, harped on themes such as the supposed despotism of chiefs and the stifling of enterprise by customary forms of reciprocity. And despite the extent to which the new legislature had bolstered Bauan power, allegiances remained as fluid as they had always been. Ma'afu in particular continued to cultivate his own power-base in eastern Fiji.[11]

In 1873 the offer of cession to the Crown was revived, and Commodore Goodenough and Consul Layard visited Fiji to investigate. Cakobau was highly ambivalent, but the negotiation gained momentum, undermining the existing independent government, and in due course an agreement was reached, which was signed by a number of leading chiefs in September 1874. Sir Hercules Robinson, governor of New South Wales, visited Fiji in HMS *Dido* to interview Cakobau and confirm his understanding. The British would accept only an unconditional cession but undertook 'to deal with the King, chiefs and people not only equitably, but most liberally'.[12] Cakobau was told that he 'would be placed in a position which would make it unnecessary for you to draw upon the people for your support, and you would be supported in a way that your rank and position entitles you to'. That the Vunivalu would be pensioned off, albeit handsomely, was made explicit in newspaper reports in Sydney, which described Cakobau as 'ex-King' when he was brought back to New South Wales for a visit, to honour him and to mark Fiji's formal incorporation into the British empire.

Cakobau, accompanied by his sons Ratu Timoci (Timothy) and Ratu Joseph, was accorded a semblance of the honours due a visiting monarch. He was given a tour of the city's neoclassical post office in Martin Place, shown the workings of gas lights, the telegraph, and the view from the roof. He travelled by train to the outlying settlement, now suburb, of Liverpool. He was for some reason taken to a paper factory, he attended a great Methodist meeting in his honour, and was otherwise feasted.[13] While toasts were exchanged, however, a virus was transmitted. Measles was prevalent in the colony at the

49 Cakobau on the *Dido*, stereo view.

time, and Cakobau was infected. His case was apparently relatively mild, but others including his sons carried the contagion back to Fiji.

Though a chief medical officer had been appointed, the incumbent was new to the post and had done nothing to establish a quarantine system. At the time the arrival of a ship at Levuka was accompanied by no formalities, though the officers on board had some sense of the risk of an epidemic but were peculiarly negligent in failing to quarantine the vessel or observe any precautions at all. The ship's doctor, in fact, told Layard, then interim administrator of the colony, that all the Fijians on board carried the disease. Layard did ask whether Cakobau's sons could remain on board, but when it was suggested that this was impractical, the 'conversation then drifted to more general topics'.[14] The Fijian crew of the government boat that met the *Dido* fraternized more or less imme-diately with those on board, and very soon afterwards Cakobau, his sons and others were taken ashore to a general welcome. Over the subsequent days the Vunivalu, still recovering from his illness, was reunited with kin and met with a number of chiefs. Soon afterwards two further ships arrived from Sydney that very likely also carried infected individuals.

With the possible exception of a late eighteenth-century dysentery epidemic, known only through oral tradition, the 1875 introduction of measles was the worst disease event of Fijian history. A newspaper correspondent, aware only of the ramifications around Levuka, reported at the beginning of March that 'hundreds have already died, and the ravages of the disease still continue unabated'. Among the victims were prominent chiefs such as Roko Savenaca, Cakobau's half-brother and a former Minister for Native Affairs, and Ritova, his old adversary from Vanua Levu. 'It is really shocking', the journalist wrote, 'to witness the number of burials which take place. No less than four corpses, rolled in mats, have been carried past my own door since 8 o'clock this morning: and it is not unlikely that there may be others before the day closes.'[15] The devastation was unlikely to be limited to Fiji: shortly after the *Dido* had deposited Cakobau and his infected companions, the ship had taken on board over a hundred labourers and left to return them to various parts of Vanuatu and the Solomons.

The events were not only tragic but inauspicious, and it was in no way surprising that they prompted particular interpretations in many local minds. Though there was some illness among settler families, European susceptibility was mild relative to that of Fijians, who were therefore asking 'why do not the whites die as well as themselves'? 'They say further that the white men brought the sickness to Fiji, that the natives may all be killed, and the white men get all the land.'[16]

Negligence was compounded by sheer bad luck. Walter Carew, one of the few settlers who had a degree of rapport with inland Viti Levu people, and had formally been appointed Commissioner for the Interior, had arranged a meeting of chiefs and people at Navuso, on the Rewa river, at which the British takeover was to be presented and explained by Layard. Had the gathering taken place on the intended date, early in January 1875, no harm would have been done, at any rate none as soon or as swiftly. But a hurricane led to a postponement of the meeting, the return of the *Dido* intervened, and some of those who attended what turned out to be a great assembly of nine hundred to a thousand people came from Levuka and were already infected. Perhaps primarily because a good many of the people had confidence in Carew, the meeting went well, from the colonial perspective, and those present indicated that they would 'renounce heathenism and abandon cannibalism, to live peaceably among themselves, and to acknowledge thenceforward the supremacy of the Government'.[17] Unfortunately, a number of chiefs went on from the meeting to visit Levuka, but even had this not been the case, in the aftermath of the meeting, as participants returned to their villages, measles 'was diffused simultaneously through almost every part of the highlands'.

At this time estimates of the total population of Fiji were vague. Before the first epidemics, which were associated with wrecks or visits of trading ships in the late eighteenth century, as many as 300,000 people may well have lived in the group. For the 1870s a figure of approximately 150,000 has been considered credible, though this was supported by actual counts for only a few of the smaller settlements and islands. In the aftermath of the epidemic some statistics were reported. On the island of Ovalau 447 out of 1,546 had died; on Koro 688 out of 2,543, and in the northern Viti Levu district of Ba some 2,214 out of 7,925 inhabitants were thought to have died. The mortality rate, in other words, was over a quarter. These figures were extrapolated across the whole of Fiji, resulting in a figure of some 40,000 deaths, which both at the time and subsequently was widely accepted.[18] Horrific as this was, the impact on the population carried over some years, fertility was low, and infant mortality high.

Anatole von Hügel, a twenty-year-old traveller and ethnological enthusiast of aristocratic Austrian descent, happened to arrive in this group of islands in the aftermath of these events. He went on to travel extensively in the interior, and remarked frequently on the melancholy character of settlements emptied by the epidemic. 'We passed Viria, once an important town but now silent and deserted. . . . It is very saddening to pass these abandoned towns, formerly so prosperous and full of life, now so forlorn. The history of one seems to be that of all.'[19] At Verata he was told 'sickening stories about the time of the epidemic. How it rained in torrents and the sick and dying, tormented by the burning fever, crept alongside the deep ditches filled with putrid green water to quench their thirst and could not be persuaded to return to their huts, but lay on the saturated ground in the torrents of rain to die.'[20]

* * *

On a subsequent tour of western Viti Levu, von Hügel recorded that the chief of the coastal town of Sigatoka 'was busy notching the bamboos of the roof of the bure [in this context, the chiefly house of the village], to check off the number of those who had died during the epidemic. He counted over thirty able-bodied men that the town had lost "since it turned Christian", and that, he said, was not by any means the sum total of all deaths. This shows', von Hügel observed, 'how intimately measles and the new religion are connected in the minds of the natives.'[21]

Under these circumstances, it is not at all surprising, indeed the colonial officials of the time acknowledged that 'as might have been anticipated', many of those who had so recently adopted Christianity rejected it in the aftermath of the horror. In some cases, the heathen practices that had been proscribed were deliberately revived, in others Methodist teachers were merely sent away.

The new governor, Sir Arthur Gordon, had arrived at Levuka, and taken up residence at Nasova, which would become the headquarters of government, on 24 June 1875. Gordon was a liberal of a distinctly patrician kind. He was descended from the earls of Aberdeen, who had held high political office for generations, and his own father had been prime minister. He had a romantic view of his Scots ancestry, and saw the Fijian chiefs, clans and intrigues as having affinities with the Scots of the Middle Ages. This identification was, of course, consistent with the broader social evolutionism articulated by eighteenth-century Edinburgh and Glasgow theorists such as Adam Ferguson – peripheral peoples represented the pasts of Europeans – but the particular expression was distinctive. While modern hunter-gatherers were being relegated to the very beginnings of humanity, Fijians – together with various Polynesian peoples – would be equated with rugged and independent European peoples of the recent past.

This romanticism underpinned Gordon's celebration of the Fijian aristocracy and determination to govern through Fijian chiefs and institutions. But his affirmation of custom had definite limits. A spirit of independence might have been attractive in principle but was unacceptable in practice. Gordon asked Walter Carew to investigate the unsettled state of the interior and Carew, now described as 'Special Commissioner for Ba and Nadroga', reported in September a visit to Navatusila men, those connected with the killing of Baker some eight years earlier. 'I found them most uncommunicative,' he wrote, 'professing to know nothing, and to have heard of nothing'; they 'declared themselves to be ignorant of the name of the Buli', the official district chief, implying their non-recognition of new forms of government. Even the local missionary teacher, one Sefanaia, refused bluntly to tell Carew anything at all. He stated that if he did so he would offend the neighbouring people. Carew heard, too, that a number of teachers who had tried to proselytize at a village called Naicobocobo 'had recently had a most narrow escape of being murdered, the people ascribing the late epidemic to the anger of their heathen gods as their recent conversion to Christianity'. He told the ordained native minister of the district to back off for the time being. The mood he encountered, the missionaries' story, and other reports and rumours, convinced him that 'great trouble will shortly arise . . . unless action be taken at once'.[22]

The action Carew had in mind was not repressive but diplomatic. Over subsequent weeks he worked to convene meetings and persuade various parties in the Viti Levu interior to accept the authority of the governor and the new administration. He was a fluent speaker of standard Fijian, perhaps with some grasp of the interior dialects also, and spoke to one group 'with slight intermissions for nine hours', to another from 3 p.m. until 1 a.m. At Nasaucoko on the Sigatoka river he tried to reassure people that an armed

50 The village (in the foreground) and fort (behind) at Nasaucoko, sketch by Arthur J.L Gordon.

government camp that would be established was there simply to prevent general wrongdoing, that it was not 'a white man's camp, or a Bau man's camp, 'nor a camp of sea-coast people'. He repeatedly emphasized that no member of the official Fijian force there (the base would be manned by members of the local 'armed native constabulary', not by white soldiers) would be permitted to solicit or requisition food, but rather anything needed would be paid for. Everywhere he struggled to dissociate the new government from the coastal chiefs who, he recognized, were 'feared and detested' by those of the interior. He insisted, too, that all were 'perfectly free to accept Christianity or not'.[23]

These affirmations of the disinterestedness of the state were high-minded and may well have reflected Carew's own views, but they were views of what should have been the case, not what was. The British administration in Fiji was unavoidably identified with Bau and with other dominant chiefs, and no less aligned with them than it was with Christianity in general and the Methodist Church in particular. Ironically, given the history of evangelical dissent, the

Wesleyan mission had become, and indeed remains today, the established Church of the Fijian aristocracy and state. In subsequent years, disaffected individuals, sometimes whole clans or villages, would embrace Catholicism either simply to annoy Methodist chiefs or because they thought an identification with the French Marist missionaries might somehow exempt them from the rule of the British in Fiji.

Over several uncertain months, life at the Nasaucoko camp was peculiarly tense. Carew's appointment was administrative and he could not give orders to the armed Fijian force, which consisted largely of men from eastern and coastal Fiji, and was commanded by Captain Henry Olive. Both Olive and his men took the view that they had been sent into the district to fight; they were discontented and irritated by Carew's concern to take matters slowly, to conciliate. Olive's frustration appears to have been exacerbated by illness. He was probably bipolar and when low was 'all apathy and irresolution'. 'I dare not approach him with any suggestion, no matter on what topic', Walter Carew wrote to Gordon, and wrote repeatedly, pressing the governor to find some pretext to recall the captain, who needed, he felt, a change of scene.

Carew referred to the Fijians he was endeavouring to conciliate as 'a fierce, restless and turbulent lot of cannibals', but added that 'I myself respect these men for their daring, their activity, and love of freedom, and hospitality to those they do not suspect of being connected with their enemies.'[24] He stressed that the hill tribes were not to be underestimated: 'when once agreed on any point, their organization is not to be surpassed'. Europeans in Fiji would all have gone along with the characterization of a 'turbulent lot of cannibals', but very, very few would have said that they respected them, nor would they have credited them with any organizational or military effectiveness. Carew felt that 'the outside world in Fiji cannot understand', they had no grasp of the situation on the ground. Both the European population and probably also the Fijians who lived away from the theatre of conflict expected a quick and decisive campaign, which he considered neither possible nor desirable.

Carew did well to conciliate as many people as he did, over six to seven months in late 1875 and early 1876. But the damage – in the form of measles – that had already been done, together with the deep-seated antagonisms among various interior peoples and between them and the predatory matanitu of the coast, made it probably inevitable that even careful and extended reassurance from a sympathetic if effectively disingenuous Englishman would not forstall the kind of 'disturbance' that had been anticipated and feared. Throughout the early months of 1876, there were rumours that the Nasaucoko fort would be attacked – at one time reports reached Levuka that it had been, the constabulary and the Europeans massacred. In fact, there was no assault, but in March there were increasing signs that some kind of uprising was likely. People from villages friendly to the government, who had supplied Nasaucoko with food, were harassed. And then in mid-April, over a week, the 'devils' or 'tevoro' attacked and burnt at least twelve pro-government villages. Among early reports was a letter from one Sala Seru, the *buli*, or officially appointed district chief, in the village of Vatukarasa. 'Evil has arrived in our district,' he wrote:

> They from Batiri are clubbed; all the towns until you arrive at Korotogo are burned.
>
> A great number of men are clubbed; I do not correctly know the number. . . . The man found some who had been clubbed, one old woman, and two, a mother and child; one old woman shot in the neck, and one able-bodied man shot dead; and one speared with a tabevatu.
>
> The attacking party were from Taviuni, Nadrala, Vatuvoko, and all the devils in this district, or on this side. The magistrate (native) from Tavuni was shot, and said to have been dragged off to be cooked.
>
> Our district is ruined. On this (Monday) morning this thing happened.
>
> I beg of you some more paper and envelopes that I may continue writing to you. I have no more paper.
>
> I write this letter in great haste.
>
> My love to you.[25]

Further communications described how villagers had retreated and barricaded themselves inside caves, but that 'cannibals' had taken up position outside, and in one instance 'occupied themselves during the whole night in firing upon the defenceless occupants'.[26] This may have been untrue or only partially true, but there was no doubt that rebels had made a coordinated assault and killed a considerable number of people in settlements allied to the government. Luki, the Roko Tui Nadroga, the official district chief of the western province of Nadroga, quickly brought together a small force, ventured up the Sigatoka river and made an immediate retaliatory attack.[27] Na Bisiki, one of the rebel leaders, was reported killed. Carew wrote that he had been an 'atrocious scoundrel . . . their tower of strength, and a most determined cannibal . . . at the root of all the mischief'. His death, he considered 'most fortunate', but a week later it transpired that the information was false, that Na Bisiki was well and active. Though, following the assault from Nadroga, his men had been forced to withdraw, it seemed now that 'the Kai Colo are boasting great things again'.[28]

It took considerably longer for the government to bring its troops together. The governor took the view that what was in fact an army, but would be described as a police force, should be made up not of a small detachment of Royal Engineers that was stationed in the colony, nor of settlers, but rather of locals under the command of British officers. All provinces were asked to supply volunteers, and animosity toward the hill peoples was such that many districts had no trouble finding considerably more men than they had been asked for. Some two thousand Fijians, divided into distinct forces that undertook separate campaigns into the 'disaffected' districts, would in due course assist the administration's suppression of the insurrection, which got under way in May 1876.

In the interim, however, 'loyal' chiefs continued to act independently, raiding and burning villages identified with the 'tevoro', or 'devils'. It was evident, too, that despite Carew's effort to separate the issue of conversion to Christianity from that of recognition of British rule, the two were entirely conflated. ' "Lotu" ', Carew noted, 'is not a Fijian word; it means religion, possibly in Samoa'. (In fact, it was Tahitian, and had come to refer to Christianity in the early stages of the LMS venture there, and had then been introduced by missionaries into western Oceania.) 'But with these people it means nothing more than rebellion or no rebellion. To be *lotu* is to recognize the Government, to be *vaka tevoro* is to murder, etc.'[29]

This, presumably, was how 'tevoro' were characterized by Christian Fijians. While rebels did fight and kill, in conformity with the long-standing customary celebration of warrior prowess, fighting and cannibalism had now acquired new meanings: they were acts of defiance, of resistance to colonial rule. Interior people defined their own action in explicitly political terms, one group declaring that they constituted 'a "matanitu vaka ira," i.e. separate government ... having broken from their rightful [pro-Government] chief, Tui Conua'.[30] On this occasion, and on others like it, Carew and his colleagues in the administration would make decisions about what had been customary, about who deferred to whom, about the boundaries of lands. Yet whether a certain man was the 'rightful' chief of a certain group of people would chronically prove contentious. A few years earlier, a witness to a Cakobau government inquiry, irritated by questions about the customs regarding succession to chiefly office, declared that their custom had always been to fight about it. But this fluidity in indigenous affairs would be intolerable to the British regime, which struggled to document and fix customs, rights and relationships of all sorts. What was never acknowledged was that this fixing entailed taking sides, which the colonial regime did most spectacularly and brutally in the case of the so-called 'little war', but would carry on doing in a variety of ways for decades afterwards.

During May parties from both sides carried on raiding the other and many villages were burnt. In some of the 'loyal' villages attacked by rebels, the *sulus*, the sarong-style European fabrics that Christian Fijians generally wore, were torn off men and women, to refute or reverse their new religious identification and all it implied. There continued to be differences of opinion among the British. Some were in favour of sending tabua, whale's teeth, to all the rebels, entreating them to 'soro', to express their submission in a customary fashion. But chiefs such as Na Bisiki and Mudu of Qalimari were trenchantly opposed to Church and government and had already rejected such action at many meetings among the peoples of the district. And attitudes in the administration had hardened in favour of exemplary and repressive action. Despite Gordon's inclination to support Fijian custom, he excluded the idea of resolving the conflict in a Fijian way, if that meant that rebel men might merely surrender and go unpunished. He considered it unfortunate that the worst that had been done (at any rate judicially) to any offender in the past had been to exile them for a period. He considered it necessary to insist upon the absolute power of the state. He instructed his subordinates: 'Procure submission wherever you can; punish the obstinate; make prisoners where possible; do not empty the land.'

The governor was repeatedly vexed by the practice of government forces, which was to burn rebel villages at every opportunity. He considered the tactic uncivilized, and was no doubt right in thinking that in the longer term it would do more to undermine than strengthen colonial rule – those who suffered could only be more deeply estranged from the British. He issued a formal government order prohibiting the practice, but conceded defeat even as he drafted the document, allowing exceptions where there might be 'strong reason' for burning, or where it might be 'impracticable' not to do so. The practice was deep-seated among both Fijians and colonial forces – it had been a routine element of customary warfare, as it was of punitive colonial ventures across the Pacific. Both his subordinates and Fijian allies – who were, naturally enough, seizing the opportunity to fight their own battles – did, as it happened, find it 'impracticable' not to burn rebel villages. Over the months of conflict at least dozens of settlements and their gardens would be destroyed.

Here again Gordon would have liked to set aside the hallmark of his policy, to conduct business in conformity with Fijian custom. He wished he could dissociate the repression from routine warfare, and instead have it recognized and understood, by those who were loyal and disloyal alike, as an assertion of the law. He would fail, in the case of the particular policy, but would certainly fail also, to present the campaign as anything other than the subjugation of one group of tribes by another, another that was allied with, that as it were included, the British and Christian regime.

The campaign gained momentum in June. The Qalimari were driven out of villages in the lower Sigatoka and their stronghold, the fort of Matanavatu, was assaulted and taken in the middle of that month. Soon afterwards the chief Mudu and others considered 'ringleaders' were captured and taken down to the coast. Gordon swiftly made arrangements to conduct trials, and a court was set up in the coastal town of Sigatoka. The trials were conducted by his nephew, Arthur J.L. Gordon, who was an assistant commissioner and had led the recent and successful campaign. Gordon himself sat, he wrote, 'on the divan a little in the background'. Whether he was trying to affirm that there was some separation between executive power and the judiciary, or conceding that there was next to none, is unclear. Several of the Roko Tuis were present as 'assessors', ostensibly to act somewhat like a jury, but of the thirty-six men who were indicted, virtually all freely admitted the particular offences.

Mudu, identified as 'the chief fomenter of the late troubles', was charged with conspiring with other chiefs 'to set on foot murderous raids upon peaceable subjects of the Queen . . .', with bearing 'arms in such raids', with being an accessory to 'killing and slaying', and having killed and slain 'with malice aforethought' various individuals himself. When he was given the opportunity to speak in his defence, 'Mudu made a long and very curious statement with respect to intrigues with the Sabeto chiefs', which Gordon found was 'wholly irrelevant to the charges against himself, which he freely admitted'.[31] This, needless to say, reminds us that relevance is not measurable, not a fact, but an issue liable to be construed differently by the different parties to any particular conflict. And perhaps in terms that are not only different, but incommensurable, in a conflict that is cross-cultural, even in this case multi-cultural, given the extent to which long-standing disputes between different Fijian peoples, as well as a contradiction between Fijian dissidence and colonial rule, were at play. Mudu surely rehearsed a history of local relationships and 'intrigues' precisely because, from his perspective, it was relevant, it accounted for his conduct. For him, and no doubt for some of his antagonists, the conflict had been about something other than what the British had recognized. Or rather, what they recognized represented just one layer, one expression of an old and manifold set of troubles. But even had Gordon grasped the salience of some set of ancient and ongoing troubles, such a history would have been in no way admissible; it was superseded by colonial distinctions between the legal and illegal. Hence Mudu's statement was 'wholly irrelevant', amounted to no sort of excuse, and provided no grounds for mercy.

Of the thirty-six men tried, one was acquitted. A witness was brought forward that Kai Vinaka had been forced to accompany the rebels; he was one of a dozen or so men among the prisoners from the village of Tabu ni Vonu who, it was said, had been taken away and forced to fight. All of the others were sentenced to death, about a third to 'Death, but recommended to mercy', generally because they were known to have participated in the fighting, but not to have killed anyone themselves. Gordon spent the evening after the trial considering the sentences. 'Where so many richly deserved death, it was difficult to select', he wrote. He had 'hoped to keep the number down to ten or twelve, but if any at all were to be executed, I found it impossible, with justice and fairness, to bring it below fifteen.'[32]

Name.	Charges.	Plea.	Evidence.	Judgment.	Sentence.	Remarks.
Matalau of Nadrala	1. That at divers times and places, between the 12th day of April and the 23d day of June in the present year, to wit: at Batiri, on the 17th of April, and elsewhere, he did bear arms against the duly constituted authorities of this Colony. 2. That at divers times and places, between the 12th day of April and the 23d day of June in the present year, to wit: at Matanavatu, he has, by force of arms, resisted the arrest of certain persons charged with the crime of murder; and was accessory to the unlawful killing and slaying of divers of Her Majesty's subjects, killed in the endeavour to make such arrests. 3. That he was accessory to the killing and murdering of divers of Her Majesty's peaceable subjects in the said Colony, to wit: Batikobulu, Jinnia, Seruaya, Navue, Salome, Namoli, Tonasiga, Tovidrin, Wagaiwai, Takuieri, Sidrai, Qaidawarau, and Cairisa. 4. That he did, on the 17th of April last past, at Batiri, of malice aforethought, kill and slay one Salome, against the peace of Her Majesty and the said Colony.	Guilty. I killed Salome. I killed her with a club.	Pleaded guilty	Guilty	Death	Executed.
Na Walu, of Nadrala	1. That at divers times and places, between the 12th day of April and the 23d day of June in the present year, to wit: at Batiri, on the 17th of April, and elsewhere, he did bear arms against the duly constituted authorities of this Colony. 2. That at divers times and places, between the said 12th day of April and the 23d day of June in the present year, to wit: at Matanavatu, he has, by force of arms, resisted the arrest of certain persons charged with the crime of murder; and was accessory to the unlawful killing and slaying of divers of Her Majesty's subjects, killed in the endeavour to make such arrests. 3. That he was accessory to the killing and murdering of divers of Her Majesty's peaceable subjects in the said Colony, to wit: Batikobulu, Jinnia, Seruaya, Navue, Salome, Namoli, Tonasiga, Tovidrin, Wagaiwai, Takuieri, Sidrai, Qaidawarau, and Cairisa. 4. That he did, on the 17th of April last past, at Batiri, of malice aforethought, kill and slay a child, name unknown, against the peace of Her Majesty and the said Colony.	Yes, I was at Batiri with those who killed the women. I did not kill any women. It is quite true I killed a child; only one though.	Admits guilt	Guilty	Death	Executed.
Taere of Nadrala	1. That at divers times and places, between the 12th day of April and the 23d day of June in the present year, to wit: at Batiri, on the 17th of April, and elsewhere, he did bear arms against the duly constituted authorities of this Colony. 2. That at divers times and places, between the 12th day of April and the 23d day of June in the present year, to wit: at Matanavatu, he has, by force of arms, resisted the arrest of certain persons charged with the crime of murder; and was accessory to the unlawful killing and slaying of divers of Her Majesty's subjects, killed in the endeavour to make such arrests. 3. That he was accessory to the killing and murdering of divers of Her Majesty's peaceable subjects in the said Colony, to wit: Batikobulu, Jinnia, Seruaya, Navue, Salome, Namoli, Tonasiga, Tovidrin, Wagaiwai, Takuieri, Sidrai, Qaidawarau, and Cairisa.	Guilty. I killed this woman at Batiri.	Admits guilt	Guilty	Death	Executed.

51 Extract from a table in Sir Arthur Hamilton Gordon's private publication, *Letters and Notes written during the Disturbances in the Highlands (known as the "Devil Country") of Viti Levu, Fiji.*

The following morning the sentences were carried out in the *rara*, the extensive open green generally found in Fijian villages. It was insisted that women and children remain inside, and that absolute silence was maintained. Two upright posts from an old house were used to support a cross-beam and form a gallows, but the hanging of the first man, Matalau, was botched. The rope broke, 'he fell on his face on the ground, and Solomoni [a Fijian constable] shot him through the head with a rifle'. Four others were, as Gordon put it, 'hanged more successfully', without 'the violent struggling one associates with the idea of hanging'. The remainder were shot in the centre of the green, before an old mound in which chiefly ancestors had been buried:

> Mudu was the first shot. He did not die like a chief. When told to kneel he did so, but immediately rose again and ran towards the people, calling to them as his 'children' (*luvequ*) to protect and help him. Not a voice replied, nor was a hand raised. Had he succeeded in exciting their sympathy, our career would have been short. He was brought back and placed seated on the ground, but he would not keep his position, and shifted round rapidly, half sideways, half crouching, so that when the party fired he was not killed outright, and had to be shot through the head.[33]

Eight other men were executed without incident, though it turned out that one, Tabuarua, convicted of poisoning, had escaped during the night.

When Gordon wrote about the campaign and its conclusion later, he thought it 'important to point out that the capital punishments thus inflicted were not, as they might at first sight appear to be, military executions. The accused were tried in the same manner as they would have been under ordinary circumstances. . . .' He would argue consistently, too, that the overall action had been a police matter rather than a military one.

These distinctions were unlikely to have been apparent to those who witnessed the 30 June executions. If Fijian societies had always been marked by violence, that violence had been mainly delivered in heat and rage. This cooler mass killing was alien to the understandings of these Islanders. It might be assumed that they found the proceeding peculiarly shocking, and they may well have done, but the fact of the matter is that there is no way of reconstructing the states of mind of those who witnessed this at once silent and extravagant ritual. Some among the crowd were allied with the victors and perhaps had no particular feeling for enemies, men themselves known to have been violent. But many were prisoners from the rebel tribes, commoner followers who would in due course be deported or released. They had seen the lives of kin, of chiefs – who people throughout Fiji were in general reverential of, and deeply attached to – terminated in this unprecedented and unusual fashion. If the moment of formal colonization had been marked by the carnage of the measles epidemic, and its consolidation by this carefully staged atrocity, the new world must surely have seemed to them to be a savage and desolate one.

Late in the evening Charles Eyre, one of Gordon's minor officers, arrived. He had returned from a visit to the captured stronghold of Matanavatu. He was 'in raptures' about the countryside, the beauty of the fort's situation and surroundings. Indeed one of the stranger features of the reports and

52 Highland Viti Levu prisoner, photographed c.1876–7.

memoranda from the 'Little War' campaign is their mingling of stories of atrocities with lyrical accounts of the Fijian environment, which on the drier western slopes was considered by some to be reminiscent of England. And this was the substance of late conversation on 30 June. 'Nothing was said about our day's work', Gordon wrote the next day. But 'During the night, a woman began talking to the ghost of Matalau – very weird and ghastly.'[34]

* * *

Operations in the central highlands continued until around the beginning of September. Na Bisiki was captured. This man, Carew considered, had been the most formidable of the government's opponents. For two years he had 'exercised a species of direct terrorism over the tribe to which he belonged, and was a man of great determination of character, and of undaunted courage' who had done more than anyone to fortify 'the obstinacy of the tribes of this region in their outbreak and persistent defiance of the authorities'. Such was his mana, and force of personality, that Carew feared that no one would testify to the chief's direct involvement in any offence, prejudicing his conviction. Yet a verdict was pre-empted by a handcuffed Na Bisiki attempting an extraordinary escape, while surrounded by constables, and as evidence was presented against him. He at first succeeded in breaking away, but only as far as the top of a bluff on the outskirts of the village, where he was shot dead.

In the course of the same trial almost eighty men were convicted of various offences connected with the uprising and sentenced, typically to two to three years' hard labour. Five were executed, as were five further men in a separate trial at Nasaucoko in October. At the same time Gordon declared a general amnesty and the campaign over.

* * *

The files of colonial correspondence intersperse reports of the Viti Levu war with papers dealing with a host of topics. Some, such as those concerned with the future location of the colony's capital – which was to be moved from Levuka to Suva, on the mainland – were essentially practical. Others touched on much deeper questions of colonial policy – particularly on the extent to which Fijian custom and law might be enshrined in colonial administration and regulation. Gordon was committed to the view that they should, and saw himself almost as grafting a rational and civilized form of colonial government onto a Fijian society, a hierarchy of chiefs, that existed already, and needed only to be purged of its barbaric elements, elements that among Christian Fijians had been largely consigned to history by the mission.

If this understanding – that proposed an obligation to respect the customs of the Islanders – was in principle good, and surely preferable to the premises of many colonial regimes, it demanded and stimulated something of an inquisition, which in its various branches would keep colonial officials, both European and Fijian, busy for decades. What exactly were these customs that were to be preserved and protected? What, for example, could chiefs customarily demand from their people? How were legitimate offerings and expressions of respect to be distinguished from the exactions of an overbearing despot? If it was obvious that cannibalism and widow-strangling would be (and had already largely been) abolished, despite having been customary, many practices fell in a grey area – it was either unclear whether they actually were customary, or arguable that they might have been, but were sufficiently detrimental to Fijian welfare to be proscribed anyway.

Fiji would, in other words, not be merely a colonial possession, it would not simply be ruled, but actually and exhaustively *governed*, in the sense that the ostensible rationality of the state and its agents would be dedicated to describing and regulating many domains of life, work and behaviour. The business assumed greater momentum, and could be cloaked in benevolence, with growing official concern over the decline of the Fijian population, which, it was erroneously assumed, had a plethora of causes independent of introduced disease. (The measles epidemic was understood as a one-off event rather than as one having medium-term effects on fertility.) Certain forms of marriage, drinking kava, forms of customary exchange that stifled a spirit of enterprise, the keeping of dogs, were all in one way or another blamed for poor health.

The 'insanitary' character of Fijian life was rigorously inspected. New regulations in 1885 concerned the constructed of new houses. Landholders could no longer simply erect a dwelling wherever they wished. Proposals had to be submitted to the chief and elders of the village, who would consider whether the site was unhealthy or unsuitable, and might direct a would-be builder to another location if they considered it necessary. No house could be built without a raised foundation. No ditch could be dug without a free outlet. Chiefs were obliged to check that the pitch of the roof met an appropriate standard, that posts and beams were sound, and so on and so forth. More radically, certain villages that lay in what were judged to be insanitary situations were relocated and amalgamated. In a good many cases these villages were or had been associated with dissent, and relocation made them easier of access, easier to observe.[35]

* * *

This broadly intrusive effort was resisted in small ways by many villagers, and people were constantly being fined for minor transgressions of one regulation or another. But it was also responded to more powerfully and imaginatively, in ways that the colonial administration found hard to fathom and hard to manage.

In 1886 the minister John Bates Thurston reported that 'events of an unusual character were transpiring in the mountainous parts of Colo East'. A party of 'strange men' had appeared. They had faces blackened as had been customary in wartime, they carried guns, they were dressed in barkcloth, implying a reversion to heathenism, and they performed a sort of drill 'under the command of persons whom they termed "sartini" or serjeants'. It transpired that they were adherents of a man named Dukumoi, but who had adopted the name Navosavakadua, the Fijian translation of the chief justice's title, 'he who speaks but once', whose word is final. Carew reported that he was propagating 'a very ingenious and dangerous compounding of Fijian mythology and belief with the teachings of the Old and New Testaments'. He referred to a tradition concerning Degei, the prominent god sometimes described as 'the Fijian creator', whose great dove was killed by his twin grandsons, the two young chiefs Nakalasabasai and Namakaumoli. In retribution their lands were laid waste and they were sent into exile. Their subsequent fates were unknown, but Navosavakadua revealed that they had in fact sailed their canoe to the land of the white men, who wrote about them in the Bible. The sacred book had been deceptively mistranslated by missionaries, who referred to the two as Jesus Christ and Jehovah, rather than by their Fijian names.

The two, Navosavakadua prophesied, were to return, and a new era in Fiji would begin. Adherents of what colonial officials called the Tuka cult would have life eternal, and would recover their ancient power and prestige. In the meantime they were to drill like soldiers and to carry out particular rituals in spirit houses. Navosavakadua's teachings entailed novel geographic identifications: 'They have named the various spots around Nakawadra respectively Roma (Rome), Ijipita (Egypt), Kolosa (Colossians), &c.' Navosavakadua also told his followers that white men as well as Fijians believed that the two chiefly brothers would return. Surveyors 'going about with chains and looking through glasses, pretending to measure land, are in reality looking for them', as were men-of-war at sea.[36]

A.B. Brewster was another planter turned colonial official, with some paternalistic fondness for 'the hill tribes of Fiji', about which he later wrote a travel book-come-anthropological monograph. He was considered knowledgeable and was charged with investigating the affair. He observed in conclusion that:

It may be urged that Navosavakadua is mad and therefore harmless, but it is apparent that there is a good deal of method in his madness. Witness for instance the large amount of presents he has received. His votaries are continually presenting pigs, tabuas, masi and yaqona [cloth and kava], and to such an extent as to very much rouse the jealousy of the Roko Tui Ra [the colonially appointed provincial high chief]. Again his movement was organized with a great deal of skill, his followers being divided into bands of what were called soldiers commanded by 'satinis' and in such villages as believed in him were 'betes' [priests] who regularly reported him in the way Wesleyan Native teachers report to their superior officers.[37]

This characterization emphasized the irrational mimicry of colonial institutions, but Navosavakadua's rites and projects were far more deeply seated than Brewster or any other European understood. He was a priest of the land, and in this area priests had long performed rites that consecrated warriors, that rendered them invulnerable. His narrative of revelation aspired to create a new world in which the empowered and blessed state was extended among his followers at large, who brought gifts and drank sacred waters, identifying themselves with the priest, as people within a potent vanua. This understanding privileged the land and the autochthonous cults and forms of authority that belonged to it. It was opposed to what had become the dominant and conventional Fijian polity, which was constituted around the avowedly greater sanctity of the immigrant chief.[38]

To the core, Navosavakadua's teaching and his practice affirmed the status of the *taukei*, the common owners of the land, as against the immigrant chiefs of the sea, who were now closely identified with Christianity and government. There was more to this challenge to the lotu than the affirmation of ancestral gods and customary ways that had been central to the resistance of hill peoples in 1875–6. Navosavakadua asserted that the Christianity of the Wesleyans and their Fijian adherents was predicated on lies about the names and origins of gods. In truth the gods were gods of the land, of his own Kauvadra landscape specifically. To honour them was to honour the precedence of the place, and indeed implied some reversal of the hierarchies that had come to constitute the colony. 'All existing affairs would be reversed; the whites would serve the natives, the chiefs would become the common people and the latter would take their places.'[39]

Colonial officials such as Brewster considered Navosavakadua mad and characterized his teaching as crazy superstition, but nevertheless felt there was a real threat to the stability of the colony. The priest had already been deported once, during an earlier phase of resistance to the Roko Tui Ra, the officially appointed provincial high chief. Since, in 1885, he was responsible for no violence, and could only be charged with conduct calculated to create a breach of the peace, he was initially sentenced only to a year's hard labour, but in 1887 the ordinance 'To Provide for Confining Disaffected or Dangerous Natives to particular localities' was introduced specifically to deal with him, and he was exiled to Rotuma. Rotuma formed part of the Crown colony but was distant, and culturally quite distinct from Fiji. The priest would be a stranger and a closely monitored guest, and would, it was anticipated, have no opportunity to pursue political or ritual agitation. Whether Navosavakadua was reconciled to these circumstances or not cannot be established, though he married on the island and lived there until his death in 1897.

Navosavakadua's deportation did not, however, bring an end to either the particular practices that the colonial regime considered dangerous or to dissidence in the Colo provinces in general. There were many 'outbreaks' – officials resorted to disease metaphors – of Tuka-related activity in subsequent years. In 1891 and 1914 reports of a revival of rites prompted vigorous policing, involving the flogging or sundry punishment of many individual villagers and the relocation or deportation of several whole village communities. Other leaders emerged, often claiming an affiliation with Navosavakadua, and people punished for engaging in rites, or defecting from the dominant Church to local movements, found in due course that the government could do nothing if they turned to Christian faiths such as Seventh-Day Adventism. Implicitly rather than explicitly opposed to the Fijian hierarchy and government, such sects created a sphere of autonomy, a space for local imagination and local action.[40]

* * *

Gordon and his successors frequently acted repressively, so far as the people of the Viti Levu west and interior, and certain other 'disaffected' groups, were concerned. But Gordon considered himself a liberal among colonial policy-makers, and indeed he was, in the important sense that he considered it more vital to sustain the Fijian community than to frame policy around the interests of settlers. Settlers and their allies, such as merchants based in Australia, never ceased to agitate for land, and against the system of taxation in kind, which positively discouraged Fijians from doing what most had no inclination to do anyway, which was leave their villages to work on plantations for Europeans. Under a different regime, whether British or that of any other European power, the Fijians could easily have found themselves dispossessed like indigenous peoples the world over. Though Gordon's executions of rebels remain shocking, they were at least not succeeded by confiscations of tribal territories of the kind that commonly took place in the aftermath of conflict in New Zealand, New Caledonia and elsewhere.

Yet there was a corollary to this paternalistic protectionism. Gordon was contemptuous of the white settlers then resident in Fiji, many of whose small enterprises were indeed hopelessly under-capitalized. But he needed them, or some other enterprise to flourish, since it was his task to make the colony cover its costs, which would be impossible unless exports got off the ground. Though Gordon hoped that after a generation or so Fijian communities would 'advance', it could only be anticipated that the Fijian contribution to tax revenues would be very modest for many years.

If there was a lack of investment there was also a lack of labour, and it appeared unlikely that recruitment from Vanuatu and the Solomons could fill the gap. The deservedly bad press that the trade had received made it impossible for someone in Gordon's position to promote it, and once kidnapping was suppressed, it was unlikely that Fiji would ever attract sufficient numbers of Islanders anyway. Queensland paid better, had additional attractions such as the entertainment offered by the port towns, and was by this time well established as the preferred place for Islanders to work. Some Islanders continued to be recruited for Fiji, and some of them stayed on and settled among Fijians, but the answer to the colony's larger 'labour question' had to come from elsewhere. Even before he arrived in Fiji, Gordon had probably decided to seek labourers from India, who had been recruited for decades to work in other colonies such as Natal and Mauritius. There was already a well-established system of officially sanctioned recruiting depots and agents; it was comparatively straightforward to add Fiji to the colonies of destination.

Like the trade in Islander labour before and in parallel with it, Indian indenture was chronically controversial, for many good reasons. Regulation did nothing to ameliorate diverse injustices and improprieties that began when poorly informed or gullible recruits were lured into depots, injustices that carried on as contracts were formalized, as men and women were shipped and in due course subjected to plantation regimes, which many inspectors considered onerous if not more blatantly exploitative. The growth of the Fijian sugar industry saw labour fully institutionalized, however. The experience of the plantation 'lines' would later be recalled and memorialized with horror by survivors and descendants who remained in Fiji, in due course amounting to near half the colony's population. They came, with considerable justification, to understand their suffering as a price paid to sustain the Fijian population,

Fijian society and Fijian ownership of Fijian land. If the political trouble that eventually followed had many layers to it, if it reflected deep intra-Fijian fissures that had so many years earlier motivated Navosavakadua and his followers, it was nevertheless the case that Gordon and his successors had given the colony a deeply contradictory constitution, at once liberal and illiberal, protective and oppressive. But the awkward order would not be sustained by the British alone. It was also the willingness, indeed the enthusiasm on the part of a Fijian elite, to collaborate that maintained stability through much of the twentieth century, and the Indo-Fijian elite that in due course emerged pressed for reform, but broadly supported that stable order too. The negotiation of the Fijian nation in the twentieth century is another story, but it is notable that its tensions precluded real reckoning with the colony's beginnings. The events of the 1876 war in the Viti Levu interior remain known, to some degree, in the communities that were most affected, but there are no monuments on the battlefields and no memorials to the dead.

CHAPTER TEN

✦

Our paradise became a hell

In Wellington in early 1881 Sir Arthur Gordon met one William Churchward, a former army officer seeking a colonial appointment of some sort, and encouraged him to act as 'Adviser and Chief Secretary' to Malietoa, then considered 'King of Samoa'. As job offers went, this was not great – there was no salary attached, unless Churchward was somehow able to persuade Malietoa to impose taxes to fund one – but he agreed to travel to Apia, the main settlement on Samoa, to take up the post, anticipating rather that he might become the British consul when that role became vacant. Gordon was meddling: he had been interested in incorporating both Samoa and Tonga into the Crown Colony of Fiji, but as was his wont he masked the imperialistic impulse in a spirit of charity, emphasizing to Churchward that he would be in a position to do 'an immense deal of good – and a great deal of harm!'.[1]

Churchward appears to have done not much of either, in a political sense, during his four-year stint in Samoa, but he did make a considerable, if largely inadvertent contribution to Samoan social life. Keen on his recreations, he considered it regrettable, during his first couple of years in the islands, that Samoans exhibited no interest in joining the British residents in an occasional game of cricket. In Tonga the game had been embraced with such enthusiasm that playing more than one day a week had been prohibited, and the Tongans in Samoa, who often played with Churchward and friends, eventually gave the Samoans the idea that they too ought to take it up. What Churchward described as a 'deputation' approached himself and the Apia magistrate, another Englishman, seeking instruction which they were more than keen to provide.

> For a time all went on very smoothly, but the quiet and serious English style did not suit them long. One by one, innovations of their own and Tongan manufacture crept into the game, until soon nothing remained of cricket *pur*

et simple, but the practice of one man bowling a ball to another man trying to hit it.[2]

The innovations included the enlargement of teams to forty or one hundred a side – to however many could be rounded up – and a distinctive style of bat, closely resembling a type of ancestral club. But more importantly the game was made the occasion for inter-village feasting. Play would be preceded by a grand procession headed by the umpires, the players wearing wreaths and garlands, who would perform dances and drills, directed by 'officers' 'generally dressed in full naval uniform, with swords and cocked-hats complete', who would dash up and down the lines, directing the performance. Behind them would come women and children, 'also in gala dress', bearing the feast for players and spectators alike. According to Churchward, the 'antics in the field beggar description. Each different club would have a distinct method of expressing its joy at the dismissal of an adversary from the wickets; some of them, of a most elaborate nature, must have taken much careful drilling in private.'[3]

The game, now known as *kirikiti* or *kilikiti*, has flourished ever since, and continues to be played by Samoans in New Zealand as well as Samoa itself.[4] Though like any sport it often still expresses local rivalries, the game in the 1880s had a more particular political slant, it being identified as a British activity rather than simply a European one. The quasi-military ceremony that accompanied it included, at any rate on some occasions, salutes in front of the houses of the Apia magistrate and the British consul. These were expressions, not of any especially positive respect for or interest in the British Crown, but of a snub – of anti-German sentiment.

From the late 1850s on the Germans had made Samoa the base for their enterprises in the Pacific. In the early 1870s agents of the formidable Hamburg firm of Godeffroy and Son had taken advantage of a demand for firearms among Samoans, and rapaciously acquired land on a massive scale. Though the contracts that both they and various German, Australasian and British competitors used were vague and misleading – they omitted details of price which would be subject to surveys undertaken at an unspecified future date – some Samoans were equally manipulative, disposing of lands that were in no sense theirs to sell, or rushing to sell, to pre-empt perhaps estranged relatives and co-owners. Some lands were certainly sold several times over, and when sales were investigated European claims added up, in total, to more land than physically existed in the islands, including many inhabited villages. The Samoans were in no sense naïve, they understood what sale meant. But, as in many other parts of the Pacific, and indeed of the colonized world, the dispersed and non-exclusive nature of ownership as well as the rushed and deceptive process made nonsense of any claim that land had in general been legitimately acquired.[5]

Late nineteenth-century Samoan politics were notoriously complicated. But in fact the field of contention was like that of many other islands and archipelagoes in the Pacific. Everywhere, long-standing local struggles were played out in dealings with foreigners, while commercial, political and strategic rivalries among foreigners were conversely played out through dealings with Islanders. This articulation of indigenous and foreign contests may sound complex, and indeed the flow of events was like the movement of a kaleidoscope – different patterns and relationships emerged at each turn. Yet the dynamic was actually still more complex than this implied. On top of the interacting indigenous and foreign rivalries, pre-existing relationships with Tongans and Fijians, and internal discord, between British missionaries and British settlers, for example, among other involvements, enriched an already fertile field for multifarious engagements and strategies.

If there were parallels to Samoan conflicts across the Pacific, Samoan milieux did have, however, a peculiar capacity to bewilder Europeans, or at least those Europeans who ever went to the trouble of trying to understand what underpinned the conflicts of the last decades of the nineteenth century. Just as Tongan kingship had earlier perplexed Cook and succeeding European visitors, the Samoan polity was easily assumed to be a simple, quasi-feudal kingship or chieftainship that it was not and never had been. Inherited rank was important to status in Samoa, as it was in many other Oceanic societies, but political office was something different and resulted from a distinctive electoral process. Certain groups of orators would meet, deliberate and bestow titles upon individuals – generally male but potentially female – on the basis of their mother's rank and the strength and political prestige of her place of origin. There were many low-level titles and four 'royal' ones. Hence the European assumption that a high chief might be the leader of a large tribe was in this case erroneous; title-holders were not like the lairds of Scottish clans. They certainly always had particular local affiliations, but they were supported for various reasons by coalitions of districts.[6]

In principle there was no single Samoan king or queen, but if a single person was elected to all four titles he or she became Tupu and was hailed as O le Tafa'ifa, 'the Four-Sided One'. While oral traditions agreed that a single dynasty had retained this status from the early sixteenth to the early nineteenth century, the succeeding period was, as it had been in Tonga, one of greater fluidity and conflict. Conflict was fuelled at the local level by polygyny – aristocrats had a number of successors with rival family affiliations – and at a wider level as alliances among major districts were formed and reformed.

The arrival of John Williams and the London Missionary Society had been fortuitous, both for the mission itself and the cause of Malietoa Vai'inupo, who was able to use the new faith to consolidate his near pre-eminence. But he died in 1841, barely a decade after mass conversion, and armed conflict between more powerful lineages and parties resumed, some of it involving antagonism between the adherents of the lotu Tahiti (the LMS) and those of the lotu Tonga (the Methodists, primarily Samoans with strong Tongan affiliations). Not just European individuals, but the western powers as nations, became increasingly embroiled in the evolving conflict in the 1870s and 1880s. The Germans, Americans and British each considered that they had major interests in the islands, and were represented by consuls who negotiated with each other and with Samoans, and who sometimes agreed and sometimes disagreed, as to which prospective Samoan 'king' was to be recognized, or rather, how the claims of contending parties were to be balanced by agreement upon not only a king but a vice-king.[7]

The formal position as it was from time to time restated was that a native Samoan government had to be supported, that none of the three foreign powers would seek to annex the islands, and that none would assume pre-eminence. However, a treaty of early 1879 did give Germany special status, declaring German land claims valid and final, but this treaty conflicted with others made between Samoa and the United States, and Samoa and Britain. Gordon visited Samoa later in 1879 and while he was there negotiated what has not been acknowledged as such, but was in fact a partial colonization, the declaration that Apia, the main anchorage and settlement, was a 'municipality' with its own, European-led administration. This administration consisted of the three consuls and a few other prominent planters. Most crucially, the town had been recognized as a neutral space by Samoan warriors, who were not to pass through it armed, or fight over it, irrespective of whatever conflict might be raging elsewhere. But the municipality enacted legislation too, understandably enough embracing the sale of alcohol, port regulations and taxes, but extending also to 'fast riding', weeding, fireworks, dogs and cricket (which could not be played on or 'within 8 fathoms of' the public road).[8]

Malietoa Tavaloa, who had previously been accorded and then deprived of pre-eminence, was recognized as king, but then died in November 1880. In 1881 two contenders for the succession, Malietoa Laupepa and Tamasese, were, after a good deal of fighting, apparently reconciled and declared king and vice-king respectively. The arrangement broke down, was reaffirmed, but then broke down again. Malietoa Laupepa, together probably with the majority of Samoans, was more distrustful of the Germans than of other foreigners – not surprisingly given that the Germans were far more active economically than either the British or Americans, and were rapidly planting lands that had been speculatively acquired with coconuts (copra was now being exported to Europe to be processed into soap), coffee, cocoa and cotton, and had introduced some fifteen hundred labourers to work them, who from time to time chased Samoans off lands that they believed were their own.[9] Hence there was a good deal of well-founded local suspicion that the ultimate German aim was to annex the islands, hence too perhaps the popularity of cricket.

The Germans for their part had never been keen supporters of Malietoa and in 1885 began actively to undermine his regime, expelled Malietoa Laupepa from

53 Malietoa Laupepa, photographed c.1880.

Mulin'u, a district on the edge of Apia which had developed into the seat of government, and raised their own flag there. They expressed support for Tamasese instead, even though he held only one out of the four titles required by a Tafa'ifa. Foreigners were alarmed when Islanders began to play their own game. The Hawaiian king, Kalakaua, had been interested for some years in creating some union of island nations, with Hawaii in a leading role. He was supported by his then premier, Walter Murray Gibson, a notorious opportunist and fraudster, whose interest was above all commercial. In 1886–7 they were in contact with Malietoa, proposing not merely a treaty of friendship but a confederacy of independent kingdoms in the Pacific – that might embrace Tonga and Kiribati (the Gilbert Islands) also. Following a letter stating Malietoa's willingness – his unconditional willingness – to join a confederacy, the Hawaiians had constructed an embassy and threw a party on a grand scale for several hundred Samoan chiefs and people. Malietoa, who was among the more devout Samoan Christians, left early, but the usual prohibition upon supplying alcohol to Samoans was ignored, and a riotous all-night event was reported censoriously in New Zealand and elsewhere. The excess of the occasion owed a good deal to the European or part-European John Bush, Kalakaua's minister plenipotentiary to the kings of Samoa and Tonga, who appears to have been drunk more often than not. Though Malietoa felt that he had much to gain from an alliance with the Hawaiians, he reportedly told a member of the delegation that if they had come to teach his people to drink, he wished they had stayed away.

Kalakaua had bought an English ship that he fitted out as a warship, renamed the *Kaimiloa* and despatched to the South Pacific under the command of one George Jackson, once a British naval officer, but more recently the head of a reform school for Hawaiians. The officers and crew were Hawaiians, some of them former pupils or inmates from Jackson's school, and were accompanied by a Hawaiian band and Joseph Dwight Strong, a competent painter who had been appointed 'government artist' by Kalakaua. The *Kaimiloa* arrived off Apia, sent their band and crew ashore, and in due course held meetings with Malietoa, but also, in secret, with Tamasese. Indeed, they partied with Tamasese to the acute annoyance of the Germans.[10] These political initiatives antagonized the other two 'Powers' for different reasons, but quickly collapsed, not as a result of that opposition but because of political changes within Hawaii itself. Other settlers led a push to remove Gibson, who had to flee, and the new cabinet recalled the *Kaimiloa*, which was in due course sold at a heavy loss. Not only the ship, but in effect Hawaii's pan-Pacific ambitions, were relinquished.

Later in 1887 Tamasese was able to marshall sufficient support to oust Malietoa. He formed a new administration involving Eugen Brandeis, who acted as premier, and worked closely with the DHPG, the company that had taken over Godeffroy and Son's business after its collapse, and the German consulate. The regime vigorously pushed its advantage, imposing a new and onerous poll tax upon ordinary Samoans, who were cheated out of what would have been the market price for what they paid in copra, and going as far as to deport Laupepa to the Marshall Islands. Tamasese unwisely claimed the Malietoa title and began accumulating, through levies and coerced exchanges, Malietoa fine mats, in effect expressions of entitlement. These steps were inflammatory, and with other measures they alienated the population, who came out in support of another prominent chief, Mata'afa Iosefa. Open war then broke out between his followers and the diminishing party that still backed Tamasese. Simultaneously, a conference of the three interested 'Powers' took place in Washington, at which Samoans themselves were unrepresented, and which was notably inconclusive, though marked by German manoeuvring in the direction of annexation.[11]

* * *

In 1886 John Bates Thurston, Colonial Secretary and later governor of Fiji, had remarked on the 'chronic state of unrest' in Samoa that formed 'the leading feature of their local politics'. A private letter written in 1892 had the flavour of a bad joke: to 'pacificate' Samoa one would have to set up a military government, 'make it a felony to own or edit a newspaper, deport all novel writers, and for ten years allow no one to call his soul his own'.[12] Thurston had in mind not 'novel writers' in general but Robert Louis Stevenson in particular, whose writings on what would otherwise have been arcane and obscure colonial affairs were reaching wide audiences through *The Times*. Stevenson had been in the Pacific intermittently since June 1888. Notoriously prone to illness, and not doing well in the United States, he wanted to try a complete change of climate, but was attracted also by the romance of the sea and the islands. He and an entourage chartered a schooner, the *Casco*, leaving San Francisco in late June 1888. He would spend time in the Marquesas, Tuamotus and Tahiti, before giving up the ship at Honolulu and becoming close to King Kalakaua there. A second cruise in a trading vessel, the *Equator*, would take him to Kiribati and in due course Samoa, where he resolved to settle.

Stevenson's first encounters with Islanders were in the Marquesas. Like Sir Arthur Gordon, he quickly associated them with the Scots. Such understanding and rapport with people at Nukuhiva as he had been able to acquire, Stevenson considered, owed much to the fact that he had 'some knowledge of our Scots folk of the Highlands and the Islands. Not much beyond a century has passed since

54 Portrait of Mata'afa Iosefa taken by Thomas Andrew in 1896.

these were in the same convulsive and transitory state as the Marquesans of to-day.'[13] Stevenson's analogy had an edge quite different to Gordon's, however. Gordon evoked an attachment to clan and custom that he admired, or at any rate romanticized, in both Fijians and his ancestors, and it would have been surprising had the writer of historical romances not thought in these terms too. But what Stevenson began with was the predicament of the recently colonized:

> In both cases an alien authority enforced, the clans disarmed, the chiefs deposed, new customs introduced, and chiefly that fashion for regarding money as the means and object of existence. The commercial age, in each,

succeeding at a bound to an age of war abroad and patriarchal communism at home. In one the cherished practice of tattooing, in the other a cherished costume, proscribed. In each a main luxury cut off: beef, driven under cloud of night from Lowland pastures, denied to the meat-loving Highlanders; long-pig, pirated from the next village, to the man-eating Kanaka.[14]

The slender evidence for Marquesan cannibalism reminds us that Stevenson did his bit to reproduce certain stereotypes of Pacific life, but in his case the

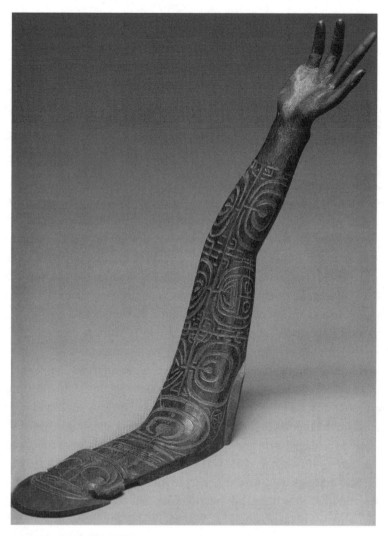

55 Carved arm with tattoo designs, collected by Robert Louis Stevenson during his visit to the Marquesas Islands.

hackneyed images are like pieces of flotsam and jetsam, on the surface of an uncertain but deeper understanding. With a degree of genuine rather than merely rhetorically assumed modesty, Stevenson admitted his own limitations as a cross-cultural actor and observer. In the Marquesas he misrecognizes gestures and dispositions, he makes faux pas, he suffers anxieties that prove groundless. Most importantly, though, he deprives a gullible set of readers of any expectation that they may now read of a primitive people or an exotic culture. What he witnessed, what he can report, is the upshot of around a century of generally deleterious contact. He evokes a conversation with a young mother in the Anaho valley who wants to hear him talk about England, but who goes on to lament depopulation, 'the decease of her own people'. Stevenson was affected, imagining that in future centuries 'their case as ours, death coming in like a tide, and the day already numbered when there should be no more Beretani [Britain], and no more of any race whatever'.[15] Though the image of the fatal impact was itself a colonial stereotype of another sort, Stevenson was responding to the very real depopulation, the very real demoralization, of the Marquesas at the time.

* * *

Stevenson encountered entirely different circumstances in Kiribati, then the Gilbert Islands. Since the mid-century the engagement of the high chiefs of the atoll of Abemama with the wider world had been highly singular. Before then, the regular visits of traders had deposited a beachcomber community on the island, and ships seeking coconut oil were increasingly active. Barter was unregulated, and on a small island (with a land area of no more than about 16 square kilometres) beachcombers, with their drunkenness and demands for food and women, were still more disruptive and irritating than elsewhere. It is nevertheless extraordinary that in 1851 the principal chief Tem Baiteke took the simple step of having every white resident of Abemama and the neighbouring atolls – some fifty men – killed. Enough was enough.[16]

Tem Baiteke had a trusted adviser and advocate, Richard Randell, a trader polygamously married to Kiribati women, resident on another island. He was the source of the reports of the massacre that reached the outside world. They emphasized the degenerate and troublesome character of the victims, and no punitive action against the chief was ever considered, let alone carried out. Randell also acted as a go-between, encouraging a relationship between Tem Baiteke and the New England missionaries, by then long established in Hawaii, who were increasingly active, following the London Missionary Society model in sending out Hawaiian missionaries to the Marquesas as well as various parts of Micronesia.

The chief's most important step was to establish a tightly regulated trading station. This was situated on an islet, which was rigorously maintained as a sole point of entry and trading station. Vessels were brought in by a pilot, foreigners brought their goods into a shed and laid them out, Islanders arrived with coconut oil, had it measured out, and then took their preferred items away. Young women and gifts were sent on board ships, but seamen appear not to have been welcomed ashore, and the chief himself only rarely visited ships or agreed to meet white visitors. In establishing this singularly orderly commerce, Tem Baiteke had also suppressed local institutions somewhat like the Samoan *fono*, the meetings of orators, at which matters were debated and more or less democratically resolved. The new regime was distinctly auto-cratic, sustained by violence, and repressive in its attention to the interests of the population. No alcohol was permitted to be traded, and those who made their own toddy suffered corporal punishment.

Tem Baiteke was succeeded by his son, Tem Binoka, who was less deft polit-ically and had to deal with unrest, but nevertheless maintained the regime. He went as far as to invite a missionary teacher to reside on the island, not out of any genuine interest in Christianity, but because he was insatiably curious about the outside world. He was in his forties when Stevenson visited. He was a formidable personality, often bizarrely clad in a woman's dress, a naval uniform, or a 'masquerade costume' of his own invention. 'I see him now come pacing toward me in the cruel sun,' Stevenson wrote, 'solitary, a figure out of Hoffmann.'[17]

Stevenson was astonished both by the rigorous regulation of Abemama society and the king's larger-than-life personality. 'He is greedy of things new and foreign,' he wrote:

House after house, chest after chest, in the palace precinct, is already crammed with cloaks, musical boxes, blue spectacles, umbrellas, knitted waistcoats, bolts of stuff, tools, rifles, fowling-pieces, medicines, European foods, sewing-machines, and, what is more extraordinary, stoves: all that ever caught his eye, tickled his appetite, pleased him for its use, or puzzled him with its apparenty inutility. And still his lust is unabated. He is possessed by the seven devils of the collector. He hears a thing spoken of, and a shadow comes on his face. 'I think I no got him,' he will say.[18]

But if this rapacious interest in the commodities of the globe led the high chief to be exploited by those traders able to arrive with something that he lacked, something that interested him, Tem Binoka was no more naïve about the conduct of commerce than he was about the government of his own island. He listed to Stevenson all the captains and traders that he knew, dividing them into three classes – ' "He cheat a litty" – "He cheat plenty" – and "I think he cheat too much." '[19] There are moments of mockery in Stevenson's character-ization of the chief, but Tem Binoka's stature and sheer extravagance exceed them all. He comes across as his own man, a careful autocrat, comfortable at once with the customary status he has invented, and his inquisitive modernism. At times he dresses ludicrously, but he has an ironic intelligence that is at least a match for Stevenson's own.

* * *

If, in the Marquesas and Kiribati, Stevenson was a better than average travel writer, in Samoa he became a different kind of commentator altogether. In late 1890 he had finally found a place to settle, an estate in the hills behind Apia, which he named 'Vailima'. He gardened, he read, he wrote, but above all he became absorbed by Samoan folklore, Samoan affairs, by Samoans. He had dashed off novels such as *The Wrecker* (1892) and was uncertain about what he ought to work on next. 'Lives of the Stevensons? *Historia Samoae*? A History for Children?'[20] Within weeks he was working intensively on what he called a pamphlet, in fact a short book of substance, that he would call *A Footnote to History: Eight Years of Trouble in Samoa*. 'I recoil from serious names,' he remarked, but he had a sense of urgency, he wanted the book in print while it might make a difference to the rapidly evolving conflict.[21]

On 2 January 1892 he planned to visit Blacklock, the American consul, with 'some questions to ask him for my History'. He went from there to Vailele 'where I had also to cross-examine the plantation manager about the battle there'.[22] The next day he was rewriting his draft on an engagement that had taken place on the coast at Fangalii, four years earlier, to take account of the new information. The events he described were extraordinary. The 'Powers' had until then manip-ulated matters by arming their preferred factions, holding out inducements, and from time to time humiliating or undermining the chiefs they opposed. When it came to war they had let the Samoans get on with it, and suffer the losses. But so concerned were the Germans to maintain Tamasese that in mid-December 1888 they landed their own forces, ostensibly to protect a German plantation but intending to attack supporters of Mata'afa Iosefa.

Their tactics, Stevenson considered, had been poorly conceived. Two parties from the naval ships *Olga* and *Elbe* were landed in the dark, and expected to fight through dense brush known to and occupied by their enemies. 'The thing was a bluff, and it is impossible to bluff with stealth.'[23] The Germans reached the plantation and its principal house but were virtually trapped within it, and subjected it to continuous fire from Samoans close around. The Germans ventured out several times, to attack the attackers, while the Mata'afa's men, in Stevenson's judgement, 'showed themselves extremely enterprising', venturing beyond cover, and threatening to surround the soldiers who came out of the house. The Germans were running out of ammunition, but once it became light the *Elbe* shelled a nearby village, prompting Mata'afa's followers to disperse. The Germans seized the opportunity to withdraw to the ships themselves. This 'unfortunate movement' gave the operation 'an irremediable air of defeat'. Some of the subsequent reports despatched by Reuters described a 'repulse', the Germans having been 'driven back to their boats'.[24] This was not strictly accurate but it did magnify the incident, enlarging its significance to that of a major setback. Though many Samoans had died, the Germans had lost some 56 out of a landing party of 140. Of the German dead, the heads of a good many had been taken, in conformity with Samoan warrior custom. 'All Samoa drew a breath of wonder and delight' at this humiliation of a formidable imperial nation, Stevenson reported.[25]

Over the ensuing months the Germans engaged in ineffective reprisals. A naval build-up off Apia, involving seven ships from the three 'Powers' as well as a host of partisan traders, raised the real threat that instability on a Polynesian island would lead to an outbreak of war. This was forestalled by one of the more famous incidents of Samoan history, a devastating hurricane that wrecked every ship but one in the harbour at the time. Tamasese's 'king-ship' irretrievably lost, the Washington conference was in due course reconvened in Berlin, the Germans having accepted the failure of the campaign they had pursued. While Samoans at this time were overwhelmingly supportive of Mata'afa Iosefa, Germany blocked his nomination as king and pressed to reinstate Malietoa Laupepa instead.

Laupepa himself at first supported Mata'afa, but then acquiesced to the proposal of the three imperial nations. Yet he lacked broad support in Samoa and his followers began a campaign against the districts that were uncompromising in their backing of Mata'afa. This was in the end largely successful and Mata'afa, like Laupepa before him and ten other dissident chiefs, were all exiled to the atoll of Jaluit in the Marshalls. In August 1898 he was allowed to return, coincidentally, around the time of Laupepa's death. The following year, a further Berlin conference resolved finally to partition Samoa between Germany and the United States. In the decade that remained to him, Mata'afa's pre-eminence among chiefs was acknowledged but the Germans would neither forget nor forgive the heads taken in December 1888, and would not permit him to be described as king. Stevenson witnessed none of this. He had died suddenly at Vailima on 3 December 1894.[26]

* * *

In earlier sections of this book I have drawn attention to the travels of Islanders. The modern history of the Pacific was made up not only of a succession of meetings with European visitors and intruders, who ventured into and impacted upon local lives, but it was shaped in all sorts of ways by Islanders who voyaged and encountered each other, who voyaged to colonial ports, to America and Europe itself, and made their own sense of the world they found.

To the travels of Islander sailors, the enterprises of Islander missionaries, and the expatriate experience of indentured workers, must be added the involuntary exile of those deported by French, British and German colonial regimes. Bouarate, Navosavakadua, Laupepa and Mata'afa were only a few among many who at one time or another were removed to islands within the Pacific, but to Islander milieux, within which they were strangers. Some like Laupepa and Mata'afa returned, others such as Navosavakadua never did. We know little about how deportees passed their time, still less about what they made of their experience. Given the near impossibility of substantiating any speculation, it may make no sense to broach the topic at all. Yet all these men made something of exile. Those who returned home re-entered local political worlds, and acted afterwards, in ways influenced by exile and by what they had made of it. At the very least, it can be said that they had the chance to reflect on circumstances from a distance, that they were compelled to see their own society from the outside, from a 'distance' and an 'outside' that were not abstract, but places on an imperial map. Deposited on Rotuma and Jaluit, Navosavakadua and Laupepa experienced for themselves something of the hostile reach and range of imperial power.

* * *

Though Stevenson's life and some of his writings sustained the romance of the South Seas, his legacy is arguably more singular. *A Footnote to History* was unprecedented among the writings of Europeans on the Pacific. The accounts of voyages and travels aside, missionaries turned folklorists had published studies of manners and customs and compilations of traditions, many of which would be valued by scholars, and Islanders themselves, for accounts of beliefs and rites that were lost locally, in the aftermath of conversion to Christianity. But these studies presumed that the traditions described belonged to an older, simpler order; they took the lives of Islanders to be antecedent to those of Europeans. Missionaries had also written histories of their own enterprises, and books that combined folklore with the wonderful movement 'from darkness to light'.

Stevenson's book was something else altogether. It was a history but not a progressive one, not a self-congratulatory narrative of missionary triumph, nor a tale of settler nation-making, like W.D. Alexander's *Brief History of the Hawaiian People* (1899). It was a contemporary history of political conflict, with a paradox at it heart. In his opening paragraphs, giving his readers a point of entry into Samoan events, Stevenson dramatized a struggle between epochs, between the age of finance and that of communism, between great European powers and men who were Christians and cricketers but otherwise 'the contemporaries of our tattooed ancestors who drove their chariots on the wrong side of the Roman wall'.[27] This announced the need for a detour into the world of Samoan custom and character – of which Stevenson's grasp was adequate if ultimately superficial. Yet what followed, and the very premise of the undertaking, was different. Samoan events and actions were considered political events and actions, like those of London, Paris and Berlin, that made up the wider and more familiar drama of world affairs. Stevenson's title was apologetic, and he aired doubts that the book would be read. But its substance was unapologetic and uncompromising. His readers were required to follow, absorb and reflect upon the actions of Laupepa, Tamasese, Mata'afa and others, as they were accustomed to studying those of Napoleon, Bismarck and Gladstone.

This contemporary history was shorn of the touch of caricature, the lighter tone, that prevailed in *In the South Seas* and in the bulk of travel writing of the time. To assimilate it to a European register and genre was of course, in one sense, to write ethnocentrically, to pass over the ways Samoans themselves might have perceived and understood the history, which would have been different. But if this was an ethnocentrism, it was one that demanded much of Stevenson's European and North American audience. It demanded that they go the distance, that they immerse themselves in a complex set of circumstances and happenings, that they consider them as seriously as any more familiar contentions, nearer home.

A Footnote to History had, needless to say, shortcomings of all sorts. It was overtly partisan in favour of Mata'afa, for one. And it would prove exceptional. Nothing similar would be written about the evolution of Tahitian or Fijian politics for close to three-quarters of a century, until professional historians, the best of them anthropologically minded, got to work in the postwar decades. The book remains important as an expression that Islanders could be approached, not for the singularity of their 'culture', nor for the quirkiness of their manners, ill-adjusted as they were to the 'modern world', but because

Europeans and Islanders were at last recognized as inhabitants of the same world and the same time, caught up in events that gained momentum and unravelled, that changed lives and ended them, on both sides.

* * *

In its progression from region to region, the European colonization of the Pacific neatly reversed the voyages of settlement that Islanders had, tens of thousands of years earlier, embarked upon themselves. The first islands that formally became British were among the last reached by Polynesians, those of New Zealand. The Polynesian archipelagoes were engaged with in many ways through the early and middle decades of the nineteenth century, prior to trade and mission intrusion in Melanesia, which was an older, much longer settled region, in indigenous terms. And when Europeans began to move into Melanesia they moved from south and east to west and north, reversing the route of the early Oceanic settlers. In due course, in the late 1870s, merchants and missionaries turned their attention to the Bismarck Islands, to New Ireland and New Britain, which had been the islands that Islanders had settled when they first ventured beyond the great land mass of 'continental' New Guinea.

The Bismarcks were entered, in effect, from Samoa. The missionary George Brown – one of a newer generation, from a well-educated, professional family – had spent his early twenties in New Zealand, joined the Methodists, and then worked for fourteen years in Samoa. He was fluent in Samoan, anthropologically minded, and moved to follow the example of the great missionary pioneers. The LMS was at the same time establishing its first stations in Papua, and Brown toured the Australian colonies to raise support and funds for a new mission in the Bismarcks. He initially settled Samoan and Fijian teachers on the Duke of York Islands in the strait between New Britain and New Ireland, and he himself established a station on the Gazelle Peninsula in 1877.

This was a very different environment to any the missionaries in the Pacific had entered before. The population was vast and the culture entirely unfamiliar. Yet the distinctiveness of New Britain societies had the potential to work in favour of the mission. Prominent men among the Tolai were active traders, who managed local markets through which goods flowed between the coast and interior, and accumulated and deployed shell monies that were measured in colonial parlance by the fathom. A modern study in economic anthropology was entitled *Capitalism, Primitive and Modern*; the people seemingly constituted an exception to the rule of a stark clash between local communism and global finance evoked by Stevenson for Samoa, which most of us would take as a truism of the colonial confrontation.[28]

In New Britain and for that matter elsewhere in New Guinea, missionaries would be more closely associated with traders than had been typical in Polynesia, indeed they would trade actively themselves. This at once created a point of engagement between them and the locals, but also rendered them a threat. New sources, new goods made them significant to Tolai, for they both fuelled and destabilized pre-existing relationships. When a party of Fijian missionaries ventured inland from Blanche Bay in early April 1878, the prominent man Talili and his associates understood this as a provocation. He was not a priest whose rituals were threatened, but a master of trade who saw men, he understood, intent on taking over local exchange networks. The leader of the visiting group, one Sailesi and three other Fijians, were killed, their bodies cut up and distributed for consumption among Talili's allies.[29]

Brown learned of the events and hurried to the settlement where the missionaries' widows and children were grieving. They wailed inconsolably in the customary fashion. 'Both widows and children were expostulating with the deceased, and asking why they had left them.'[30] ' 'Twas little use trying to speak any trite words of comfort,' he wrote at the time, and acknowledged that 'many horrible accounts of their death . . . made our blood boil'. In his autobiography these words were omitted, he emphasized instead his distress, that he prayed 'with great earnestness to God that He would give me wisdom sufficient for our great need'.[31] He could have abandoned the mission, but dismissed that course of action in favour of mounting a swift retaliatory operation. The remainder of Islander teachers were moved to do so, he might have forbidden them, but they would then have been so dispirited as to have given up their work. The few white settlers in the area feared, or at any rate told him they feared, that they would be unsafe if the assault passed unpunished. So Brown recruited friendly Tolai, the settlers, and his Fijian and Samoan missionaries, and organized a two-flanked attack on a number of villages known to have been involved, either in the attack or in the cannibalism of the victims. What took place was quite unlike the ineffective, usually misdirected shelling operations that had often been undertaken by naval vessels. From 18 to 21 April 1878 a succession of raids took place, and close to one hundred local warriors and at least a few women were killed. Houses were burnt and heavy fines in shell money demanded by way of compensation.[32]

Brown tried to manage both the fighting and the subsequent exchanges in what he understood to be the customary fashion. Though his local 'auxiliaries' were told that there was to be no killing of women or children, and that none of the enemy were to be consumed, these prohibitions had only been partially observed, he was forced to acknowledge afterwards. Yet Brown's peacemaking appears to have been adroitly conducted. He took and received gifts, accepted apologies, and agreed to send the mission teachers that the people now, it seems, wanted. What had been inflicted upon them had been 'an earthquake, not a fight', some of the formerly hostile men conceded – and since this was and is a region of considerable seismic activity, the metaphor was vivid.

In subsequent years, Talili continued to begrudge the mission presence and resist it in less overt ways, but the raid had, more broadly, the effect of affirming the power of the mission. It was not, however, this sheer strength that secured conversions, but the way that strength was appropriated locally. The lotu was represented as a form of magic, and that magic was seen as an item of property, which entered into local trade. Once he had acquired it, one Tolai bigman could sell it on to another, and encourage one of Brown's army of Fijian or Tongan teachers to travel with it. Within a few years the Methodists had several thousand adherents, and though some Tolai would embrace Catholicism, Christianity in one form or another was pervasive within a few decades.

But the Blanche Bay incident, when first reported in Australia, provoked great controversy. The Methodist Church and its missionary board were acutely embarrassed, not least because they had long criticized the punitive operations of various labour recruiters and traders. They did not feel they could censure Brown but deeply regretted 'that no other course seemed to him to be open'.[33] A majority, perhaps, believed that it would have been better to abandon the mission than to secure it at such cost.

Captain Purvis of HMS *Danae* made some enquiries the following year. He took the view that Brown 'could hardly have acted otherwise than he did', but reflected also upon underlying causes of the violence.

1. The Samoan and Fijian teachers are mostly ignorant of the language of those they are supposed to teach.
2. Their habits (with the exception of wearing some clothes), houses, and manners, are the same as the natives.
3. Their conduct towards the natives is most overbearing, this more especially applies to the Samoans.
4. The Aborigines [i.e., the Tolai] look upon them as being of the same race as themselves, and will not be dictated to by them.
5. The chiefs make a large profit by carrying trade to the bush tribes, and whenever they see the teachers trying to push inland they think it is for the purpose of taking the trade out of their hands.[34]

It has generally been assumed that Islander teachers were more effective than white missionaries because they were closer to the people they evangelized. But within Polynesia there were much greater cultural affinities than between Samoans or Fijians and the peoples of the Bismarcks. Whether Purvis was correct in stating that Tolai saw Fijians and Samoans as 'being of the same race' as themselves is hard to judge. Either way, just as the Rarotongan Ta'unga's writings on the peoples of the Isle of Pines reflected many of the prejudices of white missionaries, Brown's Samoans may well have felt that Tolai, whose culture was profoundly different to their own, were beneath them, not least because they were heathen. Mission histories and modern oral histories smooth out many tensions, many awkwardnesses of local translation and negotiation, that were very much part of this seemingly successful evangelization.

* * *

Even before Brown established the New Britain mission, the great German firm, Godeffroy and Sons, which was active in Micronesia as well as Samoa, investigated possibilities in the same region and set up a permanent trading station in the Duke of Yorks in 1876. An independent German trader, Eduard Hernsheim, set himself up a network over the same years, embracing Palau, the Marshall Islands and New Britain. One of the challenges was fostering demand among Islanders for European commodities, and one of the responses the establishment of 'smoking schools': pipes and tobacco were at first distributed freely, but the practice indeed did catch on, enabling the traders to extract copra among other exports on a grand scale, though the profitability of all of these enterprises declined after the 1870s.[35]

Emma Forsayth, part-Samoan, part-American, and Thomas Farrell, her Australian settler husband, initially ran one of Godeffroys' stations but established their own enterprise. Emma, later notorious as 'Queen Emma of the South Seas', with a great estate, mansion and supposedly regal lifestyle, saw the potential in New Britain of the German firm's approach in Samoa. She embarked on massive purchases of land, in general for arms and ammunition, which raised the same issues of what sale meant and who was entitled to sell as had arisen in Samoa and everywhere else. Forsayth was, however, careful to prepare and preserve documentation that was considered to meet legal standards, and typically refrained from actually planting lands for some years after purchase. The early 1880s saw a land rush, and thousands of acres passed into colonial hands within a few years.[36]

Over these years colonial schemes were being hatched everywhere in relation to every conceivable part of the Pacific that was not yet unambiguously part of another nation's sphere. Given the largely uninvestigated nature of the island of New Guinea and its vast size, it is hardly surprising that the apparent opportunities stimulated scheming and fantasy in equal measure. Though the Dutch had claimed the western half of the island since the late 1820s, the east remained a possession of no one but its inhabitants, though settlers in Australia, and in Queensland in particular, campaigned for annexation, as they were agitating similarly for either the colonial or imperial government to annex the then New Hebrides, the Solomons and sundry other territories.

Private ventures were ambitiously conceived. In 1883 one H.R. MacIver, a former soldier, sought subscriptions, aiming to raise £250,000 for a 'New Guinea Exploration and Colonization Company', conceived as a successor to the East India and Hudson's Bay companies. The intention was to purchase lands and to settle on them working people who had 'no means of livelihood' in England itself. Though this notion – that those who were surplus to the labour market of the crowded metropolis could find prosperity while civilizing supposedly unproductive regions on the periphery – was a resonant one in much imperial propaganda, the scheme received short shrift from the colonial office. MacIver – who had cited the 'success' of the Congo in support of his plan – was told that if he went ahead and acted in defiance of the government, the Royal Navy would 'interfere for the protection of the native inhabitants'. When he then changed tack and represented the enterprise purely as a trading venture, the colonial office pointed out that his publicity emphasized the scope for and promise of agricultural settlement, that it appeared fraudulent. Neither MacIver nor his deputies would quite take no for an answer, and for a year or more the colonial office were reporting, and attempting to quash, revivals of the scheme in various guises.[37]

This enterprise in the end went nowhere, but one that was considerably more ambitious in conception, but if possible less realistic in its planning, actually was successful in raising funds, recruiting settlers and sending ships to the Bismarck Islands. The author of what was known as the Free Colony of Port-Breton, even as New France, was one Charles Bonaventure du Breuil, who called himself the 'Marquis de Ray'. He in fact did come from a minor aristocratic family that had lands in Brittany and had wide though not notably successful colonial experience – he had tried farming and similar ventures in the United States, Senegal, Madagascar and Indochina. He was forty-five years old in 1877 when he began running advertisments for a lucrative investment scheme, loosely clad in patriotic and civilizing rhetoric. He thought at first of a site on the north-west Australian coast, apparently unaware that the region was part of a British colony, established fifty years earlier. He then turned to island Melanesian locations and in due course resolved on New Ireland, and indeed was able to sell tracts of land to some three thousand speculators and potential settlers in France. The interest enabled him to raise the price of land, first from five to ten francs, then twenty and fifty francs per hectare. He envisaged importing indentured Indian and Chinese labourers; he established spin-off ventures that would cultivate sugar, maintain a shipping line, and mine copper, and all of these attracted further investors. What made the venture a success at this initial stage was a vigorous marketing operation: du Breuil ran conferences, was no doubt an effective speaker, got a fortnightly newspaper, *La Nouvelle France*, off the ground, and had an extended promotional tract, as well as a succession of prospectuses, printed and widely distributed. He at no point received official support, which was paradoxically beneficial in that he was able to claim that the colony would be a Catholic one, capitalizing on the unpopularity of the anti-clerical ministry of the time.[38]

From late 1879 onward, some eight hundred settlers, French, Belgian, Italian and German, would join a succession of vessels, mostly under a

56 Copy of a certificate of title to one hectare of land in the free colony of Port-Breton, from A. Baudouin, *L'Adventure de Port-Breton et la colonie libre dite Nouvelle-France* (Paris, 1885).

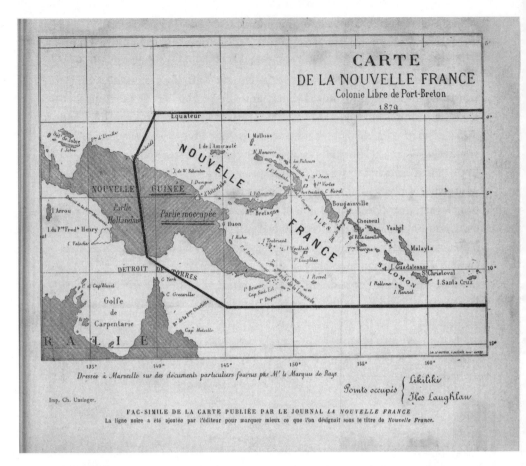

57 Copy of the map published in the journal *La Nouvelle France,* from A. Baudouin, *L'Adventure de Port-Breton et la colonie libre dite Nouvelle-France* (Paris, 1885).

Liberian flag, that headed for New Ireland. The first was the *Chandernagor,* which carried close to ninety but settled a small party separately on the Laughlan Islands in Milne Bay. The bulk tried first to land at the site initially selected, Port Praslin, known from Bougainville's 1760s and Duperrey's 1820s voyages. They soon relocated to Metlik, a short distance down the coast, unloaded supplies there, and began surveying streets and tracts of land. The massive investment in the venture was reflected in expensive and elaborate pieces of equipment, as well as a huge supply of bricks, intended for the construction of a cathedral, but in more basic respects the settlers were poorly equipped. George Brown reported that 'they had scarcely any axes and the few spades with which they were supplied appeared to be of the worst possible material'.[39] Brown's colleague Benjamin Danks described the colony as 'the maddest of all the mad schemes of the Nineteenth Century'.[40] He had responded to an appeal for aid and went to Metlik, to relocate those settlers who wished to move to the mission station at Port Hunter in the Duke of Yorks. He found the encounter with the sick, exhausted and hungry men and women harrowing. 'Bandaged legs, pale emaciated faces, eyes sunk down . . . some were mere skeletons and were supported for the time being only by the hope of getting away.' Once Danks explained that he would evacuate whoever wished to come, most hurried to assemble their possessions and were ready to leave within five minutes.

Though a ship was chartered from Sydney to bring food supplies, Metlik was abandoned in August 1880, about the time a second ship, the *Génil*, arrived. This had had a voyage extraordinary for its discontent among the prospective settlers and their abuse by the captain, a vicious character named Gustave Rabardy. The entire group had deserted at Singapore, but Rabardy had recruited a couple of dozen Malay labourers and carried on to land at least them. A third ship, the *India*, arrived with a much larger, mainly Italian party in late October 1880. They were better provisioned, and for a few weeks it seemed they might actually establish a viable settlement, but disease, bad weather and food shortages then led to a collapse of morale. The *Génil* had gone to Australia to obtain food, but returned only much later than promised and just missed the *India* on 20 February 1881, which evacuated the settle-ment, taking the survivors to New Caledonia. More than half later went on to Australia and formed the nucleus of a settlement that would become known as New Italy in northern New South Wales. Yet a further ship from Europe, the *Nouvelle Bretagne*, would carry another party of prospective settlers. Octave Mouton, son of a Belgian recruit, wrote long afterwards of their arrival at Port Breton on 15 August 1881:

> what a delusion, our paradise became a hell rather than a land of promise, some of the passengers were so much affected that they cried of disappoint-ment [the] small harbour was no more than a little bay . . . at the time of our entrance there was no cloud to be seen, only rain and such rain, this rain lasted at least forty-eight hours, before it cleared, then we were able to see what we came to . . . one of [the settlers] named Pitoy was nearly out of his head when he asked where shall find my 1800 hectares, there he was pulling his hair and crying the poor devil was to be pitied.[41]

The settlers realized that the Arcadian landscapes which had been represented to them in the marquis's promotional literature were not to be found (they derived in fact from illustrations in *L'Univers pittoresque*, a popular geographic encylopaedia). They reconciled themselves to attempting to garden, they struggled to survive on eggs and stocks of biscuits and haricot beans, but like their predecessors began to die from malaria. A succession of ship's captains had been appointed governors of the colony, of whom Rabardy would be the last. He committed suicide, or at any rate died under mysterious circumstances, about the time the settlement was finally evacuated with the help of Emma Forsayth's partner, Farrell. Not acting altruistically, he appropriated a good deal of the abandoned property around the settlement, but then helped Mouton's family, among others, establish themselves on New Britain.

The grotesque failure of the 'free colony' was symptomatic of an absolute gulf between understandings of the Pacific in Europe and circumstances in the Pacific itself. Yet investors, in Australia in particular, remained intensely interested in acquiring land in New Guinea, and it was rumoured in 1883 that a Sydney-based syndicate was actively doing so. Annexation was vigorously advocated by the Australian colonies, indeed Queensland went ahead to claim most of the eastern half of the island in 1883. The act was declared null and void by London, but the pressures accumulated. The conduct of the labour trade remained politically volatile, yet the colonial administrators felt they had to create a context in which regulated recruiting could take place, they felt they had to assure planters and investors from Queensland to Fiji that labour would come from somewhere.[42]

If the politicians in London did not want to incur the expense and yet another colonial administration, they were on the other hand anxious to preserve a British sphere in the south-western Pacific, against the French who had strong interests in Vanuatu, and more particularly the Germans whose enterprises in the Bismarcks and elsewhere in New Guinea were increasingly important. But, ironically, the very public Australasian campaign for annexation prompted the Germans to act, and in mid-1884 a newly constituted and officially recognized Neu Guinea Kompagnie despatched a scientific expedition that at the same time took possession of much of northern New Guinea. Britain quickly moved to establish a 'protectorate' that incorporated the south-eastern half of the island. The powers were involved in horse-trading for months, but the lines of partition were agreed upon in April 1885, though revised in various ways in succeeding years, particularly as part of the deal that made western Samoa German in 1899.

This process, these negotiations were entirely different to those that had proceeded in New Zealand and in Fiji, in the lead-up to the agreements that resulted in what was called 'cession' to Britain in 1840 and 1874 respectively. In those cases considerable numbers of settlers had already entered the territories in question. Their presences, and unregulated land acquisitions, constituted a problem to which, in a sense, colonial administration represented a solution. It was a 'solution' that created further and larger problems but it was one that at the time some Islanders reluctantly accepted, and others for their own reasons positively welcomed. If the circumstances were invidious, if the debates that resulted in indigenous acquiescence were flawed, if the treaties were misleading or mistranslated, it can at least be said that a process took place that some Islanders, some inhabitants of the islands in question, were aware of, and in which they were able, in however unsatisfactory a way, to intervene.

Nothing like this had happened when the French had grabbed New Caledonia and nothing like it happened either when the Germans and British grabbed New Guinea. These declarations, which superseded native sovereignty, largely preceded even a precise knowledge of the relevant coastlines, let alone any understanding of the vast inland and upland territories. They preceded any but the most superficial observations of the peoples of an extraordinary and diverse country. Only coastal groups such as the Tolai and the people around Port Moresby had been engaged with to any serious extent, and even those for barely a decade. Those who at best had cruised the coasts had no notion that, for example, there were populations of tens of thousands in Highlands valleys who had been agriculturalists for as long as anyone in Asia or Europe. Such peoples had, at a stroke, been incorporated into the empires of Germany and Britain, yet these empires were expressed, on Melanesian soil, as yet by no institutions, no official residents, no police. On the map, the colonization of New Guinea by European powers was complete. On the ground, it had not even begun.

Epilogue

During the nineteenth century the minority of Islanders whose lives were long, by the standards of the time, witnessed extraordinary changes. A Tahitian villager, say a boy, born in the 1780s, would experience as a child a customary order already energized by exchange with Europeans, yet already dislocated by introduced disease and depopulation. His life as a young man might not be too directly affected by the political turmoil that so preoccupied the missionaries, the Pomare dynasty and their opponents: many common men, it is true, were intermittently called upon to fight, but these engagements were occasional, and much of the time subsistence life in more out of the way settlements carried on as it had.

Yet in due course the revolutionary introduction of a Christian order, backed by the chiefs, and organized to sustain their kingdom, had its ramifications everywhere. Architecture, dress, sex, work and the daily routine were all reshaped. In his sixties this same man would experience a second wave of colonization, the establishment of a French administration, which by his seventies would sustain a thoroughly Europeanized port town in Papeete, a host of outlying settlements, and a landscape of roads rather than paths. The world into which this man had been born was now a world away, an object not only of his own nostalgia but of the nostalgic researches of colonial folklorists and ethnologists, who laboured to reconstruct the beliefs and customs of 'ancient Tahiti'.

A young man or woman born in the vicinity of Noumea, in New Caledonia, in the 1840s would similarly lead a life with its beginnings in essentially indigenous milieux, milieux to be sure that knew of or engaged with the missionary project. A boy or girl might very well have a male relative who had worked as a crew-member upon a European trader, yet have grown up with the drama and threat of ceremony and vengeance, aware of the grandeur of great feasts. Yet this person even in their twenties or thirties would inhabit an Australianized 'bush', a settled land in which Kanak had suffered marginalization. Yet he or she might make a viable life, as a stockman, even as the wife, of some French, Irish, or Australian farmer.

In western Oceania change came later but came when it did, much more rapidly. Until the early 1870s Solomon Island societies, particularly those of 'bush' people, of the interior of the larger islands, had only second-hand contacts with the Europeans whose exchanges with coastal peoples were anyway irregular. But once the labour trade gained momentum, the passage and the plantation assumed enormous significance even for those who remained at home. A Malaitan boy born in, say, 1860 would have had an infancy more or less unmodified by anything Europe had to offer or impose, but might then suffer the rigours, and capitalize upon the advantages, of work on a colonial continent. He might, by his thirties, have joined the evangelical mission, maybe even embraced the life of a teacher, becoming we might even say one of the first members of a literate Melanesian middle class. The expatriate Melanesian world, which afforded such possibilities, would be abruptly truncated with the end of indenture and the deportation of Islanders, at the beginning of the twentieth century.

From the formal historical perspective, the last decades of the nineteenth century were marked by a wave of annexation, by the almost pervasive establishment of formal colonial rule. The process had begun as early as the 1840s and 1850s, with the acquisitions of west Papua, New Zealand, Tahiti, the Marquesas and New Caledonia by Holland, Britain and France. Fiji was ceded to Britain in 1874; eastern New Guinea was divided between Germany and Britain in 1884; Rapa Nui was annexed by Chile in 1888; the Cook Islands came under British administration in the same year; and parts of the Solomon Islands became a British protectorate in 1893. The Hawaiian kingdom was occupied by the American military in 1893 and formally annexed in 1898; the Samoan islands were partitioned between Germany and the United States in 1899, and an Anglo-French condominium was established to rule the New Hebrides, later Vanuatu, in 1906. Thus recited, the history has a semblance of inevitability, but the Tongan kingdom was reformed as a constitutional monarchy in 1875 and retained formal independence throughout the period, albeit firmly within a British sphere of influence. There had, of course, been codes and laws and governments established, led by coalitions of chiefs, missionaries and settlers, in Tahiti, Fiji, Samoa and Hawaii, among other places, and we might imagine histories, ones not so profoundly different to those that actually happened, which could have featured the independent development of one or more of these Islander kingdoms.

The story was different in western Oceania. Though there were chiefs and paramount chiefs, notably in New Caledonia, the extensive exchange networks that linked people across regions were not hierarchically structured, hence the preconditions for wider political unity, for the formation of modern, but independent, political entities were lacking. Colonial powers did not take emergent nations over from indigenous elites, they did not even go through the form of negotiation, but rather simply took possession, and only subsequently, and often slowly, established administrative control. Which is to say that formal colonization, the assumption of sovereignty over Islanders' societies by European states, was not the event it was made out to be. In some cases, Islanders inhabited a colonial world decades earlier. Already, at the very beginning of the nineteenth century, Pomare among other Society Islanders was confronted by the demands of commerce and Christianity, and thinking through what was to be gained and lost through engagement with them. In other contexts, notably in Highland New Guinea, but also in the interiors of larger islands throughout island Melanesia, people retained great autonomy, and refused to adopt Christianity, for decades after the imposition of colonial rule. In some cases they refuse still. While many of those who did convert would not today accept that they thereby renounced 'custom'.

If Europeans were struck from the outset by the observation that some Islanders were the subjects of kings, and others inhabited seemingly simpler societies, the less hierarchical orders were consistently misread. Yes, their political forms were fluid and local, but the relationships that made them up were never localized. To the contrary, Islanders across the great ocean were engaged in elaborate systems of trade with close neighbours and more distant partners, which immersed them in gift-giving, diplomacy, commerce and contest, long before Europeans intruded and brought their own offerings and made their own demands. True, some peoples were caught up in interaction and trade to a greater degree than others, but with very few exceptions, such as the genuinely isolated inhabitants of Rapa Nui, the 'local' lives of Islanders had involved the extra-local for a long time – from the start, we should say, recalling the archaeology of voyaging and trade. If the term 'native' implies embeddedness in a small-scale, bounded community, it has to be said that Islanders were never natives.

The experience of empire was the enlargement of all this. The argument here is in no sense that empire was other than exploitative, indeed brutal – recall the killings on board the *Carl*, to single out but one episode. Yet it was also the creation of a cosmopolitan arena, which extended and elaborated upon the deeply inter-social character of Islander society. As commerce accelerated, Islanders saw more and more of each other. They interpreted what they saw in parts of the Pacific that were new to them, they found ways of making sense of the ports and cities beyond the Pacific that they also visited. They communicated these imaginings, their sense of wider worlds, to kin, to other Islanders, who never left home, but nevertheless began to conceive of what they did, in relation to Britain, to Europe, to the ways of Asian and African peoples they met off ships or in the course of their own travels.

We – historians among others – may think we know empire, a European project with a beginning and an end, marked by the establishment and disestablishment of presumptuous forms of government. But empire as it was experienced in the Pacific and elsewhere was something that came before this and that reached beyond it. It was conspicuously violent, yet replete with possibilities, marked out by travels, possible travels, and travels of the mind. Empire was powerfully suggestive, it prompted people to rethink themselves, their lives and their futures – most obviously, but not only, as they underwent 'conversion', which of course meant less or more, in different places and times.

Empire involved, and involves, straightforward matters that we know – the appropriation of lands, the command of labour, the killings of those who resist. But it was always, at the same time, and equally profoundly, something other than what we know, a more elusive matter of imagination, and activity inspired by imagination. This dimension of empire was never clearly or fully documented. It surfaces, sometimes only obliquely, in documented histories, histories that I have tried to re-examine and re-think, all too selectively, here. In this sense, too, empire's echoes and effects are not done and dealt with: they are everywhere unresolved and with us still.

Notes

Introduction

1. Archibald Menzies, 'Journal 1791–1794', BL Add. Ms. 32641, 4–5; W. Kaye Lamb (ed.), *The Voyage of George Vancouver, 1791–1795* (London, 1984), I, 307–8, n.3. Another rich journal for this voyage, that of the clerk Edward Bell (Alexander Turnbull Library, Wellington), reports Kualelo's experiences at a number of points.
2. Lamb, 307.
3. Menzies, 'Journal'.
4. The most popular twentieth-century history of the Pacific was Alan Moorhead's *The Fatal Impact: An Account of the Invasion of the South Pacific* (London, 1966). But many more recent, and academically reputable books, such as Steven Roger Fischer's *Island at the End of the World: The Turbulent History of Easter Island* (London, 2005), reproduce the same broad approach.
5. Pacific Islands history began to move in this direction in the 1960s, and senior practitioners of the period, such as J.W. Davidson, were also advisers on transitions to self-government. From 1966 'ethnohistory' featured regularly in the *Journal of Pacific History*, though two-sided understandings were expressed more ambitiously, and for a wider public, only somewhat later, notably in Anne Salmond's *Two Worlds: First Meetings between Maori and Europeans 1642–1772* (Auckland, 1991).
6. The problems and limitations of reconstructing Islanders' histories via a primarily European documentary archive were cited and reflected upon by most scholars in the field from the 1960s on, though Greg Dening, influenced by anthropologists such as Clifford Geertz and Victor Turner, was most imaginative, in opening up questions on the nature of cross-cultural history, and historical knowledge itself, in *Islands and Beaches: Discourse on a Silent Land* (Melbourne, 1980) and subsequent works. Klaus Neumann's *Not the Way it Really Was: Constructing the Tolai Past* (Honolulu, 1992) remains the most provocative interrogation of the conventions of historical writing in the Pacific context.
7. I am conscious that this term has been the focus of sustained debate, stimulated notably by Kwame Anthony Appiah's *Cosmopolitanism: Ethics in a World of Strangers* (New York, 2006). This history is broadly consistent with Appiah's challenge to the dichotomous thinking that juxtaposes the West and the rest, moderns and locals, and so forth (*Cosmopolitanism*, xxi), but is concerned above all to demonstrate that milieux remote in time and space from today's hot spots of global culture were marked by cosmopolitan experience, to a previously unconsidered degree.
8. Menzies, 'Journal'.
9. Matthew Spriggs, *The Island Melanesians* (Oxford, 1997), 223–6.
10. Among the best overviews of the sixteenth- to eighteenth-century voyages is O.H.K. Spate's *The Pacific since Magellan* (Canberra, 1979–88); this includes useful citations to

the various scholarly publications of expedition journals, many published by the Hakluyt Society, as well as secondary studies.

11. David A. Chappell's *Double Ghosts: Oceanian Voyages on Euroamerican Ships* (Armonk, New York, 1997) is a useful but uneven survey. Jean Barman and Bruce McIntyre Watson, *Leaving Paradise: Indigenous Hawaiians in the Pacific Northwest, 1787–1898* (Honolulu, 2006) is impressively researched.

12. These various cases are discussed in chapters 1 and 2 below.

13. Louis-Antoine de Bougainville, *Voyage autour du monde* (Paris, 1771); Denis Diderot, *Supplément au Voyage de Bougainville* (Paris, 1796); Anne Salmond, *Aphrodite's Island: The European Discovery of Tahiti* (Auckland, 2009), 110–23.

14. The work was used to promote the blockbuster 2005 exhibition, *Joshua Reynolds: The Creation of Celebrity* at Tate Britain. See also *Cook and Omai: The Cult of the South Seas* (Canberra, 2001). The older standard study is E.H. McCormick's *Omai: Pacific Envoy* (Auckland, 1977). Mai again loomed large in *Between Worlds*, a 2007 exhibition on native visitors to Britain at the National Portrait Gallery, London.

15. Nicholas Thomas, *Discoveries: The Voyages of Captain Cook* (London, 2003), 261–3.

16. Lamb, *The Voyage of George Vancouver*, 421–5, 448–9.

17. My discussion of Oceanic archaeology relies heavily upon Matthew Spriggs, *The Island Melanesians*; and Patrick Vinton Kirch, *On the Road of the Winds: An Archaeological History of the Pacific Islands before European Contact* (Berkeley, 2000). These are the best recent syntheses, but more recent research (reported in the journal *Archaeology in Oceania* among other places) has needless to say altered certain understandings. See also Stuart Bedford, Sean P. Connaughton and Christophe Sand, *Oceanic Explorations: Lapita and Western Pacific Settlement* (Canberra, 2007).

18. Relevant studies in historical linguistics include M. Ross, A. Pawley and M. Osmond (eds.), *The Lexicon of Proto-Oceanic* (Canberra, 1998) and (a synopsis) Andrew Pawley, 'The Prehistory of Oceanic Languages: A Current View', in P. Bellwood, J.J. Fox and D. Tryon (eds.), *The Austronesians: Historical and Comparative Perspectives* (Canberra, 1995).

19. Andrew Pawley, 'Rubbish-man, Commoner, Big-man, Chief? Linguistic Evidence for Hereditary Chieftainship in Proto-Oceanic Society', in Jukka Siikala (ed.), *Oceanic Studies* (Helsinki, 1982).

20. Among the richest evocations of the manifold qualities of priestly and chiefly roles in Pacific societies is Raymond Firth's classic, *We, the Tikopia* (London, 1936).

21. Peter Bellwood, 'Hierarchy, Founder Ideology and Austronesian Expansion', in Bellwood, Fox and Tryon (eds.), *The Austronesians*.

22. T. Lee et al., 'Prehistoric Inter-Archipelago Trading of Polynesian Tree Snails Leaves a Conservation Legacy', *Proceedings of the Royal Society* (B) 274 (2007), 2,901–14. Thanks to Diarmaid Ó Foighil (University of Michigan, Ann Arbor), for drawing this information to my attention.

23. See, e.g., Jim Allen, 'Pre-Contact Trade in Papua New Guinea', in R.J. May and Hank Nelson (eds.), *Melanesia: Beyond Diversity* (Canberra, 1982); Geoffrey Irwin, 'Chieftainship, Kula and Trade in Massim Prehistory', in J.W. Leach and E.R. Leach (eds.), *The Kula: New Perspectives on Massim Exchange* (Cambridge, 1983); Shankar Aswani (ed.), *Essays on Head-Hunting in the Western Solomon Islands*, special issue, *Journal of the Polynesian Society* 109 (1) (2000).

24. Among the best-known instances is the spread of the cult of 'Oro in Society Islands in the Pre-European Period. See, e.g., Douglas L. Oliver, *Ancient Tahitian Society* (Honolulu, 1974), chapter 22.

25. Clements Markham (ed.), *The Voyages of Pedro Fernandez de Quiros, 1595 to 1606* (London, 1904–5); Dening, *Islands and Beaches*, 9–11; Spriggs, *The Island Melanesians*, 226–40.

26. Andrew Sharp (ed.), *The Journal of Jacob Roggeveen* (Oxford, 1970).

27. Recent discussions of this background include Thomas, *Discoveries*, chapter 2; and Salmond, *Aphrodite's Island*.

28. Epeli Hau'ofa, *We Are the Ocean: Selected Works* (Honolulu, 2009), 65. Hau'ofa (1939–2009) was one of the Pacific's most inspiring and radical intellectuals. His 1993 essay, 'Our Sea of Islands', an affirmative account of Oceanic identity, and an argument that Islanders were as much linked as separated by the sea, was much debated but has proved enduringly influential. With other writings it has appeared in *We Are the Ocean*.

29. Thomas, *Discoveries*, enlarges on this argument.

30. George Forster, *A Voyage Round the World* (ed. Nicholas Thomas and Oliver Berghof, Honolulu, 2000), 334.

31. 'The Diary of Máximo Rodríguez', in Bolton Glanvill Corney, *The Quest and Occupation of Tahiti by the Emissaries of Spain* (London, 1919), III, 89.

32. Hau'ofa, 'Our Sea of Islands'.

33. For the maritime-historical background see Spate, *The Pacific since Magellan*, III, 173–6, 273–8; and for a more focussed account of the development of commerce in Hawaii and its consequences, Patrick Vinton Kirch and Marshall Sahlins, *Anahulu: The Anthropology of History in the Kingdom of Hawaii* (Chicago, 1992), I, 36–45.

34. H.E. Maude, *Of Islands and Men: Studies in Pacific History* (Melbourne, 1968), chapter 5.

35. John Gascoigne, *Joseph Banks and the English Enlightenment* (Cambridge, 1994); Patricia Fara, *Sex, Botany and Empire* (London, 2003).

36. The single most important primary account, and the most revealing concerning the cross-cultural interactions, is *The Journal of James Morrison* (ed. Owen Rutter, London, 1935; forthcoming as *Mutiny and Aftermath*, ed. Vanessa Smith and Nicholas Thomas, Honolulu). Among many studies, Greg Dening's *Mr Bligh's Bad Language* (Cambridge, 1992) has been particularly influential.

37. The classic account of the castaways and deserters known in the Pacific literature as beachcombers is Maude's 'Beachcombers and Castaways', *Of Islands and Men*, chapter 4. More recent discussions include Vanessa Smith, *Literary Culture and the Pacific* (Cambridge, 1998), chapter 1.

38. Oliver, *Ancient Tahitian Society*, chapter 28.

39. For a valuable recent overview, see Patrick V. Kirch and Jean-Louis Rallu (eds.), *The Growth and Collapse of Pacific Island Societies: Archaeological and Demographic Perspectives* (Honolulu, 2007).

40. D.E. Stannard, *Before the Horror: The Population of Hawaii on the Eve of Western Contact* (Honolulu 1989).

41. Robert F. Rogers, *Destiny's Landfall: A History of Guam* (Honolulu, 1995).

42. There is no single listing of early ships' visits to the Pacific, but various monographs provide details for specific islands and archipelagoes, e.g., for the Marquesas, Dening, *Islands and Beaches*, 296–301; for the Solomons, Judith A. Bennett, *Wealth of the Solomons* (Honolulu, 1987), appendix 1; Patrick O'Reilly and Edouard Reitma, *Bibliographie de Tahiti et de la Polynésie française* (Paris, 1967), 20–226. More special-ized finding aids, such as Robert Langdon (ed.), *Where the Whalers Went* (Canberra, 1984), are also relevant.

43. For the Solomon Islands, see Bennett, *Wealth of the Islands*, chapter 2; for New Guinea, J.L. Whittaker et al. (eds.), *Documents and Readings in New Guinea History* (Milton, Queensland, 1975), includes much significant material.

44. George Smith, *The Life of William Carey* (London, 1885); Andrew Porter, *Religion versus Empire? British Protestant Missionaries and Overseas Expansion, 1700–1914* (Manchester, 2004), 41–5.

45. William Carey, *An Enquiry into the Obligations of Christians to use means for the Conversion of the Heathens* (Leicester, 1792), 81–2.

46. The most relevant study in this context is W.N. Gunson, *Messengers of Grace: Evangelical Missionaries in the South Seas* (Melbourne, 1978). Jean and John Comaroff's historical anthropology, *Of Revelation and Revolution* (Chicago, 1991–7), in which the London Missionary Society's (LMS's) activity in southern Africa looms large, is rich and suggestive.

Chapter 1: A plan of great extent and importance

1. William Wilson, *A Missionary Voyage to the Southern Pacific Ocean, performed in the Years 1796, 1797, and 1798* (London, 1799). There has been no general account of the LMS other than an official history more than a century old (Richard Lovett, *The History of the London Missionary Society, 1795–1895*, London, 1899), but W.N. Gunson, *Messengers of Grace: Evangelical Missionaries in the South Seas* (Melbourne, 1978), provides an enormously valuable social history, which also discusses the formation and work of the Wesleyan Methodist Missionary Society, among other evangelical bodies. Sujit Sivasundaram, *Nature and the Godly Empire: Science and Evangelical Mission in the Pacific, 1795–1850* (Cambridge, 2005), relates missionary writing to popular science, while Anna Johnston's *Missionary Writing and Empire, 1800–1860* (Cambridge, 2003) compares primarily LMS accounts of Polynesia, Australia and India. There is, needless to say, a very considerable literature dealing with histories of conversion, individual missionaries, etcetera.
2. Wilson, *A Missionary Voyage*, XCIX
3. Wilson, *A Missionary Voyage*, XCIX.
4. Geoff Quilley and John Bonehill (eds.), *William Hodges, 1744–1797: The Art of Exploration* (London, 2004).
5. W. Henry, LMS South Seas Journals, Box 1, Folder 3; Wilson, *A Missionary Voyage*, 76–7.
6. I refer to Alfred Gell's influential analysis, *Wrapping in Images: Tattooing in Polynesia* (Oxford, 1993). Crook's observations and experiences are discussed in Thomas, *Marquesan Societies: Inequality and Political Transformation in Eastern Polynesia* (Oxford, 1990), as well as in Dening, *Islands and Beaches*. His important 'Account', long a key source for enquiries into early Marquesan society and culture, has recently been published as William Pascoe Crook, *An Account of the Marquesas Islands 1797–1799*, ed. by Greg Dening, Hervé-Marie Le Cleac'h, Douglas Peacocke and Robert Koenig (Papeete, 2007).
7. Wilson, *A Missionary Voyage*, 141.
8. The complex pre-European political history was effectively distilled by H.G. Cummins in 'Tongan society at the time of European contact', in Noel Rutherford (ed.), *Friendly Islands: A History of Tonga* (Melbourne, 1977). Later studies include Judith Huntsman (ed.), *Tonga and Samoa: Images of Gender and Polity* (Christchurch, 1995).
9. 'John's' real name was Andreas Cornelius Lind.
10. Wilson, *A Missionary Voyage*, 97.
11. Wilson, *A Missionary Voyage*, 102.
12. The best early account of kava drinking and the ceremony – and of much else in Tongan life – appears in John Martin, *An Account of the Natives of the Tonga Islands* (Edinburgh, 1827), II, 125ff. The book was based on information provided by William Mariner, a young beachcomber, in the group from 1806 to 1810.
13. Wilson, *A Missionary Voyage*, 107.
14. Wilson, *A Missionary Voyage*, 248.
15. Phyllis Herda, 'Gender, Rank and Power in 18th-Century Tonga', *Journal of Pacific History* 22 (1987), 195–208.
16. 'Journal of the Missionaries on Tongataboo in the Friendly Islands', *Transactions of the Missionary Society* 1 (1804), 257.
17. James Orange, *Life of the Late George Vason of Nottingham* (London, 1840). This work substantially reproduces Anon., but written by Vason, *An Authentic Narrative of Four Years at Tongataboo* (London, 1810). Page references here are to a republication, ed. David G. May (Nuku'alofa, Tonga, 1998). This text and the beachcomber genre in general are discussed by Smith, *Literary Culture and the Pacific*, 36–42.
18. *Orange, Life of the Late George Vason*, 68, 78.
19. 'Journal of the Missionaries', 261. 'Peppy, a native of Owhyhee [i.e., Hawaii]' had also arrived on the *Mercury*, the American trading ship that brought Beak and five other beachcombers.

20. 'Journal of the Missionaries', 281, 290–1. For discussion of these events see Niel Gunson, 'The Coming of Foreigners', in Rutherford, *Friendly Islands*, 99–105.

21. 'Journal of the Missionaries', 313–16.

22. William Wilson, 15 March 1802 (London Missionary Society, South Seas Letters, Box 1, folder 4; School of Oriental and African Studies, London). See also Orange, *Life of the Late George Vason*, 102–10.

23. Crook, *Account*, 106.

24. Crook, *Account*, 110.

25. Edmund Fanning, *Voyages and Discoveries in the South Seas 1792–1832* (Salem, 1924); extract in Crook, *Account*, 159–64.

26. For Keatonui, see chapter 2 below, and Thomas, *Marquesan Societies*.

27. Crook, *Account*, 132–6.

28. The comparative study of Polynesian political systems was the great theme of the anthropology of Oceania before, and throughout, the twentieth century. Theoretically influential studies included Marshall Sahlins's *Social Stratification in Polynesia* (Seattle, 1958) and Irving Goldman's *Ancient Polynesian Society* (Chicago, 1970). Patrick Vinton Kirch's *The Evolution of the Polynesian Chiefdoms* (Cambridge, 1984) gave theoretical reconstructions a base in empirical archaeology. My early book, *Out of Time: History and Evolution in Anthropological Discourse* (Cambridge, 1989), challenged the scholarship and the assumptions that lay behind theories such as Goldman's.

29. Crook, *Account*, 142.

30. 'Temoteitei', *Evangelical Magazine*, December 1799, 261–2.

31. For Stevenson, see chapter 10 below, and Smith, *Literary Culture in the Pacific*. Dening's interest in the beachcomber motif extended throughout his writing: see also *Performances* (Chicago, 1994) and *Beach Crossings* (Melbourne, 2004).

32. *Morning Chronicle*, 19 July 1808.

33. Joseph Fox, *An Appeal to the Members of the London Missionary Society* (London, 1810). Just one copy of this tract appears to be extant; it is in the British Library.

34. Fox, *An Appeal*, 21. Controversy around Tapioi's story also appeared in several numbers of *The Gospel Magazine*, e.g., November 1807, 511–16; February 1808, 37–9, etc., and apparently in *The Instructor*, which I have been unable to trace. There are in addition unpublished letters in the LMS SSL, Box 1.

35. Wilson, 15 March 1802, LMS SSL.

36. Everard Im Thurn (ed.), *The Journal of William Lockerby* (London, 1925), XXXIX–XL.

37. Rhys Richards, 'Indigenous Beachcombers: The Case of Tapeooe, a Tahitian Traveller from 1798 to 1812', *The Great Circle* 12 (1), 1–14, tells Tapioi's story in part but did not have access to sources such as Fox's *Appeal* and various magazine articles.

38. Fox, *Appeal*, 46–9.

39. Fox, *Appeal*, 60–2.

40. Fox, *Appeal*, 38.

41. Henry Bicknell to Joseph Fox, Morea, October 1812, LMS, SSL, Box 1.

42. See, for example, the mode of reconstructing Maori understanding in Anne Salmond's *Two Worlds*.

43. The key source for this phase of Tongan history is Martin, *An Account*.

44. *Transactions of the Missionary Society* 3 (1813), 283–4.

45. Martin, *An Account*, I, 211.

46. The best sources for this history are C.W. Newbury (ed.), *The History of the Tahitian Mission* (London, 1961), which includes invaluable contextual and editorial material, in addition to the missionary John Davies's history of the enterprise; and Oliver, *Ancient Tahitian Society*.

47. *Oracle and Daily Advertiser*, 19 October 1799.

48. Newbury, *History*, 70n.

Chapter 2: The Typees fought us to the last

1. Judith A. Bennett, *Wealth of the Solomons* (Honolulu, 1987), 26.
2. Such characterizations date, in certain forms, to the eighteenth-century French geographer, Charles des Brosses (*Histoire des navigations aux terres australes*, Paris, 1756–7); but were refined in twentieth-century anthropology particularly through an influential, though ultimately widely criticized essay by Marshall Sahlins, 'Poor Man, Rich Man, Big Man, Chief: Political Types in Melanesia and Polynesia', *Comparative Studies in Society and History* 5 (1963), 285–303. Responses included Bronwen Douglas's 'Rank, Power, Authority: A Reassessment of Traditional Leadership in South Pacific Societies', in her *Across the Great Divide: Journeys in History and Anthropology* (Amsterdam, 1998).
3. Simbo in particular was described with considerable eloquence by A.M. Hocart in a series of essays published in the 1920s, e.g., 'The Cult of the Dead in Eddystone of the Solomons', *Journal of the Royal Anthropological Institute* 57 (1922), 71–112; 259–305. Unpublished sections of what amounted to an ethnographic monograph on the area are in the Hocart Papers, in the Alexander Turnbull Library, Wellington. More recent studies by archaeologists and anthropologists including Peter Sheppard, Tim Thomas, Christine Dureau and Debra McDougall are represented in Shankar Aswami (ed.), *Essays on Head-Hunting in the Western Solomon Islands, Journal of the Polynesian Society* (109) (2000). Edvard Hviding, *Guardians of Marovo Lagoon* (Honolulu, 1996) incorporates historical anthropology in a present-day ethnography of maritime life.
4. Hocart, 'Notes on White Men – Mandegusu', Alexander Turnbull Library, Wellington; Christine Dureau, 'Recounting and Remembering "First Contact" on Simbo', in Jeannette Marie Mageo, *Cultural Memory: Reconfiguring History and Identity in the Postcolonial Pacific* (Honolulu, 2001).
5. David Porter, *Journal of a Cruise made to the Pacific Ocean* (1815). All page references here are to the edition of R.D. Madison (Annapolis, Maryland, 1986). Madison's introduction and annotations are those of a naval historian with little interest in Polynesian dimensions of the story, but the edition is extremely useful for the main text, from Porter's first edition, and supplementary chapters from the second, in which the main narrative was censored in the wake of controversy around Porter's actions. With the exception of a short journal by the midshipman Feltus, who was killed in a fracas at a late stage of the Nukuhiva occupation (Pennsylvania Historical Society), Porter's book appears to be the sole extant account of his voyage; an extensive collection of Porter family papers in the Library of Congress, Washington, adds little to an understanding of the expedition. I draw here on my own previous work, Thomas, *Marquesan Societies*.
6. Porter, *Voyage*, 314.
7. Porter, *Voyage*, 329
8. Porter, *Voyage*. 349.
9. Porter, *Voyage*, 354.
10. Porter, *Voyage*, 364–5.
11. Porter, *Voyage*, 397.
12. Porter, *Voyage*, 400.
13. Gamble's misadventures are described in chapters 19–20 in the second edition of Porter's *Voyage*.
14. For discussion, see Thomas, *Marquesan Societies*.
15. Nicholas Thomas, *Entangled Objects* (Cambridge, Mass., 1991).
16. Dorothy Shineberg, *They Came for Sandalwood: A Study of the Sandalwood Trade in the South-West Pacific 1830–1865* (Melbourne, 1967), is the classic study, but one concerned, as the title indicates, primarily with the later development of the trade in Melanesia. Kirch and Sahlins, *Anahulu*, I, 58–60, incorporates some discussion in the Hawaiian context.

17. R. Gerard Ward, 'The Pacific Bêche-de-Mer Trade with Special Reference to Fiji,' in Ward (ed.), *Man in the Pacific Islands* (Oxford, 1972), 91–123.

18. Camille de Roquefeuil *Journal d'un voyage autour du monde, pendant les années 1816, 1817, 1818, et 1819* (Paris, 1823), I, 275.

19. See Kirch and Rallu, *The Growth and Collapse of Pacific Islands Societies*, 160–76, for an archaeological perspective on past demography.

Chapter 3: If King Georgey would send him a vessel

1. Steven Hooper, *Pacific Encounters: Art and Divinity in Polynesia 1760–1860* (London 2006), 80–8; Nicholas Thomas, *Oceanic Art* (London, 1995), 151–64.

2. Lilikala Kame'eleheiwa, *Native Land and Foreign Desires: Pehea La e Pono ai?* (Honolulu, 1992), 25–40.

3. Velerio Valeri, 'The Conqueror Becomes King: A Political Analysis of the Hawaiian Legend of 'Umi', in Antony Hooper and Judith Huntsman (eds.), *Transformations of Polynesian Culture* (Auckland, 1985).

4. *Historical Records of Australia*, Ser. I, vol. 8, 624–7.

5. Otto von Kotzebue, *A Voyage of Discovery into the South Sea and Beering's Straits . . . undertaken in the Years 1815–1818* (London, 1821), 301, 306–9.

6. Kotzebue, *A Voyage*, 324–5.

7. Marshall Sahlins and Patrick V. Kirch, *Anahulu: The Anthropology of History in the Kingdom of Hawaii* (Chicago, 1992), I, 36–54, esp. 43.

8. Sahlins, *Anahulu*, I, 60.

9. The fragmented and widely dispersed evidence concerning the *Argo* and Slater's movements was carefully pieced together by Everard im Thurn and Leonard C. Wharton, 'Introduction', in Im Thurn and Wharton (eds.), *The Journal of William Lockerby . . . & Other Papers* (London, 1925), xxxiii–xxxix.

10. *Sydney Gazette*, 28 October 1804.

11. Im Thurn and Wharton, 'Introduction', xlvii–lv.

12. The section that follows is based on Lockerby's own account, in Im Thurn and Wharton, *The Journal*.

13. Im Thurn and Wharton, *The Journal*, 17–19.

14. *The Journal*, 19–20.

15. *The Journal*, 22.

16. *The Journal*, 34.

17. *The Journal*, 40–5.

18. The argument put forward, influentially but controversially, by William Arens in *The Man-Eating Myth* (New York, 1979), was followed up by Gananath Obeyesekere, *Cannibal Talk: The Man-Eating Myth and Human Sacrifice in the South Seas* (Berkeley, 2005). Earlier essays by Obeyesekere were responded to by Sahlins in 'Artificially Maintained Controversies: Global Warming and Fijian Cannibalism', *Anthropology Today* (2003) 19 (3), 3–5; others joined the debate in issues 19 (5) and (6) of the same journal.

19. Im Thurn and Wharton, *The Journal*, 46–50.

20. *The Journal*, 50.

21. *The Journal*, 71.

22. *The Journal*, 72.

23. Dillon's extraordinary career is reconstructed in J.W. Davidson's posthumously published *Peter Dillon of Vanikoro* (ed. O.H.K. Spate, Melbourne, 1975).

24. For Dillon's later account, see Peter Dillon, *Narrative and Successful Result of a Voyage in the South Seas . . . to ascertain the actual fate of La Pérouse's Expedition* (London, 1829), I; see also Davidson, *Peter Dillon*, chapter 2.

25. Dillon, *Narrative*, I, 12.

26. *Narrative*, I, 17–18.

27. *Narrative*, I, 23.
28. *Narrative*, I, 35–6.
29. See, e.g., Greg Dening, *Islands and Beaches* (Melbourne, 1980).
30. Im Thurn and Wharton (eds.), *The Journal*, 212.
31. *Missionary Herald*, April 1821, 114. This event, needless to say, has been much analyzed and discussed. See Sahlins, *Anahulu*, I, 57, for key references.

Chapter 4: Not a vestige of idolatry was to be seen

1. A number of similar incidents and arguments are reported in *Transactions of the Missionary Society* [*TMS*] 2 (1804), 326–31.
2. *TMS* 2, 348–9. See also C.W. Newbury (ed.), *The History of the Tahitian Mission* by John Davies (London, 1961), 62–7.
3. For Society Islands religious history, see, e.g., Teuira Henry, *Ancient Tahiti* (Honolulu, 1928), esp.121–6; Douglas L. Oliver, *Ancient Tahitian Society* (Honolulu, 1974), 909–13; and, a summary, Thomas, *Oceanic Art* (London, 1995), 158–9.
4. *TMS* 2, 327.
5. *TMS* 2, 330–1.
6. *TMS* 2, 141. The missionary letters from this period (some published in *TMS*, also in manuscript, LMS SSL Box 1) are replete with references to Islanders arriving or departing on commercial vessels, and to the Hawaiians whom Pomare made his constant companions.
7. *History of the Tahitian Mission*, 121.
8. James Montgomery, *Voyages and Travels round the world by the Rev. Daniel Tyerman and George Bennet*, second ed. (London, 1841), 31; *History of the Tahitian Mission*, 223; *TMS* 2, 279.
9. *TMS* 2, 317, 343.
10. Niko Besnier's fascinating ethnography, *Literacy, Emotion and Authority: Reading and Writing on a Polynesian Atoll* (Cambridge, 1995) suggests manifold ways in which the written and printed word has been highly charged for recent generations of Polynesians. His findings, obviously, cannot be projected back into the early nineteenth century, but are suggestive, for the varied potencies that scripts have possessed for peoples of the Pacific.
11. For fuller discussion, see Nicholas Thomas, Anna Cole and Bronwen Douglas (eds.) *Tattoo: Bodies, Art and Exchange in the Pacific and the West* (London, 2005).
12. The most precise and concise account of this history is in Newbury's 'Introduction', *History of the Tahitian Mission*. Oliver, *Ancient Tahitian Society*, chapters 30–2, is a fuller, blow-by-blow account, to 1815.
13. *History of the Tahitian Mission*, 153, 156.
14. *History of the Tahitian Mission*, 177.
15. *TMS* 2, 313–14. William Ellis, *A Vindication of the South Sea Missions from the Misrepresentations of Otto von Kotzebue* (London, 1831), 38.
16. Oliver, *Ancient Tahitian Society*, 1135.
17. On the general theme, see Peter van der Veer (ed.), *Conversion to Modernities: The Globalization of Christianity* (New York, 1996).
18. *History of the Tahitian Mission*, 190–3.
19. *History of the Tahitian Mission*, Appendix II.
20. *Quarterly Chronicle of Transactions of the London Missionary Society* 2 (1825), 211–12.
21. Otto von Kotzebue, *A New Voyage round the World, in the years 1823–, 24, 25, and 26* (London, 1830), I, 151.
22. Von Kotzebue, *New Voyage*, I, 147, 159, 168–9.
23. Ellis, *Polynesian Researches* (London, 1829).
24. *New Voyage*, I, 153–45.
25. Ellis, *A Vindication*, 47–9.

26. Richard Moyle (ed.), *The Samoan Journals of John Williams, 1830 and 1832* (Canberra, 1984), 3.
27. John Campbell D.D., *The Martyr of Erromanga, or the Philosophy of Missions* (London, 1842), 196, 198.
28. *The Martyr of Erromanga*, 197.
29. Niel Gunson, 'John Williams and his Ship: The Bourgeois Aspirations of a Missionary Family', in D.P. Crook (ed.), *Questioning the Past* (St. Lucia, Queensland, 1972).
30. John Williams, *Missionary Enterprises in the South Sea Islands* (London, 1838), 53.
31. *Missionary Enterprises*, 97.
32. Bourne, quoted in Williams, *Missionary Enterprises*, 112–13.
33. Richard Gilson, *The Cook Islands 1820–1950* (ed. Ron Crocombe, Wellington, 1980), 21.
34. Aaron Buzacott, quoted in Raeburn Lange, *The Origins of the Christian Ministry in the Cook Islands and Samoa* (Christchurch, 1997), 5.
35. Williams, *Missionary Enterprises*, 144–51.
36. Moyle (ed.), *The Samoan Journals*, 9–10.
37. *The Samoan Journals*, 68. For discussion see Vanessa Smith, in Jonathan Lamb, Vanessa Smith and Nicholas Thomas (eds.), *Exploration and Exchange: A South Seas Anthology 1680–1900* (Chicago, 2000), 217–21.
38. Dening, *Islands and Beaches*; Thomas, *Marquesan Societies*.
39. Gilson, *The Cook Islands*, chapter 3.
40. Williams, *The Samoan Journals*, 280–1.
41. *Farewell to Viriamu* (London, 1838).
42. Thomas, *Discoveries*, 239–41.
43. Dorothy Shineberg, *They Came for Sandalwood: A Study of the Sandalwood Trade in the Southwest Pacific 1830–1865* (Melbourne, 1967), 18–25.
44. Ebenezer Prout, *Memoirs of the Life of the Rev. John Williams, Missionary to Polynesia* (London, 1843), 388–92.
45. Bernard Smith, *European Vision and the South Pacific*, 2nd. ed. (New Haven, 1985), 318–21; on representations of Williams's death, see also Sujit Sivasundaram, *Nature and the Godly Empire: Science and Evangelical Mission in the Pacific 1795–1850* (Cambridge, 2005), chapter 4.
46. Albert J. Schütz (ed.), *The Diaries and Correspondence of David Cargill, 1832–1843* (Canberra, 1977), 19.
47. Schütz (ed.), *The Diaries and Correspondence*, 41.
48. *The Diaries and Correspondence*, 95.
49. *The Diaries and Correspondence*, 125.
50. *The Diaries and Correspondence*, 186.
51. J.W. Davidson, *Peter Dillon of Vanikoro* (Melbourne, 1975), 290–3.
52. Schütz (ed.), *The Diaries and Correspondence*, 224.
53. Schütz, 'Introduction' and editorial comment in *The Diaries and Correspondence*, esp. 244–6, is excellent on Cargill's personality and the likelihood that this depression was exacerbated by dengue fever.

Chapter 5: Haunted by the example of Cook

1. The modern edition is Johann Reinhold Forster, *Observations Made during a Voyage Round the World* (ed. Nicholas Thomas, Harriet Guest and Michael Dettelbach, Honolulu, 1996); John Martin, *An Account of the Natives of the Tongan Islands* (Edinburgh, 1827); William Ellis, *Polynesian Researches* (London, 1829) appeared first in two volumes and then in four (London 1831); it was reprinted in both England and the United States several times in the 1830s. All of these works are discussed in Jonathan Lamb, Vanessa Smith and Nicholas Thomas (eds.), *Exploration and Exchange: A South Seas Anthology 1680–1900* (Chicago, 2000), and e.g., in Rod Edmond, *Representing the South Pacific: Colonial Discourse from Cook to Gauguin* (Cambridge, 1997).

2. Helen Rosenman (trans. and ed.), *An Account of Two Voyages to the South Seas* (Melbourne, 1987), is invaluable for Dumont d'Urville's biography and the context of the voyages, as well as an abridgement that provides a refreshing alternative to Dumont d'Urville's padded-out and pompous original publications. See also John Dunmore, *From Venus to Antarctica: The Life of Dumont d'Urville* (Auckland, 2007), a short, straightforward biography, and Susan Hunt, Martin Terry and Nicholas Thomas, *Lure of the Southern Seas: The Voyages of Dumont d'Urville 1826-1840* (Sydney, 2002), an exhibition catalogue.

3. Thomas Forrest, *A Voyage to New Guinea and the Moluccas* (London, 1779). On the wider history of west Papua, which largely falls outside this book's scope, see Clive Moore, *New Guinea: Crossing Boundaries and History* (Honolulu, 2003), chapter 3.

4. Dunmore, *From Venus to Antarctica*, 58-9.

5. Rosenman, *Two Voyages*, I, 31-2.

6. Rosenman, *Two Voyages*, I, 71.

7. Rosenman, *Two Voyages*, I, 99.

8. See, for the earlier phases of Hongi's activity, Anne Salmond, *Between Worlds: Early Exchanges Between Maori and Europeans, 1773-1815* (Auckland, 1997), 437-45; and more generally James Belich, *Making Peoples: A History of New Zealanders* (Auckland, 1996), 156-64.

9. Rosenman, *Two Voyages*, I, 108-15.

10. Rosenman, *Two Voyages*, I, 118-26.

11. Rosenman, *Two Voyages*, I, 132.

12. Dunmore, *From Venus to Antarctica*, 130-40.

13. Forster, *Observations*, 153.

14. Dumont d'Urville, 'Notice sur les îles du Grand Ocean et sur l'origine des peuples qui l'habitent', *Bulletin de la Société de Géographie de Paris* 17 (1832), 1-21. For discussion see Nicholas Thomas, *In Oceania: Visions, Artifacts, Histories* (Durham, 1997), chapter 5; *Journal of Pacific History* 38 (2) (2003) (a special issue incorporating a translation of the 'Notice').

15. Grégoire-Louis Domeny de Rienzi, *Océanie, ou cinquième partie du monde* (Paris, 1836-7).

16. James Cowles Prichard, *Researches into the Physical History of Mankind*, 3rd. ed. (London, 1836-47); Horatio Hale, *United States Exploring Expedition: Ethnography and Philology* (Philadelphia, 1845); For further discussion see Thomas, *In Oceania*, 145-51; Bronwen Douglas, 'Art as Ethno-Historical Text', in Nicholas Thomas and Diane Losche (eds.), *Double Vision: Art Histories and Colonial Histories in the Pacific* (Cambridge, 1999); and, for the broader context, George Stocking, *Victorian Anthropology* (New York, 1987).

17. Dumont d'Urville, *Voyage pittoresque autour du monde* (Paris, 1834-5); Dumont d'Urville, Carol Legge (trans.), *The New Zealanders: A Story of Austral Lands* (Wellington, 1992).

18. For a readable recent history, see Nathaniel Philbrick, *Sea of Glory: The Epic South Seas Expedition 1838-1842* (London, 2004).

19. Charles Wilkes, *Narrative of the United States Exploring Expedition* (Philadelphia, 1845), I, xxix.

20. Wilkes, *Narrative*, I, 313.

21. Wilkes, *Narrative*, I, 326.

22. For discussion of Fiji and the Bau-Rewa conflict in this period, see Marshall Sahlins, *Apologies to Thucydides: Understanding History as Culture and Vice Versa* (Chicago, 2004).

23. Wilkes, *Narrative*, III, 128.

24. Wilkes, *Narrative*, III, 265-71; Philbrick, *Sea of Glory*, chapter 10.

25. Wilkes, *Narrative*, III, 271-86.

26. William Reynolds, *The Private Journal of William Reynolds: United States Exploring Expedition, 1838–1842*, ed. Nathaniel Philbrick and Thomas Philbrick (New York, 2004), 195.
27. Reynolds, *The Private Journal*, 145.
28. Hale, *Ethnography and Philology*, 50.
29. Primary accounts of these voyages include Robert FitzRoy, *Narrative of the Surveying Voyages of His Majesty's Ships Adventure and Beagle* (London, 1839); John Lort Stokes, *Discoveries in Australia* (London, 1846); J. Beete Jukes, *Narrative of the Surveying Voyage of HMS Fly* (London, 1847); John Macgillivray, *Narrative of the Voyage of HMS Rattlesnake* (London, 1852); John Elphinstone Erskine, *Journal of a Cruise among the Islands of the Western Pacific* (London 1853); Andrew David (ed.), *The Voyage of HMS Herald* (Melbourne, 1995).
30. Jukes, *Narrative*, I, 217.
31. Jukes, *Narrative*, I, 223–4; 229.
32. Jukes, *Narrative*, I, 232.
33. Jukes, *Narrative*, I, 265–6.
34. Jukes, *Narrative*, I, 270.
35. Jukes, *Narrative*, I, 271–8. The ornamented skull appears to have been destroyed, along with other material in the Royal College of Surgeons collections, by a bomb in 1941. Douglas Newton, *Art Styles of the Papuan Gulf* (New York, 1961) identifies the men's house as Buniki, on the Bamu river. I am grateful to Elizabeth Bonshek for drawing attention to this; for further detail see her contribution on the *Fly* in Lissant Bolton, Nicholas Thomas, Elizabeth Bonshek and Julie Adams (eds.), *Melanesia: Art and Encounter* (London, 2011).
36. Jukes, *Narrative*, I, 276, 278.
37. Jukes, *Narrative*, I, 291.

Chapter 6: The smell of burning flesh is not nice

1. Hugh Laracy, *Marists and Melanesians: A History of Catholic Missions in the Solomon Islands* (Canberra, 1976), 17–22.
2. James Belich, *Making Peoples: A History of New Zealanders* (Auckland, 1996), 179–80.
3. Nicholas Thomas, *Marquesan Societies* (Oxford, 1990).
4. Greg Denings, *Islands and Beaches: Discourse on a Silent Land* (Honolulu, 1980), chapter 6; C.W. Newbury, *Tahiti Nui: Change and Survival in French Polynesia 1767–1945* (Honolulu, 1980), chapter 4.
5. Maurice Leenhardt, *Notes d'ethnologie néo-calédonienne* (Paris, 1930); James Clifford, *Person and Myth: Maurice Leenhardt in the Melanesian World* (Berkeley, 1982).
6. R.G. and M. Crocombe (eds.), *The Works of Ta'unga: Records of a Polynesian Traveller in the South Seas 1833–1896* (Canberra, 1968), 108.
7. Bronwen Douglas, *Across the Great Divide: Journeys in History and Anthropology* (Amsterdam, 1998), chapter 3.
8. Julian Thomas (pseudonym of Stanley James), *Cannibals and Convicts: Notes of Personal Experience in the Western Pacific* (London, 1886).
9. For an interesting perspective, see the catalogue to a Sydney exhibition dedicated to the work of one former Communard who later settled in Sydney and was influential in colonial design: Ann Stephen (ed.), *Visions of a Republic: The Work of Lucien Henri, Paris, Noumea, Sydney* (Sydney, 2001).
10. Henri Rivière, *Souvenirs de la Nouvelle-Calédonie* (Paris, 1881), 11, 13.
11. Rivière, *Souvenirs*, 79.
12. My understanding is indebted, above all, to Bronwen Douglas's chapter, 'Winning and Losing? Reflections on the War of 1878–9 in New Caledonia', in Douglas, *Across the Great Divide*. Other influential studies include R. Dousset, *Colonialisme et contradic-*

tions: *étude sur les causes socio-historiques de l'insurrection de 1878 en Nouvelle-Calédonie* (Paris, 1970).

13. Rivière, *Souvenirs*, 109.
14. Rivière, *Souvenirs*, 110–14.
15. Rivière, *Souvenirs*, 115, 119.
16. Rivière, *Souvenirs*, 123–4.
17. 'Gunga', *Narrative of a trip from Maryborough to New Caledonia, with details of the late revolt* (Maryborough, 1878), 4.
18. *Cannibals and Coverts*, 79.
19. Rivière, *Souvenirs*, 145–9.
20. Charles Amouroux and H. Place, *L'Administration et les Maristes en Nouvelle-Calédonie: Insurrection des Kanak en 1878–79* (Paris, 1881), 14.
21. *Cannibals and Converts*, 85.
22. *Cannibals and Converts*, 90–3.
23. Douglas, *Across the Great Divide*, 207–9.
24. Douglas, *Across the Great Divide*, 215–17.
25. 'Rapport sur les causes de l'insurrection canaque en 1878', printed in Dousset, *Colonialisme et contradictions*, 159.
26. Amouroux and Place, *L'Administration et les Maristes*, 131.
27. Louise Michel, *Légendes et chants de gestes canaques* (Paris, 1885); see also Bullitt Lowry and Elizabeth Ellington Gunter, *The Red Virgin: Memoirs of Louise Michel* (Alabama, 1981). I am unable to substantiate the story that Michel sent the rebel chief Atai a scarf or a piece of her scarf as a token of support.
28. J.W. Anderson, *Notes of Travel in Fiji and New Caledonia* (London, 1880), 221.
29. P. Lambert, *Moeurs et superstitions des Néo-Calédoniens* (Noumea, 1900), 67.
30. The most recent and valuable publication is Roberta Colombo Dougoud, *Bambous kanak* (Geneva, 2008).

Chapter 7: A new phase of piracy

1. For an up-to-date archaeological discussion, see Patrick Vinton Kirch, *On the Road of the Winds* (Berkeley, 2000), 233ff. P. Bahn and J. Flenley, *Easter Island, Earth Island* (London, 1992), drew out the larger ecological implications of the island's story, as did, more popularly, Jared Diamond in *Collapse: How Societies Choose to Fail or Succeed* (New York, 2005).
2. See particularly the work of Matthew Spriggs, including 'Landscape, Land Use and Political Transformation in Southern Melanesia', in P.V. Kirch (ed.), *Island Societies: Archaeological Approaches to Evolution and Transformation* (Cambridge, 1986) and *The Island Melanesians* (Oxford, 1997).
3. James Cook, *A Voyage toward the South Pole and around the World* (London, 1777), I, 288.
4. Steven Roger Fischer, *Island at the End of The World: the Turbulent History of Easter Island* (London, 2005), 72, quoting unpublished research by Grant McCall.
5. Greg Dening, *Islands and Beaches: Discourse on a Silent Land* (Honolulu, 1980), 295–301.
6. Frederick William Beechey, *Narrative of a Voyage to the Pacific and Beering's Strait* (London, 1831), 43–53.
7. Fischer, *Island at the End of the World*, 76.
8. I am indebted, for my overall understanding of Peruvian slaving in the Pacific, and for most of the specific information in this section, to H.E. Maude, *Slavers in Paradise: The Peruvian Labour Trade in Polynesia 1862–1864* (Canberra, 1981).
9. Maude, *Slavers*, 2–4.
10. Maude, *Slavers*, 8–11.
11. Maude, *Slavers*, chapter 3.

12. Greg Dening (ed.), *The Marquesan Journal of Edward Robarts* (Canberra, 1974), 266–7.
13. *Messager de Taiti*, 28 février 1863; Maude, *Slavers*, 15–18.
14. *Messager de Taiti*, 21 février 1863; *Sydney Morning Herald*, 14 April, 25 August 1863.
15. For the series of reports, see *Messager de Taiti*, 28 février, 14 mars 24 mars, 4 avril, 23 mai and 20 juin 1863.
16. Maude, *Slavers*, 138.
17. Maude, *Slavers*, chapters 16–18 *passim*.
18. James Cowan, 'The story of Niue', *Journal of the Polynesian Society* 32 (1923), 241–2.
19. Fischer, *Island at the End of the World*, 83.
20. Fischer, *Island at the End of the World*, 114.
21. See particularly Katherine Routledge, *The Mystery of Easter Island* (London, 1919), and Alfred Métraux, *Ethnology of Easter Island* (Honolulu, 1940).
22. Fischer's monumental *Rongorongo: The Easter Island Script: History, Traditions, Texts* (Oxford, 1997) provides an absorbing account of the European recognition, investigation of, and preoccupation with, the art form, as well as documentation of known extant tablets. However, I am not fully in agreement with Fischer's interpretation of rongorongo history, nor am I in a position to assess the adequacy of his effort to decipher the script.
23. Herman Melville, *Moby Dick, or the Whale* (New York, 1851; ed. Tony Tanner, Oxford, 1988), 491.
24. William J. Thomson, *Te Pito te Henua, or Easter Island* (Washington, 1891), 513.
25. Thomson, *Te Pito te Henua*, 514.
26. Thomson, *Te Pito te Henua*, 515.
27. Thomson, *Te Pito te Henua*, 516.
28. Kirch inclines toward this view (*On the Road of the Winds*, 275), but it is not generally accepted, see, e.g., Eric Kjellgren, *Splendid Isolation: Art of Easter Island* (New York, 2001), 50.
29. For broader discussion of these propensities, see Nicholas Thomas, *Entangled Objects: Exchange, Material Culture and Colonialism in the Pacific* (Cambridge, MA, 1991), chapter 3. For the specific examples, see Samoan clubs in the form of whale blubber knives, Sean Mallon, *Samoan Art and Artists* (Nelson, 2002), 95; for recreations of ships (on land), Charles Wilkes, *Narrative of the United States Exploring Expedition* (Philadelphia, 1845), II, 137.
30. For this reason I find implausible Fischer's suggestion that Rapanui were stimulated to create a proto-script because they witnessed the Spanish preparing a deed of cession in 1770 (*Rongorongo*, 552). The stimulus is likely to have occured, I suggest, much nearer the time the boards were first seen by Europeans.
31. Compare, for example, the swiftly changing religious climate in Tahiti, discussed by Niel Gunson, 'An Account of the Mamaia or visionary heresy of Tahiti, 1826–1841', *Journal of the Polynesian Society* 71 (1962), 209–43.

Chapter 8: Man-o'-war all same old woman!

1. Dorothy Shineberg, *They Came for Sandalwood: A Study of the Sandalwood Trade in the South-West Pacific, 1830–1865* (Melbourne, 1967), chapter 7.
2. Shineberg, *They Came for Sandalwood*, 100ff.
3. Shineberg, *They Came for Sandalwood*, 134–5.
4. K.R. Howe, 'Tourists, Sailors and Labourers: A Survey of Early Labour Recruiting in Southern Melanesia', *Journal of Pacific History* 13 (1978), 28–31.
5. Howe, 'Tourists, Sailors and Labourers', 31–2.
6. John Elphinstone Erskine, *Journal of a Cruise in the Western Pacific* (London, 1853), 366–7.
7. Peter Corris, *Passage, Port and Plantation: A History of Solomon Islands Labour Migration, 1870–1914* (Melbourne, 1973), 11–12.

8. Rev. J. MacNair to Commodore Lambert, 22 October 1868, in *Further Correspondence respecting the Deportation of South Sea Islanders* (papers presented to the House of Lords, London, 1871), 4–5.

9. John McDonnell to the Colonial Secretary, in *Further Correspondence*, 7–8.

10. Commander Palmer to Commodore Lambert, *Further Correspondence*, 41.

11. *Further Correspondence*, 7.

12. Marilyn Strathern, *No Money on our Skins: Hagen Migrants in Port Moresby* (Canberra, 1975).

13. Palmer to the Earl of Belmore, *Further Correspondence*, 19–20.

14. Captain George Palmer, *Kidnapping in the South Seas, being a Narrative of a Three Months' Cruise of H.M. Ship Rosario* (Edinburgh, 1871), 156.

15. Shineberg, *They Came for Sandalwood*, 197.

16. The key documents relating to the case of the *Carl* appear in several collations of British Parliamentary Papers, e.g., *Copies or Extracts of any Communications of Importance respecting Outrages Committed upon Natives of the South Sea Islands* (London, 1873), 220–45. Other accounts from the period include Albert Hastings Markhan, *Cruise of the 'Rosario' amongst the New Hebrides and Santa Cruz Islands exposing the Recent Atrocities Connected with the Kidnapping of Natives in the South Seas* (London, 1873), chapter 10; and A.B. Brewster, *King of the Cannibal Isles* (London, 1937), 213–37.

17. Markhan, *Cruise of the 'Rosario'*, 117.

18. *Report of the proceedings of H.M. Ship 'Rosario', during her cruise among the South Sea Islands between 1st November 1871 and 12th February 1872* (Parliamentary Paper, C.542, London, 1872), 9.

19. *Further Correspondence respecting the Deportation of South Sea Islanders* (Parliamentary Paper, C.496; London, 1872), 34.

20. The point was raised at the time: *Copies or Extracts . . . respecting Outrages*, 210.

21. *Further Correspondence*, 35.

22. The following standard works provide good accounts of the more regulated conduct of the trade: Deryck Scarr, 'Recruits and Recruiters: A Portrait of the Labour Trade', in J. W. Davidson and Deryck Scarr (eds.), *Pacific Islands Portraits* (Canberra, 1973); Corris, *Passage, Port and Plantation*; W.E. Giles, *A Cruize in a Queensland Labour Vessel to the South Seas* (ed. Deryck Scarr, Canberra, 1968). For a more recent, critical account, see Tracey Banivanua-Mar, *Violence and Colonial Dialogue: The Australian-Pacific Indentured Labour Trade* (Honolulu, 2007).

23. William T. Wawn, *The South Sea Islanders and the Queensland Labour Trade* (ed. Peter Corris, Canberra, 1973), 8–9.

24. Wawn, *South Sea Islanders*, 10.

25. Wawn, *South Sea Islanders*, 9.

26. Wawn, *South Sea Islanders*, 16.

27. Wawn, *South Sea Islanders*, 245.

28. *Papers relating to recent Operations of HMS 'Opal' against Natives of the Solomon Islands* (Parliamentary Paper, London, 1887); Douglas Rannie, *My Adventures among South Sea Cannibals* (London, 1912), 197. Accounts of the incident are collated by Roger M. Keesing, 'The Young Dick Attack: Oral and Documentary History on the Colonial Frontier', *Ethnohistory* 33 (1986), 268–92.

29. Rannie, *My Adventures*, 200.

30. Rannie, *My Adventures*, 202; J. Cromar, *Jock of the Islands* (London, 1935), 235–6.

31. *Papers relating to recent Operations*, 17.

32. *Papers relating to recent Operations*, 18–19.

33. Keesing, 'The Young Dick Attack', 279.

34. Keesing, 'The Young Dick Attack', 278.

35. Keesing, 'The Young Dick Attack', 284.

36. Rannie, *My Adventures*, 204.

37. Keesing, *Melanesian Pidgin and the Oceanic Substrate* (Stanford, 1988).
38. Keesing, 'Plantation Networks, Plantation Culture: The Hidden Side of Colonial Melanesia', *Journal de la Société des Océanistes* 42 (86), 163–70.
39. Corris, *Passage, Port and Plantation*, 127–9. Much important work has been done on the Melanesian presence in Queensland, including the subsequent history of communities there; see, e.g., Clive Moore, *Kanaka: A History of Melanesian Mackay* (Port Moresby, 1985); Patricia Mercer, *White Australia Defied: Pacific Island Settlement in North Queensland* (Townsville, 1995); and Banivanua-Mar, *Violence and Colonial Dialogue*.

Chapter 9: The whites would serve the natives

1. Frederick J. Moss, *A Planter's Experience in Fiji* (London, 1870), 24–5.
2. Deryck Scarr, 'Cakobau and Ma'afu: Contenders for Pre-eminence in Fiji', in J.W. Davidson and Deryck Scarr (eds.), *Pacific Islands Portraits* (Canberra, 1973), remains a good guide to a confusing series of developments; the earlier history of Bau's ascendancy is most fully addressed in Marshall Sahlins, *Apologies to Thucydides: Understanding History as Culture and Vice Versa* (Chicago, 2004). Earlier forms of Sahlins's arguments appeared in *Islands of History* (Chicago, 1985), chapters 2 and 3; and in *Culture in Practice* (New York, 2000).
3. There are several histories by missionaries, notably including Thomas Williams and James Calvert, *Fiji and the Fijians, II: Mission History* (London, 1858), and J. Waterhouse, *The King and People of Fiji* (London, 1866).
4. 'Report of Colonel Smythe, R.A., to Colonial Office', appendix II in Berthold Seemann, *Viti: an Account of a Government Mission to the Vitian or Fijian Islands, 1860–1861* (London, 1862), 424.
5. 'Report of Colonel Smythe', 427.
6. 'Report of Colonel Smythe', 429.
7. Scarr, 'Cakobau and Ma'afu', 113.
8. A.B. Brewster, *The Hill Tribes of Fiji* (London, 1922), 26–32; Deryck Scarr, *A Life of Sir John Bates Thurston, I: I, the Very Bayonet* (Canberra, 1973), 69.
9. Fred Wesley, 'Living in the Shadow of Cannibalism', *Fiji Times*, 28 September 2008.
10. Brewster, *Hill Tribes*, 31.
11. Scarr, 'Cakobau and Ma'afu', 118–19.
12. *Sydney Morning Herald*, 27 October 1874. See also *Correspondence Respecting the Cession of Fiji* (Parliamentary Paper, C1114, London, 1875).
13. *Sydney Morning Herald*, 21 December 1874.
14. R.A. Derrick, '1875: Fiji's Darkest Hour – An Account of the Measles Epidemic of 1875', *Transactions and Proceedings of the Fiji Society* 1 (1955), 5.
15. *Sydney Morning Herald*, 17 March 1875.
16. *Sydney Morning Herald*, 17 March 1875.
17. *Letters and Notes written during the Disturbances in the Highlands (Known as the 'Devil Country') of Viti Levu, Fiji, 1876* (Edinburgh, 1879), I, vi.
18. Norma McArthur, *Island Populations of the Pacific* (Canberra, 1967), 6–10.
19. Jane Roth and Steven Hooper (eds.), *The Fiji Journals of Baron Anatole von Hügel, 1875–77* (Suva and Cambridge, 1990), 29.
20. Roth and Hooper, *The Fiji Journals*, 164.
21. Roth and Hooper, *The Fiji Journals*, 216.
22. *Letters and Notes written during the Disturbances*, I, 10–12.
23. *Letters and Notes written during the Disturbances*, I, 95.
24. *Letters and Notes written during the Disturbances*, I, 22.
25. *Further Correspondence respecting the Colony of Fiji* (Parliamentary Paper, C.1404, London 1876), 131–2.
26. *Letters and Notes written during the Disturbances*, I, 95.

27. *Letters and Notes written during the Disturbances*, I, 91.
28. *Letters and Notes written during the Disturbances*, I, 121.
29. *Letters and Notes written during the Disturbances*, I, 140.
30. *Letters and Notes written during the Disturbances*, I, 105.
31. *Letters and Notes written during the Disturbances*, I, 420.
32. *Letters and Notes written during the Disturbances*, I, 420.
33. *Letters and Notes written during the Disturbances*, I, 440.
34. *Letters and Notes written during the Disturbances*, I, 441.
35. *Further Correspondence relative to the Colony of Fiji* (Parliamentary Paper, C.1826, London, 1877), 47–8; for broader discussion see also Nicholas Thomas, 'Sanitation and Seeing: The Creation of State Power in Early Colonial Fiji', *Comparative Studies in Society and History* 32 (1990), 149–70.
36. *Correspondence relating to the Native Population of Fiji* (Parliamentary Paper, C.5039, London, 1887), 73–80.
37. *Correspondence* (C.5039), 80.
38. My understanding of Navosavakadua's life and legacy is profoundly indebted to Martha Kaplan, *Neither Cargo nor Cult: Ritual Politics and the Colonial Imagination in Fiji* (Durham, 1995).
39. Brewster, *The Hill Tribes*, 237.
40. Further discussed in Nicholas Thomas, *In Oceania: Visions, Artifacts, Histories* (Durham, 1997), chapter 2.

Chapter 10: Our paradise became a hell

1. William B. Churchward, *My Consulate in Samoa: a Record of Four Years' Sojourn in the Navigators Islands* (London, 1887), 3.
2. Churchward, *My Consulate*, 143.
3. Churchward, *My Consulate*, 146.
4. Though intriguingly, Tongans now play only conventional cricket.
5. The best general history is R.P. Gilson, *Samoa 1830–1900: The Politics of a Multi-Cultural Community* (Melbourne, 1970); see also Malama Meleisea, *The Making of Modern Samoa* (Suva, 1987). For the developments focused on here, Meleisea's 'Introduction' to the Pasifika Press edition of Stevenson's *A Footnote to History* (Auckland, 1996) provides an excellent and lucid distillation of a very complex series of events.
6. Gilson, *Samoa*, chapter 2.
7. Gilson, *Samoa*, chapters 11–12.
8. *Correspondence respecting the Affairs of Samoa 1885–89* (Parliamentary Paper, C.5629, London, 1889), 88–100.
9. Gilson, *Samoa*, 377.
10. Ralph S. Kuykendall, *The Hawaiian Kingdom, III: The Kalakaua Dynasty* (Honolulu, 1967), 335.
11. Gilson, *Samoa*, chapter 15.
12. Deryck Scarr, *Fragments of Empire: A History of the Western Pacific High Commission* (Canberra, 1967), 72.
13. Robert Louis Stevenson, *In the South Seas, being an Account of Experiences and Observations in the Marquesas, Paumotus and Gilbert Islands* (London, 1900), 11.
14. Stevenson, *In the South Seas*, 11.
15. Stevenson, *In the South Seas*, 26.
16. This section draws upon H.E. Maude's 'Baiteke and Binoka of Abemana: Arbiters of Change in the Gilbert Islands', in J.W. Davidson and Deryck Scarr (eds.), *Pacific Islands Portraits* (Canberra, 1973).
17. Stevenson, *In the South Seas*, 279, referring to the romantic author E.T.A. Hoffmann.
18. Stevenson, *In the South Seas*, 281.

19. Stevenson, *In the South Seas*, 283.
20. Stevenson, *Vailima Letters: being Correspondence addressed by Robert Louis Stevenson to Sidney Colvin, November 1890–October 1894* (London, 1895), 108.
21. Stevenson, *Vailima Letters*, 114.
22. Stevenson, *Vailima Letters*, 132.
23. Stevenson, *A Footnote to History: Eight Years of Trouble in Samoa* (Auckland, 1996), 99.
24. *Correspondence respecting the Affairs of Samoa*, 268–9.
25. Stevenson, *A Footnote to History*, 105.
26. Meleisea, 'Introduction', xiv–xvi.
27. Stevenson, *A Footnote to History*, 1.
28. T. Scarlett Epstein, *Capitalism, Primitive and Modern: Some Aspects of Tolai Economic Growth* (Canberra, 1968).
29. Helen Bethea Gardner, *Gathering for God: George Brown in Oceania* (Dunedin, 2006), chapter 4.
30. *George Brown, D.D. Pioneer Missionary and Explorer, an Autobiography* (London, 1908), 254.
31. Brown, *Autobiography*, 254.
32. Brown, 'Journal of the Rev. G. Brown, 1877–78', Mitchell Library, Sydney, MS A1686-13, extracts in J.L. Whittaker, N.G. Gash, R.J. Lacey and J.F. Hookey, *Documents and Readings in New Guinea History* (Milton, Queensland, 1975), 418–23.
33. Methodist Church of Australasia papers, in Whittaker et al., *Documents*, 425.
34. Captain Purvis, in Whittaker et al., *Documents*, 426–7.
35. Stewart Firth, 'German Firms in the Western Pacific Islands, 1857–1914', *Journal of Pacific History* 8 (1973), 14.
36. Clive Moore, *New Guinea: Crossing Boundaries and History* (Honolulu, 2003), 116; Peter Hempenstall, *Pacific Islanders Under German Rule: A Study in the Meaning of Colonial Resistance* (Canberra, 1978), 123–5.
37. *Correspondence respecting New Guinea and Other Islands* (Parliamentary Paper, C.3863), 34–44.
38. Peter Biskup, 'Introduction', in *The New Guinea Memoirs of Jean Baptiste Octave Mouton* (Canberra, 1974).
39. Brown, *Autobiography*, 363.
40. Whittaker et al., *Documents*, 405.
41. Biskup, *The New Guinea Memoirs*, 49–50.
42. Moore, *New Guinea*, 133–9.

Acknowledgements

Nearly thirty years ago I began anthropological and historical work in the Pacific, a fascinated but naïve student. Niel Gunson, who supervised my doctoral thesis at the Australian National University, gave me a sense of historical craft that I have struggled to honour ever since. I cannot mention everyone who at one time or another inspired or encouraged me, but the writing of sections of this book has reminded me how much I owe Roger Keesing (1935–93) and Jonathan Friedman. My greatest debt is of course to those who hosted me, particularly in the Marquesas, Fiji, and Niue – so-called 'informants' who became friends and in some cases collaborators. Since 1993 much of my research has followed art in New Zealand; though they do not feature in any direct way in this book, conversations with New Zealand artists, especially Robert Jahnke, John Pule, Jim Vivieaere, Mark Adams and Lisa Reihana have been vital to my imagining of the colonial age in the Pacific. As were the writings of, and a few discussions I was fortunate to have with, Epeli Hau'ofa (1939–2009), the great radical intellectual of the new Oceania.

This particular book was written and researched over a three-year period, 2006–9, with the support of a Leverhulme Trust Major Research Fellowship. I am deeply appreciative of the Trust's generosity; *Islanders* could certainly not have been completed without the time and space for reading and writing that the award gave me. Colleagues at the Museum of Archaeology and Anthropology in Cambridge have been supportive of my need for periods away to get the book finished; I must especially thank Robin Boast, Wendy Brown, Mark Elliott, and Anita Herle for making it all possible. I also thank them, and all my colleagues at the Museum, for making the place an enormously stimulating environment for research, not least on colonial exchanges and their legacies.

I am grateful to my friends and colleagues, Lissant Bolton, Peter Brunt, and Sean Mallon, for many discussions and for their interest in my work. When this book was only half-written, I was able to present the core of its argument to a Pacific studies group in Ann Arbor, Michigan, convened by Damon Salesa; the occasion renewed my sense of the project, and I am enduringly grateful to Damon, as well as to Vanessa Agnew, Vicente Diaz, and Susan Najita. I also thank Bronwen Douglas and Matthew Spriggs, especially for their comments on sections of the book, but also for talk about Pacific topics, off and on over more than twenty years.

Most of all I have to thank Annie Coombes for her love and encouragement. This book owes much to our many conversations about colonial histories, but is more profoundly also the upshot of a shared life, shared travels, shared amusements. Since 2004, Nicholas Coombes-Thomas has been part of that life, and this book is marked, too, by his presence, his laughter, and his curiosity.

London

May 2010

Index

Tahiti, 7, 12, 17, 59, 79, 83, 147, 152, 194, 200, 294
  barter, 80
  beachcombers, 24, 40
  Bounty loaded at, 21
  Cook, 6, 15, 16, 21, 33, 129
  drawings, 18
  emigration from, 191
  emigration to, 19–20, 200
  environment, 186
  European influences, 24, 99, 101–2, 127–8, 130, 149
  feathers, 74–6
  France in, 163, 243, 295
  human sacrifice, 26, *27*
  labour recruitment, 211, 222
  language, 16, 56, 98, 101, 129
  literacy, 206, 207
  missions, 19, 42, 49, 55–6, 96–9, 101–9, 112–15, 148, 202, 244, 256, 294
    LMS, 31–5
  politics, 56, 74–7, 101–2, 283
  population, 102, 115
  religion, 97–9, 103–4
  sexual activity, 88
  slave raiders, 194–6
  Stevenson in, 275
  travellers from, 4–5, 17–19, 20, 25, 36, 54, 93, 182, 188, 237, *see also* Tapioi
  violence, 22, 52, 55, 61
Tahiti Iti, Tahiti, 96
Tahuata, Marquesas, 43–4, 47, 72, 114–15, 162
  LMS, 34–5
Taiohae Bay, Nukuhiva, 45, 47, 71
  Porter, 60–4, 67, 70, 72
    smallpox, 197
Taipi, Marquesas, 47, 68, 69, 70
  and Porter, 64–7
Taiwan, 8
Talange'enia (Malaitan), 235
Talanoa (conversation), 37, 38
Talaunga'i (Malaitan), 235
Talili, chief, New Britain, 285–6
Tama ('Sam', Hawaiian), 44
Tamafaiga, chief, Samoa, 113
Tamaha (Tahitian), 67
Tamasese, chief, Samoa, 272–5, 280, 281
Tamatamihi (Rapa), 195
tangata manu cult, Rapa Nui, 205–6
Tanna, Vanuatu, 237, 246
  labour recruitment, 211, 212, 216–17, 219, 226, 246

Williams murder, 117–20
Tano Manu (Tahitian), 36
Tanoa, leader, Bau, 123
Taole (Niuean), 198–9
tapa (sacred material), 207
Tapioi (Tahitian), 25, 52–4, 80–1, 96, 188
  Kelso trial, 48–51
tapu (taboo), 45, 59, 77, 141, 142, 245
  abolition, 95
taro, 10, 11, 165, 242
Tasmania, 132, 139
tatau, see tattooing
tattooing, 6, 16, 35, 42, 44, 60, 147, 200, 202
  banned, 277
  meaning of, 101
Taufa, chief, Tonga, 135, 136
Taufa'ahau, chief, Tonga, 243
Ta'unga, teacher, 164, 167, 214, 287
taura (shamans), 103, 104
Tavea, Fiji Islands, 85
Tavea island, 83
Taviuni, Fiji, 255
Te Weherua, Maori, 19–20
Teinae, chief, Tahuata, 35
Tem Baiteke, chief, Kiribati, 278–9
Tem Binoka, chief, Kiribati, 279–80
Temoana, chief, Nukuhiva, 163
Temoteitei (Marquesan), 45, 47–8
temples, 12, 67, 74
Teouma cemetery, Vanuatu, 9
Teremba, New Caledonia, 167–8, 171
Teresa, 193
Tetuanui (Tahitian), 19
Thomas, John, 136
Thomas, Nicholas, 72, 185
Thomson, William, 202–4
Thurston, John Bates, 247, 264, 275
Tiaiarapu, Tahiti, 102
Tierra del Fuego, 146, 153
Ti'i, first man, 98
Tikopia, Solomon Islands, 91–2, 93
Times, The, 275
Tjibaou, Jean-Marie, 163
tobacco, 79, 82, 287
Tofua, Tonga, 21
Tokalau Islands, 193, 198
toki (adze), 41
Tolaga Bay, New Zealand, 133
Tolai, New Britain, 284, 285–7, 293
Tom (Tahitian), 36
Toma ('Tomma', Tahitian), 51, 52
tomahawks, 59